D0906338

No. 1315
$19.95

THE
MASTER CRAFTSMAN'S ILLUSTRATED WOODWORKING MANUAL
—with projects

BY LEWIS H. HODGES

TAB BOOKS Inc.

BLUE RIDGE SUMMIT, PA. 17214

Other TAB books by the author:

No. 974 *66 Weekend Wood Furniture Projects*
No. 1102 *How To Build Your Own Fine Doll Houses & Furnishings*
No. 1240 *Building Antique Doll House Furniture From Scratch*

FIRST EDITION

FIRST PRINTING

Library of Congress Cataloging in Publication Data

Hodges, Lewis H.
    The master craftsman's illustrated woodworking manual—
with projects.

    Includes index.
    1. Woodwork. I. Title.
TT180.H62   684'.08   81-9202
ISBN 0-8306-0035-3   AACR2
ISBN 0-8306-1315-3 (pbk.)

Cover photo of "Craftsmen at work" courtesy of Baker Furniture Co., Holland, Mich.

Contents

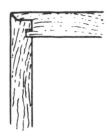

Preface

Woodworking has always been the most prevalent and rewarding of the craft activities. As a building and furniture material, wood is, by far, the best understood. It is part of our natural heritage, and Yankee ingenuity has made the most of it. For too long we have taken wood for granted. But even with today's high prices, wood is probably the best bargain around. Unlike oil, coal and gas, lumber is a *renewable resource.*

The fascination of working with wood is, unlike metal, no two pieces of wood, regardless of size or shape, are exactly alike. There is no other material, either man-made or developed synthetically, that has more desirable working characteristics. Perhaps no other material has the versatility of wood. It can be found almost everywhere. It is easy to handle. It can be shaped, bent, formed, smoothed and finished. It presents interesting grain patterns, varied coloration and surface texture. Wood is generally warm to the touch, while metals are usually cold. Hardware, abrasives, adhesives and fasteners (nails, screws, etc.) are usually no further away than the corner hardware store.

This book is designed for the typical home craftsman and the small woodworking and cabinetmaking entrepreneur. It also is an excellent reference for the industrial arts and vocational education teacher as well as for Junior Achievement and 4-H Club leaders and members.

Special emphasis is placed on the selection, safe use and maintenance of tools—both hand and power—and on the selection of materials involved. The entire continuum of processes from early design concepts and planning to the final finishing operation is included. I assume that the woodworker has some fundamental knowledge of the tools and machines described herein, although the craftsman might not have these tools in his own shop.

There are many misconceptions concerning wood. There are still many people who believe in "dry rot." Even insurance experts contend that steel beams are more fire-resistant than wood beams, when the reverse has been demonstrated many times. Steel will sag and collapse in a fire while a wooden beam will hold up exhibiting only a small coating of char. The menace of insects has often been grossly exaggerated. The word "termite" strikes terror to the hearts of the average homeowner, but this tunnel-building insect, which has caused untold damage in the past—particularly in the southern states—can be barred effectively from buildings by a few precautionary measures, such as metal shields and preservative treatment of wood. (In addition, wood can be soaked in two chemicals, alternatively, to form a chemical reaction. These chemicals are *sodium arsenate* and *copper sulfate,* which react to form *copper arsenate,* an insoluble toxic, which permanently resides in the wood.)

Although wood has been with us since time immemorial, science and technology have paid considerable attention to its improvement in terms of machinability, adaptability and preservation.

Scientific experiments conducted at the Forest Products Laboratory at Madison, Wisconsin, report that wood has been successfully cut and shaped with the laser beam and with water jets under the extreme pressure of many thousands of pounds per square inch.

Polyethlene glycol 1000 developed by Dr. Stamm at Dow Chemical is used to stabilize green wood so that the wood resists shrinking. It has been reported that one company which specializes in high quality carvings has reduced its carving losses from about 60% to less than 3%. At the same time it has increased its production because of the lubricating properties of polyethylene glycol 1000.

Chemicals are used to render wood fire-resistant. These chemicals, under high pressure, are forced into the wood. Some woods treated with these chemicals are not only fire-resistant, but also emit a gas which acts as a fire extinquisher.

The same Dr. Stamm mentioned earlier devised a system called *Impreg* by which thin layers of plastic *(phenolic resin)* could be forced into thin layers of veneer. The same thin sheets of plastic were used to adhere layers of veneer together. This method produced a wood-based product that resists all tendency to warp, swell or shrink.

Later came a process even more revolutionary. Called *Compreg,* it used the same methods used in making Impreg, but in addition it used high pressure to remove nearly three-fourths of the air from the wood cellular structure. Club propellers used in World War II to test military aircraft engines were made of Compreg. Knife handles made of Compreg stand up indefinitely after repeated washing in an automatic dishwasher.

A huge machine like a mammoth paper cutter slices through large logs, thus eliminating the need for wasted lumber—sawdust. This method makes it possible to obtain nearly 30% more lumber from a log.

Safety should be an ever-present factor in the mind of the woodworker. Good judgment intertwined with common sense in using tools and equipment will prevent most accidents. Every move made with a tool or machine should be thought out in advance. The craftsman should anticipate what might happen under a host of conditions. Contrary to what people might think, a dull tool is much more dangerous than a sharp tool. A sharp tool will always perform in a certain prescribed manner, while no one can predict what a dull tool will do.

Most modern power woodworking equipment is provided with safety devices and guards to protect the craftsman. These are fine and from the psychological standpoint are indispensable, but they never compensate for poor judgment and carelessness. Guards prevent only a few of the accidents that might occur.

Work should never be rushed in the woodshop. Haste not only makes waste, but it is the cause of many accidents.

Proper dress is very important. Goggles, safety glasses or face shields should be worn when operating woodworking machines. Long sleeves should be avoided. Finger rings should be removed before starting to work. Ties should be removed or tucked in the shirt front. Stop machines to make adjustments. Keep the area around each machine clear of clutter and debris. Do not approach too close to a person operating a machine. Expect the same from others while you are operating a piece of power equipment. Other safety precautions will be reviewed in connection with the individual machines and tools further on in the book.

This book is divided into 13 chapters. The major emphasis is on tools and their functions. Special tools and tools not covered elsewhere are discussed in Chapter 7.

Chapter 12, *Mass Production and Industrial Woodworking,* covers the area of multiple parts production and the field of furniture making and other wood products.

It would be presumptuous for me to assume that this is a totally comprehensive treatise on the subject of woodworking. No one man, however informed, could write with total authority on all the facets of the very broad area of woodworking, particularly if limited to one book. But the more enterprising and knowledge-seeking woodworker can vastly increase his/her storehouse of knowledge and skills by consulting the manufacturers listed in the appendix. *Arabic numbers in paranthese refer to items in the Appendix: Suppliers/Manufacturers.* The names and addresses of companies are listed in the Appendix.

Lewis H. Hodges

Acknowledgments

The author wishes to express his appreciation to the following companies for their generosity in supplying illustrative material for this book: Adjustable Clamp Company, American Machine and Tool Company, Belsaw Power Tools Company, Binks Mfg. Company, Black Bros., Black and Decker (U.S.) Inc., Brodhead-Garrett, Conover Woodcraft Specialties, Inc., C. O. Porter Machinery Company, Dupli-Carver and Laskowski Enterprises, Ekstrom, Carlson and Company, Emco-Lux Corporation, Foley Mfg. Company, Fox Super Shop, Inc., Frog Tool Company Ltd., Goodspeed Machine Company, J. M. Lancaster Company, Kohler-General, Kurt Mfg. Company, Mereen-Johnson Machine Company, Norton Company, Oliver Machinery Company, Parks Woodworking Machine Company, Powermatic Houdaille, Inc., Precision Concepts Corporation, Safranek Enterprises, Sand-Rite Mfg. Company, Shopsmith, Inc., Sprunger Corporation, Toolmark Company and Wetzler Clamp Company. Full addresses of these companies are listed in the Appendix.

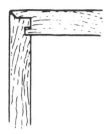

Introduction

The working environment of the home workshop or small commercial shop should be conducive to the production of quality furniture and wood projects. Shop organization of tools and materials is a "must" for an efficient work place. The larger hand tools should be placed on pegboard racks, with the silhouette of each tool enameled on the pegboard. Colored plastic, such as "Mystik Tape," may be used in place of the enamel. Sometimes the pegboard is covered with white enamel or lacquer before the silhouettes are applied to provide contrast and to aid in keeping the board clean. A good general rule to follow is, "keep a place for everything, and everything in its place."

WORKING ENVIRONMENT

The small hand tools are quite often placed in shallow drawers. A mechanic-type cabinet works fine, provided that the bottoms of the drawers are covered with "Flox," velvet, felt or flannel to prevent damage to precision tools and sharp cutting edges. The larger, lower drawers in the mechanic-type chest may be used for power tool accessories.

Each piece of power machinery should be located so that there is plenty of room around it. The circular or radial saw should be located near the entrance as it is usually the first power tool used when lumber is brought into the shop. The more affluent craftsman may have a power jointer, which should be located near the saw, and perhaps a thickness planer is added to make the triad complete. The other power tools (lathe, drill press, shaper, etc.) may be located wherever it is convenient.

The Workbench

The workbench is probably the most important tool or furnishing in the home or small commercial woodshop. Quite often it is placed in a corner and almost always against the wall. Electric outlets should be nearby for portable electric tools, and the most used hand tools should be on a pegboard within easy reach.

The workbench should be provided with at least one vise and a number of bench stops. The quick-action vise is considered by many wood craftsmen to be the best.

The purchase of a maple laminated top workbench would require a considerable outlay of cash. Even a craftsman-made bench of maple would not be exactly inexpensive. However, a very serviceable bench top can be made of two layers of ¾" plywood covered with ¼" hardboard.

According to Woodcraft Supply (204), the *Ulmia* workbench is considered the model in Europe. This German joiner's/cabinetmaker's bench is made of European red beech and is built with the same quality of craftsmanship as exhibited in a fine piece of furniture. It has a vise at the front of the left end and another across the right end. The only drawback is that the cost will put a big hole in a thousand dollar bill. For those who wish to build their own German-type bench, bench plans and vise hardware are available at Woodcraft Supply (204). Complete plans and directions for building a European workbench are included in an article by Tage Frid in *Fine Woodworking Techniques* by Taunton Press. Complete blueprints are available from Taunton Press. These orthographic drawings may be a little easier to work with than the isometrics in the article.

Constantine (41) supplies a *Danish* Workbench of solid construction, but simpler in design than the German-style bench. A unique feature of this bench is that by loosening four wing nuts, the bench may be folded and stored away when not in use.

A few suppliers and/or manufacturers of workbenches follow. The arabic numbers in parentheses refer to the Appendix.

■ Constantine (41).
■ Fair Price Tool Company (67).
■ Garden Way Research (78).
■ Leichtung (112).
■ Universal Clamp Company (186).
■ Woodcraft Supply Corp. (204).

11

Clamp Racks

Provision must be made for the larger *bar clamps*. Slots may be cut into a hardwood 2″ x 2″ or larger and fastened to the wall with anchor fasteners. If a large number of bar clamps are used, it is advisable to mount an A-frame structure on a platform provided with large casters so that it can be moved about the shop. Bar clamps are stored on both outside slopes of the "A." Small clamps may be stored under the slopes of the "A."

Lumber Racks and Shelves

Most lumber for home workshops is stored in a horizontal position; however, if the shop has high ceilings, such as provided in a portion of a garage, the lumber may be stacked vertically. The rack for horizontal storage should be of sturdy construction. The main uprights should be 4″ x 4″s or the equivalent, with 2″ x 4″ crossbars, or holes bored in the upright and pieces of pipe at least 1½″ in diameter inserted.

This type of construction allows lumber to be removed from either side of the rack or from the ends. Make sure that plywood lumber lies flat. It should never be leaned against the wall.

Finishing Materials

All finishing materials should be stored in metal cabinets with metal doors to decrease the fire hazard. This is particularly true of the more volatile liquids. Some home workshop owners and nearly all school shops color code the larger containers of volatile liquids. Here is one such code: gasoline —red containers, turpentine or mineral spirits—gray top, black bottom, lacquer thinner—yellow containers, denatured alcohol—green containers, lubricating oil—red top, black bottom and kerosene—black containers. No more than one gallon of each liquid should be stored in the home workshop at one time.

Small aerosol spray cans of finishing materials can safely be used on small projects in the home workshop if adequate ventilation is provided by opening windows or doors, but commercial or industrial type spray guns can be used only with a metal spray booth and a properly certified exhaust fan. It is best to check with the local fire marshal before installing such a system. Old paint and finish cloths should be disposed of at the end of each day or placed in metal safety containers.

Dust Control

An industrial-type respirator should be available and worn, particularly when machine sanding is being done over an extensive or prolonged period. If considerable sawing, jointing and planing are done in the workshop, it is almost a necessity to provide an industrial-type dust collecting system with metal and flexible tubing connected to the cyclone. Doyle Johnson of Crown Point, Indiana, describes a damper-controlled dust collection system using plastic drainage pipe and a clothes dryer vent hose in *Fine Woodworking,* September, 1978. However, a shop can be kept reasonably clean with a heavy-duty vacuum cleaner in the 10 gallon or 20 gallon size. Carts with handles are available to provide mobility. If the home craftsman does only a minimum of power sawing, and no surfacing or jointing by power equipment, an ordinary household vacuum will be sufficient. Accumulated sawdust should be disposed at the end of each day. A fire extinguisher should be located in a central position in the shop.

Machine Care and Maintenance

Power machines should be kept clean and well lubricated. Belts should be checked for wear and pulleys for looseness. Craftsmen with air compressors should be careful to control the pressure when cleaning machines. William G. Ovens of Potsdam, New York, points out in *Fine Woodworking,* January/February 1979 that "section 1910.242 of the Occupational Safety and Health Administration requires that 'compressed air shall not be used for cleaning purposes except where reduced to less than 30 psi'...."

Forty or 50 years ago all machinery was painted black, but currently colors are used to good advantage. Green seems to be the accepted color for the body of most machines. Pittsburgh Paint and Glass has an excellent color system, sometimes called "color dynamics," not only for machines, but also for walls, ceilings and for marking out safety zones on the floor. Operating parts on the machine are finished in colors in strong contrast to the body of the machine, and machine controls, levers and switch boxes are finished in high visibility colors.

Lighting

Fluorescent lighting is recommended for basic illumination when artificial lighting is needed. Additional individual lights will probably be needed over some machines (band saw, jigsaw, drill press etc.), and a desk-type light may be needed over the workbench for close and fine work.

Enough electrical outlets should be provided to care for special lighting and portable power tools. One master switch should control all lights and machines and it should be capable of being locked.

Power Machinery

Power equipment may be purchased in three categories: new, used and in kits. Each has its advantages and disadvantages.

Many contend that purchasing new machinery is the only way to go. For the beginner, it is probably the best way as he lacks the experience to properly evaluate used machinery or the expertise to build a machine from a kit. The overriding disadvantage of buying new machinery is the high cost.

For the experienced and discerning craftsman, used machines may be the best option. Used power tools are not only less expensive, but in many cases are of superior quality. Machinery of yesteryear was more apt to be made of heavy cast iron components, which gave far more stability and long-lasting service. Machinery currently being manufactured leans toward die castings, plastic parts, sheet metal stampings and sheet metal welded components.

The major disadvantage of buying used equipment is that due to competition the cost is nearly as great, and sometimes greater, than that of new machinery. Another disadvantage of buying used equipment is trying to locate the accessories such as guards, fences, attachments, pulleys and sharpeners.

One way of beating the high cost of power tools is to buy the unassembled main components in kit form and making the other components of wood or plywood in your own shop. More about kit-built equipment will be discussed in appropriate sections of this book.

The Cooperative Workshop

If the craftsman does not have a suitable area for a workshop in his basement or garage, he/she might consider joining a "coop" in which a number of craftsmen may share shop area and shop costs. For the beginner, this arrangement is particularly desirable as he can learn a great deal by observing others at work. Another "spin-off" is the social camaraderie such a setup provides.

SKILLED AND SEMI-SKILLED
OCCUPATIONS AND CAREERS RELATED TO WOODWORKING

Cabinetmaking is the trade or occupation around which many woodworking skills and occupations revolve. The home craftsman, as well as the small custom furniture maker, will need many, if not all, of the same skills and information as the cabinetmaker.

Cabinetmaker

The cabinetmaker can take a design idea and carry it through to its final completion using a host of hand and power tools and materials. However, the total number of these highly skilled craftsmen have decreased in recent years due to the division of labor and the use of high production machinery. In a furniture factory employing hundreds of workers, one might find only a handful of cabinetmakers. And their work might be quite different than that of the cabinetmaker in a custom furniture shop, where the cabinetmaker would build a piece of furniture from "scratch." Too often the skills of a cabinetmaker in a large furniture factory go to waste as he often is nothing more than a "glorified inspector."

A large number of workers in a furniture plant are semi-skilled machine operators and concentrate on only one aspect of the trade. They carry such titles as "dry kiln operators," "universal saw operators," "spindle carvers," "back knife lathe operators," "band saw operators," etc.

All other workers are in the categories of unskilled or low-skilled workers. The workers in these jobs can be trained in a matter of hours—in some cases even minutes. Their work involves sanding, sponging, moving or stacking component parts or "tailing" a production machine. The "tailer" removes work from a machine after it passes through the production phase.

There are at least three ways in which a person may become a cabinetmaker:

■ Informal training.
■ Vocational trade schools and cooperative training.
■ Formal apprenticeship.

Informal training usually takes place when an unskilled or semi-skilled worker demonstrates outstanding skill, attitude and desire to climb the company ladder. He is often taken under the wing of a cabinetmaker or supervisor and gradually develops skills approaching that of a cabinetmaker. The major stumbling block to this approach is that it usually takes many years of on-the-job experience and outside study on one's own to reach a high degree of efficiency.

In the last 40 years trade training in high schools, community colleges and technical institutes, and cooperative on-the-job training in which the student works part-time in the industry, have become quite popular.

A typical program of this nature is spelled out as follows. The seventh or eighth grade junior high school student takes woodworking which is part of a general shop program. Little work is done on the power tools as the emphasis is on the proper handling of hand tools.

In the ninth or 10th grade machine woodworking, mechanical drafting and blueprint reading are often included.

During the 11th grade a student takes *shop mathematics* and *vocational cabinetmaking* for 2½ to three hours per day. This course is taught by a vocationally certified instructor who has had considerable experience in the woodworking industry.

The 12th grade program calls for half of each day to be spent in a cooperative on-the-job training in industry. One period of the other half day is spent in related technical information class in which safety, first aid, social-economics problems and labor relations are covered, along with problems related directly to cabinetmaking and woodworking.

The trainee may continue his instruction at a community college, technical institute, adult evening school or in a formal apprenticeship program. In most cases credit is given for previous training, thus shortening the apprenticeship period.

Finish Carpenter

The *finish carpenter*, inside carpenter or trim man uses many of the same tools and skills that the cabinetmaker uses, but to a more limited extent. His work is generally confined to hand tools, although occasionally power tools are used. There are many more finish carpenters than cabinetmakers as carpentry is the largest skilled trade group in America.

Millworker

The *millworker* is employed in woodworking, furniture or mill workshops where large quantities of standardized parts and components are produced. Much of his work involves the adjustment of machines and the sharpening of knives for the machines. He is sometimes known as the "setup" man. The millworker is capable of operating all woodworking machines.

Boat Builder

The *boat builder* is familiar with the same tools and skills as the cabinetmaker, particularly on larger boats that require extensive interior cabinetmaking.

Wood Patternmaker

The wood *patternmaker* in some ways is at the pinnacle of the woodworking trades. He works to much closer tolerances than the cabinetmaker, and his hand and finger dexterity must be beyond reproach. His technical skills must be finely honed as he has to interpret drawings, blueprints and technical specifications. The patterns he makes are used for foundry castings; therefore he must know the characteristics of the metal being cast, but also must select the best wood for making the patterns. To the outsider his work appears to be of the puttering kind as he might confine his efforts to a piece of wood no bigger than a bread box for many days or even weeks. The wages of a wood patternmaker are generally higher than that of a cabinetmaker or millworker.

SEMI-PROFESSIONAL SKILLS RELATED TO WOODWORKING

The *furniture designer* is a combination artist and draftsman. He often submits a series of sketches, often in color, to his client—the furniture maker. The client looks over these renditions and selects the one that impresses him the most. After the selection is made, the furniture designer or his assistant makes the working drawings—usually full-size—and develops the specifications in consultation with the client. Many furniture designers are free-lance designers, while others are hired full-time by large companies. National and international free-lance designers, who have reputations as well-known creative experts in their field, many times become wealthy individuals.

Although *interior designers* might not know the difference between a band saw and a band aid, they must be able to identify and evaluate different woods, and be knowledgeable about different periods of furniture. They must be able to select and recommend all the items in a total home environment, and know how these items are best arranged for a pleasing and comfortable aesthetic effect.

PROFESSIONAL SKILLS RELATED TO WOODWORKING

The *architect* designs homes, churches, schools, and commercial and industrial buildings. He must also be a wood engineer and know the structural limitations of wood. The architect sometimes designs special furniture for such structures as schools, churches, libraries, museums and municipal buildings.

Wood Technologist

The *wood technologist* is a true professional in that he must have a degree in his field which requires a minimum of four years. Many technologists also possess an advanced degree. His professional training involves intensive study in the disciplines of physics, chemistry, mathematics and engineering as well as obtaining a thorough knowledge of lumbering, wood and wood-product manufacturing.

Forester

The *forester* oversees the planting, growing and harvesting of trees. He helps control the process by which forest products enterprises are supplied with usable raw materials. He often marks trees which are to be cut, supervises the cutting and transportation of the logs, and determines whether the logs are suitable for timber, lumber or pulpwood for the paper industry. He is very conservative conscious and believes in selective cutting of trees to assure the continuous supply of this precious commodity—wood.

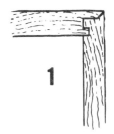

1

Designing and
Planning Woodworking Projects

Much has been written about design in the past quarter century. It is safe to say that in all probability, more has been written in this field in the last 25 years than in all the history of woodworking. As a result, there is a greater interest, awareness, and a certain amount of sophistication and creative ability as a result of this new awareness.

INTRODUCTION

The American public is acquiring a better appreciation of the beauty and refining influence of good furniture and household accessories. This broad statement is accurate in that it reflects the cultural growth of our nation. Modern taste in household items, as in music and literature, is founded on a fairly widespread understanding of fundamentals. Good furniture is furniture designed along lines of symmetry and harmony, which will forever remain beautiful, and furniture so conceived stands aloof from transitory style preference. In spite of our recent advances in design, there are still designers who have been guilty of conceiving and perpetuating ugly and atrocious monstrosities on a sometime gullible public. Furniture and wood accessories are often too heavy. Although they are strong and sturdy, often they are difficult to move about the home. Furthermore, they are wasteful of that valuable commodity—wood.

A wood craftsman who religiously copies the drawings and plans of others misses out on the most rewarding aspects of his craft. All woodworkers have creative ability to a certain extent, and these skills should be used, even if the results are not the most impressive. Only by exercising his creative talents can the woodworker eventually reach his full potential which will not only be appreciated and admired by the designers, but by all others who might observe his creative ability.

BASIC DESIGN CONSIDERATIONS

What is visually pleasing to one person is not neccessarily pleasing to another. Traditional furniture by the old masters is pleasing to many because it has stood the test of time. Others are attracted to contemporary furniture because of its clean lines and the economical use of wood. To the housewife contemporary furniture is attractive because she can visualize much less dusting and cleaning, and to the homeowners who have small homes and apartments the generally smaller scale pieces fit in better. Traditional furniture, because of its very nature, needs more "elbow room

Artistic and Aesthetic Aspects

Designing for artistic qualities is a very complex and difficult process. There are no rigid rules that one can follow, because the visual aspects are often very subtle. The principles of design are hard to define even after we know what they are. The most often stated principles of design are: *proportion, balance, rhythm, color, harmony, center of interest and texture.*

Functional Aspects of Design

In the field of design we often hear the expression "form follows function." The question one should ask is, "Does the piece of furniture do well what it is supposed to do?" A well designed chair must conform to certain fixed sizes. But these sizes vary for children and adults. An upholstered chair designed for comfort does not go well in the dining room. The chair must be sturdy enough to support the weight. It must be made of material available to the maker. It should be easy to maintain, affordable and fit into the environment in which it will be used.

The designer's very difficult objective is to achieve elegance, grace and charm without overstepping the confines of function. The function of a piece of furniture must be carefully considered before the process of design can begin.

Proper and Economical Use of Material

The competent and experienced woodworker will have no problem here. His training and experience has emphasized the characteristics and limitations of the material he uses and the unique qualities of each.

The furniture designer not only uses wood to advantage, but expeditiously uses cane, tile, metal hardware, ceramics, fabric, plastics, laminates, veneers, marquetry, inlays and ornamental trim to enhance the product.

At one time in our not too distant past, veneered plywood was considered a poor substitute for solid wood, but this is no longer true. The diminishing quantity of furniture hardwoods means that the existing supply must be conserved by using a considerable amount of it in the form of veneers. Furthermore, beautiful grain patterns of matched veneers are not possible with solid wood.

An Understanding and Skills in the Use of Tools and Equipment

The designers must be acquainted with the tools and equipment used by the cabinetmaker and woodworker. If he is not knowledgeable about the capabilities and limitations of tools and machines, he might design a product which is impossible to make or would be uneconomical to construct.

Methods, Processes and Operations

The basic operations of forming, shaping, bending, assembly and finishing should be understood by the designer. He should be acquainted with, and preferably be able to operate, circular saws, band saws, lathes, shapers, routers, drill presses, sanders, etc.

A knowledge of basic joints, and which is the best for the particular use to which it is to be put, is essential to sound basic furniture design.

STEPS IN CREATIVE DESIGN PROBLEM SOLVING

What is the problem? What needs to be designed?

Identification

Let's assume that letters, envelopes, stamps, paper clips and rubber bands can never be found when needed. Care must be taken in the beginning not to name the project—only the function of the project.

Eventually from this exercise a number of "wall letter racks" were developed. See Chapter 13 for procedures and plans for building.

Analysis

What should it do? What should it look like?

The process of analysis is a type of brainstorming by the designer. It is highly desirable that many others be brought into the process as well. The following statements might be the outcome:

■ The envelopes should not fall out.

■ The envelopes should not be easily removed.

■ The support should hang flat against the wall.

■ It should be easy to clean and wax.

■ It should be structurally sound.

■ Its cost should be reasonable.

■ The container for stamps, paper clips, etc. should be fairly shallow and items should be easy to remove.

■ The container should be easy to close.

■ The rack should fit into its environment and be pleasing in appearance.

Investigation and Tryout

What are some of the possible solutions to the problem? Solutions or partial solutions may be found by doing the following.

■ Look at existing wall racks, planters or similar accessories in homes and stores.

■ Study library project books, catalogs, magazines, etc.

■ Visit furniture museums.

■ Sketch ideas as they develop.

■ Make scale models to test ideas or make test pieces from inexpensive wood.

■ Make tentative working drawings.

■ Experiment with different materials.

■ Seek information from technical references.

■ Discuss ideas with other members of the household, other craftsmen, parents, teachers, neighbors, etc.

Evaluation

All the better ideas evolving from investigation and tryout must be carefully evaluated in terms of function and appearance. It is the time for combining ideas. Sometimes a model is required to crystallize these ideas. A scale model gives the designer a three-dimensional look into problems relative to shape, size, materials, construction and finish. Tentative working drawings, pictorial renderings and material lists can be complied.

Construction

The following questions must be answered:
— How do I make it?
— What kind of joints will be the best?
— What kind of adhesive would be the most suitable?
— How should it be assembled?
— What grades of abrasives would be right to use?
— What tools should I use, and are they in good condition?
— What type of finish would be the most appropriate?

Post Evaluation

Not until the product is complete can the solution be tested and evaluated. Actual use will help to provide some basis of evaluation. The designer must be able to answer the following. Where does the final product (solution) fall short? What can be done to improve the product? What do others think about the solution (product)?

DESIGN PRINCIPLES

The principles of design mentioned earlier are briefly expanded here.

Proportion

Proportion is the interrelationship between components of a woodworking project. A heavy oak table should not be supported by spindly or delicate legs, even if those legs were made of the strongest wood in the world. However, the average woodworker is more apt to make legs of all kinds too heavy and bulky rather than too slender.

Balance

Furniture that is balanced symmetrically will be balanced. However, if a horizontal center line is drawn through a project, the top and bottom may be exactly alike, but the upper part will appear larger than the bottom.

It is possible to obtain balance without symmetry, but this type of *balance* should be left to the experienced and professional designer. It is a subtle arrangement that is hard to achieve. This takes place when completely different components are arranged so that the product appears balanced and is therefore pleasing to the eye.

Rhythm

Rhythm is achieved by the use of repeated components or units within a project. A large wall spice cabinet with many identical drawers would be a case in point. Many ornamental carving strips used to trim and decorate furniture have reoccurring elements in its design. Parquet flooring is considered beautiful because of rhythm.

Color

Color is as important to the furniture designer as it is to all product designers—and maybe more so. Nature has provided wood with many intrinsic, beautiful colors. These colors should be captured and enhanced by using only a transparent finish. Other woods have to be stained in order to get the desired result. I am opposed to bleaching woods such as walnut and mahogany. Why destroy the natural beauty of the wood? Inlays, marquetry and *intarsia* use different colored veneers to achieve amazing results.

Primary colors are seldom used on painted, enameled or colored lacquered pieces except in small amounts. The primary colors are often mixed with white to form tints, or mixed with complementary colors to form shades of the color.

Harmony

Harmony is the ability of component parts to be compatible with each other. A chromium drawer pull would not harmonize with the drawers on a *Chippendale* chest, and an intricate carving would look out of place on a contemporary table.

Center of Interest

The *center of interest* is what the eye first sees on a project. It may be a splash of color, a small inlay, a well-done carving, an exotic grained veneer, a piece of hardware or a small turning.

Texture

Texture has to do primarily with the smoothness or roughness of the surface. On furniture, it applies more to the upholstery fabrics than to the wood. However, wood does have texture. A high gloss texture is appropriate for the piano, but would be out of place on a Danish contemporary piece of furniture.

No matter how excellent a design might be, the designer's work will come to naught if poor materials are selected, the overall craftsmanship is sloppy, and the finish is poorly selected and/or poorly applied.

TECHNIQUES USED IN DESIGNING

The *doodle method* (controlled free form) is used in designing bowls, trays, table tops and other contemporary free form patterns. An ever-curving, continuous, swirling, sweeping line is drawn on a large sheet of plain, unruled paper. It becomes readily apparent that the drawing will furnish a number of possible forms, which may be cross-hatched or darkened to bring them out (Fig. 1-1).

Doodle Method

Select one of the forms for your project. Enlarge the shape selected by drawing a vertical line, a horizontal line and two 45° lines through the center of the selected shape.

On a separate piece of paper draw the same set of straight lines. It is then easy to enlarge the shape. For instance, if the drawing is to be doubled in size, step off twice the distance with dividers equal to twice the distance of each line of the original on the new drawing. Connect the eight points freehand or with a French curve (Fig. 1-2).

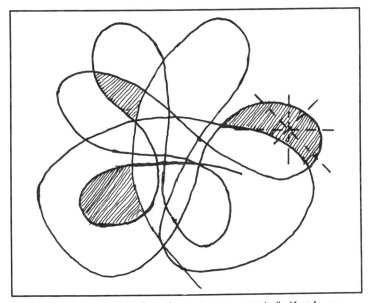

Fig. 1-1. The doodle method of creating contemporary controlled free forms.

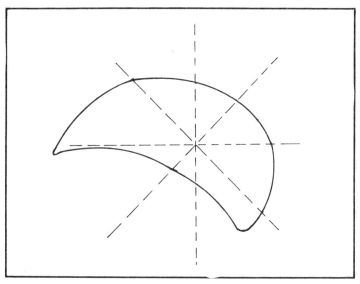
Fig. 1-2. Controlled free form (doodle method) enlarged.

Controlled Shapes From Basic Forms

Trays may be designed involving three basic geometrical shapes: the *triangle*, the *rectangle* and the *circle*. A number of tentative forms should be made full-size from each basic shape, and the final selection made from these. Sometimes sharp-pointed colored chalk is used to draw the outline because it is easier to control than a pencil (Fig. 1-3).

The Mirror Method for Designing Symmetrical Shapes

This method is used when both sides of a project or a component are symmetrical such as turned legs, turned lamp bases, turned salt and pepper shakers or pepper mills, turned candlesticks, etc. However, this method is not confined to turnings, but may be used on any project which is identical on each side. The purpose of this method is to experiment visually on the relationship between the width and length of the object before committing yourself on the final drawing.

HOW TO USE THE MIRROR TO DESIGN SYMMETRICAL SHAPES

Draw the outline of one side of the object on translucent or tracing paper. Place the mirror upright beside the drawing on the vertical axis. Move the mirror toward and away from the drawing until the right proportion is arrived at.

Draw a vertical line along the lower edge of the mirror as soon as the right position has been established. The lines should extend through the two ends of the drawing. This line then becomes the center line of the project. Fold the drawing over on the center line so the original half of the drawing is on the inside.

Trace the outline of the original half on the reverse side. The pencil graphite will be transferred to the inside opposite the original half, and the drawing will be complete when the paper is unfolded.

PRELIMINARY SKETCHES

This is a free wheeling exercise. Let your mind run wild. There is no need to worry about making mistakes. The designer can make mistakes at this stage without dire consequences. A few more minutes or another sheet of paper is about all that could happen.

Try to visualize what you would like the product to look like when finished. Draw rapidly and do not worry about neat lines, scale or proportion. It is best to hold the pencil rather loosely, some distant back from the point. Block in the object with long continuous strokes, using the elbow as a pivot point. Fingers and wrist motion are used for short lines. After the blocking-in is complete, darken the outline and details.

A small toy table is used as an illustration as it will be used to depict other principles of drawing and construction in later sections of the book (Fig. 1-4).

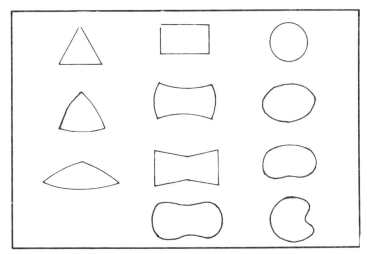

Fig. 1-3. Controlled shapes from basic forms.

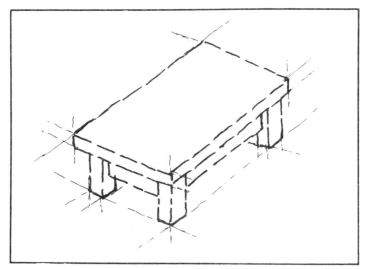

Fig. 1-4. Preliminary sketch of toy table.

PICTORIAL OR CLIENT DRAWING

A presentation drawing is often made after the initial brainstorming and preliminary sketch or sketches are made. The pictorial drawing is a refined and more sophisticated developed visual. These drawings may be freehand sketches or mechanical drawings. Quite often they are a combination of both.

These drawings are used for different purposes. The furniture designer presents them to his client (the furniture manufacturer) for his selection and approval before proceeding with working drawings. The school shop instructor may require his students to present a pictorial drawing before the student makes a final drawing. The home craftsman may crystallize his own ideas by making a pictorial idea.

Pictorial drawings come in different forms. The most common are *front view, perspective, isometric* and *cabinet.* Each is illustrated.

Front View

The *front view* is used occasionally for pictorial drawings, but it is not the most effective because of the lack of depth (Fig. 1-5).

Perspective view

Perspective views are probably the most effective as they show the object in the same way that the human eye or eye of a camera sees it. All lines, except the vertical ones, converge at vanishing points (Fig. 1-6).

Isometric View

The *isometric* drawing is probably the most popular used for the pictorial in that it is easy to draw on a drawing board. Also, it is easy to visualize the object in spite of the fact that lines do not converge. Parallel lines are actually parallel to each other.

It is easy to draw an isometric because about all that is needed is a drawing board, T-square, a 30°-60° triangle and a pencil. The three basic lines of the drawing form a "Y" with each segment of the "Y" equal to 120° (Fig. 1-7).

Cabinet View

The *cabinet view* starts with the front view. Depth is provided by adding angle lines. However, these lines should be foreshortened to about two-thirds of their actual length; otherwise the drawing will appear distorted (Fig. 1-8).

WORKING DRAWINGS

After a presentation drawing is finally agreed upon by all parties, a *working drawing* must be made. The working drawing must be complete so that the cabinetmaker or craftsman may construct the product with no assistance from the designer. The working drawing is generally an orthographic, three-view (top, front and end) drawing, but sometimes two views are sufficient. Generally an assembly drawing of the completed piece is sufficient, but sometimes detail auxiliary drawings are necessary.

All dimensions are shown on a scale drawing (less than full size), but if the drawing is made full size as often done for the furniture manufacturer, dimensions are not needed because the

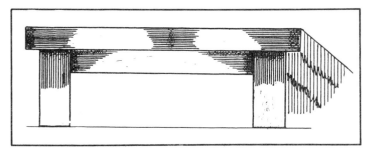

Fig. 1-5. Front view pictorial of toy table.

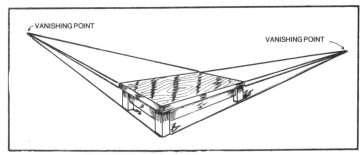

Fig. 1-6. Perspective pictorial view of toy table.

woodworkers can measure the drawing directly. The furniture designer often makes the working drawings, but sometimes this work is delegated to a draftsman's assistant (Fig. 1-9).

MECHANICAL DRAWING TOOLS

The *drawing board* should be at least 11" x 15". A person may make his own from ⅜" or ½" basswood plywood. All corners must be perfectly square.

T-Square

The *T-square* should be at least 1" longer than the long dimension of the drawing board. A craftsman may make his own, but the commercial ones with transparent plastic edges are easier to use.

Triangles

An 8" 45° and an 8" 30°-60° triangle will be useful in scribing lines at 90°, 60°, 45° and 30°. By using the two together, many more angles can be obtained.

Fig. 1-7. Isometric pictorial of toy table.

Fig. 1-8. Cabinet pictorial of toy table.

Architectural Scale

An *architectural scale* with its 12 different scales will save considerable time. The outstanding characteristic of this scale is that each graduation is deep enough so that the divider points naturally fall into the recesses when the correct dimension is reached. *Never use the architectural scale as a straight edge when drawing lines.*

Compass and Other Tools

The *compass* is necessary for drawing circles. There are a number of ancillary tools and accessories used by the draftsman such as a pencil sharpener or pointer, drawing and graph paper, assorted grades of drawing pencils, masking tape, erasers and many other things (Fig. 1-10).

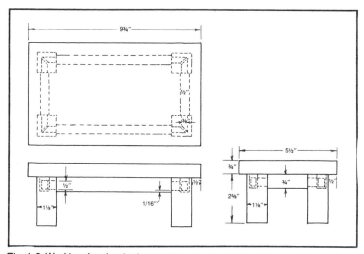

Fig. 1-9. Working drawing (orthographic projection) of toy table.

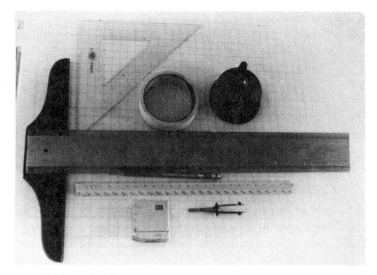

Fig. 1-10. Mechanical drawing tools.

JOB SHEETS

The *job sheet* is a companion piece to the working drawing; in fact, the job sheet requires considerable study of the working drawing before it can be completed. The job sheet organizes the work of the craftsman in a methodical, uniform manner.

A job sheet for a project with many parts would be in four parts: *introduction, bill of material, procedure, stock cutting list and/or cutting plans* and *stock bill*.

Introduction

The introductory statement explains briefly what the project is, its purpose or function and any unique characteristic of the project.

Bill of Material

The bill of material lists the *number of pieces, description, finished size* (thickness, width and length, in that order) and *material. Hardware* is listed after the wood parts. The bill of material for the toy table is in Table 1-1.

Procedure

The plan of procedure emphasizes *what* is to be done in step-by-step fashion. Each step is numbered and is in brief, outline form describing the *operation*. Each operational step should begin with a strong, active verb and should be in the imperative form. Sometimes safety precautions or technical information are added, but only after the operational step is completed.

Stock Cutting List

The sizes listed in the bill of material are finished sizes, while the sizes in a stock cutting bill are rough sizes. To the finished sizes are added about ⅜″ to the width, and about ¾″ to the length.

Cutting Plan

The cutting plan is usually developed on graph paper. The cutting plan depicts the most economical way of cutting stock to prevent waste. It is almost a necessity for cutting out a large number of parts from a sheet of plywood. Allowances should be made for saw kerfs.

Stock Bill

The stock bill is used for planning costs of wood. The formula for arriving at costs is as follows. The sizes are taken from the stock cutting list.

$$\text{Number of Pieces} \times \frac{\text{T o W e L}}{144} \times \text{Cost Per Square Ft.} = \text{Total Cost}$$

This assumes that the number of pieces are the same size, and the thickness, width and length are in inches. The word ToWeL is used only as a mnemonic device to be sure that the thickness, width and length are arranged in the proper order.

Sometimes the stock bill is incorporated in the bill of material by adding two more columns after material: Cost Per square foot and total cost. However, this method is more cumbersome than having a separate stock bill.

Table 1-1. Materials List for the Toy Table.

No. of Pcs.	Description	Size	Material
1	Top	3/4″ x 5 1/2″ x 9 3/4″	White Pine
4	Legs	1 1/8″ x 1 1/8″ x 2 5/8″	White Pine
2	Long Rails	1/2″ x 3/4″ x 8 7/8″	White Pine
2	Short Rails	1/2″ x 3/4″ x 4 1/16″	White Pine

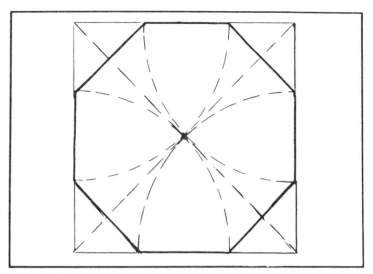

Fig. 1-11. How to lay out an octagon.

LAYOUT TOOLS

Layout and measuring tools include the compass, combination square, folding rule, framing square, large dividers, marking gauge, mortise gauge, scratch awl or scriber, T-bevel square, trammel points and the try square.

Circles or portions of a circle can be laid out directly on the wood. Small circles are made with the compass or dividers. The dividers work best if one leg is sharpened to a chisel point. Trammel points are used for large circles. Two steel points are used for scribing, but a pencil may be substituted for one of the points. Circles scribed with the dividers or trammel points should be darkened in using a hard, chisel-pointed pencil.

HOW TO LAY OUT AN OCTAGON

Draw a square equal to the size of the desired octagon. Draw a diagonal to establish the center. Draw quarter circles from each corner of the square using half the diagonal as a radius.

Connect the points where the quarter circles touch the edge of the square. The octagon is laid out with eight equal segments (Fig. 1-11).

HOW TO LAY OUT A HEXAGON

Draw a circle with a diameter equal to the distance between the opposite points on the desired hexagon. The points of the compass or dividers are set at a distance equal to the radius of the circle.

Draw an arc starting at any point on the circle. Strike two more arcs using the ends of the arc at the point where it meets the circle. Continue around the circle until the six equal segments are established (Fig. 1-12).

PATTERNS AND TEMPLATES

Patterns, full-size, are often needed when irregular curves are involved and when the drawing is less than full-size. Translucent graph paper may be placed over the small drawing and the curves drawn in. On a piece of tracing paper lay out squares so that the drawing will be full size. If the project is symmetrical, only a half drawing is necessary. The number of squares on the pattern must correspond to the number of squares on the graph paper drawing. Mark off points on the pattern which correspond to the relative position on the graph drawing. Connect these points, first freehand, followed by darkening the lines using a French curve.

A *template* is a more permanent pattern drawn on thin plywood, heavy cardboard, ⅛″ hardboard or aluminum. The edges must be carefully smoothed with sandpaper or emery cloth. Templates are necessary when making a large number of duplicate parts.

STYLES AND PERIODS OF FURNITURE

Some authorities include furniture from the landing of the Pilgrims to the Civil War under this category, which includes Classical furniture by the old masters. Others claim that Early

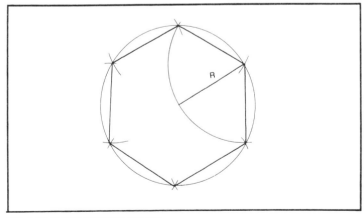

Fig. 1-12. How to lay out a hexagon.

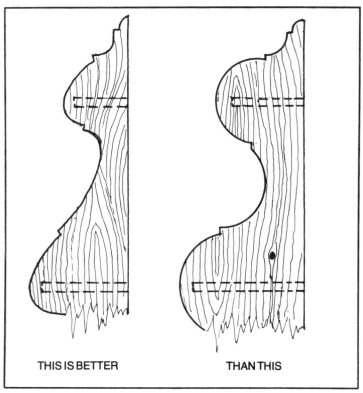

THIS IS BETTER   THAN THIS

Fig. 1-13. Changing radii for curves.

American furniture includes *Primitive, Pilgrim, Puritan, Country* and *Colonial* (William and Mary) up to about 1750. No one definite style or period emerged during this time.

Early American Furniture

The simplicity and humble beauty of Early American and Colonial pine furniture and accessories have fascinated and delighted Americans for well over 300 years. The early craftsmen designed and made objects of charm and grace, each one reflecting the individuality of the maker.

Here are a few basic rules for designing Early American Furniture.

■ The *square* is the least desirable rectangular shape.

■ Multiple squares, likewise, are not the most pleasing to the eye.

■ The most satisfying of all rectangular forms is called the *divine section* or the *golden mean* rectangle. The ratio of width to length is one to 1.618.

■ When dividing a rectangle into parts by vertical lines, it is better to divide the rectangle into odd rather than even number of parts. The center section should generally be larger than the end sections.

■ Curves are more pleasing if the radius is ever-changing rather than being a portion of a circle (Fig. 1-13).

■ In dividing a rectangle by horizontal lines (chests of drawers, shelves, etc.), it is more desirable if the drawers or distance between shelves are progressively larger toward the bottom (Fig. 1-14).

■ Drawer knobs or pulls look more balanced if they are slightly above the center of the drawer (Fig. 1-15).

■ Curves moving abruptly from one direction to another are best separated by a break (Fig. 1-16).

■ Curves should end up parallel or at right angles to the axis of the project (Figs. 1-17 and 1-18).

Classical Furniture (ca. 1750-1820)

Classical furniture or period furniture is generally considered to be the furniture designed and made by the master furniture makers, and their names were identified with their furniture.

Thomas Chippendale. Chippendale's furniture was known for graceful curves and beautiful carvings. His furniture, in addition to being very pleasing to the eye, was sturdily built as well, as a

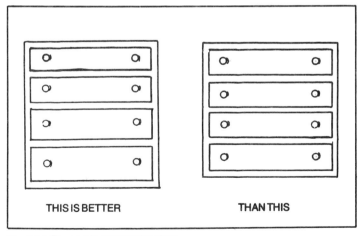

Fig. 1-14. Drawers in progressive sizes.

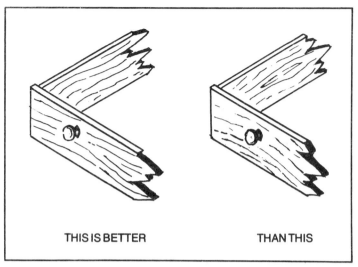

THIS IS BETTER   THAN THIS

Fig. 1-15. Drawer knobs more balanced when slightly above center.

number of his original pieces are still in use today. Although the Chippendale style is considered distinctive, his chairs were often mistaken for Queen Anne.

George Hepplewhite. Hepplewhite furniture is nearly as popular today as it was in its heyday (1770-1790). His shield-back chairs and settees were probably his best contribution; however, his furniture was rather delicate and was apt to break.

Hepplewhite and Sheraton furniture pieces are somewhat similar in design.

Thomas Sheraton. Sheraton furniture can usually be identified by the use of straight lines and squares. Sheraton often decorated his furniture with paint, inlays, carvings and many ornamental designs. Turnings were often spiral turned, fluted or reeded.

Duncan Phyfe. Duncan Phyfe furniture did not exemplify a true style or period, although it is considered so in America. Phyfe's work was largely copied from Sheraton and Directoire (forerunner of French Empire furniture). He very effectively used the cornucopia and saber-legs on his sofas, and the lyre on his chair backs.

Victorian Furniture (ca. 1840-1925)

Victorian furniture, which covered a historical period of nearly a century, was not a furniture period or style, but a

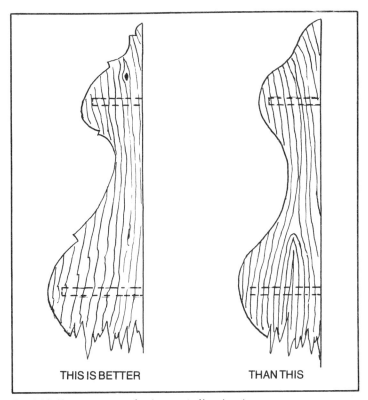

THIS IS BETTER   THAN THIS

Fig. 1-16. Abrupt curves are best separated by a breal.

composite of previous periods, styles and substyles. Victorian furniture, although influenced by the English and French of earlier periods, is definitely American in origin.

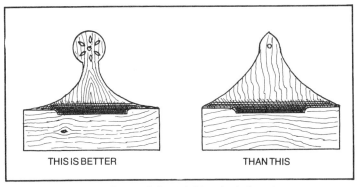

THIS IS BETTER   THAN THIS

Fig. 1-17. Curves should be parallel or at right angles to the axis.

Fig. 1-18. Early American spice drawer cabinet with recessed knobs.

Victorian pieces that sold for pennies or were given away before World War II are now valued antiques, and many are now in museums or in the possession of collectors. As a result of this recent revival, many furniture manufacturers are now making reproductions of Victorian furniture.

Traditional Furniture

Traditional furniture consists of all kinds, styles and periods of furniture not included in the category of contemporary furniture.

Modern or Contemporary Furniture

Contemporary furniture is known by its straight lines, attractive grain woods, ease in keeping clean, and scale appropriate to small houses and apartments.

Teak and walnut are the woods most often used in this furniture, the design in which, in the most part, came from Scandinavian countries. Wood is often combined with glass, plastics and metal to form very attractive and functional pieces.

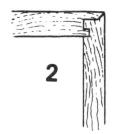

2

Materials and Hardware

Trees grow vertically (above and below the earth's surface) and horizontally (to form the limbs). Each layer formed within the trunk and root system serves a vital purpose in the total development of the organism.

Man takes note only of the particular layers within the tree that serve his needs for lumber production. These layers—found in the trunk—and the cutting methods used to obtain them should be of concern to the home craftsman. Any wood project depends not only on the skill of the craftsman who fashions the finished product, but also on the quality of the wood itself and the care taken when the wood is harvested.

HOW A TREE GROWS

A tree grows much the same way as an onion—one conical layer on top of another. Commercial lumber comes only from trees of some size—in other words, trees that have reached full maturity or nearly so.

A tree consists of the *trunk, branches* of different size and a *root system*. The top of the tree is usually referred to as the *crown*.

In size, the root system is about the same as the crown. The higher portion of the crown generally is the predominant portion because it receives more sunshine and rain, and that portion becomes the trunk. The secondary branches become just that—secondary—and many of the small ones wither, die and drop off.

Growing takes place in two places—at the very tip of the elongated cones, which increase the height of a tree, and in the *cambium layer* which is between the bark and the wood (Fig. 2-1).

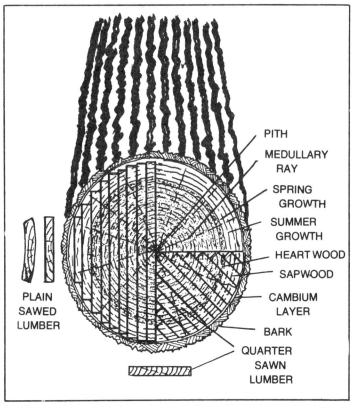

Fig. 2-1. A cross section of a tree demonstrating methods of sawing lumber.

This growth contributes to the thickness of a tree. Figure 2-2 is not drawn to scale; if it were, the height would be many times higher in proportion to the diameter of the trunk.

Burls, splated wood, bird's eye, crotch and stump woods are woods with unusual configurations. They are formed by unusual growth, chemicals, disease and by the location of the wood within the tree.

Methods of sawing or machining of wood may enhance the beauty of the finished product. Wood turned on a veneer lathe and quarter-sawn wood, for example, are quite attractive.

Annular Rings

Ordinarily, the age of a tree can be ascertained by counting the *annular rings*—spring growth plus summer growth. Usually the summer rings are counted because they are denser, darker and more pronounced. Trees that grow in the tropics and are not regulated by changes of seasons, but grow continuously throughout the year, do not have well defined growth (annular) rings.

Counting the rings on the stump or on the end of a log does not always give the correct answer. Take a look at Fig. 2-2. If we count the annular rings, we get an age of 10 years, not 15. It took the tree

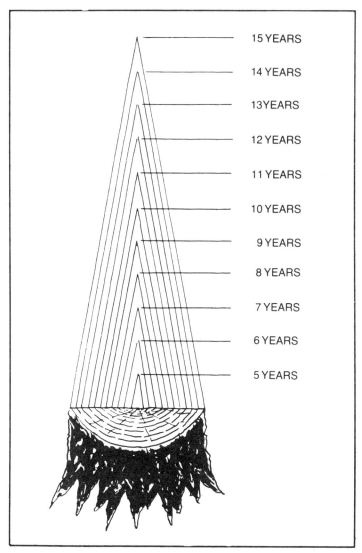

15 YEARS

14 YEARS

13 YEARS

12 YEARS

11 YEARS

10 YEARS

9 YEARS

8 YEARS

7 YEARS

6 YEARS

5 YEARS

Fig. 2-2. The cambium layer at different stages of the tree's growth.

between four or five years to reach the stump height. Only by cutting off a tree next to the ground and counting the rings do we approach the correct answer.

Tree Cross Section

A further explanation of the major parts of a tree will be discussed now. The *pith* serves no useful purpose in a tree. Pith is the very center of a tree (Fig. 2-1). It is generally soft and is apt to rot, which leaves a hollow. Sometimes honey bees take advantage of the cavities and deposit their honey there.

The wood that encircles the pith is called the *heartwood*. It is the main portion of the tree trunk and gives it strength and stability. It is no longer in the growing stage and it does not aid in carrying moisture and food to the rest of the tree. The heartwood is generally darker than the sapwood which surrounds it. The cells in heartwood are dead and are frequently clogged with dark-colored waste material which gives it some of its characteristic color. Some heartwood turns darker when exposed to the air while other heartwood turns lighter. The spring growth and the summer growth rings are more condensed in the heartwood than in the sapwood.

Sapwood is made up of spring growth and summer growth. The spring growth is generally wider than the summer growth because of more favorable growing conditions (moisture, etc.). The summer growth takes place more slowly and is apt to be darker in color and denser in texture, although sapwood in general is lighter in color than heartwood. The sapwood is important as a conductor of food and moisture to the rest of the tree.

The *cambium layer* is between the sapwood and the bark. It is a semi-liquid, cohesive substance. The main function of the cambium layer is to create cells which divide. Some of the cells form wood while others form bark. The growth takes place by cell division. New wood cells are formed on the inside and new bark cells are formed on the outside of the cambium layer.

WOOD CELL STRUCTURE

Wood cells are the building blocks which make up the structure of the wood. They grow together and are of different sizes and shapes. Most cells are elongated and are pointed at the end (Fig. 2-3).

Sometimes cells are called fibers or *tracheids*. The length of fibers varies between different species and may vary in length in an individual tree. Hardwood tracheids average about 1/25″ in length while softwood fibers are much longer.

Cells in hardwood that have large cross-sections are called *vessels*. These vessels are primarily the means by which sap is transported in the tree.

Both hardwoods and softwoods have special cells which grouped together form *medullary rays* (Fig. 2-1). They are arranged in horizontal fashion in a radial direction from the pith toward the bark. Their purpose is to conduct sap (moisture and food) across the grain. They are most noticeable in quarter-sawn surfaces.

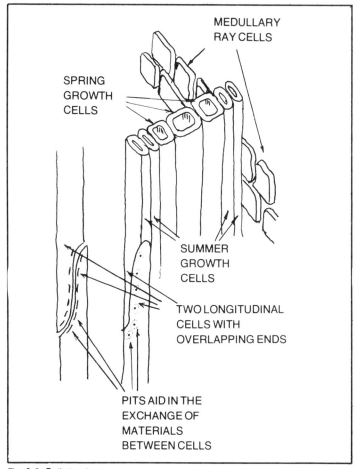

Fig. 2-3. Cell structure.

There are other cells known as *parenchyma* cells. Their main function is to store food. (See *Wood Handbook: Wood As An Engineering Material.*)

LUMBERING

Care is taken by the foresters that trees are mature before cutting. The trees are carefully inspected and marked only if they are ready for harvesting. In addition to the trees marked, because of their lumber potential, other trees are marked because they have been infected by disease and/or insects. Others are also marked to be removed in order to give elbow room to those left. This not only gives them a chance for survival, but they will grow faster.

Power saws are used to "harvest" the trees. The trunk is cut into appropriate lengths after the limbs are cut off. Very few logs are floated down rivers to the sawmill today. More often they are slid out of the woods with caterpillar tractors and then placed on trucks to be transported to the sawmill. Sawmills are located within easy driving distance to the forests from which the logs came.

The sawmill is located near water, usually a river or a lake, so that a pond can be provided to store the logs until sawing starts. This helps prevent early seasoning and thus prevents checking of the wood. It also helps to prevent infestation by insects. Logs should be sawn into lumber as soon as possible after the tree is harvested, because lumber saws easier while green.

Sometimes the logs are washed and the bark is removed before sawing takes place. Circular saws are still used to cut small logs, but the larger ones are generally sawn by huge band saws with teeth on both edges which permits the cutting of lumber in both directions while the carriage passes the saw.

In recent years mobile sawmills have been used to move into areas where there are mature trees and the lumber is cut close to the source of supply.

After the lumber is cut into boards, planks and timbers, it should be carefully stacked with narrow sticks between each layers, with space between each board for circulation of air. The stack should be up off the ground and the top should be covered to protect it from rain or snow. Lumber should be air-dried from six months to two years depending on the thickness and the species.

SAWMILLS

Dwight G. Gorrell of Centerville, Kansas, describes in the July/August 1979 issue of *Fine Woodworking* how he and his father built a two-man sawmill, with "its major components from scrap iron and parts from highway vehicles and old farm machinery."

The 52" diameter circular saw is powered by a multi-fuel spark diesel engine with a four-cylinder starting engine. A major drawback of this operation is the lack of a millpond, which means that logs cannot be skidded "through mud, gravel or rocks."

Mobile Sawmill

Northeast Ohio Machine manufactures and sells a large mobile sawmill on a large multiple-wheel trailer chassis.

Small Stationary Sawmill

The *Belsaw* sawmill is advertised as the only one-man sawmill of its kind in the world. It can be powered by a power take-off from a farm tractor or a diesel engine (25 hp or over). It is claimed that Belsaw mills are sold year after year more than all other makes of sawmills combined, primarily because of their ease of operation.

A 40" diameter, inserted tooth blade is used because teeth can be quickly removed and replaced with a wrench when worn, which minimizes filing.

A variable-speed, power feed operates with as little as 25 hp. Forward feed is variable from 0 to 1.33" in each saw revolution. The carriage backs away at triple speed after cutting.

The Belsaw sawmill handles logs up to 14' long and up to 18" in diameter. Concrete footings are recommended to provide stability and optimum performance of the saw (Fig. 2-4).

CHAIN SAW LUMBERING

The chain sawmill has become a necessity for some wood-workers due to the high cost of lumber and/or to the long distance to the sawmill. The portable chain sawmill has the distinct advantage of being transportable to the log, rather than bringing the log to the mill.

This versatile tool will pay for itself in a few days of cutting. Logs can be turned into lumber, some of which a commercial sawyer would not bother with.

Fig. 2-4. The Belsaw sawmill.

Robert Sperber, the man who designed, built and sells the Sperber chain saw sawmill, wrote a very comprehensive and enlighting article on the use of the chain sawmill in *Fine Woodworking* magazine, Fall, 1977. The article entitled "Chain Saw Lumbering: Cut Your Wood Where It Falls," explains how the saw chain is sharpened for ripping, and how the mill is pulled through the log. Crotch wood can be saved because of its interesting grain, something that would be impossible to do with a commercially owned sawmill.

Sperber discusses in detail how the slabbing rail is used for the first cut, but is discarded for sawing the remaining cuts. He points out that although quarter sawing can be done on the Sperber mill, unless the log is very large the results will be far from satisfactory. He cautions the operator that goggles, ear protection and a dust mask should be worn for safe operation of the chain sawmill.

Sperber manufactures four sizes of saws. The smallest can be operated by one man and is powered by one engine. The other three models require two engines and are manned by two people. The larger saw will handle logs up to 4′ in diameter.

Granberg Industries offers a chain sawmill that clamps on the bar of the chain saw and fits bar lengths from 14″ to 56″. They also sell a sharpening jig using a hand file. A more expensive sharpening jig using a stone instead of a file, and operated by an electric motor, is also available. It is claimed to be much faster and more accurate.

Haddon Tools makes an inexpensive, lightweight LUM-BER/MAKER which uses a 2" x 4" or 2" x 6" as a slabbing rail. The LUMBER/MAKER cuts in a vertical rather than a horizontal position. This chain sawmill does not require a special saw chain.

Sears, Roebuck sells a compact lumber making attachment, similar to Haddon's, that clamps to any chain saw guide bar up to 30" long. The following are chain saw sawmill suppliers and manufacturers: Granberg Industries, Inc. (90), Haddon Tools (92), Sears Roebuck and Co. (163) and Sperber Tool Works (170).

PLAIN SAWING OF LUMBER

Plain sawing of wood is the most common way of sawing lumber. There is not as much waste and it is much faster than quarter sawing (Fig. 2-1). Actually, when a log is plain-sawn, two or three pieces in the center of the log (the widest pieces) are quarter-sawn in that the saw cuts are parallel to the medullary rays. However, the outside pieces do not fare as well. When the wood is drying, the tension in these outside pieces is tremendous. In the drying process the internal forces in the wood apply along the annular rings. With the strength of thousands of rubber bands, the annular rings try to contract (that is, become straight lines). As a result, the board has the tendency to cup to the outside (See "plain sawed lumber" in Fig. 2-1). Naturally, the board the greatest distance from the center of the log will warp the most.

QUARTER SAWING OF LUMBER

Quarter sawing of wood is accomplished by cutting a log into four parts, longitudinally, so that the end of the log is a 90° pie-shaped segment. The quarter log is cut in such a manner that the saw cuts are parallel—or nearly so—to the medullary rays. Medullary rays conduct sap across the grain in both softwoods and hardwoods by strips of cells that run at right angles to the fibers (Figs. 2-1 and 2-3).

This sawing produces large flakes on the surface of the wood, particularly in oak. Quarter sawing is used with many other woods besides oak to prevent or retard shrinking, twisting and to prevent small checks from appearing on the surface. Wood cut in this manner will wear much longer than wood cut in other ways.

CLASSIFICATION OF WOOD

Wood is classified in two categories—*softwoods* and *hardwoods*. Traditionally, softwoods came from evergreen, cone-bearing trees that retain their leaves (needles) throughout the year.

Trees that have broad leaves and shed their leaves annually are called hardwoods. Botanically, the softwoods are called *gymnosperms*, and the hardwoods are called *angiosperms*.

There are certain discrepancies in this method of classification. Some so-called softwoods are actually harder than some hardwoods. Conversely, some hardwoods are softer than softwoods. For example, basswood classified as a hardwood is much softer than some of the pines and firs which are classified as softwoods.

Wood is also classified as *open* grain and *close* grain. Walnut, mahogany and oak are open grain woods and in the finishing process require a filler. White pine, basswood, birch, maple, poplar and redwood are only a few examples of close grain woods.

In addition, wood is classified according to thickness: *board*-lumber less than 2" in normal thickness, *dimension*-lumber from 2", but not including 5" in normal thickness, and *timbers*-lumber 5" or more in normal thickness in the least dimension.

INTRODUCTION TO CUTTING GRADES

The grade of a piece of lumber is based on the number, character and location of features that lower the strength, durability or utility value of the lumber. Among the more common visual features are knots, checks, pitch pockets, shake and stain, some of which are a natural part of the tree. The sawmill is the place where most of the grading takes place.

Softwoods

The two major categories of softwoods are *construction* and *remanufacture*. Construction lumber needs no further grading after it leaves the sawmill. There are three classifications of construction lumber.

Stress-Graded Lumber. Applies to softwood lumber 2" to 4" thick used for structural purposes.

Nonstress-Graded Lumber. Commonly called "yard lumber." It includes boards, lath, planks, etc.

Appearance Lumber. Appearance lumber includes trim, siding, flooring, ceiling, paneling, casing, base, stair strips and finish boards. Finish boards are commonly used for shelving and built-in cabinets.

Remanufacture lumber is supplied to industry and is cut to specific smaller sizes. The four grades of remanufacture lumber are: *factory; industrial clears; molding, ladder, pole, tank* and *pencil stock grade;* and *structural laminations.*

Hardwoods

Cutting grades are as follows.

■ "Firsts"—the highest grade.

■ "Seconds." Firsts and seconds are generally combined into one grade known as "FAS" (first and seconds). The percentage of "firsts" required in the combined grade varies from 20% to 40% depending on the species.

■ Selects.

■ No. 1 Common.

■ No. 2 Common.

■ "Sound Wormy." "Sound Wormy" has the same requirements as No. 1 Common and better except worm holes, limited sound knots and other imperfections are allowed in the cuttings.

■ No. 3A Common.

■ No. 3B Common.

In general the minimum acceptable length, width surface measure, and percent of piece that must work into a cutting decreases with decreasing grade.

"Firsts" call for pieces which allow 91⅔% of the surface measure to be cut into clear face material, while No. 3B Common calls for 25% of the cuttings to be sound—clear face not required.

The species of wood named for grading rules used by the National Hardwood Association (NHA) are as follows in Table 2-1, but it should be noted that two of the species are softwood (cedar, aromatic red and cypress). Cypress has a different set of grading rules.

PRACTICAL USES AND PHYSICAL CHARACTERISTICS
OF COMMON DOMESTIC SOFTWOODS AND HARDWOODS

The following information is courtesy of the Research Department of the American Wood Working Company (7).

Table 2-1. Species of Wood Named for Grading Rules Used by the NHA.

Alder, red	Hickory
Ash	Locust
Aspen	Magnolia
Basswood	Mahogany
Beech	African
Birch	Cuban and San Dominican
Boxelder	Philippine
Buckeye	Maple
Cedar, aromatic red	Hard (sugar)
Cedar, Spanish	Soft
Cherry	Pacific Coast
Chestnut	Oak
Cottonwood	Red
	White
Cypress	Pecan
Elm	Poplar
Rock	Sycamore
Soft	Walnut
Gum	Willow
Black	
Red	
Tupelo	
Hackberry	
Hardwoods (Philippine)	

Hardwoods (Tropical America other
     than mahogany and Spanish
       cedar)	

Ash, Black

■ **Uses:** Handles, dowels, blocks, balls, lamp parts.

■ **Characteristics:** Weight 39½ pounds per cubic foot dried to 12% moisture content. Medium hardness. Medium strength, splits fairly easy, good dimensional stability and is moderately decay resistant.

Ash, White

■ **Uses:** Rollers, handles, long dowels, athletic equipment.

■ **Characteristics:** Weight 41 pounds per cubic foot at 12% moisture content. Hard, high strength, moderately easy to split, good dimensional stability and moderately resistant to decay.

Aspen

■ **Uses:** Light-weight use, dowels, plugs for pipes, etc.

- **Characteristics:** Weight 25 pounds per cubic foot at 12% moisture content. Soft, medium strength, does not split easily, dimensional stability good and is not decay resistant.

Basswood

- **Uses:** Lightweight use, novelties, moldings.
- **Characteristics:** Weight 26 pounds per cubic foot at 12% moisture content. Soft, medium strength, does not split easily, good dimensional stability and does not resist decay.

Beech

- **Uses:** Substitute for hard maple.
- **Characteristics:** Weight 45 pounds per cubic foot at 12% moisture content. Hard, high strength, splits easily, dimensional stability fair, does not resist decay.

Birch, White

- **Uses:** Spools, dowels, a fine turning wood.
- **Characteristics:** Weight 36 pounds per cubic foot at 12% moisture content. Medium hardness, medium strength, does not split easily, good dimensional stability, moderately decay resistant.

Birch, Yellow

- **Uses:** Bobbins, moldings, lab equipment, finishes nicely.
- **Characteristics:** Weight 44 pounds per cubic foot at 12% moisture content. Hard, high strength, does not split easily, good dimensional stability, does not resist decay.

Cherry

- **Uses:** Furniture, food paddles, printing blocks, patterns.
- **Characteristics:** Weight 35 pounds per cubic foot at 12% moisture content. Medium hardness, high strength, splits fairly easy, excellent dimensional stability, moderately resistant to decay.

Cypress

- **Uses:** Good for outdoor use, tanks, chemical plants.

■ **Characteristics:** Weight 32 pounds per cubic foot at 12% moisture content. Soft, medium strength, splits easily, good dimensional stability, high decay resistant.

Elm, Rock

■ **Uses:** Excellent for rollers, blocks, handles, farm implements.

■ **Characteristics:** Weight 44 pounds per cubic foot at 12% moisture content. Hard, high strength, does not split easily, good dimensional stability, moderately decay resistant.

Elm, Soft

■ **Uses:** Poultry equipment, aviaries, sporting goods.

■ **Characteristics:** Weight 37 pounds per cubic foot at 12% moisture content. Medium hardness, medium strength, does not split easily, good dimensional stability, is not decay resistant.

Fir

■ **Uses:** Good construction Lumber, long softwood dowels.

■ **Characteristics:** Weight 34 pounds per cubic foot at 12% moisture content. Medium hardness, high strength, splits easily, fair dimensional stability, moderately decay resistant.

Gum, Black

■ **Uses:** Bores nicely, rollers, handles, bushings, implements.

■ **Characteristics:** Weight 35 pounds per cubic foot at 12% moisture content. Soft, medium strength, does not split easily, fair dimensional stability, not decay resistant.

Gum, Red

■ **Uses:** Intricate turnings, furniture parts, wedges, bushings.

■ **Characteristics:** Weight 35 pounds per cubic foot at 12% moisture content. Soft, medium hardness, does not split easily, fair dimensional stability, does not resist decay.

Hickory

■ **Uses:** Heavy duty tool handles, foundry blocks, wedges, etc.
■ **Characteristics:** Weight 51 pounds per cubic foot at 12% moisture content. Very hard, high strength, splits moderately easy, fair dimensional stability, is not decay resistant.

Maple, Hard

■ **Uses:** Resists abrasion, bearings, blocks, faucets, etc.
■ **Characteristics:** Very hard, high strength, weight 44 pounds per cubic foot at 12% moisture content. Splits easily, good dimensional stability, moderately decay resistant.

Maple, Soft

■ **Uses:** Spool hubs, furniture frames, novelties.
■ **Characteristics:** Weight 33 pounds per cubic foot at 12% moisture content. Hard, high strength, does not split easily fair dimensional stability, moderately decay resistant.

Oak, Red

■ **Uses:** Bungs, blocks, rollers, agricultural implements.
■ **Characteristics:** Weight 44 pounds per cubic foot at 12% moisture content. Very hard, high strength, moderately easy to split, good dimensional stability, moderately decay resistant.

Oak, White

■ **Uses:** Heavy rollers, plugs, tool handles, agricultural implements.
■ **Characteristics:** Weight 47 pounds per cubic foot at 12% moisture content. Very hard, high strength, splits moderately easy, good dimensional stability, moderately decay resistant.

Pine, White

■ **Uses:** Architectural designs, moldings, models and patterns.

- **Characteristics:** Weight 27 pounds per cubic foot at 12% moisture content. Soft, low strength, splits easily, excellent dimensional stability, moderately resistant to decay.

Poplar, Yellow

- **Uses:** Display fixtures, lamp parts, musical instruments.
- **Characteristics:** Weight 28 pounds per cubic foot at 12% moisture content. Soft, medium strength, moderately easy to split, fair dimensional stability, does not resist decay.

Redwood

- **Uses:** Good for outdoor use, tanks, moldings, etc.
- **Characteristics:** Weight 28 pounds per cubic foot at 12% moisture content. Soft, medium strength, does not split easily, good dimensional stability.

Sycamore

- **Uses:** Butcher's blocks, rollers, scientific instruments.
- **Characteristics:** Weight 34 pounds per cubic foot at 12% moisture content. Hard, medium strength, does not split easily, fair dimensional stability, moderately decay resistant.

Walnut

- **Uses:** Trophy bases, display parts, lamp and furniture parts.
- **Characteristics:** Weight 38 pounds per cubic foot at 12% moisture content. Hard, high strength, moderately easy to split, excellent dimensional stability, moderately decay resistant.

MOISTURE AND WOOD

The weight of water in wood depicted as a percentage of the weight of oven-dry wood, is called the moisture content (MC) of wood. Moisture content affects the weight, shrinkage, strength and other properties of wood.

Moisture content in the growing tree (green wood) may vary from 30% to more than 200% of the weight of the wood. Sapwood generally has a higher moisture content than heartwood, but this is not true of such trees as birch, hickory, some species of oak and black walnut. There is considerable variation in the MC between trees of the same species and within the same tree.

Moisture exists in green wood in two places: *cell cavities (lumens)* and *within the cell walls*. Moisture within the cell walls is often called "bound" moisture.

Generally, green wood is considered wood in which the cell walls are completely saturated with moisture. However, green wood usually contains additional water in the cell cavities.

The "fiber saturation point" is that point at which the cell walls are completely saturated, but no water exists in the cell cavities. The average fiber saturation point of wood is about 30% moisture content, but different species and different pieces of wood may vary considerably.

The physical and mechanical properties of wood begin to change if the moisture content of wood is lowered below the fiber saturation point, and the wood is no longer considered "green."

The "equilibrium moisture content" (EMC) is that moisture content when the wood is neither gaining or losing moisture. The EMC has a very close relationship to humidity and temperature of the air surrounding the wood (Fig. 2-5).

Wood is being constantly exposed to widely varying temperature and humidity conditions which affect the moisture content. Although the changes are slight they do, nevertheless, exist. These daily fluctuations in general affect only the wood surface. The moisture content changes can be eliminated, or at least retarded, by applying surface coatings such as varnish, lacquer, enamel or paint.

When the moisture content in wood is below the fiber saturation point, the wood shrinks while losing moisture and swells while gaining moisture. The losing and gaining of moisture takes place in the cell walls.

This swelling and shrinking has an adverse effect on the wood. It leads to checking, splitting and warping.

Wood shrinks most in the direction of the annual growth rings, only about 50% as much across the rings, and hardly at all along the grain.

No significant changes in dimensions will occur in wood, if the wood is made into furniture or installed in buildings at a moisture content corresponding to the normal atmospheric conditions at which it will be exposed. Even if the wood is not properly seasoned, minor dimensional changes are insignificant if proper design is used.

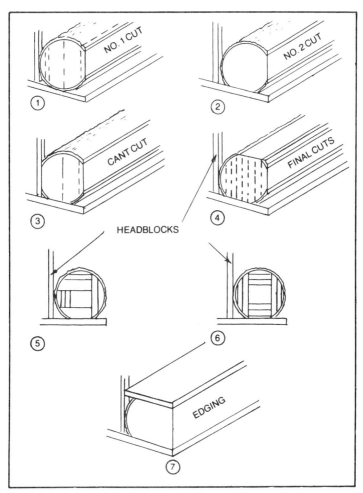

Fig. 2-5. Cross section of cell structure at different moisture contents.

The two most common methods of determining moisture content are the *oven-drying method* and the *electrical method*. The oven-drying method is probably the most acceptable method of finding the moisture content, although it is a very slow method and requires that wood be cut.

The formula used to find the moisture content using the oven method is:

$$\text{Percent of Moisture Content} = \frac{\text{Weight When Cut-Oven-dry Weight} \times 100}{\text{Oven-dry Weight}}$$

The Principal advantages of the electrical method over the oven-drying method are its speed and convenience, and the wood being tested is not cut or damaged.

Some of the newer portable electric moisture meters have solid state circuitry. One company manufactures a pocket size electrical moisture meter. The majority of these moisture detectors operate in a range from 6% to 30% moisture content.

Here are a few suppliers/manufacturers of moisture meters: Delmhorst Instrument Co. (54), Electrodyne, Inc. (63), Moisture Register Co. (128) and Valley Products and Design (188). (For full addresses refer to the number in parentheses listed in the Appendix.)

STABILIZING AND SEASONING WOOD

When green cut wood is allowed to soak in a water solution of polyethylene glycol 1000, called PEG for short (30% to 50% by weight with PEG), the wood shrinks very little when dried and, in addition, swells very little when subjected to high humidity. However, unless used with care and properly protected, wood so treated is apt to become slightly sticky at high relative humidities. (Polyethylene glycol 1000 or "PEG" has an average molecular weight of 1000 from which it gets part of its name.)

Stabilizing Green Wood

The time for adequate soaking in the solution of water and PEG depends on the thickness of the stock. Thick stock may require weeks of soaking. This treatment bulks the cell walls and this is the reason for its success.

PEG is a non-toxic, non-corrosive and non-explosive solution. The treatment has slight effect on color, gluing or the physical properties.

Solutions of water and PEG can be used over and over again by replacing the chemical used up by the repeated soakings. It is recommended that a *hydrometer* be used to make sure that the solution is up to full strength. Different percentages of the PEG solution have different specific gravities.

PEG has also been used as a chemical seasoning agent by reducing the checking of green wood during the drying process. Only light treatments of PEG solution are necessary as high penetration is not required. The disadvantages of using PEG are: its cost, that it can be used only on green wood and that wood treated with PEG is not easy to finish.

According to R. Bruce Hoadley (*Fine Woodworking* magazine Nov./Dec. 1979) in his article "PEG for the Woodworker: What You Always Wanted to Know About Polyethylene Glycol 1000," a black walnut disc 30″ in diameter and 3″ thick (presumably for a table top) might require $40 worth of PEG. Hoadley points out the many practical uses for PEG: "gunstocks for rifles, strips used as core laminations for archery bows, musical instrument parts, bases and framing, large engraving blocks and patterns." He notes, "PEG treatment is also applicable to large wood carvings and has proven useful in stabilizing waterlogged artifacts recovered by archeologists."

Supply sources for PEG include, Robert M. Albrecht (154), Constantine and Son, Inc. (41), Craftsman Wood Service Co. (45), Crane Creek Co. (48), Industrial Arts Supply Co. (102), Lamont Specialties (113), Spielman's Wood Works (171) and Wilkens-Anderson Co. (199).

Air Drying of Lumber

All wood products (furniture, flooring, trim, doors etc.) used inside a heated and/or air conditioned building require stricter controls on moisture content than wood used in unheated structures or outdoors.

The average moisture content varies in different geographical areas of the United States. In the hot, dry southwest the average moisture content for interior products is 6%, 11% in the humid southeast, and 8% average moisture content for the rest of the United States. A plus or minus 1% will not appreciably affect the wood product.

There is considerable variety in the methods of seasoning lumber. Some softwood sawmills kiln-dry the best grades of lumber direct from the saw, while the lower grades are air-dried. Some mills ship lumber without any seasoning whatsoever. Air-dried lumber may be kiln-dried at the mill, at a custom drying plant or at the final manufacturing plant.

Good air-drying conditions require certain practices:

■ The new cut lumber must be protected from the weather (rain, snow, sleet, etc.)

■ The lumber must be piled (stickered) so that good circulation of air is provided.

■ There must be weather that is favorable to good drying. If the weather is too humid or cold, drying takes place at a very slow pace which extends the time before kiln-drying can take place.

Accelerated air-drying has greatly reduced the length of drying considerably. Large fans are used to force air through the piles of lumber. Sometimes a small amount of heat is added.

Air-drying should reduce the moisture content to between 12% to 20% for softwoods and between 20% to 25% for dense hardwoods. Thoroughly air-dried lumber over an extended time period should bring the moisture content close to the equilibrium moisture content, which is between 12% to 15% for most of the United States.

Kiln Drying of Wood

The dry-kiln provides an environment where temperature, humidity and the movement of air are controlled. Seasoning takes place much faster than when wood is air-dried. In addition to drying the wood, kiln-drying kills insects, prevents or destroys fungi or stain and reduces the weight, which is an important factor when lumber has to be shipped long distances.

Kiln-dried wood should be dried to a moisture content not exceeding 12%. For furniture, it should be less.

Generally, kiln-drying practice calls for high humidity in the form of steam and low heat at the beginning of the kiln-drying process, followed by lowered humidity and higher heat during the intermediate phase, and high heat with practically no humidity near the end.

William Rice, a former kiln operator, who teaches wood science and technology at the University of Massachusettes, describes in detail, with illustrations, in *Fine Woodworking Techniques* how a woodworking craftsman can build his own dry-kiln, which will handle 500 board feet of lumber for less than $1000. He also explains what happens to "free water" and "bound water" in the cell, the three environmental factors that have to be controlled within the dry-kiln, operating temperatures, heat sources, the hygroscopic property of wood, how the kiln operates and many other aspects of kiln-drying.

OTHER WOOD OR WOOD RELATED PRODUCTS

Exotic woods are woods with particular unique grain configuration and color. Most of these woods are rather expensive and many come from foreign countries such as Africa, Brazil, India, Nigeria, Australia, Guatemala and Venezuela.

Exotic Woods

In Brazil alone, in addition to *Rosewood (Jacaranda)*, there are the following beautiful tropical woods: *Amendoim, Amoreira, Cabriuva, Canafistoula, Cavjuna, Embuia* (sometimes called *Brazilian Walnut), Ferobinho Campo, Goncalo Alves, Ipe, Marfim, Para Kingwood, Pernambuco, Peroba, Serejeira, Sucupira* and *Tulipwood.* While serving as a consultant to the Brazilian Minister of Education for over two years, I had small pieces of these species of wood turned on a lathe to use as coasters.

Flitches and Slabs

Flitch sawn slabs are logs sawed through without turning the log, producing a slab as wide as the log and retaining its natural contours. The pieces are free form as opposed to dimension lumber, and come in a variety of sizes and shapes. They are often used for coffee tables, clock sections, wall sculpture, etc. Walnut, cherry, maple and redwood burl are a few of the woods used.

Spalted Wood

Spalted wood is caused by a complex mechanism associated with decay in wood. Although hard to describe, the spalting action produces figures and colors in wood that are unmatched for its beauty. The process differs from tree to tree and does not occur in all trees. Most woods that are white in color are apt to spalt.

Parasites, bacteria and fungi all contribute to the spalting process or decaying process, but the wood must be "caught" at the right time—before actual rot takes place. Mineral deposits often cause interesting black or dark colored rings or lines in the wood.

Veneers, Plywood and Laminates

Veneers are thin slices of wood, varying in thickness from 1/42″ to 1/20″, but the two standard thicknesses are 1/40″ and 1/28″. Veneers are commonly classified as *face* veneers and *crossband* veneers.

As one might assume from the name, face veneers are used for exterior use on furniture or paneling where it is seen. Face veneers come in different lengths and widths depending largely on the size of the log and how the veneer is cut.

Crossband veneers are laid at right angles to face veneers and are entirely covered up except for the edges. Poplar is probably the most used veneer for crossbanding.

The configuration of grain in face veneers is due to the part of the tree from which it is taken and the method of cutting the veneers.

The two most common ways of cutting veneers are *rotary* and *sliced*. The rotary method involves a huge lathe. Large logs are placed between the centers. As the log revolves in the lathe, a large knife advances automatically toward the center of the log, thus peeling off large sheets of veneer of predetermined thickness. This method is used to cut crossbands and sometimes face veneer for paneling, but it does little to enhance the grain of the wood. The home woodworker will have little use for wood cut in this fashion except for crossbanding.

Sliced veneers are cut with a large paper-knife-like cutter that slices off thin sheets of veneer. Of course, thin sheets could be cut with a circular saw or band saw, but the loss in sawdust would create a situation that would not be economically feasible. Exotic figures and grain patterns are developed when burl, stump wood, crotches, butt wood and swirls are cut by the slicing method.

Very thin veneers 1/64" thick in large sheets are now available to craftsmen, and open up many new possibilities involving veneer. A flexible backing helps to prevent splitting and tearing, and aids in bending. It eliminates or reduces the need for clamps, bending forms and cauls which are ordinarily used. By using contact cement, the process is much faster and easier.

Bob Morgan Woodworking Supplies (28) has a hot melt glue sheet that is ironed on with an ordinary electric iron. After the glue is ironed on to the base material, the veneer is applied and ironed on to the glue surface.

Marquetry

Marquetry is the process and skill involved in cutting small pieces to certain defined sizes and shapes that when arranged properly become beautiful pictures and designs. These designs are then inlaid into wood objects to decorate such things as jewel boxes, coffee tables, chests of drawers, and other pieces of furniture or accessories.

Many natural wood colors are available to the marquetry worker. For additional colors, veneer is stained or dyed. Where gradual shading is needed on the marquetry picture or inlay, pieces of veneer are placed on edge in hot sand. Shading will be darker in the lower portions which are closer to the heat source.

The tools most commonly used for cutting marquetry pieces are the X-acto knife, a fret saw for hand sawing, and the scroll or jigsaw for power sawing. Beveling the edges of the veneer will aid in providing closer joints between the pieces of marquetry and the base veneer.

Parquetry

Parquetry is similar to marquetry, except that all cuts are straight. Veneers are cut into triangles, squares, rectangles, parallelograms, trapezoids, etc. Solid wood is used for floor parquetry. Making a checkerboard or chessboard is parquetry at its elementary level.

Not very many colors should be used, and the veneer grain should be straight. The many geometric designs available will provide enough interest without resorting to veneers with exotic grain patterns.

Inlays and Overlays

Inlays and *overlays* are preassembled pieces of veneer (marquetry process) mounted of sheets of heavy paper. Overlays are simply glued to the surface of the object, paper side up. After the glue is dried, the paper is removed by moistening and sanding.

Inlays require that the shape of the inlay be chiseled or routed out of the base object. The depth should be slightly less than the thickness of the inlay. The inlay is glued in, paper side up. After the glue is dry, the paper is removed by moistening, and the inlay is sanded down to the level of the base object.

Inlay Borders

Inlay borders come in many varieties and widths. Some inlay borders are simply strips of one solid wood from 1/16″ to ¼″ wide. This natural wood strip material is generally available in ebony, rosewood, satinwood, holly, etc.

Other inlay borders generally consist of two or more outside edge bands with geometric marquetry veneer pieces laid in between the edge bands. In addition to wood, celluloid strips, solid brass strips and imitation mother-of-pearl are used for inlay borders.

Inlay borders require a groove made by a saw, router or other tool. The grooved channel should be slightly less in depth than the thickness of the inlay border. The inlay borders are glued in. When dry, the border is sanded down to the level of the surrounding

64

wood. Inlay borders are usually sold by the yard (36″) and the price per yard varies greatly.

Plywood

Plywood comes in two forms: *veneer core* and *lumber core*. Veneer core plywood is made up of an uneven number of layers of veneer with adjacent layers at right angles to each other and face veneer on at least one of the two faces.

Lumber core veneer is made up of solid lumber, usually poplar; however, basswood and mahogany are also used as core stock. Each side of the core is covered by a layer of crossbanding and face veneer.

When plywood is used for cabinetmaking, the rough edges must be covered. Although veneer strips are sometimes used for this purpose, it is at best a poor choice. Solid wood strips, a little wider than the plywood is thick, are a much better solution. The wood should be the same kind as the face veneer. After solid wood strips are glued to the plywood, the wood strips are sanded down to the level of the plywood.

Plywood can be curved by sawing kerfs on the under side. This method works better with lumber core plywood. A saw kerf through everything except the final crossband and face veneer is first made on a test piece of plywood. The test piece is clamped to the bench top with the kerf on top. Measure a distance equal to the desired radius from the saw kerf. Bend the unclamped end upward until the saw kerf is closed. Measure the distance from the bench top to the lower face of the plywood at the point where the radius is marked off. The distance from the bench top to the plywood is the distance apart that the saw kerfs are made on the desired part.

Plywood has several advantageous physical characteristics. Shrinkage and expansion in one direction is countered by equal shrinkage and expansion at right angles.

Plywood does not easily split. It comes in large sheets which lend plywood to many practical applications. It is much stronger than solid lumber. Mahogany plywood less than an ⅛″ thick was used to make airborne gliders for the armed services during World War II.

Plywood is of two categories as far as materials are concerned: *softwood* and *hardwood*. Softwood plywood is used mostly for construction purposes, while hardwood plywood is used where appearance is the major consideration. Most hardwood plywoods used for cabinet construction are faced with sliced veneer rather tnan rotary cut veneer. A large proportion of hardwood plywood is completely finished before it gets to the consumer.

Plywood is also classified as *interior* and *exterior* plywood. The primary difference is in the type of glue used. Glues used for interior plywood are not moisture-proof.

Plywood generally comes in sheets 4' x 8', although hardwood plywood is sometimes available in smaller sheets. The common thicknesses of plywood are ¾", ⅝", ½", ⅜" and ¼", although thicker and thinner plywoods are also marketed.

Laminated Wood

Although solid pieces of wood can be bent under favorable conditions which usually require steam, hot water, or special heated bending irons in addition to forms, cauls and clamps bending can be accomplished easier with thin strips of wood laminated together. The bending of thin strips to the correct curvature causes little stress and damage to the wood fibers. Stronger components result because of the minimum tension caused by the bending.

Laminated pieces change shape considerably less than solid members if the moisture content varies. Small radii can be obtained with laminated components than with solid pieces. By staggering the joints in thin strips of lamination, curved pieces of almost any length can be obtained. Laminated curved stock can be formed in one single gluing and bending operation.

Resin glues are often used for laminated products, but whatever type is used it should be tested first, particularly where staining can be a problem on products where appearance is a major factor. After the glue has set, the product should be set aside for a week or more before the final shaping, sanding and finishing are completed.

Laminates are used in making structural architectural beams in buildings, tennis rackets, furniture parts, boat parts and golf clubs. The use of plastic laminates (*Formica, Micarta* etc.) and their application is of interest to the woodworker. Due to their composition and the specialized skills involved, this topic was not considered an appropriate one to explore in this book.

Particle Board and Hardboard

Particle board and hardboard used for many purposes. Particle board is composed of wood shavings, wood chips, wood flakes and sawdust. Particle board made exclusively of wood flakes is vastly superior to other particle boards. These ingredients are joined together with adhesives. The smaller ingredients are used on the surface to create a smoother surface. Particle board is used extensively for core stock in plywood. Thicknesses vary from ½″ to about 1½″. The standard size sheet is the same as for plywood—4′ x 8′.

Particle board is much softer than hardboard. It is easily shaped with standard woodworking tools and powered equipment, but due to its softness all exposed edges should be protected with solid wood or veneer. When solid wood is joined to particle board, it is best to use a standard joint such as tongue and groove, spline or dowel. Another advantage of solid wood trim is that it can be enhanced by some decorative shape.

Hardboard is made of fibers. It is harder, heavier and more dense than particle board. Hardboard is available in two textures. Both sides are smooth in one type. The other type has only one side smooth, and the other side has a screen-like texture.

There are three grades of hardboard: *service grade, standard* and *tempered*. Tempered hardboard is the strongest and hardest. It also takes finishing materials easier. The widely used "pegboard," which has a wide variety of practical uses, including methods for tool storage and arrangement, is only one of the ways of utilizing hardboard. Pegboard, perforated with holes fairly close together

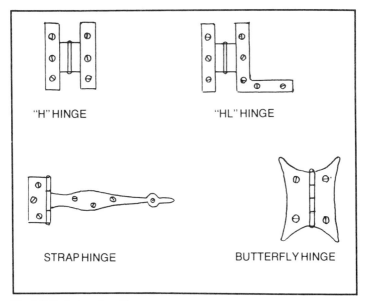

"H" HINGE   "HL" HINGE

STRAP HINGE   BUTTERFLY HINGE

Fig. 2-6. Early American hinges.

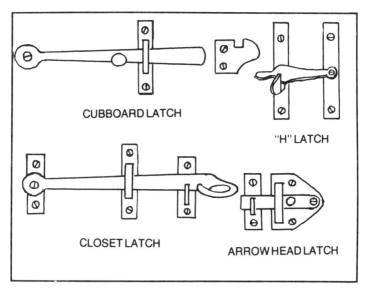

CUBBOARD LATCH

"H" LATCH

CLOSET LATCH

ARROW HEAD LATCH

Fig. 2-7. Early American latches.

into which heavy metal hooks or other supports are inserted, is widely used for displays in stores and commercial establishments.

Hardboard is used extensively in furniture construction for drawer bottoms, dust covers of the back of chests and cabinets, and for backs for televisions.

Regular woodworking tools and power equipment may be used on hardboard in the same fashion as for solid wood. Tools must be sharpened more often because of the abrasive action of the chemicals and adhesives in hardboard. For continued use over a long period, it is best that carbide-tipped blades be used on power tools. Hardboard will not need sanding except along the edges. Hardboard will take almost any type of finish and it may be applied by any of the conventional methods (roller, brush or spray). See the Appendix for some wood suppliers.

ORNAMENTAL HARDWARE

The most common pieces of *ornamental hardware* for furniture are drawer pulls, knobs and keyhole escutcheon plates. These and many other pieces of ornamental hardware will be described.

Early American Hardware

Early American hardware of the Puritan and Pilgrim era was generally made of wrought and/or forged black iron, and so it is today. Special pyramid-head screws are available for attaching hardware.

Hinges. The different types of Early American hinges are: "H" hinge, "HL" hinge, strap hinge and butterfly hinge (Fig. 2-6).

Latches. The different types of Early American latches are: "H" latch, arrow head latch, cupboard latch and closet latch (Fig. 2-7).

Pulls. The different types of Early American pulls are: spear pull, square pull and ring pull (Fig. 2-8).

Queen Anne Hardware

Queen Anne period furniture was in vogue during the first third of the 1700s. Most all Queen Anne furniture hardware of this period was made of brass. The batwing type pull and keyhole escutcheon plates are shown in Fig. 2-9. The pendant, "tear drop" type pull was also popular during this period.

Chippendale Hardware

Chippendale (Willow) handles and keyhole escutcheon plates were used on highboys, bureaus, desks, etc. from about 1730 to

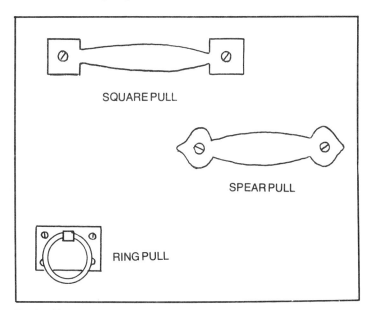

Fig. 2-8. Early American pulls.

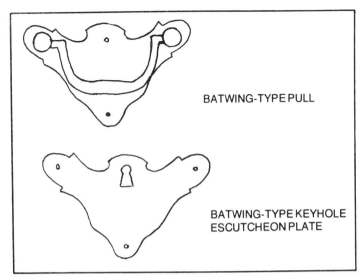

Fig. 2-9. Queen Anne hardware.

1790. These solid brass plates and handles are not engraved, and the outline of the keyhole escutcheon plates are of the same size and shape (Fig. 2-10).

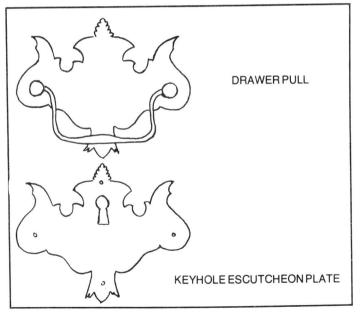

Fig. 2-10. Chippendale hardware.

Hepplewhite Hardware

The *Hepplewhite* period, and to some extent the lesser Sheraton and Adams Brothers period, was at its peak during the last few years of the 1700s and the early years of the 1800s. Drawer pulls and escutcheon plates were brass and many times were oval in shape. Round pulls were sometimes used but to a lesser extent (Fig. 2-11).

Sheraton Hardware

The *Sheraton* period was at its zenith during the early years of the 1800s. Sheraton, along with Hepplewhite and Brothers Adam, often used round or oval hardware (Fig. 2-12).

Empire Hardware

The *Empire* period extended, roughly, from the last quarter of the 1700s through the first quarter of the 1800s. During this time slot, the knob emerges as the major ornamental furniture decoration. Ring pulls, primarily of the lion's head style, were the intermediate form between oval brass pieces and the knob. Knobs were sometimes made of wood or glass, but more often were made of brass (Fig. 2-13).

Victorian Hardware

Victorian hardware was designed for Victorian furniture which was not a period or a style, but a hodgepodge conglomerate of many styles and periods, extending over nearly 100 years. As a result,

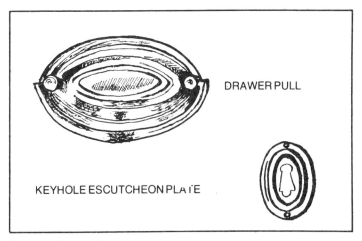

DRAWER PULL

KEYHOLE ESCUTCHEON PLATE

Fig. 2-11. Hepplewhite hardware.

Fig. 2-12. Sheraton tear-drop drawer pull.

there are many different designs of hardware, one of which is depicted in Fig. 2-14.

Provincial Hardware

French Provincial furniture can be associated with "country made" furniture. These pieces were constructed in rural areas as opposed to furniture built in the large industrial cities. Ornamentation was greatly reduced and simple lines were used in the designs. Very few inlays and carvings were used (Figs. 2-15 and 2-16).

Contemporary Hardware

The two large categories of contemporary ornamental furniture hardware are *chromium* and *plastic*. The plastic knobs, pulls, etc. are quite often made of lucite. The lucite pieces are available in colors other than clear.

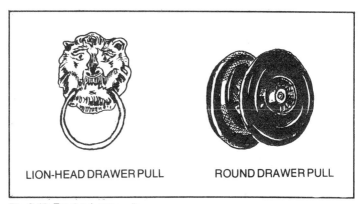

LION-HEAD DRAWER PULL   ROUND DRAWER PULL

Fig. 2-13. Empire drawer pulls.

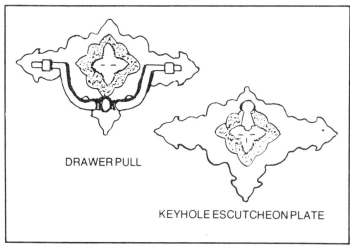

Fig. 2-14. Victorian hardware.

Campaign Hardware

This hardware, often thought of as contemporary, was a favorite of the British Army although its major purpose was practicality rather than ornamentation. The brass corners, straps and recessed pulls helped protect chests and boxes while they were transported along the campaign trail (Fig. 2-17).

NONORNAMENTAL FURNITURE HARDWARE

The following list covers nonornamental furniture hardware.

Casters

Stem Type. Wood wheels, 1 3/16″ to 1⅝″ diameter.

Shank Type. White china wheels, ¾″ to 1¼″ diameter. Brass wheels, ¾″ to 1¼″ diameter.

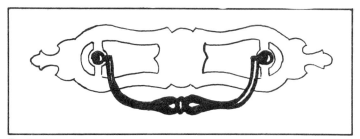

Fig. 2-15. Provincial drawer pull.

Fig. 2-16. Spanish style drawer pull.

Plate Casters. Plate size 2¾" x 3¾". Wheel size 3" x 1 5/16".

Steel Plate Caster. Hard plastic wheel. 1¼" and 1⅝" diameter wheels.

Piano Casters. Dual wheel, plate type. Plate 2¾" x 3¾".

Wheel Casters. 2" diameter, dual wheel casters.

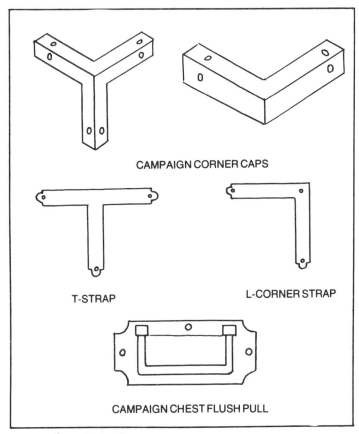

CAMPAIGN CORNER CAPS

T-STRAP

L-CORNER STRAP

CAMPAIGN CHEST FLUSH PULL

Fig. 2-17. Campaign hardware.

Catches

Brass Hook Catch ¾" to 2". *Magnetic catches*, 9 lb. to 13 lb. pull. *Spring catch. Friction catch*, ¼", 5/16" and ⅜" diameter. *Elbow catch*, brass or black. *Spring cushioned roller catch.*

Coat and Hat Hooks
Costumer Hooks, 3½" Projection
Drawer Slides

Light weight ball bearing. Nylon wheel in lengths 12, 16, 18, 20, 22, and 24".

Extension Drawer Slides

The slides come in 16", 20" and 22" lengths.

Ferrules (Sockets Without Casters)

Square Ferrules. Top inside dimensions ¾", 1" and 1¼".
Round Ferrules. Top inside dimensions ¾" and 1⅛".

Hanger Bolts

The bolts come in these sizes: 5/16" x 2½", 5/16 x 3" and 5/16 x 3½".

Hinges

Semi-concealed hinge. ⅜" inset overlapping, copper and black.
Self-closing hinge. ⅜" inset overlapping.
Fancy box hinge, ¾" x ⅝".
Combination hinge and support.
Cabinet hinge. Semi-concealed for doors ¾" thick with ⅜" offset.
Wrought brass butt hinges. Height ½" to 2"; widths: narrow, middle and broad.
Narrow cabinet hinge, fast pin, steel. 1" to 3" in length of joint. Opens to widths of 1" and 2".
Narrow cabinet hinge, loose pin, steel. 1" to 2" length at joint. 1" to 1 9/16" width open.
Continuous hinge. 48" long by 1 1/16, steel brass plated and steel nickel plated.
Table hinge, fast pin, steel. Length of joint 1" to 1½". Width open, 2⅝" to 3⅛".
Back flap and hinge, steel. Length of joint, 1½" to 2".
Cabinet strap hinge, steel, fast pin. 1" x 4" and 1 3/32" x 6".

Hooks

Screw hooks, curved, 1¼" to 2½". *Screw hooks,* square bent, 1" to 2¼". *Shoulder hooks,* ½" to 1½". Box hooks, ½", ⅝" and ¾". Gate hooks and eyes, 1½" to 4".

Lazy Susan Bearings

They come in 3", 4", 6" and 12" diameters.

Lid Supports

Desk hinge, 1¼" x 1⅞" and 2" x 3". *Joint stay,* 8" and 10" open. *Secretary drop front catch,* 2" x 1". *Secretary quadrant,* 5' across arcs, 3½" radius. *Joint support,* 7" open. *Folding support,* 10" brass. *Hinge support for slant or upright desk lids.* 1 1/16" x 7".

Locks

Half mortise lock. Full Mortise lock. Half mortise chest lock. Wardorbe surface lock. Roll top desk lock. Drawer lock. Door lock. Surface lock.

Nut Bowl and Mallet Hardware
Plates

Mending plates, steel, length 2" and 3". Width ⅝" and ¾". *T-Plates,* steel, 2½" x 2½" x ½" and 3" x 3" x ⅝". *Flat corner iron,* steel, 1½" x 3½". Width ⅜" to ⅝".

Rubber Screw Bumpers

They are found with ⅞" diameter.

Rubber Tack Bumpers

They are found with ½", ⅝" and ¾" diameters.

Screw Eyes

Small screw eyes, 11/16" to 1⅝". *Medium screw eyes,* 1 5/16" to 1 13/16". *Short shank screw eye,* ½" to 1". *Brass wire screw eyes:* regular 11/16" and 13/16"; and short shank, ½" and ⅝".

Sockets

Square Sockets With Casters. Top inside dimension ¾", 1" and 1¼".

Round Sockets With Casters. Top inside dimension ¾" and 1⅛".

Soss Invisible Hinges

They are available in brass finish only. The 100 series hinges are designed for non-load bearing installations. The 200 series are used for doors.

Table Hardware

Tilt top catch. Card table hinge. Table top guide. Folding leg Bracket. Table drop leaf support, 8" and 10" lengths. *Table leg and lid support*, 12". *Steel extension table slide.* For pull-apart tables, 20" and 30". *Table locks.* Table *leg bracket,* steel: straight or 12° angle, for tapered legs; and tapped for 5/16" hanger bolt.

Tool Chest Hardware

Snap catch. Draw bolt catch. Lock and bolt catch.

WOOD SCREWS

Screws are ideal for furniture making. The holding power of nails is considerably less than screws, but the installation of screws is more time consuming. Furthermore, screws can be replaced or removed much more easily than nails without harming the wood.

Screws are used to attach one component to another, to fasten hardware to furniture parts and to strengthen joints. Screws are available in many styles, sizes, surface decoration, different metals, types of heads and driver slots. The three most common screws used in woodworking are the *round, oval* and *flat* head. There are two kinds of flat head screws; the standard slotted and the Phillips head screw (Fig. 2-18).

The standard flat head screws are a bright, natural steel with no surface finish and are commonly called flat head bright or simply FHB.

Round head screws of steel are often finished with a gun-metal blue finish because they are often exposed. But steel is only one of the metals of which screws are made. For special purposes, they are made of brass and copper.

Oval head screws are often plated because of their ornamental nature in that they are often used to attach hardware. Chromium, cadium and nickel are the materials most generally used for plating.

An off-the-beaten-path type of screw is reported by Rob Sheppard of Calgary, Alberta, Canada in the Nov./Dec. 1979 issue

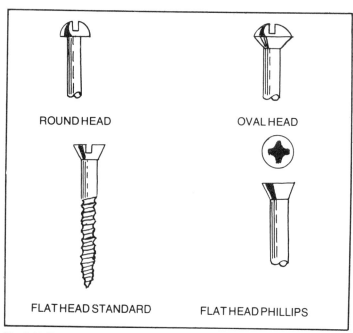

ROUND HEAD

OVAL HEAD

FLAT HEAD STANDARD

FLAT HEAD PHILLIPS

Fig. 2-18. Kinds of wood screws.

of *Fine Woodworking* magazine. Called the Robertson screw, it is similar to the Phillips screw but has a square hole in the flat head. A Robertson screwdriver tip fits snugly in the square hole, thus reducing the possibility of slipping. Greater turning pressure can be applied and only one hand is needed to drive the screw.

Screwdrivers

The standard universal screwdriver is used to drive slotted screws. It has a variety of different shaped handles. The most recent is a handle in a perfect sphere. Materials used for handles are plastic, wood and metal. The screwdriver comes in many different lengths and tip widths.

Phillips screwdrivers vary in blade lengths from 1½″ to 10″ in five different point sizes. They are also available in offset screw drivers.

Spiral ratchet screwdrivers drive screws much faster than conventional screwdrivers, but they are rather tricky to use. A person should practice using this tool for a considerable time before attempting to drive screws in a fine piece of furniture. The bit is more apt to slip off the screw, marring the surface of the wood. Occasionally injuries are involved when the finger or thumb is caught in the spiral ratchet mechanism.

There are two types of spiral screwdrivers: quick return type and manual return type. The manual return type is much easier to use.

The hand brace screwdriver bit is a good tool for driving large screws. Care must be taken to prevent turning off the head of the screw due to the extra leverage of the brace.

Offset screwdrivers are available for both slotted and recessed (Phillips) head screws. The offset screwdrivers are used to install screws in tight and cramped quarters.

Countersinks and Counterbores

Countersinks are used to flare out the holes for flat head screws so that they will be flush with the surface of the wood. The included angle is 82° and they come in two kinds: one kind for a brace and the other to fit in the Jacobs chuck of a portable electric drill or a drill press.

The *counterbore* is used to drill or bore a hole so that a plug may be inserted in the hole to cover the head of a screw. Sometimes the plugs are used for a decorative effect.

Screw-Mate Wood Drill and Countersink

The *Screw-Mate* drills a pilot hole, a shank hole and countersinks all in one operation. See Table 2-2.

Screw-Sink Combination Countersink-Counterbore

The *Screw-Sink* does the same operations as the Screw-Mate, but in addition it counterbores for wood plugs. See Arco Products Corp. (11) in the Appendix.

Plug Cutter

This hollow drill makes a clean, straight plug that matches the wood of the project and fits snugly. The plug cutter should be used

Table 2-2. Sizes of Screw-Mates.

¾" x No. 6	1¼" x No. 10
¾" x No. 8	1½" x No. 8
1" x No. 6	1½" x No. 10
1" x No. 8	1½" x No. 12
1" x No. 10	2" x No. 10
1¼" x No. 8	2" x No. 12

Table 2-3. Lengths and Shank Sizes of Screws.

	¼	⅜	½	⅝	¾	⅞	1	1¼	1½	1¾	2	2¼	2½	2¾	3	3½	4
S																	
H	2	2	2														
A	3	3	3	3													
N		4	4	4	4												
K			5	5	5												
		6	6	6	6	6	6		6								
S		7	7	7	7	7	7	7	7								
I			8	8	8	8	8	8	8	8	8						
Z				9	9	9	9	9	9	9	9	9					
E			10	10	10	10	10	10	10	10	10	10					
S					11	11	11	11	11	11	11	11					
						12	12	12	12	12	12	12	12				
							14	14	14	14	14	14	14	14			
								16	16	16	16	16	16	16	16		
									18	18	18	18	18	18	18	18	18
											20	20	20	20	20	20	20

in combination with the Screw-Sinks. Plug cutters are made for screw sizes 6, 8, 10 and 12.

Scratch Awl

A *scratch awl* or prick punch is used to mark pilot holes by extending the awl through the shank hole.

How To Drive Screws

■ Mark the center for the screw holes on the first member.

■ Select the screw according to its function: a small diameter screw for thin wood, a large diameter screw for thick wood, a longer screw if the thread end of the screw will enter end grain and a shorter screw if the thread end of the screw enters cross grain (Table 2-3).

■ Select the correct size drill for the shank hole. See Table 2-4.

■ Drill the shank hole. The screw should easily pass through the shank hole.

■ Countersink the holes if flat head screws are being used and are exposed. The head should fit neatly into the countersunk portion. The surface of the head of the screw should be flush or slightly below the surrounding wood surface. If the hole is to be counterbored for plugs, countersinking is not necessary.

■ Mark the pilot holes on the second member with a scratch awl. Be sure the two members are properly aligned.

■ Select the proper drill for the pilot hole. See Table 2-4.

■ Drill pilot holes. The holes should not be quite as deep as the threaded portion of the screw is long.

■ Select the proper screwdriver for the screw chosen. If the tip needs sharpening, be sure that the two faces are left parallel. *Never sharpen a screwdriver point to a chisel edge* (Fig. 2-19).

■ Place a little paraffin on each screw by rubbing the thread against a piece of paraffin. This is particularly apropos if the wood is hard.

■ Drive the screws home.

Table 2-4. Shank and Pilot Hole Drill Sizes for Hardwood.

Shank Size Screw Gauge #	Shank Hole Size	Pilot Hole Size
0	1/16″	1/32″
1	5/64″	1/32″
2	3/32′	3/64″
3	7/64″	1/16″
4	7/64″	1/16″
5	1/8″	5/64″
6	9/64″	5/64″
7	5/32″	3/32″
8	11/64″	3/32″
9	3/16″	7/64″
10	3/16″	7/64″
11	13/16″	1/8″
12	7/32	1/8″
14	1/4″	9/64″
16	17/64″	5/32″
18	19/64″	3/16″
20	21/64″	13/64″

Pilot holes in softwood should be approximately 1/64″ in diameter less for the smaller sizes and 1/32″ less in diameter for the large sizes

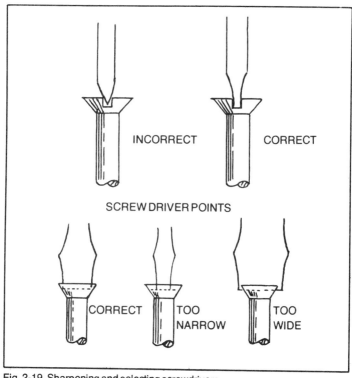

INCORRECT   CORRECT

SCREW DRIVER POINTS

CORRECT   TOO NARROW   TOO WIDE

Fig. 2-19. Sharpening and selecting screwdrivers.

■ Glue in plugs if holes have been counterbored. When glue is set, cut off plugs with a sharp chisel. The grain of the plug should run in the same direction as the surrounding wood.

NAILS

The three large classification of nails are *brads, nails* and *spikes.* The main categories according to function are *brads, finishing, casing, common* (the spike is a large common nail) and *box.*

Another off-the-beaten-path nail is the old-fashioned cut nail used to restore antique furniture. Escutcheon pins are special ornamental nails used to attach drawer pulls and keyhole escutcheon plates. There are a variety of special nails—some of which are coated—for many purposes. See Independent Nail, Inc. (100).

The brad in essence is a small finishing nail. A brad driver is often used instead of a hammer for driving brads (Fig. 2-20).

Brads and escutcheon pins are identified by length and wire gauge sizes, while other nails and spikes are identified by "penny" or "d." "Penny" or "d" is the weight in pounds of 1000 nails or spikes.

Finishing nails are used where the exposed head of a nail would be objectionable. A nail set is used to sink the small head below the surface. The hole is filled with a filler.

Casing nails are used to fasten interior trim, such as casing, from which it gets its name. The nail is similar to the finishing nail, but the head is slightly larger and is tapered, and for the same length it is slightly larger in diameter (wire gauge size) than the finishing nail.

The common nail is the most used nail, particularly where the large flat head is needed for its greater capacity to hold, and where it does not distract because of its appearance. A common nail larger than a 20d or 20 "penny" is called a *spike*. A 60d spike is about 6″ long.

The box nail is similar to the common nail, except the head is thinner. It is smaller in diameter for the same length as a common nail. Casing nails, common nails and box nails are identified in the same way as finishing nails. See Tables 2-5 through 2-7.

Old-Fashioned Cut Nails

The head designs for cut nails are *clout, hinge, clinch* (rose head), *spike, fine finish, wrought* and *common*. See Tremont Nail Co. (182). Look at Table 2-8 for sizes of old-fashioned cut nails.

Driving and Removing Nails

The *ripping hammer* with straight claws should never be used for removing nails. The common curved *claw hammer* is the hammer recommended both for driving and removing nails. Curved claw hammers vary in weight from 7 ounce hammers used to drive tacks, brads and small nails to the 20 ounce heavy weight for driving large common nails and spikes. The proper technique of hammer use will come only with time and practice.

Fig. 2-20. Brad driver.

"Penny"	Length
2d	1″
3d	1¼″
4d	1½″
5d	1¾″
6d	2″
7d	2¼″
8d	2½″
10d	3″

Table 2-5. Finishing Nails.

In general, the hammer should be held near the end of the handle, particularly for the larger nails. Shorter strokes are used for the smaller nails and brads.

If the nail has a tendency to follow the grain of the wood, or if the wood is extremely hard, it is best to drill a small hole for the nail to follow.

Tap the nail gently to get it started. Be sure that the hammer hits the nail squarely.

Drive in the nail until the head is nearly flush with the wood. For more holding ability, drive nails at a slight angle. If the nail starts to bend, it is best to remove the nail and start with a new one.

Drive the nail home, flush with the surface, with light, easy taps to prevent marring the surface of the wood. Countersink the head with a nail set if finishing nails are being used.

When removing nails, drive the nail back so that the head is protruding. Work the claws of a curved claw hammer under the head of the nail. Raise the hammer so that the handle is perpendicular to the work.

Table 2-6. Brad Sizes.

Length	Wire Gauges	Length	Wire Gauges
⅜″	No. 20	1″	No. 16
½″	No. 20	1″	No. 14
½″	No. 18	1¼″	No. 18
⅝″	No. 20	1¼″	No. 16
⅝″	No. 18	1¼″	No. 14
⅝″	No. 16	1½″	No. 16
¾″	No. 20	1½″	No. 14
¾″	No. 18	1¾″	No. 14
¾″	No. 16	2″	No. 16
⅞″	No. 18	2″	No. 14
⅞″	No. 16	2″	No. 12
1″	No. 18	2½″	No. 12

Table 2-7. Escutcheon Pin Sizes.

Length	Wire Gauges	Length	Wire Gauges
1/4''	No. 20	5/8''	No. 16
3/8''	No. 20	3/4''	No. 18
3/8''	No. 18	3/4''	No. 16
1/2''	No. 18	7/8''	No. 18
1/2''	No. 16	1''	No. 16
5/8''	No. 18	1 1/4''	No. 16

Move the handle back toward its original position and place a piece of scrap wood under the hammer head. Remove the nail until the handle is in a perpendicular position once again. The nail should be easily removed at this stage unless the nail is a long one in which

Table 2-8. Sizes of Old-Fashioned Cut Nails.

"Penny"	Length
2d	1''
3d	1 1/4''
4d	1 1/2''
5d	1 3/4''
6d	2''
7d	2 1/4''
8d	2 1/2''
10d	3''
16d	3 1/2''
20d	4''

it may be necessary to use a second piece of scrap wood. See Table 2-9 for upholstery tacks.

Blued Staples, Double Pointed. No. 10 gauge, width 1/4'', length 15/32'' blued finish.

Table 2-9. Upholstery Tacks.

Length	Wire Gauge
3/8''	No. 3
7/16''	No. 4
1/2''	No. 6
9/16''	No. 8
5/8''	No. 10
11/16''	No. 12
3/4''	No. 14

Blind Staples. Lengths ⅜″, ½″ and ⅝″. Coppered.

Corrugated Fasteners. Lengths ⅜″, ½″ and ⅝″.

Skotch Wood Jointers. An eight prong staple which joins without cutting or splintering the fibers. ⅜″ x 1″, ⅜″ x 1 5/16″ ½″ x 1 1/16″ and ½″ x 1⅛″.

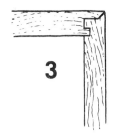

3

Sawing Tools and Their Use

The term *handsaw* refers to those tools operated by manpower rather than horsepower. No motorized saws are included in this category. Every home craftsman must develop skill with these hand-held tools to make small, delicate jobs easier and more accurate.

RIPSAW TEETH

The teeth of the *ripsaw* are like little chisels. They take out rather large rectangular chunks of wood. The ripsaw is used to cut with the grain, never across it. The channel or slit that is cut out by the teeth—as with all saws—is called the *kerf*. The alternate teeth are pointed in opposite directions to prevent the saw from binding in the cut. All saws have this characteristic to a greater or lesser degree.

Ripsaws have larger teeth than other saws, and the number of points per inch is usually 5½. (There is one more point per inch than there are teeth.) The recommended length of the saw blade is 26″, although ripsaws are available in lengths from 20″ to 28″. Some handsaws are coated with Teflon for easy cutting.

SHARPENING HANDSAWS

There are four steps in saw sharpening: *jointing, reshaping, setting* and *sharpening*. All four steps are not necessary unless a saw has been neglected for a long time.

By looking down the blade of a saw from either end, it is readily ascertained if jointing is necessary—some teeth will be shorter than others. If the saw needs jointing—and this applies to sharpening as well—it should be placed in a saw clamp. A substitute clamp can be made with two boards clamped on the two sides of the saw with the teeth slightly protruding above the boards. Tage Frid describes how you can make your own sharpening vise in the Fall/1977 issue of *Fine Woodworking* magazine.

Jointing is done by pushing a flat mill file down the length of the teeth, with the teeth perpendicular to the surface of the file. Check from time to time to see if all the teeth are even. When all teeth are touched by the file, a small, shiny spot will appear on the points of the teeth.

If it has been necessary to joint a considerable amount, it may be necessary to reshape the teeth to the same original size and shape.

After reshaping the teeth, which should be seldom required, the teeth are then *set*. Setting is done with a saw set or saw setting hammer. Each tooth is bent equally so that the saw will not bind in the wood. Not as much set is necessary when sawing dry and hard woods as when sawing wet or soft woods.

Figure 3-1 shows a craftsman setting a *Pax* saw by hand on an anvil in England. The Pax saw can be bent so that the tip of the blade almost touches the handle and it will return to the straight position when released.

The ripsaw, compass saw and keyhole saw are sharpened alike. The sharpening is done with a triangular file. Use slim taper files for saw sharpening. The length of the file is determined by the number of teeth per inch on the saw to be sharpened. Use a 7″ or 8″ file for a ripsaw (5½ points per inch). For a seven or eight point saw use a 6″ or 7″ file. For a 10 point saw use a 6″ file. For 12 to 15 point saws use a 4½″ file.

It is important that the correct handle be selected for the file chosen. The eight sizes of handles and matching file lengths are given here. No. 1, small files under 4″; No. 2, 4″ files; No. 3, 5″ files; No. 4, 6″ files; No. 5, 8″ files; No. 6, 10″ files; No. 7, 12″ files and No. 8, 14″ files.

The file handle is placed in the right hand. The point of the file is held with the index finger and thumb.

The ripsaw is filed straight across the teeth. The file is held horizontally and at right angles to the saw blade. Alternate teeth are filed in the first operation with the set of the tooth on the side of the saw opposite the craftsman. Turn the saw around in the clamp-on saw vise and file the remaining teeth after the first operation is completed. About one-half of the shiny spot should be removed in each of the two operations.

Be sure that the pressure on the file is consistent. The pressure should not be excessive. It is a good idea to practice on an old saw. Filing is done only on the forward stroke. Never drag a file across the teeth on the backward stroke. Some craftsmen count the number of strokes to obtain better consistency.

Usually filing is started at the toe (the end opposite the handle) of the saw. File only those teeth that are bent away from you.

Fig. 3-1. Setting a Pax Sheffield (England) saw.

Using the Hand Ripsaw

Large pieces of stock are placed on fairly low sawhorses. Start the saw on the upstroke. The saw should be held at about 60° to the face of the wood.

The layout line should be left on the surface by sawing close to the line on the surplus side. If the saw has a tendency to "wander" away from the line, a slight twist of the handle will bring it back in line.

Saw with long easy strokes. Let the saw do the sawing. Do not force it. When nearing the end of the cut, change to short strokes to prevent the stock from splitting prematurely.

When ripping small pieces in the vise, the stock should be held with the waste stock extending outside the vise. The heel of the saw should be held lower than the toe—about 75°.

CROSSCUT SAW

The *crosscut saw* is used to cut across the grain of the wood. The teeth are knife-shaped or wedge-shaped and the points are very sharp and pointed.

The crosscut saw has many more teeth (or points) per inch than the ripsaw. They range from eight points per inch to 12 points per inch. The 10 point saw is probably the most used. In length, the crosscut saw is sometimes called the panel saw.

The crosscut saw is sharpened in a similar manner to the ripsaw except the handle is held from 10° to 15° below the horizontal and from 60° to 65° with the blade or teeth line. A slim taper file is used for both the ripsaw and crosscut. An extra slim taper file is used to file a dovetail saw and backsaw.

Two low sawhorses should be used in crosscutting long stock, after the stock has been marked for length with a framing square and a sharp, hard lead pencil. The carpenter uses a special, wide, rectangular cross section lead pencil, but it is not suitable for fine furniture and interior cabinetmaking.

Sawing should be on the waste or surplus side of the line. From time to time the saw blade should be checked with a try square to see if the blade is sawing perpendicularly.

Start and end the sawing with short, easy strokes. The in-between sawing should be in long strokes. Again, let the saw do the sawing. The pressure should be moderate, not excessive. Short strokes at the end will prevent splintering off before the sawing is completed. Be sure to hold the waste or surplus near the end of the sawing (Figs. 3-2 and 3-3).

BACKSAW

The *backsaw* is used for fine, accurate cabinetwork. It is called a backsaw because of a steel stiffener along its back opposite the teeth. The blade is very thin, and the teeth are smaller than the teeth on a crosscut saw. Thirteen points per inch seem to be the standard. The length of the saw is generally 12″ or 14″. The backsaw is often used with a bench hook or miter box.

The stock to be cut with a backsaw is held in a flat horizontal position in the vise, bench hook or miter box. Cutting is started at a much lower angle than with the crosscut saw. As the sawing is being completed, the handle is gradually lowered to a horizontal position.

DOVETAIL SAW

The *dovetail saw* is a specially designed saw to make the finest of all cuts. It is used extensively where handmade dovetail joints are called for. It can cut both with and across the grain. The dovetail saw has smaller teeth and a thinner blade than the backsaw. The handle of a dovetail saw is similar to a file or chisel

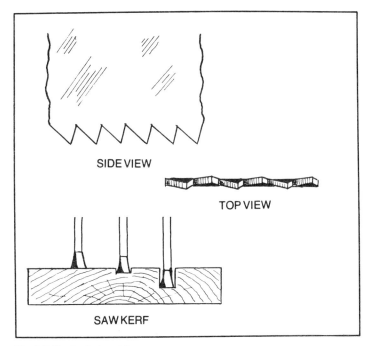

Fig. 3-2. Teeth of a hand ripsaw.

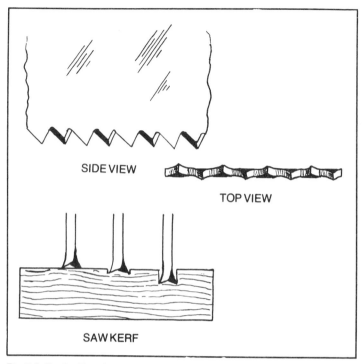

SIDE VIEW

TOP VIEW

SAW KERF

Fig. 3-3. Teeth of hand crosscut saw.

handle, while the handle of a backsaw is identical with the handle on a ripsaw or crosscut saw. A representative dovetail saw has 15 points per inch and is 10″ long.

The Blitz backsaw has a hook at the end opposite the handle for controlling the cuts. The blades are interchangeable. It is much shorter (5″) and has many more teeth (21 or 26 points per inch) than the standard dovetail saw. Although it is called a backsaw, it is most often used as a dovetail saw.

BEAD SAW

The *bead saw* is designed for very small, fine work. The saw leaves the work so smooth that little if any sanding is necessary. The depth of cut is ½″ and the blade length is 4½″. It has 38 teeth per inch and has a file/chisel-like handle.

JAPANESE SAWS

Japanese saws differ from other saws in that they cut on the *pull* stroke rather than the *push* stroke. Because of this feature, they can be designed with a much thinner blade which reduces both friction and buckling of the blade. It is not necessary to set Japanese saws.

There is a wide range of Japanese saws all the way from a tiny keyhole-like saw to a large saw known in the United States as a log saw, which is used for rough cutting on green or seasoned wood. It can be used for either crosscutting or ripping.

COPING SAW

The *coping saw* can cut short-radii, exterior and interior curves. Interior holes are made by inserting the blade through a hole. The coping saw has considerable trouble sawing stock more than ½″ thick.

The blade of a coping saw can be turned from right to left without turning the handle. The home craftsman, as well as the student in a school shop or art and craft shop, uses the coping saw with the teeth pointed toward the handle. The work is held in a horizontal position on a "V" block sawing bracket and the sawing is done near the point of the "V."

The carpenter uses the coping saw with the teeth pointing away from the handle for coping moldings and trim, which are placed in the corners of ceilings or floors in buildings.

Coping saw blades are of two kinds: the popular *pin end blade* (6 ½″ long with 15 and 20 teeth per inch) and the *loop blade* (6″ or 6½″ long with 15 to 32 teeth per inch) (Fig. 3-4). Spiral coping saw blades will saw up or down, right or left, even in circles.

HOW TO MAKE A SAWING BRACKET

Step 1 is to saw out stock. Cut one piece of ½″ x 2½″ x 7½″ of most any lumber available in your scrap box. Birch or maple are the best; however, white pine or basswood may be used. Naturally, the hard woods will stand up longer. Cut another piece ½″ x 2½″ x 4¾″.

Step 2 is to cut a "V." Drill a ¼″ in from one end of the second piece in the longitudinal center of the piece. Make angling cuts from the end to the edges of the hole.

Step 3 is to drill and countersink screw holes. On the other end of the piece mentioned in step 2, drill two holes ¼″ in from the end and ⅝″ from the sides. The holes should be slightly larger than the shank of ¾″ No. 7 flat head bright (IHB) screws, which are used to fasten the two pieces together. Drill pilot holes in the ends of the larger piece. Countersink holes on the smaller piece.

Step 4 is to sand and assemble. Sand both pieces with 220 sandpaper. Put white glue on the end of the larger piece where the pilot holes are located. Drive in the screws.

Step 5 is to saw a brace. Cut a piece of ½″ stock at 45° and the sides of a right angle 1½″ long.

Step 6 is to glue the brace. Sand the brace with 220 sandpaper and glue in the right angle formed by the larger pieces. Use white glue.

Step 7 is to finish. Spray on two or three coats of Deft or polyurethane (Fig. 3-5).

COMPASS SAW

The *compass saw* is designed to cut interior shaped holes after the blade is inserted through a drilled or bored hole. It will cut interior curves of large radii, but the coping saw or saber saw is best adapted for this purpose. The compass saw can also cut exterior curves, but certainly not with the efficiency of the band saw or bow saw.

Compass saw blades are usually 12″ long and the saw has a pistol grip. Some compass saws have interchangeable blades so that the saw may be used as a keyhole saw.

KEYHOLE SAW

The *keyhole saw* has a shorter blade (10″) and a sharper point than the compass saw. Naturally, the saw was designed to do what its name suggests—to make keyholes. Some keyhole saws have a pistol grip while others have a handle similar to a file or chisel handle. The keyhole saw will cut interior curves of shorter radii than the compass saw.

JEWELER'S SAW

The *jeweler's saw* handles rather delicate, fine tooth blades used primarily on thin metal, but it also works well on wood for cutting extremely short radii on exterior and interior curves. The jeweler's saw and the fret saw are the jigsaw puzzle maker's favorites.

There are two kinds of jeweler's saw frames—the nonadjustable and the adjustable. The nonadjustable saw frames take only the standard 5″ blade. If the blade breaks, which it often does, a new blade must be put in the frame.

The adjustable saw frame takes any size blade from 3″ to 6½″ long, which means that any broken blade that is at least 3″ long may be used the second time.

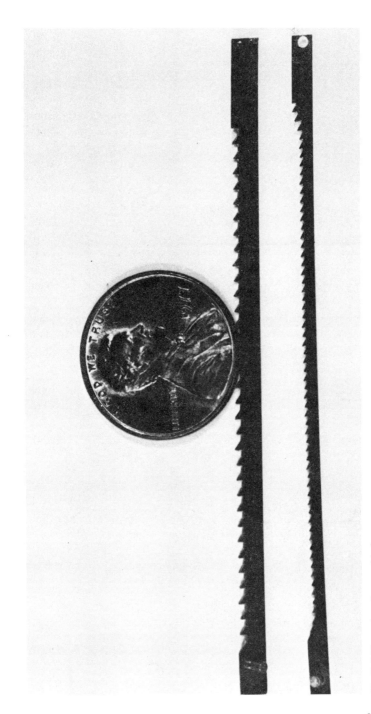

Fig. 3-4. Pin end coping saw blades.

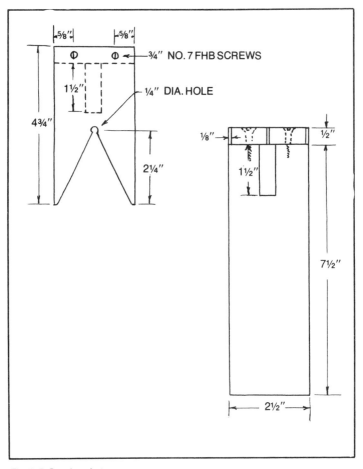

Fig. 3-5. Saw bracket.

The jeweler's saw is used with the saw bracket as is the coping saw. Thin metal should be attached to thin wood with rubber cement or double adhesive tape to give the metal support while sawing. The number of teeth on jeweler's saw blades varies from 32 to 76 teeth per inch.

FRET SAW

The *fret saw* and the jeweler's saw can be used interchangeably, but by definition the fret saw is a woodworking saw—a long, thin, narrow saw with fine teeth used in cutting ornamental woodwork. However, jeweler's saw blades have finer teeth (32 to 76 teeth per inch) while fret saw blades are from 16 to 32 teeth per inch. The blade length (5") is the same for both the jeweler's saw and the fret saw.

A deep-throated fret saw is available to make cuts up to 12" in from the edge of the work. Fret saws are used extensively for cutting marquetry designs, inlays and overlays. Marquetry craftsmen many times use the finer jeweler saw blades in their fret saws.

At least one company, Woodcraft Supply (204), markets a treadle fret saw which has changed little over the last 200 years. This foot-operated treadle machine gives the user two-handed control of the work as well as the speed of the saw. The blades for this saw vary from 18 teeth per inch to 32 teeth per inch.

BOW SAW

Tage Frid, in the Fall 1977 issue of *Fine Woodworking* , claims that, "The bow saw is my all-purpose saw. It takes longer to learn to use than other handsaws, but once you get the hang of it, you will use it for most cutting." In the same issue Frid describes how to make your own bow saw.

There are at least two sizes of bow saws (Frid refers to two others: 17¾" and 25¾" blade). The smaller one takes blades 8", 10" and 12" long. The blade is tightened with a twisted cord with an inserted toggle stick. The blade can be turned with the swivel handles so that the saw may be used like an oversize coping saw. The 12" blade, the one most commonly used, has nine points to the inch.

The larger saw takes blades 24", 28" and 32" long. The blade is tightened by a thumbscrew. The scroll blade is ⅜" wide and has nine points per inch. The fine cut blade is 1½" wide and 9½ points per inch. The fast cutting rip or crosscut is 1½" wide and has six points per inch. The fast cutting crosscut is 1½" wide and has five points per inch.

A few suppliers of bow saws are listed here. The arabic numbers in parentheses refer to items in the Appendix. Companies include Garrett Wade (79), Silvo Handware (165), Three Crowns (177), Alson Saw (137), Woodcraft Supply (204) and Frog Tool (76).

PORTABLE ELECTRIC CIRCULAR SAW

Although the *portable circular saw* is considered to be primarily a carpenter's saw for construction work, by using a special table or bench and with the portable circular saw upside down it may be used similar to a table saw.

Blades range in diameter from 4½″ to 12″. The 6½″ and 7¼″ diameter are probably the most popular.

The portable circular saw cuts from the bottom up rather than from the top down as do other circular saws. This requires that the good face of the stock is placed down, thus reducing the splintering.

The saw should be allowed to run long enough to reach full speed and the saw should be guided with both hands, if possible (Fig. 3-6).

STATIONARY POWER CIRCULAR SAWS

The stationary power circular saws have a variety of names such as table saw, bench saw, variety saw and a host of other names. These names are not consistent from one manufacturer to another; therefore, in describing the circular saws, I will use the name assigned to the saw by its manufacturer.

Chapter 3 will confine itself to the smaller saws used in the home workshop, the small custom woodworking shops and school industrial arts shops. The larger, industrial type saws used in the large woodworking and furniture making industries, and in trade and technical schools, will be discussed in Chapter 12.

The reader should keep in mind that the line of demarcation between the two categories of machines is very fuzzy. Many times the smaller machines are used in large woodworking factories for special purposes, and by the same token large power tools are occasionally found in basement or garage workshops.

One of the largest manufacturers of small and medium power tools—*Rockwell International* (155)—makes seven types and sizes of power circular saws which will be described now.

The 12″-14″ *tilting arbor saw* is a rugged machine with plenty of power to saw stock up to 5⅛″ thick. Its four-belt drive prevents any slippage between motor and saw. It is an intermediate saw that can be used in the home workshop or for heavy-duty production.

The ever-popular *Rockwell-Delta 10″ tilting arbor unisaw* has been around for a long time and is still as popular as it was when first introduced. It is used in a majority of the nation's schools and in thousands of millwork, furniture, cabinet and home workshops. It is a versatile, safe and durable machine. A large sliding table accessory attachment facilitates the cutting of large panels. The *Rockwell 10″ tilting arbor bench saw* can be purchased with a steel stand and extension wings, which makes this saw comparable to the other 10″ saws, but at a lower price.

The *Rockwell 10″ contractor's special saw* is identical to the bench saw except it has extra large extension wings to the table which are included as standard equipment.

The *Rockwell Deluxe 9″ builders' saw* comes either as a bench model or a floor model. A *9″ builders' saw* combined with a *4″* jointer is also available.

The portable *Rockwell motorized miter box* is popular with carpenters, builders and contractors. It has 90°, 45° and 22½° stops both left and right.

The Inca Swiss saw—as well as other Inca equipment—has long been a favorite in Europe by both amateur and professionals. Garrett Wade (79) has long been their agent in the United States.

Both the 7″ and 10″ table saws in the deluxe model are equipped with a mortise table. Probably the biggest disadvantage of the Inca circular saws is that angle cuts must be made with a tilting table instead of the more functional tilting arbor.

These saws, with all of their accessories, can perform the following operations: ripping, crosscutting, beveling, tonguing, grooving, dadoing, molding, tenoning, mitering, corner locking,

Fig. 3-6. Portable circular saw in use.

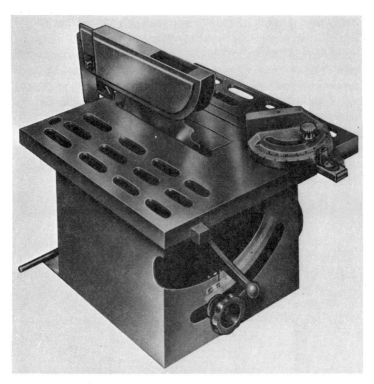

Fig. 3-7. 8" bench saw without cabinet base.

rabbeting, flat sanding, profile sanding, doweling, mortising and horizontal boring.

The American Machine and Tool company (5) builds a rugged, no-frills, 8" tilting-arbor circular bench saw for the economy-minded craftsman. It is built of cast iron and steel. At additional cost, precision, double sealed ball bearings are available. Side extensions and ripping are also available as optional accessories (Fig. 3-7).

As a step up from the less expensive machine, AMT offers a *deluxe bench saw.* Although the table is no larger than the less expensive model, it can be fitted into the cabinet, the plans of which are furnished by AMT with the purchase of one of their saws. This deluxe unit features a solid cast iron table with two (instead of one) miter gauge slots (Fig. 3-8).

A 10" table saw, with a working area with extensions, at 46" x 27" is marketed by *Conover Woodcraft Specialties* (40). Solid steel rails run the full width of the table and allow a maximum rip cut of

25″. It has a guard system which is sure and easy to use, including a kerf-splitter, anti-kickback paws and blade guard. The blade guard has metal side plates which pivot individually. This insures that both sides of the work come down flush with the table or work during angle cuts. There is a convenient Plexiglas window at the top of the guard so that close eyeballing of a cut is facilitated with safety.

This rugged, 455 pound machine has many features, such as a provision for dust collection. The miter gauge has a roller which fits into the T-slotted table. This allows extending the miter gauge head beyond the front of the table without it falling on the floor (Fig. 3-9).

Five models and three sizes of circular saws are manufactured by Sprunger Corp. (172). The three blades sizes are 10¼″, 9″ and

Fig. 3-8. Deluxe 8″ bench saw with cabinet base.

Fig. 3-9. 10" industrial table saw.

8" diameter. The 10¼" saw is available in a bench and floor model. The 9" model is a bench saw with a stand. The 8" saw comes with two different size tables. All saws have tilting arbors with the whole arbor tilting with the motor—no twisted belts. All machines are well guarded and there are many optional accessories (Figs. 3-10 through 3-13).

The Tennessee firm of *Powermatic Houdaille, Inc.* (147) manufactures a host of small and medium range power woodworking tools. The 10" tilting arbor bench saw, Model 62, is designed for a 1 to 1½ hp motor. The 10" tilting arbor floor model saw No. 66 is the same size, but it is designed to handle 1½ to 3 hp motors.

Powermatic is a stickler for safety and will not ship their saws without guards and splitters. The guard is a "see-through" guard which lets the craftsman view the work while it is being cut. The blade tilts away from the fence to guard against possible binding of material against the fence.

The guard completely covers the blade on all through cuts from narrow to full capacity. The saw is never exposed to the operator. The individual action of each guard leaf covers the blade through the entire tilt range. T-slots on the miter gauge prevent it from falling when extended beyond the front of the table (Figs. 3-14 and 3-15).

STRAIGHT CUTTING POWER CIRCULAR SAWS

Straight cutting stationary saws serve a variety of functions and have become almost a necessary item for home workshops. Without a doubt, the power circular saw is the most used tool, not only in home workshops, but in other shops (school, custom, etc.) as well.

The straight cutting circular saw performs ripping, cross cutting, mitering, beveling, grooving, rabbeting, dadoing and molding operations. It comes as close to an all-purpose tool as an individual tool can come.

VARIETY SAWS

There are two styles of variety saws: the bench saw that must be fastened to a table, stand or bench and the floor model saw, in which the saw and the base are in one self-contained unit.

The variety saw is so-called because it performs the operations mentioned. Most modern variety saws have *tilting arbors* which permit angle cuts to be made on a flat horizontal table.

Fig. 3-10. 8" bench saw with stand and accessories.

Fig. 3-11. 8″ tilting arbor saw. Rear view.

Fig. 3-12. 10¼″ floor model saw.

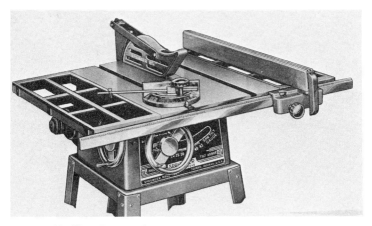

Fig. 3-13. 10¼" bench saw and accessories.

Tilting table saws are few and far between, but at one time were extensively used.

RADIAL SAW

The *radial saw* differs from the variety saw in that the saw pushes into the wood on most operations. It is easily set for cutting angles. The radial saw has become very popular in recent years.

Fig. 3-14. 10" tilting arbor saw bench model 62.

Fig. 3-15. 10" tilting arbor saw Model 66.

UNIVERSAL SAW

The *universal saw* has two saw arbors, making it possible to cross cut or rip saw without changing blades. The universal saw is never found in a homeshop, but a half-century ago it was very often found in the larger school shops and in industrial woodworking shops. The improved designs of combination saw blades have made the universal saw almost an antique.

MOTORIZED MITER BOX

This rather specialized tool greatly speeds up mitering. The motorized miter box is a valuable tool for the carpenter-builder and contractor. It would be one of the last motorized tools to buy for the home workshop.

PARTS OF THE 10" FLOOR-TYPE CIRCULAR SAW

The popular 10" floor-type circular saw has the following parts.

Base. The base houses the motor and is generally provided with an outlet that can be attached to a dust collector system or device.

Table. The table is the major part of the saw. It has a perfectly flat surface, although in most cases two grooved slots are machined to provide a track for a miter gauge.

Miter Gauge. The miter gauge is used for crosscutting. It can be used on either side of the saw. The miter gauge may be set for making angle cuts.

Ripping Fence. The ripping fence is set parallel to the saw blade and the name suggests its function.

Adjusting Wheels. One adjusting wheel controls the depth of the cut, while a second one controls the angle of arbor tilt.

Arbor. The arbor is the threaded spindle on which the saw blade is placed. The saw blade is secured with a washer and nut.

Guard And Slitter. The best guard is the one that completely guards the saw in any position. The individual action of the two leaves cover both sides of the saw through the entire tilt range. Some guards are provided with a "see-through" plastic window.

The slitter opens up the saw kerf and keeps it open so that the work does not bind. On some saws the blade tilts away from the fence to guard against possible binding of material against the fence.

If the saw being used is not properly guarded, the craftsman should consider purchasing a *Brett-Guard*. This transparent guard is made of shatter-resistant Plexiglass so that the operator can see what he is doing at all times. This guard, which prevents physical contact, also guards against flying chips and sawdust. There are a few operations that cannot be performed with the Brett-Guard in place. There are three sizes of Brett-Guards: one for 8″ and 10″ blades, one for 12″ and 14″ blades and one for 16″ blades.

SAFETY PRECAUTIONS

Never stand directly back of the saw. Always stand to one side or the other of the saw. The kickback of a saw will drive a board with the force and deadliness of an arrow.

■ Free hand sawing should never be attempted with the circular. The work should be supported by the ripping fence, the miter guard or by specially designed jigs.

■ Never allow anyone or anything to distract you from your work on the saw. The circular saw is one of the most dangerous of the shop tools and it never gives you a second chance.

■ Always use a push stick when ripping narrow pieces. A very good pushing device can be made with two pieces of ⅛″ thick hardwood which straddle the ripping fence and are held together with a ¾" piece of wood. A handle can be attached to the piece of wood for better handling.

■ Use feather boards when it is necessary to hold the work tight against the table and/or the fence. They are good guards against injury. They are almost a necessity when sawing long, thin and/or narrow pieces (Fig. 3-16).

■ The saw should be set so that only ⅛" to 3/16" of the blade extends above the stock.

■ A stop block should be attached to the rip fence when sawing multiple parts.

■ The saw should be completely stopped before making adjustments.

■ A roller support or an extra person should "tail" a saw when ripping long stock.

■ Keep ties tucked in and sleeves rolled up.

CIRCULAR SAW BLADES AND KNIVES

Saw blades are in two categories—carbide tipped and regular steel saw blades.

Carbide Tipped Saw Blades

The most common carbide tipped saw blades are the following.

Plywood, Plastic And Cutoff Blade. Recommended for smooth cuts in laminated plastics (Formica, etc.) veneers and plywood. It can also be used as a cutoff saw on hardwoods.

"S" Style Planer Combination Saw Blade. For smooth finish when ripping, crosscutting or mitering. It has four cutting teeth to every raker tooth.

Standard "C" Style Combination Saw Blade. A combination rip and cross cut with alternate bevel giving a smooth finish.

Safety Combination Saw Blade. A free cutting, fast blade for general purpose cutting.

Regular Steel Saw Blades

The following are regular steel saw blades.

Hollow Ground Plywood Saw Blade. Designed for cutting all types of thin plywood without splintering. Needs no sanding.

Flat Ground Plywood Saw Blade. Ideal for cutting veneer, plywood and laminates. Used for making miniatures and dollhouse furniture (Fig. 3-17).

Hollow Ground "S" Planer Combination Saw Blade. For fast cutting in any direction of the wood grain.

Flat Ground "S" Planer Combination Saw Blade. The teeth are set for clearance. Performs about the same as the hollow ground "S" blade.

Cut Off (Crosscut) Saw Blade. For general crosscut sawing across the grain. The teeth are set for clearance.

Ripsaw Blade. Flat ground for ripping only (cutting with the grain). Teeth set for clearance. Easy to sharpen.

All Purpose "V" Combination Saw Blade. A flat ground all purpose saw: rips, crosscuts and miters.

Chisel Tooth Combination. A flat ground, chisel tooth saw for fast rough general purpose sawing. Used by construction workers for cutting heavy construction gauge plywood.

The majority of saw blades fit a ⅝" diameter arbor, but saw blades over 10" in diameter fit either a 1" or 1⅛" arbor. Some of the smaller blades (6" and 7¼") have universal arbors which provide ½" round, ⅝" round and 13/16" diamond holes.

DADO HEAD

The *dado head* is used to cut dadoes and wide grooves which are wider than the saw blade is thick. The standard dado head consists of two outside cutter blades which together cut a ¼" dado. For dadoes wider than ¼", inside chipper blades are used. If the

Fig. 3-16. Feather boards used for cutting long, narrow, thin stock.

Fig. 3-17. Flat ground plywood saw blade.

combination of outside cutter blades and inside chippers do not make the desired width of cut, adjustments can be made with paper washers (Fig. 3-18).

Standard dado heads generally come in sets, although it is possible to purchase separate outside cutters or inside chippers. The sets are numbered 1, 2, 3, 4 and 5 and come in 6″, 8″, 10″ and 12″ blade diameters in regular or carbide tips. The five sets are described in Table 3-1.

There are also available adjustable dado sets which may be set for different width cuts without being removed from the saw arbor. One *quick-set dado head* (30) is easily adjustable to widths from ¼″ to 13/16″. This type of dado head is seldom, if ever, used in the woodworking industry.

MOLDING HEAD AND CUTTER

The *molding head* and *cutter* converts the variety or radial saw into a jointer, planer and shaper. The molding head holds the

Fig. 3-18. Outside dado cutters with paper adjustment washers.

matched and balanced cutters securely without vibration. There are a large number of cutters available in many shapes and sizes.

SAW "THROATS"

Saw "throats" should conform somewhat to the size and shape of the blades and cutters being used. The standard "throat" on most saws is too narrow for a dado head and too wide for a plywood saw. Narrow and thin pieces need adequate support as they are pushed through the saw.

Extra saw "throats" can be made from hardboard or masonite. In Fig. 3-19 the regular aluminum "throat" is on the left, a homemade dadoing "throat" is in the center, and a plywood saw throat is on the right (Fig. 3-19).

HOW TO RIP WITH THE CIRCULAR SAW

—Plane one edge of stock straight and square. If a jointer is available, it is by far the quickest and most efficient.

Table 3-1. Five Standard Dado Head Sets.

Set Number	1	2	3	4	5
Number of Cutters Per Set					
Outside Cutters 1/8"	2	2	2	2	2
Inside Chipper 1/16"	1	1	1	1	1
Inside Chipper 1/8"	1	1	2	2	2
Inside Chipper 1/4"		1	1	2	4
Width of Cut	7/16"	11/16"	13/16"	1 1/16"	1 9/16"

111

Fig. 3-19. Saw "throats."

—Test the board to see if it lies flat on the saw table. If it does not lie flat, correct the situation with a hand plane, jointer or planer.

—Adjust the fence to the correct width, either by setting the fence to the measurement on the scale or by measuring the distance from the right side of the blade to the ripping fence with a rule. The latter method is the most accurate.

—Clamp the fence securely. Test it to be sure.

—Lower or raise the saw blade so that it extends from ⅛″ to 3/16″ above the stock.

—Place the guard and slitter or Brett-Guard in position.

—Turn on the motor and allow it to attain full speed.

—Place the straight and square edge of the stock against the ripping fence.

—Advance stock against the saw slowly and steadily. After the saw has entered the wood, the piece can be advanced somewhat faster.

—Stand only to the side of the saw. Watch both hands at all times.

—Let the pieces run off the back edge of the saw. Use a roller or a second person if the piece is extra long. Never reach over the saw to catch the piece.

—Use a push stick and/or feather boards when ripping narrow pieces.

112

—When ripping very thin stock, such as a veneer, it may be necessary to clamp a wood auxiliary fence to the existing rip fence to prevent the thin wood from running under the regular fence.

HOW TO CROSSCUT WITH THE CIRCULAR SAW

—Move the ripping fence from the saw or far enough to the right to prevent interference.

—Put the miter gauge in position in the table slots.

—Raise the saw blade to extend over the top of the stock ⅛″ to 3/16″.

—Place a piece of wood from the scrap box against the miter gauge and run through the saw.

—Test squareness of stock with a try square. If the piece is not square, keep adjusting the miter gauge until it is square.

—Mark the required length on the good stock with try square and sharp pencil, if only one piece is required.

—Cut the required piece. If duplicate pieces are to be made, clamp the clearance block to the ripping fence (Fig. 3-20).

—Position stock firmly against the miter gauge. Be sure that the good face is against the table and the good edge is against the miter gauge.

—Hold stock against the miter gauge with your left hand and advance the miter gauge and stock through the saw with the right hand.

HOW TO RESAW WITH THE CIRCULAR SAW

Set the piece on edge which is to be split or to be reduced in thickness. Set the saw for ⅛″ more than one-half the width of the board. This applies only if the maximum height of the blade is equal to or greater than one-half the width of the board.

Set the ripping fence for the desired cut and push the piece through the saw. Reverse the piece end for end and push through again. Make sure the same face is placed against the fence. A feather board is most helpful in this operation.

If the width of the board is greater than twice the maximum height of the blade, make the two cuts as before. Finish sawing the remaining piece with a band saw or handsaw.

HOW TO SAW MITERED ANGLES

For simple angles, adjust the miter gauge to the desired angle. Pencil mark the point on the stock where the cut is to commence. Remove the ripping fence or push it out of the way. Adjust saw to

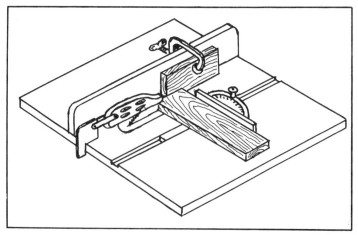

Fig. 3-20. Crosscutting short duplicate pieces with clearance stop block.

the correct depth (thickness of stock plus ⅛″ to 3/16″). If the guard has been removed, place it in position. Make a trial cut with a piece of scrap wood.

Measure the angle with a protractor or check with a T-bevel. If the angle is not correct adjust until the adjustment is made. Only the miter gauge is used to cut simple angles.

Compound angles are made in the same fashion as simple angles, except the arbor of the saw has to be tilted to get the second angle of the compound cut.

HOW TO CUT A RABBET

■ Dimension the stock to the required size.

■ Mark the rabbet on the end of the stock.

■ Set the ripping fence equal to the width of the rabbet.

■ Position the blade so that the teeth will barely touch the marked line at right angles to the saw.

■ Try out the cut on a piece of scrap wood.

■ Make an adjustment to correct any discrepancies.

■ Saw the first cut on all pieces.

■ Stop the saw and turn the first marked piece on edge.

■ Set the saw for depth of cut. The working face should be against the fence. The saw blade should intersect the first cut at a right angle corner.

■ Securely hold the piece (or pieces) against the ripping fence and make the necessary cut or cuts. Generally it is not necessary to make a trial run for the second cut.

114

If there are a large number of pieces to be rabbeted, it is best to use a feather board (Fig. 3-21). This method is used when a dado head is not available. When cutting a rabbet with the dado head, the cut is usually made on the edge of the stock which is on the side opposite the ripping fence. A rabbet may be cut across the end of a board as well as along the edge.

The dado head can be used for cutting rabbets as explained above and, of course, it can be used for cutting dadoes which are grooves cut across the grain away from the end of boards.

The dado head can be used for cutting grooves (sometimes called the plough) which are with the grain and are away from the edges of the board. The dado head can also be used to cut a gain (sometimes called a stop or blind dado) which is identical to a dado,

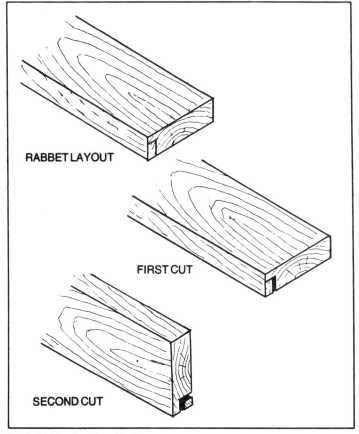

RABBET LAYOUT

FIRST CUT

SECOND CUT

Fig. 3-21. How to cut a rabbet.

except the cut does not extend clear across the board. The dado head is very helpful in cutting lap joints and tenons.

HOW TO CUT A DADO

Lay out the dadoes on the edge of the stock. Make sure they are the same size as stock (shelves, etc.) which will be inserted.

Place the two outside cutter blades and the necessary chipper blades on the saw arbor and tighten. Insert the dado "throat" into the table top.

Set the saw for correct depth and make a trial run on a piece of scrap. If the depth and width are correct, continue cutting the required piece (pieces). If two or more pieces are to be dadoes, it is best to set up stops.

Hold the stock against the miter gauge with the left hand, and advance stock and miter gauge toward the saw with the right hand. The dado can also be cut with a regular blade by pushing the material through the saw a number of times. The groove is cut in the same fashion as the dado except the groove is parallel to the grain. The stock is advanced by holding the stock against the rip fence (Fig. 3-22).

HOW TO MAKE A GAIN, BLIND DADO OR STOP DADO

A *gain, blind dado* or *stop dado* are different names for the same joint; however, the gain may describe a cut going either with the grain or across the grain. The other two terms apply only to joints across the grain.

■ Carefully lay out the joints on the edges of stock to be cut. Lay out a left and a right if the pieces are to be used in shelves or cupboards. The layout marks are placed on the edges that will be advanced over the dado head first.

■ Adjust the dado head to the proper depth. Be sure to use with the proper throat.

■ Position the miter gauge.

■ Determine the exact length of cut.

■ Lay out the distance from the first tooth above the slot on the front of the dado head to a point on the rear of the table equal to the length of the cut.

■ Identify the spot with a pencil mark.

■ Clamp tightly a stop block on the surface of the saw at the identification mark. The block should be at right angles to the saw.

■ Make a trial run with scrap stock.

■ Advance the material into the dado head slowly. Hold firmly against the miter gauge.

■ Turn off the switch when the stock reaches the stop block.

■ If all is well, make the necessary cuts on all the pieces.

■ If necessary, square up the curved corner with a chisel and mallet (Fig. 3-23).

HOW TO CUT TENONS

There are numerous ways to cut tenons: a wide dado head and miter gauge, side of tenon cut with a band saw, or making a shoulder cut with a regular circular saw and cutting cheeks of tenon by standing the piece on end. The method to be described now is the only way that perfect tenons can be cut every time without an expensive industrial tenoner, even though the pieces to be tenoned are not of consistent thickness.

If you do not own a commercial tenoning jig, one can be made that is satisfactory. The upright and the bridge piece over the fence should be made of hardwood or plywood. The piece that rides against the back of the fence is made of hardboard or masonite. This back piece could also be made of hardwood, but hardboard or masonite will slide a little easier. The jig should be 6″ to 8″ long and about the same in height.

Cut a piece of pipe for the spacer collar that will barely slide over the saw arbor. It should be cut slightly longer than required and filed or ground down to the exact thickness of the desired tenon.

Place the inside chipper blades, outside cutter blades and spacer collar on the saw arbor. Note that the usual arrangement has

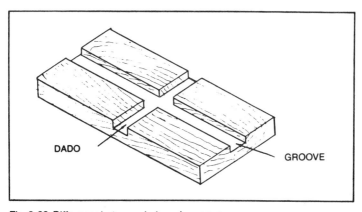

Fig. 3-22. Difference between dado and a groove.

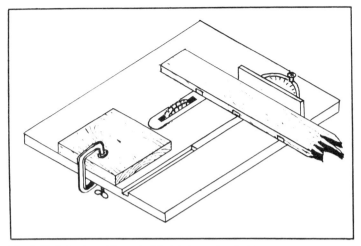

Fig. 3-23. Setup for cutting gain, blind dado, or stop dado.

been *reversed*. The outside cutter blades are in the inside, and the inside chipper blades are on the outside.

Set depth of the dado head to the length of the tenon. Clamp the stock in an upright position to the tenoning jig with a pad, under the clamp part to prevent marring the stock.

Push the stock slowly through the dado head, but only after testing the cut on a piece of scrap stock. Turn off the saw before removing the stock from the jig (Fig. 3-24).

CIRCULAR SAW MAINTENANCE

Remove rust from the table saw as soon as it starts. If the saw is not to be used for some time, apply a thin coat of grease to the top.

Do not attempt to oil or grease motor bearings. Modern motor bearings are sealed with a permanent lubricant. Periodically check the ripping fence to make sure it is absolutely parallel with the saw.

Inspect the belts from time to time. Make sure that grease or oil does not come in contact with belts.

Check guards and slitter from time to time. Remove the sawdust from the base of the saw periodically if a dust collector is not available. Check tilting saw arbor periodically to make sure that it can be tilted to the full 45°.

BAND SAW

Band saws vary in size from the 10″ and 12″ (wheel diameter) with an ⅛″ blade that creates rather fine scroll work to huge 75′

118

long blades with 16″ wide blades. These huge saws have teeth on both edges of the blade for sawing giant logs in both the forward and backward passes of the log carriage.

The 14″ band is probably the most popular in the home workshop, as well as in pattern shops, small school shops, custom cabinet shops, maintenance shops and small furniture shops. In vocational schools, technical institutes and large furniture plants, band saws vary from 36″ to 42″ in wheel diameter. The blades most commonly used are ⅜″ to ¾″ wide. The gauge thickness of band saw blades varies according to wheel size. The thinner blades are used on the smaller band saws. The skip-tooth saw is used to saw faster in certain kinds of woods, and due to its hardness will last

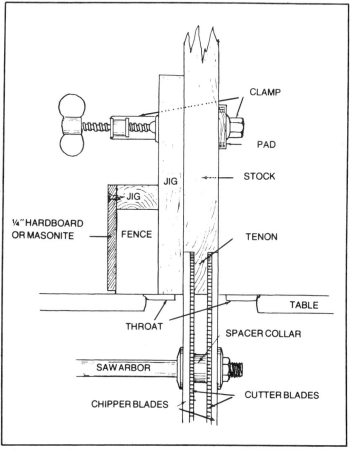

Fig. 3-24. Cutting tenon with reversed dado head.

longer. However, when it gets dull the blade has to be thrown away as it cannot be resharpened.

The band saw is a safer saw to use than the circular saw because there is no chance of a kickback. There are certain precautions, however, that must be taken. Round stock, such as dowels, must never be cut unless pieces are securely clamped in a "V" block. Irregular surfaces that rock on the band saw table should be avoided. Watch both hands at all times. The distance between the top surface of the work and the top guide should never be over ⅜".

One of the first things that a craftsman must learn about a band saw is how to fold the blade. There are many methods that may be used but they all arrive at the same result—a three-loop circle that can easily hang over dowel pegs when not in use. The best way to learn how to fold a band saw blade is from another craftsman. A movie or a series of photos or drawings do not seem to do the trick in most cases.

The major function of the band saw is to cut outside, irregular curves. There are, howver, many other operations that a band saw can perform, the most important of which is resawing. *Resawing* is the process of placing stock on edge and pushing it through the band saw. This method provides two thin boards in place of one thick one. A wider blade and a special fence are used for resawing. In a pinch, the band saw can be used for ripping if a special fence is clamped to the band saw table.

Before sawing on a band saw, turn on the switch and stand back a few seconds. Watch and listen for any unusual signs or sounds. Are there any clicking noises that indicate a blade is about to break? Is the saw "wandering" or running erratically in the guides, which might mean that the upper wheel is not tilted correctly?

When properly adjusted, the blade should run close to the guide wheels in the upper and lower guides. When the pressure of cutting is put on the blades, the guide wheels should spin rapidly.

In the Nov./Dec. 1979 issue of *Fine Woodworking* a very fine analysis of band saws appears. It is entitled "A Survey of Small and Medium-Sized Band Saws" and describes and compares 21 different band saws varying in size from 9⅝" (blade to column) to 24½". It also records maximum depth of cut, maximum blade width, blade speed, blade guides, whether the saw has tension gauge or brake, type of cover (hinged or removable), size of table, angle of table tilt, whether the frame is aluminum, cast iron or steel, overall dimensions, motor horsepower, weight of saw with motor, price per pound and total price.

The width of the band saw blade determines the size of the curve that may be cut. The narrower the blade, the smaller the circle. The blade widths indicate the smallest diameter of circle that can be cut with that blade: ⅛″ blade, smallest circle ½″ diameter; 3/16″ blade, smallest circle 1″ diameter; ¼″ blade, smallest circle 1½″ diameter; ⅜″ blade, smallest circle 2″ diameter; ½″ blade, smallest circle 3″ diameter; and ¾″ blade, smallest circle 3½″ diameter. The blade has to be slightly twisted to cut these curves.

The power wheel of the band saw is the lower wheel, and is connected directly or indirectly through pulleys and belts, to the motor. This wheel needs no adjustment.

The upper wheel has two adjustments. It can be raised or lowered and tilted. Tilting allows the blade to track properly without running off the wheel, and raising and lowering adjusts to slight differences in length of blades as well as putting the proper tension on the saw. Most band saws are provided with a spring tension device that prevents the breaking of blades, and the device indicates the proper setting for different width blades.

Each wheel is covered with a rubber band which helps to preserve the blade and the set of the teeth. Regular band saw blades for wood cutting have alternate teeth set in opposite directions.

To remove an old blade and put on a new blade, the covers over both wheels are removed. The tension on the upper wheel is relieved and the wheel is lowered. Take out the throat insert and remove the pin from the slot that leads from the throat to the edge of the table. Remove the blade from the two wheels and turn it 90° so that the blade will be easily removed from the throat and slot.

Place the new blade through the slot, turn 90°, over the two wheels, tighten the tension spring to the same setting, and then turn the wheel over by hand. If the blade tracks correctly—as it should unless the tilting adjustment has been tampered with—replace the guards and turn on the switch for two or three seconds. Be sure to listen for any clicking sound which indicates that there might be a crack in the blade. *Do not run the band saw without cover guards in place.*

If a different width blade has been installed, it will be necessary to readjust the guides—both below and above the table. The guide pins should ride just back of the teeth, and the wheel support should be back of the blade from 1/64" to 1/32" before any pressure is placed against the blade.

Cutting With a Band Saw

Long sweeping curves can easily be made with the band saw, but the shorter curves present a problem as it is not always convenient to put on a narrower blade when the problem arises. When the problem arises, saw kerfs, close together, should be made up to, but not quite touching, the short curve. When the sawing is made to the short curved line, these wedge-shaped pieces will fall away without cramping or burning the saw blades, and it also eliminates the "backing-out" problem (Fig. 3-25).

Backing a saw out of a cut should be avoided if at all possible. If the saw cannot be backed out with the motor stopped, turn on the saw and *very slowly* back the stock away from the blade. If care is not taken, it is possible to pull the blade off the wheels.

The best tool for effective band sawing is between the ears of the craftsman. Each cut should be carefully thought out before sawing. Otherwise the craftsman may end up with the stock hitting the column before the cut is completed, which means the slow and inefficient "backing out" as mentioned earlier.

When cutting long curves, square up stock. It must lay flat on the band saw table. Make a pattern and draw the curved design on the stock.

Back off the screw that holds the upper guide to the guide post. Position and clamp the upper guide so that it is approximately ⅜" above the stock.

Turn on the switch for two or three seconds to make sure it is running correctly. Permit the saw to attain full speed.

Advance work into the saw. If possible, start the cut in waste stock. Make the short cuts before the longer ones, so that waste will fall away when long cuts are made. The saw should barely touch the outside of the line. Advance the work at a fairly fast rate, but avoid crowding or twisting the saw.

Sawing Duplicate Parts

There are at least four methods of sawing duplicate parts. With the *rubber cement method,* stack the pieces to be sawn with the design marked on the top piece. Cement all pieces together. The rubber cement should only be applied to waste stock.

For the *nailing method* stack the pieces with the design on top and nail through waste stock only. Care should be taken to avoid sawing into the nails.

With the *wedging method,* stack pieces with the design on top and make two or more saw kerfs into waste stock. Drive wedges into the saw kerfs to hold the pieces together. The wedges should be as wide as the stack is high.

If the design is on the end of a rectangular shaped piece, a box-like container can be made with an open end. Place the stack in the container with the design on top and make the necessary cuts.

Duplicate circles can be cut on the band saw by making an auxiliary table for the saw table that has a sliding member so that different diameter circles may be cut. A sharp pointed nail or brad driven into the sliding member is the pivot point on which the stock is turned into the saw.

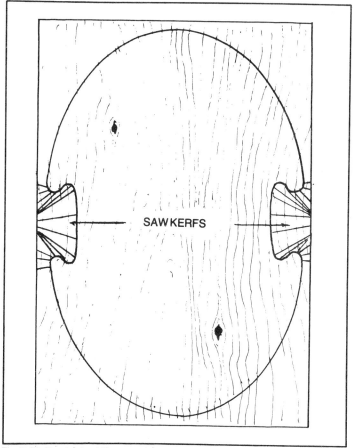

SAW KERFS

Fig. 3-25. Saw kerfs aid in sawing cricket stool top.

Compound Curve Sawing

Compound curve sawing requires two operations or sets of cuts at 90° to each other. One method requires that after the first cuts are made, the waste is glued to back up the stock for the final cut. Another method involves nailing the parts together after the first cuts. I prefer the method of leaving surplus intact at the end of the piece which holds the pieces together until a third cut is made. The first and second sets of cuts extend about ⅛" below the lower end of the leg (Fig. 3-26).

Suppliers/Manufacturers

Rockwell International (155) manufacturers 10", 14" and 20" band saws along with a large assortment of accessories.

The *Craftsman 12"* band saw manufactured by Sears, Roebuck and Co. (163) does double-duty as a saw and a sander. The blade is replaced by a medium-fine ½" wide sanding belt for finishing. Circle cutting attachments are available as accessories. A unique feature is a built-in light as an intergral part of the saw.

The *Inca Model 310,* 10½" band saw by Garrett-Wade (79) has a frame which is one single casting and heavily ribbed for stability. It has a movable brush fitted to the lower wheel to remove sawdust to give longer tire life. The teeth of all blades over ¼" wide extend over the tire, again to prolong the life of the tire.

Du-er Tools (59) manufactures three sizes of band saws: 12", 24" and 26". The blade on the two larger models rides on four wheels instead of the usual two.

Emco-Lux Corp. (65) manufactures a three wheel, three speed, belt driven band saw with a throat size of 14.3". There also is a band saw as part of a multi-purpose power tool which will be discussed later in this chapter.

Poitras, Danckaert Woodworking Machine (143) manufactures a 24" band saw equipped with a dust chute and foot brake. Parks Woodworking Machine (134) manufactures an 18" band saw of heavy fabricated steel, 12" capacity under guide, hinged doors for easy accessibility to the blade.

Sprunger Corp. (172) manufactures 10" and 14" wood-cutting band saws. The 10" saw has an optional frame height riser accessory which increases the depth of cut from 6" to 12". The body and table are heavily ribbed for greater rigidity (Fig. 3-27).

Powermatic Houdaille (147) manufactures two 14" band saws. One is for woodcutting only and the other can be used on wood or metal (Fig. 3-28). Powermatic also manufactures a 20″ woodcutting saw and a 20″ wood, metal, plastic cutting saw.

Conover (40) is the supplier of the 14″ band saw in Fig. 3-29. It has a solid, heavily constructed, cast iron frame, and the throat dimension (the distance from the blade to the frame) is a full 14″. The table tilts 15° to the left and 45° to the right. The blade is totally enclosed except where actual cutting takes place.

JIGSAW OR SCROLL SAW

The *jigsaw* and scroll saw are the same power tools, although there is a tendency toward calling the larger industrial types scroll saws instead of jigsaws. In essence, the jigsaw is a motorized coping saw.

The most popular size jigsaw is the 24″ which has set pulleys on the saw and motor to provide different speeds. The size of a

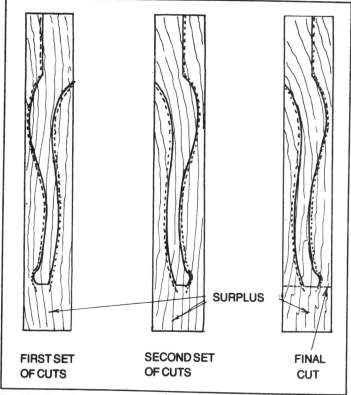

FIRST SET OF CUTS   SECOND SET OF CUTS   FINAL CUT

SURPLUS

Fig. 3-26. Compound curve cutting of Queen Anne leg.

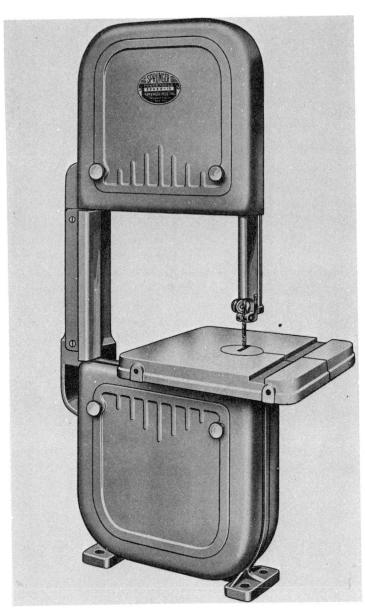

Fig. 3-27. 10″ Band saw.

jigsaw is the distance from the blade to the supporting arm. The blade is held between an upper and lower chuck. The lower chuck moves up and down and is connected to the power source. The

Fig. 3-28. 14″ woodcutting band saw, Model 141.

Fig. 3-29. 14″ woodcutting band saw.

upper chuck is connected to a tension spring which is enclosed in a tubular sleeve. The jigsaw is capable of sawing both interior and exterior cuts.

The jigsaw saws much slower than the band saw. The jigsaw cuts only on the downward stroke, while the band saw cuts continuously. The band saw will also cut much heavier stock. The advantages of the jigsaw are the ability to cut curves with small radii, to cut fine lines, and to cut both interior and exterior curves.

The teeth of a jigsaw blade points downward, which assists in holding the work to the table along with the spring hold down. The work should be pushed slowly into the blade. If the work starts to chatter, ease up on the rate of speed at which you are pushing the work into the blade.

128

Blades

Jigsaw blades come in two types: the *blank end* and the *pin end*. The blank end blades are used in most of the larger jigsaws. They are also in two different lengths—5″ and 6″. See Table 3-2.

Cutting Intarsia With the Jigsaw

Intarsia is the art of combining different kinds and colors of wood or other materials to fit a carved-out recess in solid wood. Only jeweler's saws are used because the kerf must be as small as possible.

The outline of the design must be traced very accurately. The saw should be set at a slow speed, and the outline of the design must be followed with care. All interior cuts should be made first.

After the design is completely sawed, the piece of intarsia is laid on the solid wood and maked with a very sharp, hard lead

Table 3-2. Jigsaw Blades.

No.	Thickness	Width	Teeth Per Inch
515	.020	.110	15
510	.020	.110	10
407	.028	.250	7
36	.010	.055	18
5M5	.020	.070	20
520	.020	.110	20
3M5	.020	.070	15
2M5	.020	.085	15
310	.028	.187	10
415	.028	.250	20
Blank End, 6″ Long Blades			
6/0	.007	.014	80
5/0	.008	.016	75
4/0	.009	.018	65
3/0	.010	.020	60
2/0	.010	.020	57
1/0	.011	.025	52
1 J	.012	.026	47
2 J	.014	.028	42
3 J	.014	.030	39
4 J	.015	.032	37
5 J	.015	.033	35
5 J	.016	.034	32
8 J	.024	.044	26
10 J	.016	.054	30

pencil. The design on the solid wood is recessed with a router and/or carving chisels. The depth of the recess should be about 1/64" shallower than the intarsia is thick.

Glue the intarsia piece into the solid wood. Sand the intarsia flush with the solid wood after glue is set.

Sawing Marquetry With the Jigsaw

The difference between intarsia and marquetry is not very great. Marquetry designs are set in veneer the same thickness as the marquetry and then the whole assembly is glued to solid wood. In most cases, the end result is either a picture for wall decoration, or used as a furniture decoration.

Although a craft knife or hand fret saw may be used for cutting marquetry, the jigsaw or scroll saw can do the job more accurately, with greater speed and with less effort.

Make a paper pattern of the marquetry. Mount the pattern on the background veneer which is the larger single color in most instances—the sky on pictorials. Use rubber cement on the back of the pattern.

Tape the oversize patch piece of veneer into the background veneer and pattern. The correct position can be ascertained by holding the pieces of veneer to a strong light.

Drill a small hole through the pattern and both pieces of veneer. Insert a jeweler's saw blade through the hole.

Insert the lower end of the blade through the throat in the table and into the lower chuck. Tighten the lower chuck and place the upper chuck over the upper end of the blade and tighten. The guide for the blade is then let down until it meets the veneer.

Raise the left side of table from 10° to 12°. Prepare for sawing by putting on a headband magnifier and turning on the light. The "no hands" magnifier with a built-in light is ideal. See Brookstone (32) in the Appendix.

Test the blade for proper tension and check to see if the teeth point toward the table and are on the front side of the blade. Start cutting and rotate the combined pattern, background veneer and veneer patch in a counterclockwise fashion. Continue cutting until you are completely around the piece, unless a sharp corner is reached, in which case the motor is stopped and the saw is eased slowly around the corner by turning the pulley on belt by hand.

Turn on the motor after going around the corner and continue sawing. Raise the guide when the cutting is completed and the motor is turned off.

Untighten the upper jaws and then the lower jaws. Pull the saw blade very carefully from the veneer pieces.

Remove the tape from the veneer patch insert. Place the insert patch into the background veneer and tape in place. Naturally, it will fit because both pieces are sawed at the same setting, and the angle cut has eliminated any kerf gap. Continue cutting the other patches.

Sawing Internal Curves With the Jigsaw

Bore or drill one or more holes large enough for the blade to be pushed through. These holes should be in the center portion of the part to be cut out. Keep the holes as far as possible away from the scribed lines.

Remove the blade from the jigsaw. Place the hole just bored over the throat of the jigsaw between the upper chuck and lower chuck. Insert the blade through the hole in the wood (teeth pointed downward) and place the ends of the blade in the two chucks. Tighten the blade.

Start sawing. The sawing should angle gradually toward the line to be sawed.

If it is necessary to saw sharp corners, it is best to cut clear to the corner and then back off and cut a well rounded corner into the part at right angles to the one already cut. Run the saw to the nearest hole and cut to the corner from the opposite direction.

Jigsaw Maintenance and Precautions

■ Make sure that the SAE oil used in the crank case meets the manufacturer's specifications.

■ Check belts for condition and tension. Remove any oil or grease at once.

■ Periodically check the jaws on the chucks. The thumbscrews should never be tightened with pliers.

■ Periodically oil all moving parts.

■ The throat plate insert should be removed if worn.

■ The teeth of the blade should be pointed down when inserted into chucks.

■ Pull the belt by hand to make sure the blade is set correctly before turning on the motor switch.

■ Always set the tension spring for the correct setting.

■ Ascertain if belt guards are in place.

■ Check the sawdust blower to see if it is working properly.

Other Uses for the Jigsaw

The jigsaw may be used for filing, sanding and saber sawing. Saber saw blades are held in the lower chuck only. This method speeds up the work when many internal cuts are to be made. A new cut can be made simply by lifting the guide post.

Suppliers/Manufacturers

The following jigsaws and scroll saws are listed from the largest to the smallest in the home workshop category. For the craftsman who wants the ultimate in a heavy-duty, high performance jigsaw, the *Hegner* (German made) *Multicut-2* may be the answer. The secret of its success is said to be incredible blade strength obtained by a completely new patented attachment and tensioning system. This system practically eliminates blade breakage. The "gooseneck" (distance from blade to overarm) is 14.37″. It will cut through almost 2″ (1.97″) in either soft or hardwood, 1.18″ of hard plastic, 0.47″ of copper, brass or silver, 0.39″ of medium hard steel, 0.59″ of hard aluminum or cast iron and 1.57″ of Plexiglas. The blade can be turned 90° so length of stock is no problem. The saw has a chip removal bellows that is maintenance free, and the saw can be tilted to 45°. A special clamp locking device accessory allows blades to be changed very rapidly. The Hegner can use the standard 5″ jigsaw and jeweler's saw blades. A larger *Hegner Polycut-3* will saw up to 2.16″ thick, softwood or hardwood and plywood. It is designed for industrial and institutional use rather than for home workshops.

The *Vega 26″* scroll saw, supplier Brodhead-Garrett (30), has a heavy steel tubing frame which the manufacturer contends has greater strength and stiffness than conventional cast iron. The table tilts 45° to either side and front and back. The machine speed control is lockable so that very low speeds can be assured when beginners are using the machines. The Vega will cut up to 1½″ of wood with the 5″ blade and up to 2½″ with the 6″ blade.

The *Rockwell* (155) *24″* scroll saw has been around a long time and was (and is) the old standby in many schools and shops for a half century. It was originally known as the Delta. The current model has a wrap-around guard to protect the fingers, and is available with a variable speed control as well as the four-speed belt and pulley model. The table tilts 45° right and 15° left for normal bevel cutting and 45° front for bevel cutting for extra long stock.

With the *Powermatic Houdaille* (147) *24″* scroll saw, *Model 95,* as the Rockwell saw, one has the available option of a variable speed or four-speed model. It will cut material up to 1¾" thick. The overarm may be removed so that a saber saw may be used with any size panel. The table tilts 45° right, 15° left, and the saw is equipped with a chip blower. Motor, controls and stand are extra accessories and must be ordered separately (Fig. 3-30).

The *Sprunger Corp.* (172) *20"* jigsaw has an automotive-type drive shaft with bearings on both ends for smooth vibration-free operation. The table tilts 45° and 30° left. The entire chuck and assemblies rotate as one to change cutting direction 90° for ripping long stock. It has an integral light and air blower, and will cut up to 2" of material. The speed is not variable. It has a constant speed of 2575 strokes per minute. The basic machine may be purchased without stand, light, pulleys, belt, belt guard, switch, motor mount and motor (Fig. 3-31).

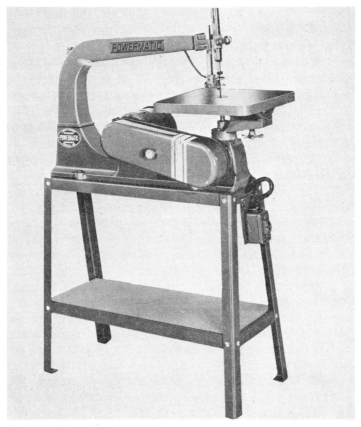

Fig. 3-30. 24" scroll saw, Model 95.

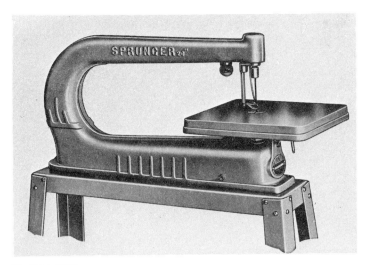

Fig. 3-31. 20″ jigsaw.

The *Dremel Moto-Shop* (57) is a favorite of the miniature and model maker. This 15″ jigsaw has a disc sander attached to it which increases its capability. In addition, a flexible shaft and accessories are available at extra cost. Drilling, routing, deburring, grinding, sharpening and carving are operations possible with this extra attachment.

This multi-purpose saw will cut up to 1¾″ thick softwood, and ½″ thick hardwood. The table raises and lowers to utilize the full length of the blade, and also tilts 45° on both sides of the perpendicular. The saw will cut to the center of a 30″ circle.

When cutting thick wood, the blade guard may have to be removed. It should be replaced when cutting thinner stock.

Jigsaw blades for the Dremel have a pin in each end and the distance from pin center to pin center is 2¾″. Blades are generally available in three grades: *fine, medium* and *coarse.* The coarse blade is wider and has 16 teeth to the inch. It should be used for straight cuts and curves with larger radii. An assortment of blades should be kept on hand at all times. Although they seldom break, they become dull and should be changed when any indication of this nature is noticed. It is false economy and a waste of time and effort to work with a dull blade when the cost factor is so low. The Dremel jigsaw is a happy and practical compromise between the tiny vibrating jigsaw and the larger, heavier jigsaw with a separate motor (Fig. 3-32).

Sawing a Small Object on the Dremel Jigsaw

Draw an outline of the piece on self-adhesive paper with a sharp pencil. It is much easier to follow a line more accurately if fine lines are on white paper than to follow lines on wood.

Place this drawing on the stock to be cut with the adhesive side next to stock. Rubber cement may be used with the pattern inscribed on plain paper.

Adhere the pattern, with double-face adhesive or rubber cement, and the stock to a much larger piece of scrap, soft wood about ¼″ thick. A circular piece between 3″ and 4″ in diameter is ideal because the craftsman then has complete control of the work. The larger protective and control piece will also prevent splintering out on the underside of the workpiece.

Saber and Bayonet Saws

The *saber saw* is like a miniature, upside down, portable jigsaw with only one chuck fastened to the motor. This feature means that the blades must be much stiffer than coping saw or jigsaw blades.

There are many types and sizes of blades available for the saber saw. Many of the blades will cut materials other than wood. The number of teeth vary from six for wood to 32 for metal. When purchasing saw blades, be certain to get those that will fit the machine. Saber saw blades will not fit all makes of saber saws.

Fig. 3-32. The Dremel Moto-Shop 15″ jigsaw and disc sander.

If the home craftsman does not possess any curve-cutting equipment, he should consider buying only the best quality saber saw which generally has the greatest versatility. The quality saws have a tilting base for angled cuts, variable speed motor, and enough power to saw through a two-by-four if need be.

One distinct advantage of the saber saw is that it will cut internal (inside) cuts without drilling or boring holes. This makes working with paneling much easier. This type of sawing is called *plunge* sawing. The saw is tilted up on the front end, and the saw blade is slowly lowered into the work, thus cutting its own hole. It is best to try this procedure on waste stock first as this technique takes some practice.

The *bayonet* saw is the "big brother" of the saber saw. It is heavier, more powerful and has to be operated with both hands. The more expensive models have two speeds and also an option switch for selecting either orbital or reciprocating blade motion. The blade of the bayonet sticks out in front of the motor, while the saber saw points downward.

COMBINATION POWER WOODWORKING TOOLS

Home craftsmen many times become very emotional when discussing the pros and cons of the combination power tool. The opponents contend that the constant shifting of the motor from tool to tool takes up too much time. They feel that individual tools with their own separate motors are the only way to go.

Many proponents argue that the combination tool is, for them, a godsend, inasmuch as their available space is much too restricted for individual tools. One manufacturer claims that his combination machine takes up no more space than a bicycle.

The multi-purpose Shopsmith (16 4), invented by a German engineer, Dr. Hans Goldschmidt, who with his wife fled Nazi Germany in 1937, has long been a favorite of home craftsmen. The current 5-in-1 *Shopsmith Mark V* has many improvements over the original Shopsmith invented shortly after World War I.

The unique Shopsmith Mark V multi-purpose tool provides five major tools in one. It combines a 10″ table saw, a horizontal boring machine, a 16½″ drill press, a 12″ disc sander and a 34″ lathe. It employs a single table, spindle, stand and motor and requires less storage space than a bicycle according to their literature (Fig. 3-33).

The Shopsmith Mark V woodworking system provides nine power tools in a compact area. With Shopsmith you can start with the Mark V multi-purpose tool and grow with the system as you progress. Adding a *band saw, jigsaw, jointer* and *belt sander* is easy and economical since they can be mounted on and powered by the Mark V. The four additional tools can be stored on a convenient wall shelf. Power stands are also available for independent operation. Shopsmith brings the enjoyment of woodworking within family budget limitations with a system to grow with (Fig. 3-34).

The Shopsmith as a Table Saw

The *Shopsmith Mark V 10"* table saw can perform the same operations as other saws of the same size, such as crosscutting, ripping, mitering, tapering, cutting compound angles, rabbeting, dadoing, grooving, tenoning, panel sawing, chamfering, panel raising, molding and much more (Figs. 3-35 and 3-36).

Fig. 3-33. Complete Shopsmith Mark V.

Fig. 3-34. Shopsmith Mark V nine tool woodworking system.

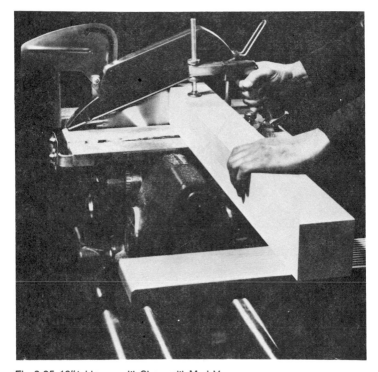

Fig. 3-35. 10″ table saw with Shopsmith Mark V.

Fig. 3-36. Shopsmith Mark V as a panel saw.

The Shopsmith as a Band Saw

The throat depth of the *Shopsmith band saw* is 10½" and the maximum vertical cutting clearance is 6". The saw will cut external curves, resaw stock, and do compound cutting, mitering, bevel cutting, multiple part cutting, pad sawing, pattern sawing and parallel curve cutting (Fig. 3-37).

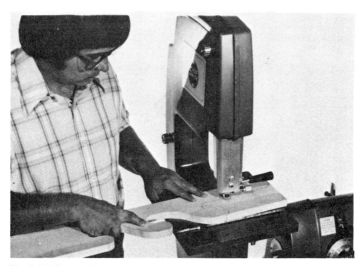

Fig. 3-37. Shopsmith band saw.

The Shopsmith as a Jigsaw

The *Shopsmith jigsaw* can be mounted on the Mark V or on a separate stand. It can do internal curve cutting as well as external curve cutting. It is an excellent tool for inlaying, intarsia and marquetry. This tool may also be used for saber cutting, filing and sanding (Fig. 3-38).

The Shopsmith as a Lathe

The *Shopsmith lathe* will perform all the operations that a lathe of comparable size will accomplish. Spindle turning, faceplate

Fig. 3-38. Shopsmith jigsaw on separate stand.

turning, fluting and reeding, and spiral turnings are a few of the operations that can be done on this lathe.

The variable speed control on the Mark V offers a speed range of 700 to 5200 rpm at the turn of a dial. It is 34″ between centers with a 16½″ swing (Fig. 3-39).

The Shopsmith as a Router

The *Shopsmith router arm* is ideal for the duplication of designed patterns. The overarm holds the router firm while the operator guides the workpiece. The pin in the table surface fits the slot of the fixture which produces an exact duplicate (Fig. 3-40).

Routing can also be done with the *Shopsmith drill press*. The variable speed, quill action for depth control and rip fence provide added convenience and accuracy (Fig. 3-41).

Fig. 3-39. Shopsmith Mark V as a lathe.

141

Fig. 3-40. Shopsmith router arm.

Fig. 3-41. Routing with Shopsmith Mark V.

142

The Shopsmith as a Horizontal Boring Machine

A *horizontal boring machine* is one useful tool you just cannot buy unless it's an expensive industrial model. It provides precision doweling the way it's done by furniture manufacturers. For drilling to any depth into the end of very long pieces, it's the only tool. This horizontal boring machine is one of the five major tools combined in the Shopsmith Mark V multi-purpose tool (Fig. 3-42).

Fig. 3-42. Shopsmith Mark V horizontal boring machine.

The Shopsmith as a Mortiser

A special accessory for the *Shopsmith Mark V vertical drill press* eliminates tedious hand work for mortising. The big 18⅜" x 14" full tilting table with lock-on self-aligning rip fence and miter gauge provides drilling convenience and versatility. The mortising attachment is slipped over the collar on the quill and secured with an Allen setscrew (Fig. 3-43).

The Shopsmith as a Vertical Drill Press

In a vertical position the Shopsmith drill press is used as a regular drill press. The quill has a feed of 4¼" and is returned to its starting position by a coil spring enclosed in the headstock. It drills to the center of a 16½" circle (Fig. 3-44).

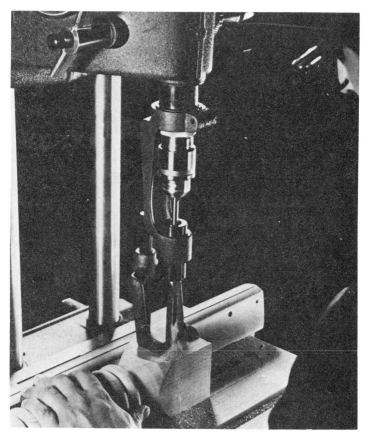

Fig. 3-43. Mortising with Shopsmith Mark V vertical drill press.

The Shopsmith as a Jointer

The *Shopsmith jointer* can be used separately or with the Shopsmith Mark V. The jointer is designed to do accurately and quickly many operations that are ordinarily done by hand. In essence it is a motorized hand plane that is used to make straight and square edges that can be glued. Besides straight jointing, the jointer can be used for rabbeting, beveling, tapering, chamfering and recessing (Fig. 3-45).

The Shopsmith as a Drum and Disc Sander

The drum sander accessory is powered by the auxiliary spindle on the Shopsmith Mark V. The versatility of the Mark V

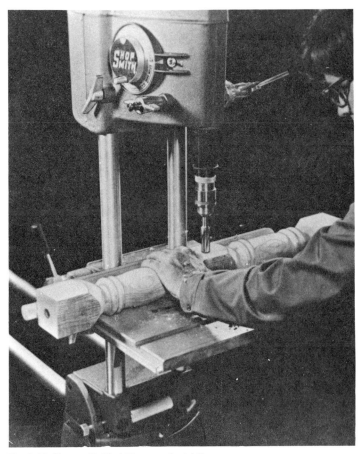

Fig. 3-44. Shopsmith Mark V as a vertical drill press.

Fig. 3-45. Shopsmith jointer.

provides the availability of the disc sander operation while drum sanding (Figs. 3-46 and 3-47).

The Shopsmith as a Belt Sander

The *Shopsmith 6″ belt sander* is ideal for straight line sanding preventing swirl marks (Fig. 3-48). *Fox Super Shop* (74), a subsidiary of Fox Industries, Inc. is a new product that has been three years in development. The company is presently establishing dealer and distributor programs. Fox claims that the Super Shop is the finest multi-purpose power tool in the field. It works in metal as well as wood. With accessories it can perform 15 operations with the following: 10″ heavy duty power table saw, ⅝″ wood or steel vertical drill press, all purpose stationary router, 12″ heavy duty disc sander, high speed shaper, professional 17″ x 34″ wood lathe, horizontal boring machine, a vertical milling machine,

Fig. 3-46. Drum sanding with Shopsmith Mark V.

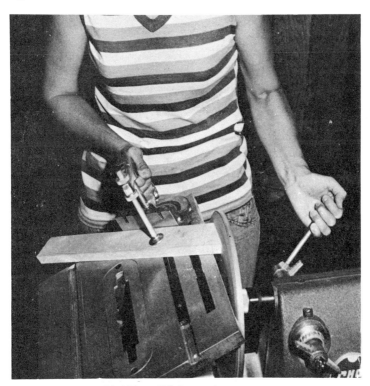

Fig. 3-47. Shopsmith Mark V as a 12" disc sander.

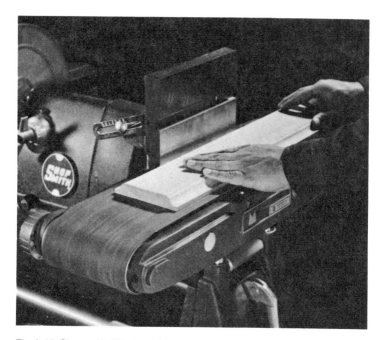

Fig. 3-48. Shopsmith 6″ belt sander.

Other Tools

The *Emco-Lux Corp.* (65) supplies two combination wood-working tools: the *Emco/Rex* and the *Emco/Super* and an individual band saw known as the *Emco BS-2*. The machines are manufactured by Emco Maier of Austria.

The Emco/Rex and the Emco/Super perform essentially the same operations, but the Emco/Super is larger with a more powerful motor. Operations are circular sawing, band sawing, grooving and coving, disc sanding, molding, mortising, planing, combing, form sanding, wood turning and flexible shaft work (Figs. 3-51 and 3-52).

The *Emco BS-2 band saw* is a three-wheeler with a 14.3″ throat and a cutting height of 5.7″. It has three cutting speeds for metal, plastics and wood. The table is 15.7″ x 15.7″ and can be boring machine, a vertical milling machine, a metal spinning lathe, a horizontal metal chucker, a 6″ jointer, a molding machine, a 6″ planer, a 15″ metal or wood band saw and a 16″ x 34″ metal lathe. It is powered by a large 1½ hp motor with a variable speed control from 30 to 7200 rpm (Figs. 3-49 and 3-50).

Fig. 3-49. Fox Super Shop multi-purpose (15 in 1) power tool.

Fig. 3-50. Fox Super Shop multi-purpose power tool with Tony Fox at the controls.

Fig. 3-51. Emcostar Rex combination power woodworking tool.

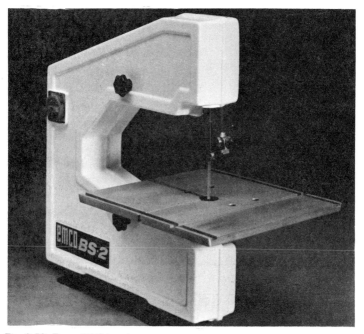

Fig. 3-52. Emco BS-2 band saw.

150

Fig. 3-53. Top view of the combination planer/molder/saw.

Fig. 3-53. Sideview of the combination planer/molder/saw.

Fig. 3-55. Combination planer/molder.

tilted to 45°. Emco-Lux also manufactures a wood turning lathe and jointer (not shown) (Fig. 3-53).

The *Belsaw* (21) *planer/molder/saw,* three-in-one combination power tool planes stock up to 12¼″ wide and up to 6″ thick; the machine molds up to face width of 12″ and edge molds up to 6″ wide, and saws up to 2½″ thick. The power feeds 12′ per minute. Two to three horsepower motors are used for general work and three to five horsepower motors for commercial work (Figs. 3-54 and 3-55).

The *Foley Manufacturing Co.* (70) *combination planer/molder* has the same specifications as the Belsaw planer/molder/saw except it does not have a saw (Fig. 3-56).

Elu Machine Co. (64) manufactures a combination table saw and a miter saw. As a table saw the motor and saw are below the table. As a miter saw, the saw and motor are above the table. The saw has a 10″ saw blade and is powered by a 1.4 hp motor. As a miter saw it will cut stock 2 3/16″ thick by 5½″ wide. It tilts from 0° to 45°.

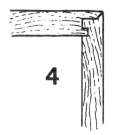

4

Planing, Jointing, Molding and Shaping Tools

Planing tools are used essentially to smooth the surface of the wood. This smoothing process involves more than flat pieces or outside surfaces. Corners, edges and inside surfaces all must be smooth and free from rough wood and splinters.

HAND-HELD PLANES

The popularity of hand-held planes is due, in part, to the fact that they are inexpensive when compared to their motorized cousins. Hand-held planes can serve the same purpose and do the job as well. However, this process requires more work and time and, perhaps, more skill on the part of the craftsman.

Block Plane

The *block plane* differs from other planes in that it is designed to be used in one hand. There are very few parts in this small plane, and the plane iron is set much lower than others. The bevel of the cutting edge is turned up instead of down. The block plane is used to plane and grain. It would be the last purchase for the home workshop as the smoothing plane or the jack plane can do the same operation nearly as well.

Regardless of which of these three planes mentioned are used for planing end grain, certain precautions should be made to prevent the splitting of the wood.

Here are steps on how to plane end grain. Plane toward the center of the end of stock from both ways instead of clear across the end, or cut a small 45° chamfer in the waste stock with a chisel. Or, put a piece of scrap stock behind the piece to be planed. Secure both pieces at the same height in a vise. Thus, the splitting will take place on the scrap piece.

Block planes vary in length from 6″ to 6⅝″. The blade width varies from 1¼″ to 1⅝″.

Jack Plane

The *jack plane* is an all-purpose plane that can be used for many tasks. You might call it the "jack of all trades" planes. If the craftsman can only afford one plane, this is the plane to purchase.

The jack plane is usually 14″ long with a 2″ wide blade. There are 18 parts to a jack plane as compared to only three for the block plane. The plane iron can be easily shifted so that it will not cut too deeply on either cutting corner.

When squaring up stock with the jack plane, plane a working face. Check with a square or straight edge to make sure the surface is flat. Plane only *with the grain*. If the wood has a tendency to "roughen up," try planing in the opposite direction.

Plane a working edge square to the working face. Test squareness with a try square or straightedge.

Plane a working end square to the working face and the working edge. Check frequently with a square.

Mark the required length and square a pencil line across the board. With a backsaw or crosscut saw, cut off the waste material close to the line just marked. Plane this second end square with the working face and working edge.

Mark the required width. If the required piece is fairly narrow (under 6″), use a marking gauge. If the piece is wide, use a panel gauge. Cut off the waste stock with a ripsaw held close to the scribed line. Plane the stock to proper width. Check the width at both ends. This second edge should be square with the working face and the two ends.

Mark the thickness with the marking gauge. Accentuate the line with a chisel-edge, hard-lead pencil. Cut a chamfer on the second face on both edges and the ends until the chamfer nearly meets the thickness line. The chamfer will act as a guide when planing the board to thickness. It will not be necessary to watch the line on every stroke of the plane.

Fore Plane

The *fore plane* is generally 18″ long with a plane iron somewhat wider than that found on a standard jack plane. Boards are often jointed on the edges with the fore plane before gluing.

If the home craftsman is thinking about a second plane to add to his tool inventory, he is well advised to select the longer jointer plane rather than the fore plane.

Jointer Plane

As its name suggests, the *jointer plane* is used almost exclusively for jointing edges of boards, particularly before gluing. The length of jointer planes runs from 22″ long upward to nearly 3′.

Smoothing Plane

The *smoothing plane* looks like a "chopped off" jack plane. The bed is much shorter and extends only to the back of the handle. Smoothing planes are 8″ or 9″ long.

This plane is especially useful on small pieces. It should be kept very sharp and very close to the plane iron cap to produce a small, silky shaving almost of the same quality as that produced by a well-sharpened scraper.

Router Plane

The *router plane* differs radically from all of the previously mentioned planes. It has two round, identical handles and an oblong base with a narrow, adjustable blade extending through the base between the handles.

The router plane is used to smooth the bottom of rabbets, grooves and dadoes. The home craftsman might better invest his money in a power router rather than the hand router described. The power router can perform many more operations. By purchasing an inexpensive accessory table, the router can be used as a shaper.

Rabbet Plane

There are a number of planes used for cutting rabbets. One plane can be used with either the left or right hand. The *bullnose rabbet plane* has the plane iron near the front, and extending across the whole plane. Thus, the plane may be used in corners.

There is a *combination plane* that can be used both for regular and bullnose planing. *Bullnosing* is the process of smoothing the bottom of a cut or groove that does not extend clear across a piece of stock.

Spokeshave

As one would suspect, the *spokeshave* was originally used to make spokes for wheels. It can be used effectively for rounding

155

corners of stock and for cutting chamfers. It can get into places that would be impossible for a plane.

The spokeshave has two wing-like handles. It has a plane iron and cuts in the same fashion as a plane. The spokeshave and cabinet scraper are similar in appearance.

Universal Plane

This tool is designed to do all kinds of planing jobs and works particularly well on moldings. A universal plane is a rather expensive tool and one that is hard to keep sharpened and adjusted. The biggest objection is the fact that it is rather difficult to use without considerable practice. Money that might be spent on this tool might better be spent on a power router, which will do the same job faster and better.

Circular Plane

This plane has a flexible, steel-spring bed and is designed to plane convex and concave curves of many sizes. It is a rather difficult tool to use, and the same operations can be done with other tools more efficiently.

Trimming Plane

The *trimming plane* is a small, light plane, handy for modeling and odds and ends of light work. This miniature plane is only 3½" long.

SPECIAL HAND PLANES

As the name suggests, the *scraper plane* is a combination scraper and plane. It looks like a plane and is used like a plane, but the cutting action is like a scraper. Particularly useful on curly and cross-grained hardwoods, it comes in a variety of sizes from 2¼" to 6½" long. See (40) (68) and (204) in the Appendix.

Palm Plane

This plane is often called the *Conover palm plane* as Conover (40) is the major manufacturer of palm planes. The body is of cast brass and the Conover plane is only 2¼" long.

Conover palm planes come in three styles. The *smooth* model has a flat sole which is ideal for all general smoothing operations. The *scrub* model has a convex sole which is excellent for removing large amounts of stock or making concave surfaces such as are

156

found in sounding boards of musical instruments and on moldings. The *beading* plane with its concave sole is invaluable in violin making, special moldings and cabinet work. See (40) and (204) in the Appendix.

Blind Nailer

The true cabinetmaker will never use a nail unless he has no option. If he does use a nail, he makes every effort to conceal it, and one of the best devices for this effort is the *blind nailer*. The blind nailer carefully raises a small curl or ship of wood. The nail is driven into the groove and the ship is glued back down over the head of the nail.

The Conover blind nailer, as well as the palm plane, is made of brass (Fig. 4-1). See (40) and (68) in the Appendix.

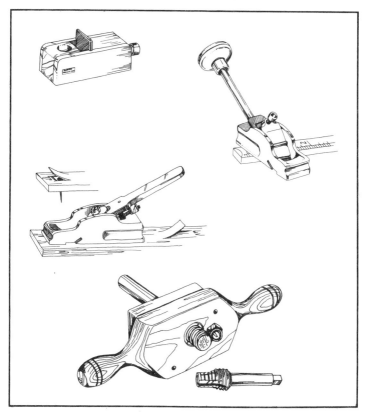

Fig. 4-1. Scraper plane, palm plane, blind nailer and thread box and tap, from top to bottom.

Violin Maker's Finger Plane

The body of this 2¼" long brass tool has a ½" wide blade and weighs only 4 ounces. An extension handle that fits into the palm of the hand supplements the push of the fingers. See (32).

Brass Whale Finger Plane

This little gem is shaped like a whale and the forefinger rests in the whale's upturned tail while in use. The base and blade are convex in shape. It is available in ⅜", ½" and ⅝" width blades. See (204).

Hollowing Plane

The cast iron, 1" blade tool enables the craftsman to rough out a hollow or contour easily with or across the grain. The overall length is 3½" and the sole has a radius of 12" in length and ⅞" in width. See (204).

Primus Plane

The body and sole of all *Primus* planes are made of wood. The woods used are beech, hornbeam and lignum vitae. Hornbeam and beech are used for the bodies, and hornbeam and lignum vitae are used for the soles. Primus planes are available in jack planes, smooth planes, try planes and rabbet planes. See (68).

SHARPENING A PLANE IRON

All plane irons are sharpened in the same way. If a plane iron is very dull and nicked, it will require regrinding as well as whetting.

When *grinding*, hold the bevel side down against the grinding wheel, and place the index finger on the under side to slide against the rest on the grinder. Take a few passes across the edge of the grinding wheel to see if the correct angle has been established. If not, slide the index finger until the right angle is found.

The bevel on most plane irons is about twice the thickness of the plane iron. During the grinding process, check often for squareness and for overheating. If the iron starts turning dark in color, dunk it in water.

When the grinding is complete, a wire edge can be removed by rubbing the edge against a piece of wood or by subsequent whetting.

Start *whetting* on the coarser side of the oilstone. Use kerosene of light oil on the oilstone face to prevent the pores of the oilstone from clogging. Check from time to time during the whetting process to make sure that the heel of the bevel, as well as the cutting edge, is being whetted. Also check for squareness.

Turn the stone over and whet the iron on the finer side. Sight along the blade edge to make sure there are no shiny white patches which indicate dull spots. Run the thumbnail along the edge to check for minute nicks.

Honing is done after the whetting and imparts a razor-like edge. Honing is sometimes done on a leather strap, but the best method is to buff the edge on a buffing wheel using buffing compound or jeweler's rouge. When the plane iron removes the hair on the back of your arm, you know it is ready to put back in the plane.

POWER PLANING TOOLS

The terms planer, surfacer and thickness planer are used interchangeably. Planers that will handle stock 12″ wide and wider are rather expensive, but many home craftsmen own these tools, because they can start with rough stock and plane any thickness needed down to ⅛″.

Most planers are power fed. The planer operator should go to the back of the planer to catch long pieces as they come through. Otherwise, the end of the board coming through last is apt to be thinner than the rest.

The grain direction should be checked before inserting stock into the planer or the surface may be badly checked and rough. Short pieces of stock should be pushed through the planer, one piece close behind the other. Generally, slightly angled pieces will go through the planer easier.

Planers vary in size from those that can handle from 7″ wide stock to 52″; larger planers can surface stock up to 9″ thick. Many smaller planers have a roller-type feed mechanism which draws the stock into the planer knives. Larger planers have a moving table, somewhat like a conveyor belt, which works the stock through the planer.

Contrary to popular conception, the planer by itself will not remove the twist or warp in stock. (There is one exception: Oliver (135) manufactures a "Straitoplane," a large, expensive industrial planer that will remove twist and warp.)

Normally there are two adjustments on a planer: one to adjust the rate of feed and the other to lower and raise the bed for different thicknesses of wood. Soft wood and narrow pieces can be fed through the planer at a faster rate than wide hard wood.

The Knife Or Cutter Head. The *cutter head* has at least three knives and is cylindrical in shape.

The Pressure Bar. The *pressure bar* is on the outfeed side of the cutter head and presses the wood against the bed of the planer after the cutter head has reduced the thickness of stock.

The Outfeed Rolls. After the stock passes under the pressure bar, the smooth lower and upper feed rolls pick up the stock and continue to move the stock.

The Infeed Rolls. The upper *infeed roll* has teeth like a gear which move the stock with more traction than would a smooth roll. The upper infeed roll is often made up of sections which are spring loaded. This feature makes adjustments for any difference in the stock thickness fed into the planer.

The Chip Breaker. The *chip breaker*, located between the cutter head and top infeed roll, is often constructed in sections. The chip breaker not only helps prevent the wood from splintering, but also holds the wood against the planer bed until the cutter head does its work.

Dust And Chip Collection. All planers, regardless of size, should have a dust and chip collector. The smaller planers can be serviced with the smaller shop vacuum models. They are available in 10, 20, 28 and 55 gallon sizes. The larger planers should use a cyclone dust collector system.

Operating the Planer

■ Set the bed of the planer to remove approximately 1/16" from the thickness of stock.

■ Ascertain grain direction. Cutterhead must cut with the grain, not against it.

■ Check to make sure that one face of stock is perfectly flat. If not, run the stock through the jointer or plane by hand.

■ Turn on the switch.

■ Push the long stock straight into the planer until the infeed rolls pick it up. Short stock is pushed in at a slight angle.

■ Go to the outfeed end of the planer and hold the boards as they come through. If the boards are not supported by a person or roller stands, the pressure bar is apt to be pushed up resulting in a depression in the end of the board.

■ Rerun stock through the planer in the same relative position if more stock is to be removed. If the second cut is made on the opposite face, recheck grain direction.

■ If some pieces are thicker than others, run them through first, so that eventually all stock is the same thickness.

■ Thin stock must be "sandwiched" with a thicker piece before running through the planer.

Powermatic Planer Parts and Controls

Powermatic Houdaille manufactures five sizes of planers: 12", 16", 18", 20", and 24". With the exception of stock capacity, they are essentially the same (Figs. 4-2 and 4-3).

Frame. The frame is precision machined from extra heavy cast iron.

Table Bed. Normally the bed and upper wedge are joined by acme-thread screws mounted on enclosed thrust bearings to raise and lower the table.

Cutterhead. The knives are staggered to create a spiral cutting concept on the Powermatic. This exclusive design reduces noise during planing operations.

Sound Curtain Container. Curtains of acoustical material at the entrance and exit areas serve to contain sounds generated within the machine.

Variable Speed Control. The *Variable speed control* adjusts the rate at which stock is carried through the planer. The 12"

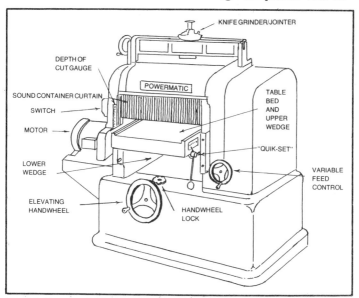

Fig. 4-2. Powermatic plane parts and adjustments.

Fig. 4-3 12" planer, Model Q100, "The Quiet One."

planer's rate is 18' per minute. The 16" and 18" rate of speed is from 15 to 37' per minute. The 20" planer rate is 20 to 50' per minute, and the 24" planer is 20 to 100' per minute.

Elevating Handwheel. The handwheel lowers and raises the table to adjust for difference in thickness.

The Depth Of Cut Gauge. The *depth of cut gauge* is fine for rough planing where precise thickness is not necessary. For exact thickness, use vernier calipers.

The Handwheel Lock. The handwheel lock secures the handwheel so that vibration will not disturb the setting.

"Quik-Set." The "Quik-Set" feature offers lever controlled table roll height adjustments from 0″ to .040″ at a touch. "Quik-Set" eliminates friction and constant under-the-table roll adjustments.

Knife Grinder/Jointer. The knife grinder and jointer is an optional accessory. The distinct advantage of this piece of equipment is that knives on the cutterhead may be jointed and sharpened without removing knives from the cutterhead.

Planer Manufacturers

A heavily constructed planer supplied by Conover (40) will handle stock up to 12″ wide and 6″ thick. This solid cast iron planer has a table surface of 13″ by 28¼″. The thickness scales are in both metric and English measurements. This sturdy machine and two horsepower motor will feed stock through the machine at the speed of 300″ per minute (Fig. 4-4).

Fig. 4-4. 12″ x 6″ surface planer.

A longtime favorite of the small workshop owner and the home craftsman is the sturdy 12" x 4" planer by Parks Woodworking Machine (139). It has a positive gripping, serrated infeed roll and a smooth outfeed roll. Parks claims it has over 40,000 planers in shops all over the world. The 12" x 4" planer is available in both the bench model and the floor model. The feed rate is 16' per minute. Parks also manufactures a 20" x 6" planer and a 13" x 5" planer (Fig. 4-5).

Williams and Hussey Machine Corporation (201) manufactures a small, simply designed, 7" molder-planer, which is ideal for the home craftsman who cannot afford the larger models. It will plane stock up to 14" wide by reversing the stock. It is available in both the hand-fed and power-fed models. The output capacity is 15' per minute with power feed. Hand-fed models may be later converted to power-fed models by attaching power drive assemblies.

As a molder, the Williams and Hussey molder-planer will produce more than 98% of all types of molding and pattern materials used today. It will make ¾" pattern cuts in one pass through the macnine (Fig. 4-6).

Garrett-Wade (79) supplies a Swiss made combination jointer and thickness planer. It combines a 10¼" capacity for edge jointing or surface planing, with a 10¼" x 6¼" capacity for automatic feed thickness planing.

Poitras, Danckaert Woodworking Machine Co. (143) makes a 12" x 6" planer and a 24" x 10". The variable feed and table adjustment are hydraulically powered.

John Harra Wood and Supply Co. (106) is a supplier, of the Makita 12" planer-jointer and the 15⅝" planer. These Japanese manufactured tools are both powered by a two horsepower motor.

Rockwell International (155) manufactures an 18" x 6", a 13" x 6" planer, and the unique and revolutionary *uniplane*. It will handle stock up to 6" wide with a depth of cut ⅛". It will plane, joint, bevel, chamfer, trim and taper with complete safety.

Analysis of Small Planers

An excellent survey of small planers 10" to 14"—the size generally used by the home craftsman—was done by Lelon Traylor in the March / April, 1979 issue of *Fine Woodworking*. Most of the planers described in this chapter are included. Traylor's breakdown in terms of price per pound is interesting, but it is only one of many factors to consider when purchasing a planer.

Fig. 4-5. 12″ x 4″ planer.

Precautions When Using A Planer

■ All stock should have one perfectly flat surface before planing.

■ Be sure that the planer cuts with grain—never cross grain.

■ Get someone to help with long stock.

■ Turn off the switch and lower the table bed, if the stock refuses to go through the planer.

■ Do not push the stock through the planer if it has large knots or splits.

■ Used lumber or painted lumber should not be pushed through the planer.

■ Do not run lumber through the planer if it is not 2″ or 3″ longer than the distance between the infeed rolls and outfeed rolls.

■ Do not turn on the planer until it is adjusted for stock thickness.

■ Avoid running stock of different thickness through the planer.

■ Stand to one side of the stock being pushed through the planer—never directly behind it.

■ Never look into the cutterhead area while stock is being planed.

■ Never let your fingers get into the table bed area; they are apt to be severely pinched.

THE POWER JOINTER

The *jointer* is also a planing tool. You might describe it as a motorized hand plane. The jointer is a more flexible tool than the planer and will plane edges, chamfers, tapers and bevels as well as face. The jointer complements the planer and the circular saw. The planer and circular saw would have rough going if it weren't for the jointer. It provides a straight edge and a true flat working face,

165

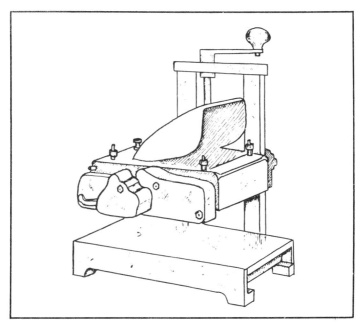

Fig. 4-6. Williams and Hussey 7″ molder-planer.

which are necessary for processing the stock on the planer and circular saw.

Sizes of Jointers

Jointers generally are available in four sizes or widths of cuts: 4″, 6″, 8″ and 12″. The 6″ and 8″ are the most popular in schools, small cabinet shops and pattern shops. The 12″ model is seldom found except in millworking or large industrial woodworking manufacturing shops. The 4″ jointer has its limitations, but in a home workshop it certainly will earn its keep.

Jointer Components

The *base* is the foundation on which the other members rest. Its weight adds a great deal to the stability and helps to cut down on vibration and chattering.

The Fence. Most edging is done when the fence is 90° to the table. Always check with a square because the tilt gauge cannot always be relied upon. Move the fence from time to time so that stock does not ride in one spot on the knives. The fence may be tilted for beveling and chamfering.

166

The Depth Gauge. The depth gauge indicates the difference in level between the front infeed table and the rear outfeed table. This difference is the depth of cut. The front table adjusting hand wheel raises and lowers the front infeed table. For close work the depth of cut should be measured with a scale or vernier calipers. The depth of cut of the final pass over the jointer should always be shallower than other preliminary cuts. On the small jointers the last cut should be 1/32″ or less.

The Rear Outfeed Table. The rear outfeed table should be the exact height of the jointer knives in their uppermost position. Once the correct position is ascertained, the rear outfeed table should be locked unless the knives have to be sharpened. If the rear outfeed table is too low, the stock will drop down near the end of the pass and a notch will be cut from the stock. If the rear outfeed table is too high, the stock will be tapered or else it will not be possible to shove the work across the knives.

The Rabbeting Ledge. The guard must be removed to cut a rabbet (a groove along the edge of stock). Set the fence for the width of the rabbet. Set the depth gauge to 1/4″ to 1/3″ the depth of the rabbet. After each pass, set the front infeed table deeper and continue until the correct depth is reached. One-eighth to 3/16″ is about the maximum depth that a small jointer can cut in one pass (Fig. 4-7).

Jointing A Surface

Adjust the depth gauge to cut 1/16″. Place the concave side of the stock (if board is twisted or warped) down on the table bed, infeed side; check for grain direction.

Push the stock slowly into knives. Watch your fingers at all times. Push the last few inches over the knives with a push stick. Use feather boards when jointing thin or narrow stock.

Jointing An Edge

Check the stock for direction of grain. Make sure the fence is set for 90°. Replace the guard if it has been removed. Set depth gauge for the desired cut. Place the true working face against the fence.

Push stock over the cutterhead. Alternate your hands so that pressure is placed on the stock while it is over both the infeed and outfeed table. The slower the cut the smoother will be the wood, but too slow an advance over the knives will heat up the knives, which is apt to remove the temper from the knives. It is also apt to burn the wood. Use a push stick for short and narrow pieces.

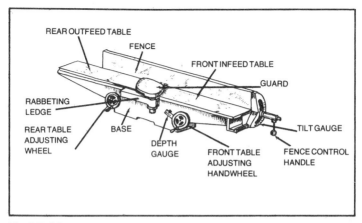

Fig. 4-7. Jointer components.

Jointer A Taper

Carefully mark on the stock where the taper begins. Place stock on the infeed table with the small end of the taper away from knives.

Place the mark where the taper begins about ⅜″ past and above the knives and rest the untapered part on the outfeed table. With the stock in this position, fasten a stop block on the infeed table so that it barely touches the end which is to be tapered.

If the taper is small, set the depth gauge for the amount of taper. If the taper is large, set the depth gauge for some fraction of the taper.

Set the tapered end against the stop and turn on the motor. Move the guard to open position and lower the stock very slowly into the knives. Push the stock over the knives with a push stick, making sure that the tapered end remains in firm contact with the infeed table all the way. Continue until full taper is established.

A stop taper is made in the same way as just described except that the taper does not continue to the end of the stock, but at some predetermined point which is marked on the stock. Stop blocks aid in controlling the cut. When the end of the cut is reached, the stock should be carefully raised away from the cutterhead. Watch your fingers at all times, because a push stick cannot always be used in this situation.

Short tapers are made in much the same fashion as long tapers, except a pad of scrap stock must be nailed or braded to the stock so that the pad and stock will slide along the outfeed table together. The stock will be elevated for the correct angle cut.

Jointing A Bevel

Tilting the fence, one way or the other from the perpendicular, is necessary for cutting bevels. Set the angle with the tilt gauge. Make the necessary passes with the stock until beveling is completed.

Jointing A Chamfer

A chamfer is done in the same manner as beveling except a smaller amount of wood is removed. Inasmuch as the fence can be tilted both ways from the perpendicular, it is not necessary to joint against the grain.

Jointing A Rabbet

Remove the guard from the jointer. Set the fence for width of the rabbet. Set the infeed table for depth of cut or some equal proportion of it.

Push stock over the cutterhead. Watch your fingers.

Continue lowering the infeed table and making cuts until full depth is reached, unless the depth is reached on the first pass.

Jointing End Grain

This operation is very seldom needed. When needed, only very light cuts should be made. There is a definite tendency for the wood to split out near the end of the cut. To prevent splitting, joint approximately 1″ on one edge of stock and then reverse the stock before completing cut.

Sharpening Jointer Knives

The steps in sharpening jointer knives are *grinding* and *honing*. The grinding of knives is seldom needed, and when needed it should be turned over to a professional. There are home craftsmen who grind their own knives, but the expense of the sharpening equipment, and the time spent in learning to grind properly, plus the fact that the sharpening equipment is seldom used, do not add up to a good investment of time and money.

Honing of jointer knives is something that a home craftsman can do and should do. Honing can be done many times before it is necessary to grind.

Honing Jointer Knives

Remove the fence after pulling the plug on the motor. Lower the front table and wipe off the knives and cutterhead. Lock the cutterhead with wooden wedges so that the knives does not rotate.

Position a flat oilstone, slipstone or carborundum stone on the ground bevel of the knife to be sharpened. Whet the knives by stroking the knife edge. Remove the wire edge with a fine slipstone. Continue until all knives are honed. Replace the fence and raise the front table.

Setting Jointer Knives After Grinding

—Place one of the jointer knives into one of the cutterhead grooves.

—Position the heel of the ground bevel from 1/16″ to 3/32″ above the lip of the cutterhead.

—Tighten lightly the clamping screws at each end of the knife.

—Place a wooden straightedge on the rear outfeed table with its edge extending over the cutterhead close to one end.

—Rotate cutterhead back and forth by hand through a 90° arc. During the rotation the jointer knife will move the straightedge.

—If the straightedge is raised from the bed of the jointer, the knife is projecting too much. If the knife does not engage the straightedge at all, the knife is not projecting enough.

—Check the other end of the knife in the same way.

—To check further, place a mark on the straightedge where it lines up with the front edge of the outfeed table.

—Rotate the cutterhead. The jointer knife will move the straightedge. Mark this position. You now have two marks on the straightedge.

—Test both ends of all knives. When the distances moved are the same for all settings, the knives are set correctly.

—Tighten all the clamping screws.

—Position the outfeed table.

—Replace guard.

Precautions

—Never joint stock that is too short. About 1′ is the minimum length.

—Use a feather board for thin or narrow stock.

—Use the guard for all operations where a guard can be used. Rabbeting operations do not permit a guard, therefore, the operator must be particularly careful during this operation. A good rule to follow is to *keep your hands at least 5″ away from the cutterhead*.

—Never joint narrow stock cross grain.

—Use a push stick when called for.

—Joint only with the grain of the wood.

—Never touch the rear outfeed table adjustment unless knives are to be honed, ground, or replaced.

—Shut down the motor if there are any unusual sounds or vibrations.

Powermatic Houdaille Jointers

Powermatic manufacturers two jointers: the 6″ and 8″ models. The 6″ model has a 48″ table and the 8″ has a 64″ table. The swivel fence permits skew or shear cutting. A combination of an Allen wrench and end wrench permits fast and accurate knife setting. Both models have three high speed, heat treated steel knives (Figs. 4-8 and 4-9).

Sprunger Corporation Jointers

Sprunger manufactures three jointers: the 4″, 4½″ and 6″. The table of the 4″ jointer is 4½″ wide and 20″ long, the 4½″ jointer has a table 5″ wide and 31″ long, and the 6″ jointer has a table 7″ wide and 43″ long. These jointers have dual control and fence lock (Fig. 4-10).

Fig. 4-8. 6″ jointer, Model 50.

171

Fig. 4-9. 8" jointer, Model 60.

Emco-Lux Corporation Jointer and Planer

Emco-Lux supplies a combination jointer and planer made in Austria. It has a width of 10¼" and the table is 36 3/16" long. It is made of aluminum cast alloy, cast iron and steel. It has an automatic

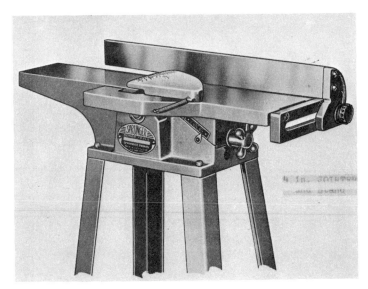

Fig. 4-10. 4" jointer and stand.

feed which will plane 19⅛" of stock per minute, as well as a kickboard guard. This unique machine has scales in both metric and English measurements (Fig. 4-11).

American Machine and Tool (AMT) Company Jointer

American Machine and Tool Company manufactures an inexpensive, 4" width, 22" table jointer with 10 year full service guarantee. It is all cast iron and steel with a precision ground table (Fig. 4-12).

Conover Woodcraft Specialties Jointer

Conover features a heavy duty, industrial type 12" jointer with a 58" table. Conover furnishes a jig for aligning the blades to a uniform height. This large jointer would be ideal in a school shop or custom woodworking plant (Fig. 4-13).

Fig. 4-11. Emco Rex B20 combination jointer and thickness planer.

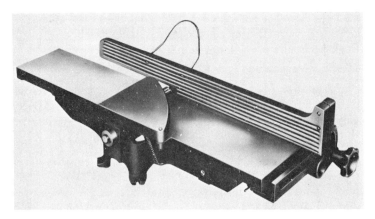

Fig. 4-12. AMT 4" jointer.

Rockwell International Jointers

Rockwell manufactures three jointers: a 4" deluxe model, a 6" deluxe long-bed jointer and an 8" long bed jointer. The 4" jointer has a 27¼" table, the 6" a 42½" table, and the 8" has a 66" long table. The two larger models have 24 volt safety control systems.

Poitras-Danckaert Woodworking Machine Company Jointers

Poitras manufactures three jointers: a 6" jointer with a 48" table, an 8" jointer with a 60" table and a 12" jointer with a 74" table. Jos. Poitras and Sons, Ltd. of Quebec, Canada, manufactures these fine machines, and they are supplied and serviced by Danckaert Woodworking Machine Co. of Atlanta, Ga.

PORTABLE POWER HAND PLANES

If it is easier for Mohammed to go to the mountain than for the mountain to go to Mohammed, it is also easier to carry the planer (in a strict technical sense, it might better be called a jointer) to the work if the work to be planed (or jointed) is large, heavy or cumbersome. The portable electric plane is used primarily by carpenters and construction workers.

Spiral, high-speed steel cutters, revolving up to 21,000 rpm produce a smooth, even surface. Carbide tip blades are available for long life. Sharpening attachments are available for most models.

In essence, the portable power hand plane is a bottom-side up jointer, and the adjustments are quite similar. It has a tilting fence which may be used for beveling. The fence may be removed for surfacing.

Rockwell International (155) makes two models of power planes. The smaller model, called the *Porta-Plane*, cuts to a width of 2 13/32″ and a depth of 3/32″. The larger model, the *Versa-Plane*, cuts to a 3″ width and a depth of ⅛″. The Porta-Plane is 16″ long and the weight 9¼ pounds, and the Versa-Plane is 18″ long and weighs 15 pounds.

MOLDING TOOLS AND MACHINES

There are two types of hand molding tools: the molding scrapers and the molding planes. Constantine and Son, Inc. (41) supplies a molding scraper. With its interchangeable blades, it provides eight different molding designs.

Fig. 4-13. 12″ long bed jointer.

Molding planes are known by many different names—universal planes, combination planes, multiplanes—as well as molding planes. One of the best is the *record multiplane*. See (68). There are 24 cutter blades included with the plane. Ploughing, rabbeting, housing, tonguing, beading, sash molding and slitting are a few of the operations performed by this plane. The plane is fitted with spurs allowing cross grain cutting to be accomplished. It has an adjustable fence and depth gauge.

Portable Electric Drill

The *portable electric drill* may be used as a molding machine. Constantine (41) supplies molding cutters that are adaptable to the electric drill or flexible shaft. The ¼" shank allows the cutters to be used in the drill press or router. The cutters are made of manganese alloy tool steel and are available in the following shapes: fancy cove cutter, adjustable bevel cutter, beading cutter, Roman Ogee-cutter, cove cutter, radius cutter and rabbet cutter.

Coastal router rasps, supplied by The Fine Tool Shop (68), come in eight different shapes. These eight rasps, plus the rasp handle, two adjustable disc guides, a ¼" electric drill and two-hand control, make molding an easy job. The eight rasps are: narrow slot rasp, double slot rasp, wide slot rasp, convex rasp, 45° profile rasp, 75° profile rasp, heavy duty mill rasp and concave rasp.

The Circular Saw as a Molding Machine

Brodhead-Garrett (30) supplies a molding head and cutters that convert the circular saw or radial arm saw to a molding machine. The 20 cutters are as follows: 201 glue joint, 202 "Ogee" window and door stop, 203 ¼" flute and ½" cove, 204 90° flute ornamental and combination, 205 curved flute and 3/16" quarter round, 206 1" flute and ½" radius, 207 5/16" quarter round and 5/16" cove, 208 3/16" and 3/8" quarter round and 1/4" bead, 209 5/8" cove, 210 panel cupboard door, 211 Muntin, 212 5/16" bead and 5/16" cove, 302 1" planer and jointer, 303 tongue, 304 groove, 350 cabinet door lip, 351 combination 1/4" and 1/2" quarter round, 352 three 1/4" beads, 354 Cloverleaf screen mold and 355 base mold. The numbers refer to Fig. 4-14.

The Router as a Molding Machine

The portable router consists of a base which is adjustable in height, a motor with speeds up to 20,000 rpm, a collet type chuck, and handles or knobs to control the router. By turning the router upside down and inserting it into a specially constructed table, the router becomes essentially a small shaper. As a router, the work remains stationary and the router is moved against the work. As a shaper, the work is pushed against the router cutter. As a router, it should be fed into the work in a counterclockwise direction, or from left to right.

If the motor has a tendency to labor, it is best to cut down on the depth of the cut even if it means that more passes have to be made. Router bits and their uses are as follows.

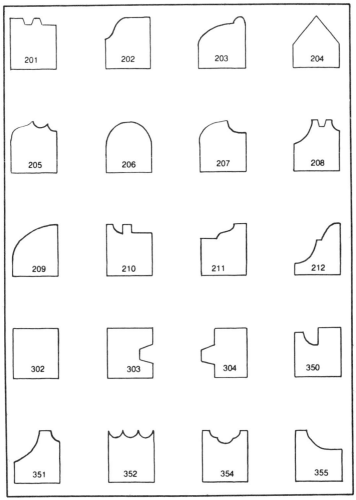

Fig. 4-14. Molding cutters for circular saw and radial saw.

Carbide Tipped Groove Forming Round Nose. Cuts rounded grooves used in a variety of applications ranging from doors to columns.

Raised Panel. A wide, shallow cutting bit for raised panel effect in one pass.

Traditional. Especially attractive where a wide, shallow decorative cut is needed. Flat bottom gives a raised effect to panels using this design. Also recommended for edge forming.

Classical. A beautiful decorative grooving. Also recommended for edge forming.

Beading. Used extensively for provincial design indoors.

Classical Bits. Add classic beauty to the project with beautiful decorative edging.

Raised Panel Bits. Clean simple lines accentuate an attractive surface.

Ogee Bits With Fillet. One bit produces three different cuts. Graceful lines of the Ogee cut can be attractively accented by one or two fillets by lowering depth setting.

Ball Bearing Pilot Guide Router Bits. The ball bearing pilot guide on router bits prevents marring and the burning of work.

Rounding Over Bits-Two Flutes. For decorative edging and drop leaf table joints. For smooth uniformly rounded edges. Lower depth setting produces rounded corner with decorative bead.

Cove Bits, Two Flutes. For decorative edging and period furniture.

Chamfering Bits, Two Flutes. For decorative edging and concealed joints.

Rabbeting Bits, Two Flutes. For fast, smooth rabbeting cuts without use of router guides.

Roman Ogee Bits. For decorative edging and period furniture.

Beading Bits, Two Flutes. For decorative period furniture.

Three Flute Slotting Cutter. For weatherstrip and trim applications.

Provincial Design Veiner. For recessed design veining in fine cabinet surfaces.

"V" Grooving Bits, Two Flutes. Excellent for lettering, grooving and sign work.

Core Box Bits, Two Flutes. Especially effective in fluting flat surfaces.

Veining Bits, Single Flute. For decorative line work on any surface.

Dovetail Bits. For making dovetail joints.

Bits For Hinge Mortising. Fast cutting bit for making mortises when work is started at the edge.

Laminate Trim Bit. For Formica and other plastic laminates.

Ball Bearing Laminate Flush Trimming Bit, Two Flutes. For fast, smooth, accurate trim cuts. Carbide tipped.

Flute Laminate Trimmer Assemblies. For flush and bevel cuts. Carbide tipped and ball bearing. For fast, accurate trim cuts.

Flush And Bevel Three Flute Laminate Trimmer Assembly. For extra smooth finish trimming. Carbide tipped and ball bearing.

Four Flute Laminate Trimmer Assembly. Carbide tipped. Ball bearing with glue shield. For extra smooth finish trimming.

THE SHAPER

The *shaper* is a rather simple, straightforward machine, with a motor connected directly, or indirectly, through a pulley and belt system to a spindle, a mechanism for raising and lowering the spindle, and a table with an opening for the spindle. The spindle on the smaller spindles revolves between speeds of 6,000 and 10,000 rpm. Many shapers have a two-way reversible switch allowing the spindle to revolve in both directions, permitting more flexibility in the operations it can perform.

Shapers are manufactured in many models and sizes: schools, custom cabinet shops and home workshops invariably use the single spindle variety, while the large woodworking industries are more apt to use the double spindle shaper.

The table top of the shaper is attached to the sturdy base and the top usually has a groove to accommodate a miter gauge. In addition, there are numerous threaded holes into which steel pins are inserted to help guide the working stock safely to the cutter blades.

The ¾" diameter spindle is the most common, but some shapers have spindles which are interchangeable so that smaller spindles may be used.

A fence is attachable to the table and is used primarily to control straight cuts. The fence is composed of two parts which are adjustable. Each half can be adjusted independent of each other. In addition, the two halves may be opened wider to accommodate larger cutters.

When a straight piece of work is to be fed into the shaper, only part way faces of the fence are lined up in a straight line. However, if the entire length of stock is to be shaped, the outfeed half of the fence must be moved away from the cutter a distance equal to the depth of the cut.

The work must be supported as the entire piece is fed through the shaper; otherwise a big gouge will be taken out of the piece as the last few inches are fed past the shaper. In addition, the operator might be injured if he does not use a push stick (Fig. 4-15).

It is dangerous to shape pieces less than 1' long using the fence, unless pieces are securely clamped in a jig. To shape end grain on pieces less than 1' wide, the pieces should be clamped in a miter gauge or a jig. Types of cutters include the following.

Cutterhead Type. The cutterhead type uses a three-knife cutterhead like the one used on the circular saw and radial arm saw, except it is somewhat smaller. The same knives—see Fig. 4-14—used on circular saw and radial saw cutterheads may be used on this smaller cutterhead.

The Double Fly Cutter Type. Two flat profile knives are used in this type. The knives are held in grooves in a collar. This method is used extensively in woodworking industries and furniture manufacturing plants. It is by far the most dangerous of all woodworking situations. I worked summers while going to college in a woodworking plant that made wood parts for automobiles and trucks. Seventy percent of the machine operators in the large mill room had lost at least a portion of one finger, and most of the injuries were caused by shapers. Since that time, machines and safety procedures have been greatly improved.

The knives must be properly ground and balanced. They also must be properly tightened and secured because vibration may cause them to be loosened and then the knives, or pieces of knives, fly into space like bullets. Disaster can be the result. Only highly skilled millmen or cabinetmakers should use this type of cutter.

The Three-Blade Cutters. These cutters are the only kind that should be used in a school or home workshop. If used correctly, there is little chance of an accident.

There are over 50 shapes of three-blade cutters, but the most commonly used are bead, groove, jointer, lip cupboard door, drop leaf cove and bead, reversible glue joint, T tongue, G groove, base shoe, taper ease, Ogee molding and quarter round.

Shaping With Collars

Irregular shaped pieces that cannot be shaped with the fence may be shaped by using collars. The collar restricts the depth of cut when work is fed freehand into the shaper. Some collars are of the ball bearing type and prevent the wood from burning when it comes in contact with the collar. Collars are of different size and are selected according to the collars' relationship with the cutter.

Collars may be used above the cutter, below the cutter, or in between two cutters. The entire edge of the stock may not be shaped using collars, because at least a small portion of the edge must touch and ride against the collar.

The edge of stock must be perfectly smooth and held against a guide pin when starting the cut. This should be done very gradually to prevent a potentially dangerous kickback.

Shaping With The Fence

Choose the proper cutter or cutters. Cutters that match, such as tongue and groove, should be selected at the same time.

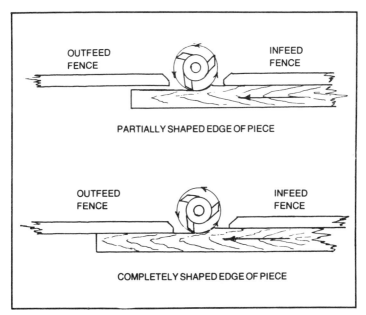

Fig. 4-15. Shaping straight stock.

Remove the nut, lock washer, collar and cutter from the spindle if it cannot be used. A flat spot on the top of the spindle allows it to be held by a wrench. Some shaper spindles are locked in place by other devices.

Slide the selected cutter on the spindle. The larger part of the three-wing cutter should be the closest to the table. This permits most of the shaping on the under side of the workpiece, which is the safest way as the workpiece acts as a guard. Be sure that the lock washer is placed under and next to the nut.

Set the fence according to the length of cut. See Fig. 4-15.

Switch on the motor. Listen to any unusual sounds or excessive vibration. Feed a piece of scrap stock through to see that the cutter is set to the correct depth.

Shaping With Patterns

Multiple pieces of irregular shapes are often shaped with patterns. Make an accurate pattern of solid wood, or plywood about ½″ thick. Make sure that the edges are smooth. Wax or paraffin is sometimes rubbed on the edges to cut down on friction.

Insert short, sharp-pointed brads into the pattern to hold the work in place. Place the pattern on the work piece and tap the pattern so brad points will enter the workpiece.

Install the desired cutter or cutters with a collar either above the cutter or below the cutter. Only the pattern rides against the collar. Sometimes a second pattern is installed on the other side of the work in order that the piece may be reversed to take advantage of grain direction.

If the piece is not shaped clear around, a jig or fixture with a clamping device is quite often constructed. Jig and fixtures are used in industry more than patterns. Special fences are another type of jig used to shape pieces that are a portion of a circle.

Shaper Manufacturers

Powermatic Houdaille (147) manufactures a single spindle shaper which accommodates four interchangeable spindles and a 1″ solid spindle for extra heavy work. The interchangeable spindles are 5/16″, ½″ regular, ½″ stub and ¾″ diameter. The spindle is driven by a two-speed "V" pulley, with speeds of 7,000 and 10,000 rpm. This Model 26 Powermatic shaper has many optional accessories to make shaping easier (Fig. 4-16).

American Machine and Tool Company (5) provides an inexpensive wood shaper kit for the craftsman who watches his pennies. The kit consists of all the necessary parts to build a *single spindle shaper* on your own stand or directly onto your workbench. Full instructions, drawings and patterns are included in the kit. This machine is designed for standard ½″ bore molding cutters obtainable at Sears and other retail outlets.

Cutters are placed directly above a cutter height adjustment wheel. A flat is provided on the top of the spindle so that the spindle can be held securely with a wrench while tightening the nut (Fig. 4-17).

The Rockwell International (155) *heavy duty wood shaper* will accept five interchangeable spindles. It will handle ½″, ¾″ and 1″ standard spindles, a ½″ stub spindle, plus an extra long ¾″ spindle with 4⅜″ capacity under the nut. Because of the wide range of cutters it will accommodate, it's a favorite in cabinet shops, furniture factories, specialty shops, school shops, sash and door companies and similar installations. Rockwell also manufactures an *overarm router/shaper* as well as a *light duty wood shaper*.

Fig. 4-16. Universal spindle shaper, Model 26.

MODEL
NO. 252

Deluxe Ball Bearing WOOD SHAPER KIT

AMERICAN MACHINE & TOOL COMPANY
Royersford, Pa.

Fig. 4-17. Wood shaper kit.

Garrett-Wade Co. (79) furnishes a Swiss made, *Inca three-speed spindle shaper*. Available speeds are 4,000, 6,000, and 8,000 rpm. The maximum spindle height adjustment is 4". This Inca shaper is powered by a 1½ horsepower motor, and many optional and useful accessories are available.

Poitras, Danckaert Woodworking Machine Company (143) manufactures two models of shapers. The *2800 B shaper* has a spindle diameter of ¾", capacity of knives 2½", vertical stroke 2½" and spindle speed of 6,000 rpm. The *3000* shaper has a spindle diameter of 1¼", capacity of knives 5", and two spindle speeds of 4300 rpm and 8200 rpm.

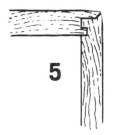

5

Turning Tools

The history of the lathe as a wood turning tool has experienced many transitions from a clumsy, wood contraption with heavy string wrapped around the work—one end of the string fastened to a treadle and the other end to a springy, flexible pole above the lathe—to the modern efficient lathe of today.

LATHE HISTORY

Inasmuch as this method caused the work to rotate in both directions, the operator had to apply the cutting tool to the work when the work was rotating toward him, which meant that turning took place only half of the time. Naturally, the work had to be longer than necessary to allow room for wrapping string around it.

Another similar version was the bow lathe. This lathe was used while the operator sat on the ground. This primitive Egyptian tool had the bow string wrapped around the work. The bow was stroked by one hand, while the other hand and feet were used to steady the cutting tool.

Jim Richey of Ponca City, Oklahoma supplies drawings and instructions on how to build your own treadle lathe of wood. It differs from the ones just described in that it has a flywheel which allows the work to rotate in only one direction. See *Fine Woodworking* March/April 1979 for details.

Richard Starr of Thetford Center, Vermont, in the same issue explains how a freewheel lathe can be built with a ratchet bicycle sprocket as the major component. He states that two lathes based on this drive system have been in use for several years in the Richmond Middle School at Hanover, New Hampshire.

PARTS OF A LATHE

The parts of the lathe are the *bed*, the *headstock*, the *tailstock*, the *faceplate*, the *toolrest* and *saddle*, and numerous locking and adjusting devices shown in Fig. 5-1. This drawing is a sketch of the very popular *Myford* lathe made in England. Its many accessories and attachments will be described later on in this chapter.

LATHE SIZE

Lathe sizes are indicated by the overall length, the maximum distance between the live center and the tail center—sometimes called the dead center—and the maximum diameter or swing, which is twice the distance from the bed to the live center. Some lathes have a gap in the bed which allows faceplate turning of bowl-like objects to be turned to a larger diameter than permissible without the gap. Some lathes have an outboard arrangement for turning faceplate work.

Wood turning lathes vary in size from the miniature Dremel with a swing of 1½″ and 6″ between centers, to the huge veneer cutting lathe used by plywood manufacturers with a 4′ swing and 8′ or 9′ between center.

LATHE SPEEDS

The standard four-step pulley and belt arrangement on many lathes has speeds varying from around 900 rpm to about 3300 rpm. Other lathes have variable speed control which is continuous over a wide range of speeds from around 350 rpm to over 3000 rpm. For large faceplate turnings and between-center turnings of over 8″ in diameter, the speed should be in the 200 to 400 rpm range.

FIVE COMMON TURNING TOOLS

The five most common turning tools are depicted in Fig. 5-2. A sixth one might be added, the *square nose*, but it is not used very often. The *skew* is used for finish cuts, but it is a hard tool to use without considerable practice.

The *gouge* is used for eliminating waste stock and for rough cutting. The *diamond* or *spear point* is used for "V" cuts and sharp corners. The *round nose* is used for scraping concave cuts.

The *parting tool* is used for making incisions for the purpose of measuring diameters with the calipers. To a certain extent, the parting tool is self-sharpening if the tool is turned over when it is dull. Long handle turning tools are easier to control than short handle ones.

186

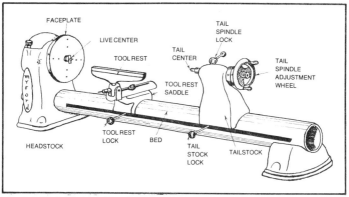

Fig. 5-1. Parts of a wood turning lathe.

OPERATIONS AND TECHNIQUES OF TURNING

The lathe is used to perform two basic operations: *faceplate turning* (salad bowls) and *turning between centers* (baseball bat). A pair of outside calipers and a steel rule or scale are necessary accessories for turning. *Never* use calipers on turning stock unless the stock has been turned perfectly round. Calipers caught by stock that is turning have caused serious injuries.

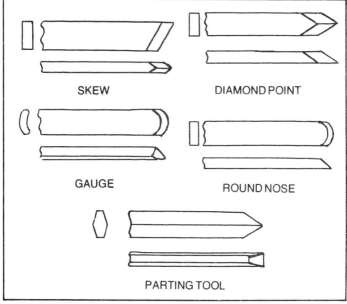

Fig. 5-2. Turning tools.

187

There are two basic techniques used in turning: the *scraping* method and the *turning* method. The turning method is very difficult and takes a long time to learn. The highly skilled professional wood turner does most of his turning with the skew. It looks so easy, but it certainly isn't. The home craftsman should stick to the scraping method.

How To Spindle Turn Between Centers

■ Mark diagonals across the corners of each of the square stock.

■ Saw two kerfs, about ⅛″ deep, on one end of the stock, following the lines just made in the first step.

■ Drill a small hole, where the diagonals cross, on the other end of the stock.

■ Remove the live center (spur center) and the dead center (tail center) from the lathe.

■ Place the live center over the end of the stock with the saw kerfs. Be sure that spurs engage the kerfs. Strike the butt end of the center sharply with a mallet.

■ Place the tip of the dead center in the small hole on the other end of the stock and strike sharply with a mallet.

■ Place centers back on the lathe.

■ Position the stock in the lathe between centers.

■ Lock the tailstock and force the dead center into the stock with the tail spindle adjustment wheel. Turn stock over by hand.

■ Cut off the corners of the squared stock with a draw shave to form a rough octagon in cross section.

■ Check the speed setting, stand to one side, and turn on the switch. If the lathe starts to vibrate, turn off the switch immediately and set for slower speed.

■ Turn the stock to the round with a large gouge. A shearing cut should be used, moving to the right with the right corner of the gouge and the left with the left corner.

■ Measure the distance between beads, coves and square parts, if any. Mark the distances on a piece of thin scrap wood. Hold the scrap wood marking template about ⅛″ from the revolving round stock and mark with pencil. *Never mark revolving stock with a steel scale.*

■ Establish diameters with outside calipers and parting tool. Hold the calipers, set at the right diameter, in the left hand and the parting tool in the right. The handle of the parting tool should extend along the forearm. Turn and measure, alternately, until the correct diameter is reached. Never force the calipers or a false measurement will be read.

■ Remove all excess waste stock with the gouge.

■ Make the necessary tapers, coves, beads, concaves, convexes, flats and "V" shaped portions with the appropriate tool.

■ Sand and finish.

How To Faceplate Turn

For large turnings, it will probably be necessary to glue up stock. Be sure joints are straight and true and the pieces are securely clamped together.

With a compass or dividers, swing a circle ¼″ to ⅜″ larger than the finished article.

Cut off the waste stock by band sawing on the scribed line just made.

Fasten the workpiece to the faceplate. There are two types of faceplate: the *screw center* faceplate and the *regular faceplate*.

The screw center faceplate has only one screw holding the workpiece. It is important that the screw center faceplate be as large in diameter as possible to adequately support the base of turning, without danger of the tools hitting the faceplate.

The regular faceplate has numerous holes for inserting screws to hold the workpiece. If there is any danger of a lathe tool hitting the faceplate, it is best to fasten a piece of scrap stock to the workpiece. When the scrap stock is glued to the workpiece, a sheet of paper is placed between the two so that the scrap piece and workpiece can be easily separated, with the point of a chisel, after the turning is completed. In addition, the scrap piece eliminates screw holes in the back or base of the turning.

Make sure that the correct faceplate has been selected. The outboard and inboard faceplate have different threads.

Attach the workpiece and faceplate to the spindle. If the work and faceplate are attached to the inboard spindle, the spur (live) center must be removed from the spindle. Of necessity, large bowls must be turned in the outboard position, which sometimes requires a special stand for the tool rest.

Make templates of the interior and exterior of turning of thin wood, hardboard, masonite or thin plywood.

Set the tool rest, just below center, across the edge of the workpiece and with a roundnose true up the edge until the piece is perfectly round. Start at a slow speed to prevent vibration. Move the tool rest across the face of the workpiece and smooth the face.

Turn the outside to the desired shape. Use templates to check work.

Turn inside to desired shape. Use templates to check work.

Sand and finish. Remove the workpiece from the faceplate.

WOOD TURNING DUPLICATORS

With the wood turning duplicator, multiple turnings exactly alike can be turned with ease. Two systems and devices will be described.

One of the simplest wood turning duplicators is manufactured by Turn-O-Carve Tool Co. (183) and is commonly named the *Model A-Base* duplicator. The duplicator is placed on top of the lathe ways or plate (if the bed is tubular) and is gently slid in the desired direction as the chisel is brought to bear against the rotating work being turned. An original turning or a profile template is placed in the frame of the duplicator a few inches above the part to be turned.

A frame holds the cutting chisel and a tracer. The chisel is set to the cutting height in the lower part of the frame, and the tracer is set to follow the contours of the original or template in the upper part of this frame.

There are no moving parts to oil or wear out. You simply line up the tool steel chisel to your lathe center by raising or lowering it in the tool post to the desired position. It is then secured in place by tightening the screws provided. The duplicator is now ready for immediate use without ever adjusting it again on the lathe. The only other requirement is the resharpening of the turning chisel when needed, which is something that need not be done very often. The tool steel chisel is an exact gauged hardness for long, heavy-duty turning.

Toolmark Co. (179) manufactures a wood lathe duplicator that will make identical wood turnings from round or flat patterns. It is of rugged construction with two 1" diameter hardened ground steel ways. It has a versatile mounting method which adapts to most any lathe. Adjustable stabilizer bushings are installed in both the lateral and transverse directions to minimize deflections. An adjustable tool holder accommodates limited vertical tool positioning and right or left hand shoulder cuts. It has linear ball bushings with bronze and felt wipers for main load bearings. The operating control hand grips are located away from the cutting area for safety.

Toolmark also manufactures the *U-Tool Woodshaver*, which introduces a revolutionary concept in wood lathe tools. It is a razor sharp U-shaped blade made of high speed hardened tool steel that

MYFORD LATHE

The *Myford ML8* wood turning, English built lathe is a traditional favorite of British turners and is rapidly becoming popular in this country. It can be purchased in the United States from Frog Tool Co. Ltd. (76) and from Russ Zimmerman (157).

The Myford lathe is cleverly designed and solidly built with fine castings and precision machined parts. It is simple to operate and versatile, with an extensive variety of accessories available.

Specifications. Distance between centers 30″, 36″ and 42″. Bed sections including 2′ can be supplied to give up to 72″ between centers. Swing over bed 8″. Left hand (outboard) swing 16″. Hollow spindle bored for No. 1 Morse taper as is the tailstock barrel. Four speeds (1425 rpm motor) 700 rpm, 7740 rpm, 1780 rpm and 2850 rpm.

Standard Equipment. Tilting motor mount for belt pulley speed change, less motor; four step motor pulley; ½″ segmented "V" belt which is easily repaired, prong or spur center for headstock; cup center for tailstock; 6″ and 10″ tool rests; inboard

Fig. 5-3. Wood lathe duplicator and lathe shield.

Fig. 5-4. English built, Myford ML8 wood turning lathe.

and outboard tool rest holders; and 6″ diameter inboard and outboard faceplates.

Special Features. One piece headstock with totally enclosed drive. Easy adjustment to angular contact ball bearings. Accurate threads and register diameter at each end of spindle for mounting chucks, faceplates, etc. Plunger indexing mechanism shaves rather than scrapes the work to the desired shape. It functions much like the skew. A hardened steel blade guard that prevents self-feeding and regulates the cut depth is a valuable components.

The Woodshaver reduces cutting loads that significantly minimize induced vibration. A very smooth shaving cut allows roughing and most work to be done at slower speeds. Higher speeds are necessary only for finishing. Only a minimum of sanding is required.

The Woodshaver has a chute-like opening that discharges the shavings downward. This significantly reduces the amount of dust and chips in the work area, increases work visibility and greatly facilitates vacuum collection. High speed hardened steel blades have a relatively long life and can be easily changed if damaged.

The smallest internal radius accessible by the U-Tool Woodshaver is ⅛″. Sharper cuts must be done with other tools (Fig. 5-3).

gives 24 fixed positions to spindle. Quick-action clamping lever control to tailstock and tool rest. Optional equipment and attachments include the following.

Miter Block (Miter Gauge). The Myford miter block enables accurate setting for angles when working with the circular saw, band saw and disc sander attachments.

Long Boring Bits. Long boring auger bits are available in 5/16″ and ⅜″ diameters with lengths of 30″ and 36″.

Fig. 5-5. Myford lathe and frog wood turning chisel.

Fig. 5-6. 12″ wood turning and metal spinning lathe #159.

Disc Sanders. Two disc sanders are available for the Myford lathe: 10″ diameter and 8″ diameter. The 10″ disc sander is fastened to the outboard end and the 8″ to the inboard end of the headstock.

Short Bed Unit. Where turning between centers is not desired, a short bed unit, less tailstock, is available for faceplate turning.

Grinding Wheel. A high quality grinding wheel is provided for normal tool grinding. It is attached to the outboard end of the headstock.

Band Saw Attachment. The band saw is mounted to the outboard end of the lathe. It has two 10″ diameter wheels and the depth of cut is 9¼″. It will cut stock up to 3¾″ thick.

Mortising Attachment. The mortising attachment will handle ¼″, 5/16″, ⅜″, 7/16″ and ½″ hollow mortise chisels and bits. There are numerous other small accessories such as special chucks, control centers and special centers, and metalworking accessories (Figs. 5-4 and 5-5).

LATHE MANUFACTURERS

Oliver Machinery Co. (135) manufactures a sturdy, 12″ combination wood turning and metal spinning lathe. This lathe would be more apt to be found in school shops rather than home workshops. It has long been a favorite of patternmakers because of the hand feed tool carriage with cross feed and compound swivel rest (Fig. 5-6).

Powermatic Houdaille (147) manufactures two 12″ lathes. Model 45 is designated as a heavy duty lathe and Model 90 is an extra heavy duty lathe.

The Model 45 has an instant set speed control. Optional straight bed and gap bed are available. The gap bed lathe allows a swing of 16″. Distance between centers is 39″.

The Model 90 has a five-position limit stop so that instructors or shop foreman may enforce preset speeds. There is also a choice of straight bed and gap bed. The gap bed allows a swing of 17″. The weight of Model 90 domestic crated with stand and motor is 550 pounds, while Model 45 is only 439 pounds (Figs. 5-7 through 5-9).

Sprunger Corp. (172) manufactures a 10″ gap bed lathe that is 36″ between centers and also a larger 12″ lathe. Both lathes have sealed heavy-duty ball bearings that never need lubrication. Each lathe has an optional sanding disc and table for the outboard end of the spindle. Lathe speeds are 875, 1150, 2250 and 3500 and are powered by ½ hp motors (Fig. 5-10).

Fig. 5-7. Heavy duty, Model 45, 39″ wood lathe.

Fig. 5-8. Extra heavy duty, Model 90 wood lathe.

Fig. 5-9. Extra heavy duty, Model 90 wood lathe with lathe shield.

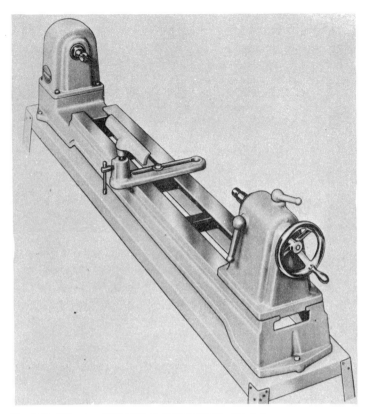

Fig. 5-10. 10″ swing, 36″ between centers wood turning lathe.

Emco-Lux Corp. (65) supplies an Austrian built wood turning lathe with a 400 mm swing (15.7+″) and 1000 mm between centers (39.37″). This rigid, robust machine has four spindle speeds of 600, 1000, 1700 and 2700 rpm (Fig. 5-11).

Fig. 5-11. Emco DB5 wood turning lathe.

Fig. 5-12. 36" between centers wood turning lathe.

American Machine and Tool (AMC) Co. (5) manufactures an inexpensive, 36" between center wood lathe. It has a large, graduated tool rest and a screw action tailstock, and a three-speed pulley.

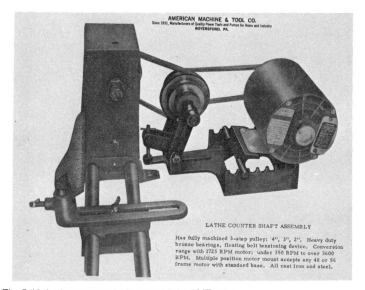

AMERICAN MACHINE & TOOL CO.
Since 1931, Manufacturers of Quality Power Tools and Pumps for Home and Industry
ROYERSFORD, PA.

LATHE COUNTER SHAFT ASSEMBLY

Has fully machined 3-step pulley: 4", 3", 2". Heavy duty bronze bearings, floating belt tensioning device. Conversion range with 1725 RPM motor: under 350 RPM to over 3600 RPM. Multiple position motor mount accepts any 48 or 56 frame motor with standard base. All cast iron and steel.

Fig. 5-13. Lathe counter shaft assembly for AMT lathe.

Optional ball bearing and bronze bearings are available. A lathe counter shaft assembly is available for the AMT lathe (Figs. 5-12 and 5-13).

Rockwell International (155) manufactures two 12" swing lathes—a heavy duty lathe and a standard lathe. The company also manufactures numerous accessories and attachments including a wood turning duplicator.

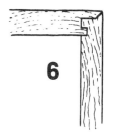

6

Drilling, Boring, Mortising, Tenoning and Routing Tools

The difference between drilling and boring, if there is a difference, is a fine line. The ordinary, mass produced drill bits available today are adequate for boring where precision and appearance are not important. We bore holes in wood; we drill holes in metal. The twist drill bits sold to many home craftsmen are designed for metal and are not intended for boring wood at all.

Experienced cabinetmakers and furniture craftsmen depend on auger bits and drills specifically designed for boring clean, smooth holes in hardwood. Properly used, these bits cut holes with more precision, more ease and give a better appearing final result.

Drill bits designed for metal have a tendency to "wander" in wood, while auger bits and other bits designed for wood are equipped with spurs and a screw point, or spurs with an unthreaded point or brad point.

The auger bits (square tang, spurs and screw point) are ordinarily used with a hand brace. Machine bits (round shank, spurs and unthreaded point or brad point) are used in drill presses and other power driven, boring machines.

Drilling and boring tools are used to make holes in wood where screws and other joining devices are needed. The size and depth of the hole depends on the type of boring tool chosen and the size of the bit inserted.

BITS

Auger bits, used for boring holes in wood by hand with a brace, are available in sizes from ¼″ to 1¼″ diameter. Sizes are indicated by a number indented in the tang of the bit. This number designates the size in sixteenths of an inch. A number 6 on the tang identifies a ⅜″ bit (6/16″).

Auger Bits

Auger bits are of two types: the *single twist* and the *double twist*. Deep holes are bored easier with the single twist drill, but the double twist cuts a cleaner hole.

Not all square tang bits are auger bits. Other boring tools, such as the *Forstner bit*, expansion bit and others are often equipped with a square tang.

The *tang* is the part that fits into the brace. A small tapered screw—feed screw—on the tip of the bit pulls the bit into the wood so the *spurs* (knife-like projections) can cut the outline of the circle. The cutting edges or *lips* cut away the rest of the hole which follows up the *twist* of the bit.

The depth of the hole can be roughly estimated by counting the number of turns that a bit makes. Each turn (revolution) of the bit will pull the bit into the wood approximately 1/16″.

Drill Bits

Drill bits, although designed for drilling metal, can be sharpened so that they perform adequately in boring wood, by sharpening to a sharper point and grinding a concave section on each lip.

Drill bits are available in *fractional* and *letter* sizes. Fractional sizes run from 1/32″ to ½″ in increments of 1/64″. Letter size bits are available in sizes from ¼″ to ½″ where a fractional size is not applicable. Fractional size drills are usually adequate for boring in metal.

Spade Bits

Spade bits are sometimes known as zip or whiz bits and are used exclusively in boring in wood. The flat, spade-shaped bits are available in sizes from ¼″ to 1″ in increments of 1/16″. The shanks of all spade bits are ¼″ in diameter so they may be used in portable electric drills. Spade bits bore faster and cleaner than many other bits. They are ideal for the home craftsman. Spade bits are available in sizes from ¼″ in diameter to 1½″.

Expansion Bits

Expansion, or expansive bits, are available in two sizes: those that bore holes from ⅝″ to 1¾″ and those that bore holes from ⅞″

to 3″ in diameter. One model of expansion bits has a micrometer dial that claims to give precision boring to 1/1000″. It also has a depth gauge which instantly shows how deeply the hole is bored.

The expansion bit is much more difficult to use than the spade bit. It has only a square tang which allows it to be used only in a brace. When boring holes 2″ or 3″ in diameter, it is almost impossible to turn the brace. The expansion bit is not a very good buy for the home craftsman.

Multi-Spur Bits

Multi-spur bits are available in sizes from ½″ to 1″ in increments of 1/16″ and in sizes 1″ to 1¼″ in increments of ⅛″. The multi-spur bit has a round shank of ¼″ diameter, so it can be used in a portable electric drill. It is a very fast, clean boring tool. It will bore a portion of a circle on the edge of a piece of wood. In addition, it will bore at an angle, overlapping or on close centers, without splitting the wood. It works well on veneers without splitting.

Forstner Bits

Forstner bits are ideal for boring flat bottom holes. They are available in sizes from ⅜″ to 1″ in increments of 1/16″. Stamp sizes are the same as those stamped on auger bits. There are also Forstner bits available in sizes from 1¼″ to 2″ in increments of ¼″.

Forstner bits are used for counterboring and (as the multi-spur) will bore a hole close or on the edge of stock without tearing. It will bore nearly through wood without the spurs or feed screw coming through and puncturing the reverse side of the stock.

Dowel Bits

The *dowel* bit that is used in a brace is simply a shortened auger bit for boring holes. It is much easier to hold the bit perpendicular to the surface of the wood. It is also advantageous whenever a shorter bit would do the job better than the standard auger bit.

There are many special dowel bits designed to be used in high-speed boring machines on mass-produced wood articles and furniture. They are available in both a right and left hand twist. Most of these machine dowel bits have a screw shank. The bits are available in carbide tips for long and continuous production runs.

Short Unispur Power Bits

This bit is specifically designed for portable electric drills and is widely used for boring in tight spots in construction work. This one-spur bit is a fast, smooth and easy-boring bit in sizes from ⅝" to 2½" diameter.

Hole Saws

Although not a true bit, it is used in portable electric drills and the drill press for making round holes. *Hole saws* are available in 50 sizes from 9/16" to 6" diameter. They are used extensively by plumbers, electricians and contractors for cutting holes for pipe and conduit.

Route Drill Bits

The *router drill* bit can be used in a fashion similar to the saber saw. It cuts its own starting hole and can move from there in any direction. It is ideal for making irregular shaped tools.

Plug Cutters

The *plug cutter* is a short, hollow bit which cuts short dowels to cover the heads of counterbored screws. It is available in ⅜", ½" and ⅝" in diameter sizes. The advantage of the plug cutter is that short dowels of the same wood as the project can be made, rather than having to rely on the standard commercial birch dowel.

Circle Cutter Bits

The *circle cutter* is a tool for cutting holes in thin metal, plastics or wood up to 8" in diamter. A small drill bit starts the hole and a cutter on an adjustable arm cuts the outside circumference. The circle cut is available with either a square shank or round shank. It is a very highly specialized tool and would be used very little by the home woodcraftsman.

Automatic Drill Bits

The *automatic drill* bit is an accessory to the automatic drill that works on the same principle as the Yankee screwdriver. It drills a hole only on the forward stroke or downward stroke. The bits are available in sizes from 1/16" to 11/64". All automatic drill bits have notched shanks. The automatic drill is a hard drill to use and has no useful purpose except in very close quarters. The hand drill is much easier to use.

Countersink Bits

The most commonly used *countersink* bit is sometimes called the rose countersink because it has many flutes around the conical point which bore a recess for heads of flat head screws and other screws of similar design. This bit has two types of shanks: one with a square shank to use in a brace, the other a round shank to use in the portable electric drill or the drill press.

Combination Wood Drill and Countersink

The *combination wood drill and countersink* performs three operations at one time. It drills a *pilot hole* for the spiral part of the screw, it drills a *shank hole* for the shank of the screw, and it *countersinks* so that the top of a flat head screw will fit flush with the wood. It is especially helpful where speed and mass production are called for. It comes in sizes from ¾" by No. 6 to 2" by No. 12 (the first number is the length of screw, and the second number the wire size or gauge of the shank).

Bit Extensions

Bit extensions are used when extra reach is needed for boring. They are available for square tang auger bits and for round shank, power tool bits.

Suppliers/manufacturers include Arco Products Corp. (11), Conover Woodcraft Specialties (40), Forest City Tool Co. (72), Greenlee Tool Co. (91), Irwin (104) and The Toolroom (180) (Fig. 6-1).

Sharpening an Auger Bit

Select an auger bit file or some other small, fine tooth file. Sharpen the lips first with an upward thrust from the first twist or throat. Keep even pressure on the file.

Retain the original angle of the bevel. *Do not file the other side of lips*. File the inside of the spurs—never the outside (Fig. 6-2).

HAND BORING AND DRILLING TOOLS

The auger bit brace can be used with a boring or drilling bit that has a square tang. The parts of a ratchet brace are head, quill, bow, handle, ratchet, chuck shell and jaws. Sizes available are (designated by the swing of the handle) 8", 10" and 12". Present-day braces are equipped with a ratchet which allows them to be used in cramped quarters.

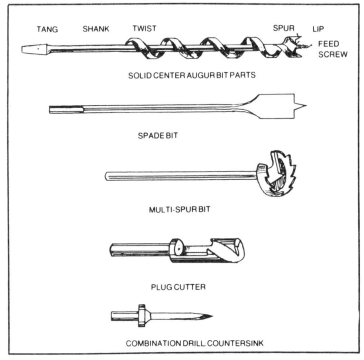

TANG   SHANK   TWIST   SPUR   LIP
                                                        FEED
                                                        SCREW
SOLID CENTER AUGUR BIT PARTS

SPADE BIT

MULTI-SPUR BIT

PLUG CUTTER

COMBINATION DRILL COUNTERSINK

Fig. 6-1. Boring and drilling bits.

Hand Drill

The "egg beater" *hand drill* is built to handle round shank drill bits ¼″ in diameter and less. It is an indispensable tool for the home craftsman, particularly if he does not possess a portable electric drill.

Breast Drill

The *breast drill* is an oversized hand drill that will handle bits up to ½″ in diameter. It has a breast plate for the operator to lean on to apply more pressure to the drill bit. The breast drill is a necessary tool when electricity is not available. The automatic drill has been discussed earlier under "Bits."

Boring With Hand Tools

Center marks are generally two pencil or scribed lines with an awl at right angles to each other. Pencil lines should be used on visible surfaces as they can be erased.

Where the two line cross, prick a small hole with a scratch awl or center punch so that the bit will center itself and will not "wander."

Material to be bored or drilled should be securely anchored with a vise or clamps.

Bits designed for boring in wood should be selected if available. Check the size. A drill bit, if it is not sharpened correctly, will cut a larger hole than the size indicated.

Special precautions should be taken when boring a hole clear through stock; otherwise, tearing or splitting will take place. Two methods which prevent splitting are as follows.

—When drilling through wood with drill bits ¼″ in diameter or smaller, place a piece of waste stock under the piece to be drilled. The only tearing will be in the waste stock.

—When boring with auger bit, place the left hand under the stock. As soon as the auger bit feed screw starts to penetrate the second side, take out the bit. Turn the board over and complete boring the hole as a center. Of course, waste stock can be placed under the location of the hole as in the first method.

Boring To Depth

Boring to depth requires a commercial depth gauge, a bit collar or a simple homemade device of wood. A square piece of

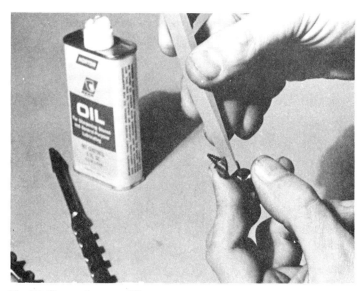

Fig. 6-2. Sharpening auger bits.

stock should be bored through the long way. The block is cut to length and the bit inserted in the hole. When the block touches the surface, it will not be possible to drill deeper, and the hole will be the correct depth.

Boring At An Angle

Boring at an angle can be accomplished by setting a T-bevel to the angle required and using it as a guide. The bit should be started straight in and gradually tilted to the angle as boring progresses. If a number of holes are to be bored at the sample angle, it is best to make a jig to guide the bit. The multi-spur bit is the best one to use for boring angled holes.

Counterboring

Counterboring is related to *countersinking*. The sides of a countersunk hole, made with a countersink bit, are at an angle. The angle is the same as the angle on the head of a flat head screw. Many times a counterbored hole is necessary to sink the head of a bolt or nut below the surface of the wood. The most important thing to remember about counterboring is *counterbored holes* must be bored before *shank holes*. To bore the shank hole first would remove wood into which the counterbore bit would have to center itself.

Counterboring is used most often to bore holes so that screw heads may be covered with dowel buttons, tapered plugs, or sections of dowels made of the same kind of wood as the project.

POWER DRILLING AND BORING TOOLS

Power tools accomplish the task of boring holes quickly and accurately. The are particularly useful when a large number of holes are required. Powered boring tools are available in both portable and stationary varieties.

Portable Electric Drills

Portable electric hand drills are available that bore from ¼" diameter to 2" diameter in wood, and up to 1" in steel. The larger models are controlled with both hands. The ¼" pistol grip, one handle model is the most popular with home craftsmen. Small drills operate at a higher speed than large ones. Many have multiple or variable speed controls, as well as reversing control.

Rockwell International (155) manufactures 18 models of pistol grip portable electric drills with ¼" and ⅜" diameter chuck capacity; six models of the *D-handle* portables with ¼″, ⅜″ and ½″ diameter chuck capacity; and nine models of the *spade handle* variety with ½″ and ¾″ diameter chuck capacity. Many have variable speed control and reversing capability. All Rockwell D-handle and spade handle drills may be converted to right angle drills with a right angle drill attachment accessory.

Conversion Units

Portable electric hand drills may be converted to the equivalent of a stationary drill attaching it to one of two units: *Portable electric drill stand* units have a heavy cast iron base with a tubular upright extending vertically from one edge of the base. The extra long arm which controls the vertical up-and-down movement of the drill affords much better leverage than could be obtained otherwise. It has an adjustable depth stop which simplifies depth drilling operations.

The *Portalign drill guide* will hold the portable drill in a perfect perpendicular position for drilling or boring. It may also be positioned for angled boring. The Portalign may be used for countersinking, boring round stock, routing, sanding and shaping, in addition to straight boring or drilling (Fig. 6-3).

Drill Press

Stationary drill presses come in two models: the *bench* type and the *floor* type. Most drill presses have from three to six speeds made possible by different size pulleys. The six speeds vary from 350 rpm to 5600 rpm. Some models have a variable speed motor, and any speed between 450 to 4800 rpm may be obtained by simply turning a dial. This eliminates the dirty and time-consuming job of changing belts on cone pulleys.

Drill presses are rated according to the distance over a board that they can reach. The 15″ drill press will drill holes in the center of a 15″ wide board.

Slow speeds are used when boring and drilling holes with large diameter bits. High speeds are necessary for small hole drilling, shaping, routing and mortising. Auger bits may be used in the drill press if the tang is cut off, and the threads on the feed screw are filed off.

Mortising may be done on the drill press with a mortising attachment, hollow chisels and hollow chisel bits. Sizes of chisels are ¼″ square, 5/16″ square, ⅜″ square and ½″ square.

Cylindrical sanding drums and sleeves are available for drill presses. Drums vary from 11/16″ in diameter and 2″ long to 3″ in

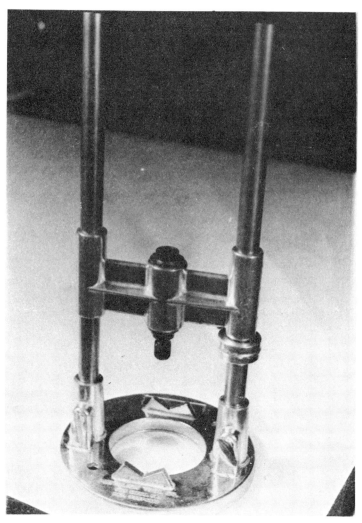

Fig. 6-3. Portalign drill guide.

diameter and 3″ long. Sleeves are available in garnet and aluminum oxide and in different size grits.

It is possible to do shaping by boosting the speed with a special high speed motor, but it is a somewhat risky setup. The spindle and quill are not built for rough usage and safety becomes a real problem.

Routing is sometimes done on the drill press at approximately 8000 rpms. When compared to the speed of a portable electric router of approximately 24,000 rpms, it is obvious that routing on a drill press would run a very poor second (Fig. 6-4).

Powermatic Houdaille (147) manufactures two 15″ drill presses. One model is a five speed step pulley version with a "Snap-Open" spring loaded guard. The other had no belts to handle when you change spindle speed. Just a twist of the accurately-calibrated variable speed control lets you choose speeds instantly while the machine is running. The step pulley model has speeds from 400 rpm to 5300 rpm. The variable speed model has speeds from 475 rpm to 4800 rpm (Fig. 6-5).

Powermatic also makes a heavy duty, 20″ drill press. This rugged machine that will stand up to day-in and day-out abuse has carefully machined spindles, sealed ball bearings, a wide variety of tables and columns, and a large number of motors and controls. Optional variable speed and step pulley models are available.

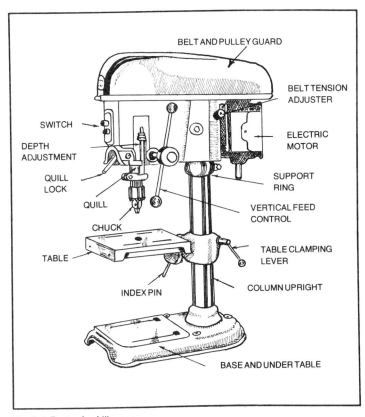

Fig. 6-4. Parts of a drill press.

Fig. 6-5. 15″ drill press, Model 1150.

Both the 15″ and 20″ drill presses have numerous accessories and attachments available, one of which is the variable speed mechanical feed unit. The feed rate is maintained for all spindle speeds. It drills to any desired depth, and is controlled by a limit-switch on a depth-stop indicator (Fig. 6-6).

Rockwell International (155) manufactures a number of drill presses. The geared head radial drill press has 12 speeds from 90 to 3360 rpm. The center of the spindle to the column is 27 9/16″ at maximum length.

The 2000 Series, 24″ drill presses provide a full 1½ hp at any speed. Rockwell also makes a 15″ and a 17″ drill press.

Sprunger Corp. (172) builds four bench type drill presses and one floor type. The small, 6″ bench type has speeds from 700 to

4300 rpm. It is powered by a ¼ hp motor. The 7″ bench type has speeds from 600 to 5200 rpm and is powered by a ⅓ hp motor. The 7½″ bench type develops the same speeds as the 7″ drill press and is powered by a ½ hp motor. The 7½″ floor type is identical to the 7½″ bench type except it is 65″ high instead of 38″.

The 16½″ radial arm drill press shown in Fig. 6-7 has a variable depth of throat from 5⅝″ to 16½″. The head swivels a full 360°. It is powered by a ½ hp electric motor. The Jacobs chuck has a capacity of ½″.

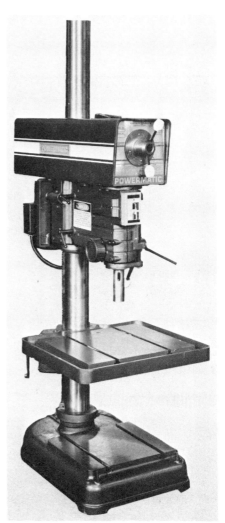

Fig. 6-6. 20″ drill press, Model 1200.

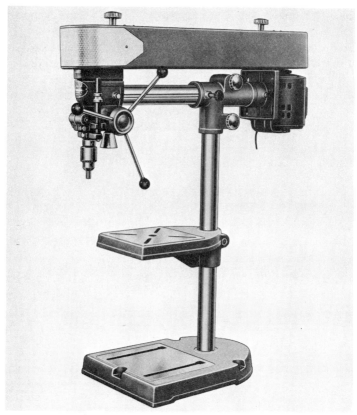

Fig. 6-7. 16½" radial arm drill press.

American Machine and Tool Co. (5) also makes a radial arm drill press. This inexpensive machine, of 32" drilling radius, has a swivel head for angle drilling, combination ball and bronze bearing spindle, ½" capacity chuck, adjustable depth stop, depth of drill indicator and is powered by either a ¼ or ⅓ hp motor (Fig. 6-8).

MORTISE AND TENON JOINTS

The *blind mortise and tenon* is one of the most used, if not the most used joints, particularly in the leg-rail construction found in tables. However, it is the most difficult to make. The mortise is generally made first as it is easier to fit a tenon to a mortise than vice versa. Figure 6-9 shows a 1½" square leg and a ¾" by 2½" rail. The mortise is never made in the center of the leg because the inside corner material would be too small and weak and would be liable to break. This, of course, means a narrow shoulder (1/16″ to ⅛″) between rail and leg which has much greater design appeal. It also provides a longer tenon. The blind mortise and tenon shown in Fig. 6-9 is in two parts: a top view and a front view.

A few general rules of mortise and tenon design are:

—The material between the top of the mortise and the top of the leg should be at least ⅜″ (more for softwoods) to assure that the top of the leg does not break out.

—In order to keep the tenon as wide as possible, make the lower shoulder cut between 1/16″ and ⅛″. This is especially true with narrow rails.

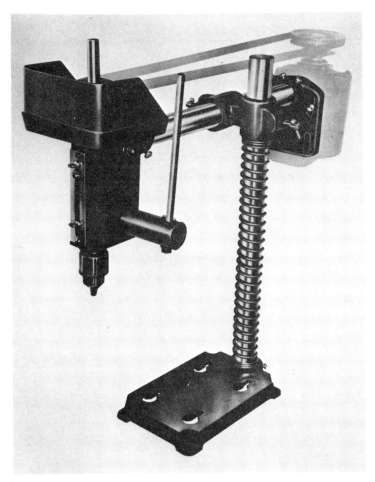

Fig. 6-8. 32″ radial arm drill press.

213

—A tenon should never be thinner than one-third the thickness of the rail. A tenon one-half the thickness of the rail is probably the best size (Fig. 6-9).

Through Mortise and Tenon Joint

The *through mortise and tenon* joint is a strong joint that can be used in many situations where the end grain of the tenon is not objectionable. It is a very easy joint to make in that three passes of a dado head (one for the mortise and two for the tenon) are all that are needed. If the setup illustrated in Fig. 3-24 is used, only two passes are needed for both mortise and tenon (Fig. 6-10).

Haunched Mortise and Tenon Joint

The *haunched mortise and tenon* joint is a blind mortise and tenon joint designed for a specific function. It is a corner joint and is most often used on paneled doors that are grooved. The shoulder, or haunch, of the tenon fits into the groove and the rest of the tenon fits into the mortise. This way, the haunch fills the groove space that would otherwise be unsightly. Figure 6-11 depicts a haunched mortise and tenon joint.

Making a Blind Mortise and Tenon With Hand Tools

The blind mortise and tenon is used extensively in furniture manufacturing, but for the amateur home craftsman it is the most difficult joint if made with hand tools. The procedure described here is for the craftsman who does not possess the necessary power tools to do the job. The blind mortise and tenon depicted in Fig. 6-9 is used as a model. Here is the procedure for making the mortise:

■ Mark ⅜″ down from the top of the leg on one of the faces to be mortised, and square a line with a try square across the end of the leg. See Fig. 6-12A.

■ From the line just made, measure down 2″ which establishes the length of the mortise and mark another pencil line across the leg. See Fig. 6-12A.

■ Extend these lines across the adjoining end of the leg (at right angle to the first face). See Fig. 6-12B.

■ Place all four legs on a flat surface and square up the ends with a carpenter's square.

■ Continue the lines of the leg just marked across the other three legs with a carpenter's square and pencil.

■ Turn the three legs 90° and mark the second mortise.

■ Set the marking gauge for 5/16 and scribe a line between the pencil lines on all eight mortises. See Fig. 6-12A.

■ Set the marking gauge for an additional ⅜″ and scribe the width of the mortise on all eight mortises. See Fig. 6-12A.

■ Set the marking gauge for ½″ and scribe a center line through the center of each of the mortises.

■ Insert an auger bit, a trifle smaller than the width of the mortise (in this case a 5/16″ auger bit which as a "5" stamped on

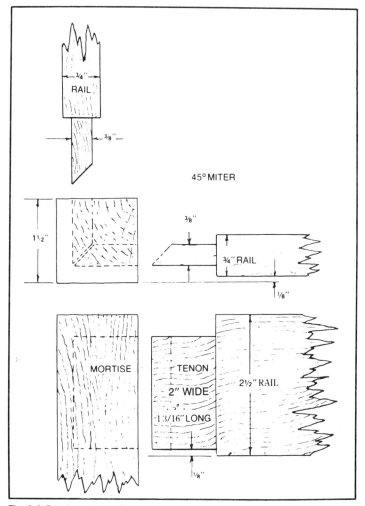

Fig. 6-9. Blind mortise and tenon.

215

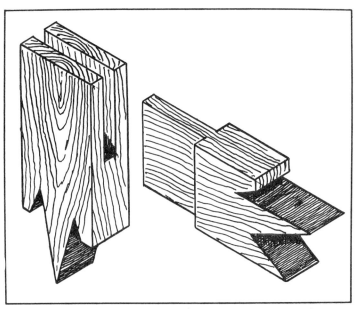

Fig. 6-10. Through mortise and tenon.

the tang), into a brace and bore a row of holes down the length of the mortise. *Do not overlap the holes.* A depth gauge is attached to the auger bit to control the depth. Be sure that the feed screw is lined up with the center line.

■ Chisel out the waste wood from the sides using a firmer socket chisel which may be used with a mallet. Keep just inside the lines.

■ Chisel out the ends with a narrow, deep-mortise chisel.

■ Chisel to the lines with a sharp, paring chisel.

Here is the procedure for making the tenon:

■ Saw rails to correct size, making sure that tenons are included. It is easy to forget the tenons when working from a drawing or blueprint.

■ Lay out the length of tenons from the ends of the rail.

■ Scribe a line around the rail from this line with a try square. See Fig. 6-13.

■ Set the marking gauge for 3/16″ (one half the difference between thickness of rail and the thickness of tenon) and scribe a line "1" down both edges of the rail and across the end.

■ Set the marking gauge for 9/16″ (3/16″ plus ⅜″) and scribe a line "2" down both edges of the rail and across the end. *Be sure the marking gauge is held against the same face while marking* "1" *and* "2".

■ Set the marking gauge for ⅜″ (the distance from top of the rail to the top of the tenon) and scribe a line "4" on both faces and across the end.

■ Set the marking gauge for 2⅜″ (the distance from the top of the rail and bottom of the tenon) and scribe a line "3" on both faces and across the end. (Notice that the gauge is set from the top of the rail in both cases).

■ Place the rail in a vise and saw "cheeks" of the tenon, keeping just outside of the lines.

■ Saw shoulder depths while work is still in the vise.

■ Place the rail in the miter box and saw down to the "cheek" cuts and down to shoulder cuts.

■ Fit tenon to mortise with a sharp, paring chisel.

■ Miter the ends of tenons in the miter box (Fig. 6-13).

MORTISING AND TENONING WITH POWER TOOLS

The hollow mortising chisel is held in place by a chisel holder which is fastened to the quill of the drill press. The revolving mortise bit is secured in a spindle collar. The hole in the spindle is usually ½″ in diameter and bushings are slid over the shank end of the bit to make it fit the hole.

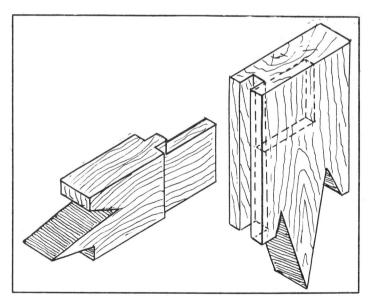

Fig. 6-11. Haunched mortise and tenon.

217

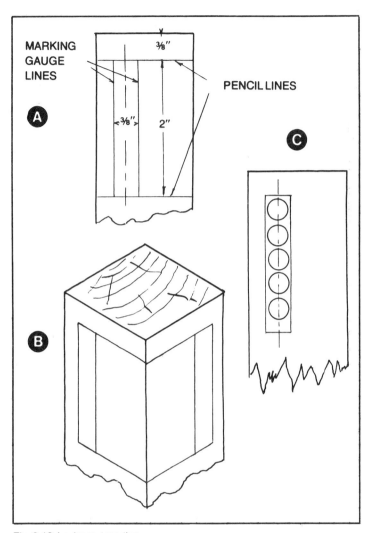

Fig. 6-12. Laying out mortise.

Fastened to the drill press table is a fence which is required to hold the mortise straight and true. On the top edge of the fence is a casting which holds adjustable hold-downs. This casting in addition supports J-shaped rods which hold the work against the fence.

The revolving bit is slid through the hollow chisel from the lower or cutting edge. The correct size bushing is then slipped on the shank of the bit. The chisel, bit and bushing are then pushed up through the hole into the chisel holder. Be sure that both chisel and bushing rest against the shoulders provided. The chisel is secured in place by setscrews in the chisel holder. Set the lower end of the bit between 1/32″ and 1/16″ from the cutting edge of the chisel and tighten the screws in the spindle collar. If there is no clearance between the lower end of the bit and the lower end of the chisel, both the bit and the chisel will burn badly in operation and lose their temper. However, if the clearance is over 1/16″, the sawdust and chips may be oversize and will not work up through the chisel.

Cutting a Mortise Using the Drill Press Attachment

This same procedure may be used for other hollow chisel mortises. Lay out the mortise on the workpiece.

Adjust the fence to the necessary position. Set fence exactly square with chisel by using a try square. If the fence is not square with the chisel, the mortise will be rough with a saw tooth design.

Mark the depth of the cut on the end of the workpiece and lower the bit and chisel to this line. Set the depth stop in this position so that the bit and chisel will not cut too deep. Adjust the hold-downs and J-shaped rods to hold work securely to the table.

Start the cut by bringing the chisel and bit down against one end of the mortise. Make the first cut. As all four sides of the chisel are in contact with the wood, this cut will require more strength than subsequent cuts.

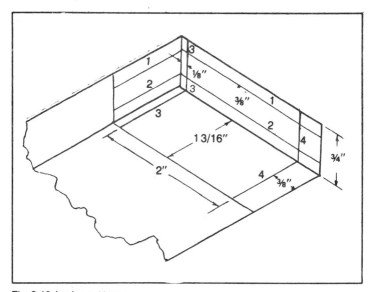

Fig. 6-13. Laying out tenon.

Lift the bit and chisel frequently, particularly when cutting hard wood, to allow the chisel and bit to cool down and the sawdust and chips to work through the chisel. If the craftsman does considerable mortising with the setup, a foot control is a good investment. It allows the worker to use both hands on the workpiece, and over a long production run it is much less fatiguing.

Move the chisel to the second cut, which is from two-thirds to three-fourths the width of the chisel, and make the second cut. Continue until all cuts are made.

The drill press should be run much slower for hardwoods than for softwoods. Mortising chisels and bits are available in ¼", 5/16", ⅜" and ½" sizes.

A few suppliers/manufacturers of drill press mortising attachments are Brodhead-Garrett (30), Rockwell International (155), Sears Roebuck (163) and Woodworker's supply (211).

Hollow Chisel Mortiser

The *hollow chisel mortiser* is designed for one purpose and one purpose only—to cut mortises. It is sometimes described as the machine that drills square holes. Although hollow chisel mortises are seldom found in home workshops, there are a few that are comparatively inexpensive when compared with industrial models. See Yates-American (214).

The hollow chisel mortiser usually has a power head of a motor which moves vertically along slides.

The table may be moved both horizontally and vertically and tilted. Some tables move transversely (in and out). The fence has holding devices similar to the ones found on the drill press mortising attachment.

Some mortisers are equipped with a power feed system which requires little effort on the part of the operator. The hollow chisel mortiser mortises with greater ease and efficiency than the drill press mortiser attachment.

Chain Saw Mortiser

The *chain saw mortiser* is strictly a mass production tool and is, by far, the fastest mortiser. It differs from the hollow chisel mortiser in that it makes a mortise with a round, semicircular cut at the bottom of the mortise.

The majro part of this machine is the chain. It is made up of links of steel with each link shaped like a saw tooth in the outside or cutting edge.

The chain runs over a guiding bar with a ball bearing sprocket wheel over the lower end. The upper end of the chain is driven by a powered sprocket.

The table is movable in three directions: up and down, back and forth, and in and out. The workpiece is moved up against the chain rather than the chain moving down into the work.

Two other types of mortisers are the reciprocating type and the oscillating bit type. The oscillating bit mortiser works something like a router. The mortise it creates has square sides and flat bottom, but the ends are rounded.

Powermatic Houdaille (147) manufactures a hollow chisel mortiser with a universal table with 45° right or left tilting, 14″ vertical and 12″ longitudinal table adjustment. It has a built-in fan to keep the work clean and a quick-acting eccentric clamp which permits fast stock change with complete accuracy in high production operations (Fig. 6-14).

Powermatic also manufactures a chain saw mortiser. This machine has a heavy, reinforced cast iron base to eliminate vibration.

It has a built-in chip blower, a continuous oiling system, a mortise chain bar that is easily adjusted and an adjustable chip breaker. It has a 6″ depth stroke which is easily controlled by a foot lever (Fig. 6-15).

THE ROUTER

The router as a molding machine was discussed to a considerable extent in Chapter 4, so that aspect of router operation will not be repeated in this section. For those who do little routing or feel that a motorized router is too large an investment, the hand router or router plane is an acceptable second choice.

The router plane differs radically from all other planes. It has two round, identical handles and an oblong base of cast iron with a narrow, adjustable knife and a chisel edge extending through the base between the handles.

The router plane is limited in its use as it is restricted to smoothing the bottom of rabbets, grooves and dadoes.

Portable Electric Router

The portable electric router—in essence a small upside-down shaper— is a high speed (up to 22,000 rpm) power tool, which in many ways had displaced the shaper. Sanding is practically eliminated when using this extremely smooth, chip-free routing,

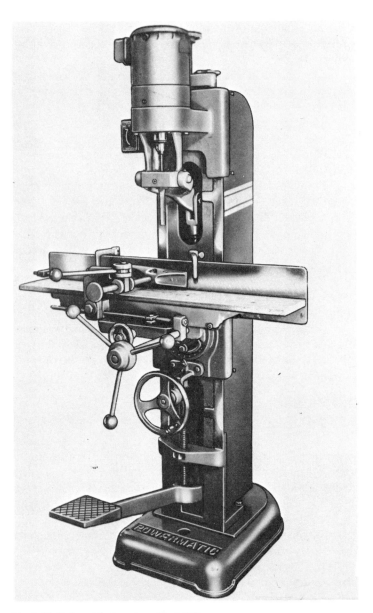

Fig. 6-14. Hollow chisel mortiser, Model 10.

molding, planing and shaping device. The portable electric route is made more versatile by the many attachments available, such as the dovetail template, shaper table and router edge guide.

The portable electric router is made up of an electric motor which is fastened to an adjustable metal base. The shaft of the motor is attached to a chuck (collet type) which holds the numerous

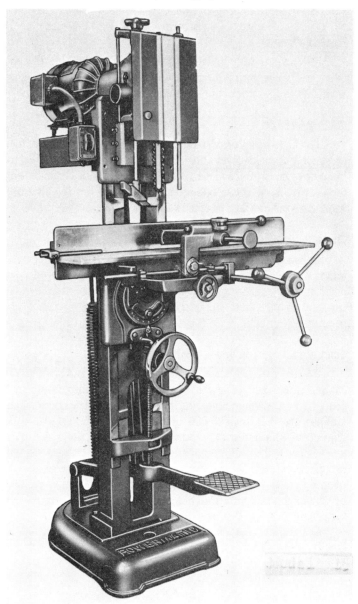

Fig. 6-15. Chain saw mortiser, Model 15.

router bits. The motors vary from the small fractional horsepower models to the heavy duty 2 hp or more. Many electric routers have a micrometer depth adjustment, a cooling fan, and two knobs or a knob and handle for better control.

Freehand Routing

Freehand routing is done by controlling the bit by conscious effort. No guides or pilot tip bits are used. The operator must be aware of the direction of the bit rotation at all times.

Routing An Edge

The edge of a project (table, chest, bench, picture frame) may be shaped or molded with bits equipped with a pilot tip, which of itself does no cutting and prevents the cutting blades from cutting too deeply. Some cutter bits are made with ball bearing pilot tips which prevent the burning of the wood.

Guide Routing

Adjustable routing guides are available which are easy to attach to the router. They are used for straight or curved edge planing, parallel grooving, dadoing or slotting operations. They are used for applications where critical accuracy and precision are required.

General Procedure for Using the Router

The hardness and consistency of the material and the depth of cut determine the rate at which a router can be fed into the stock. A router motor, when revolving freely without a working load, attains a speed of about 20,000 rpm. When the router is fed into the workpiece, the motor slows down. If the motor slows down too much because the router is fed into the work too fast, the motor will overheat and damage may occur. If the motor has a tendency to overheat, shut if off for a while and let it cool off. Another cause of overheating is dull bits. Dull bits must be sharpened or exchanged for a sharp bit.

Conversely, the router should not be fed into the work too slowly. If the cutter is allowed to stay in one spot too long, not only will the wood be burned, but the bit is apt to overheat and destroy the temper in the bit.

Always keep in mind that the router bit revolves clockwise when viewed from above, which means that the router must be moved *counterclockwise* around the edge of a workpiece. Following are accessories for the portable electric router.

Dovetail Template. An easy to use dovetail template for cutting perfect dovetail joints

Router Edge Guide. An easy to mount adjustable guide for accurate work.

Hinge Butt Template. An easy to operate template for mortising a door and butt of any length and hinge size.

Laminate Trimmer. The laminate trimmer features a dual edge guide for both flush and bevel trimming.

Bit And Cutter Sharpening Attachment. The attachment includes arbor, grinding wheel, ¼" bit adapter, wrenches, tripod router stand, etc.

Shaper Table Attachment. Special tables are available for almost all types and makes of routers which convert the router into a shaper. The router is mounted with the check through an opening in the table. The regular check is sometimes changed to a larger spindle that will carry larger cutters.

Black and Decker and Rockwell International Routers

Black and Decker (26) manufactures two routers: the 7625 model and the Routermate Deluxe (Figs. 6-16 and 6-17).

Rockwell International (155) manufactures seven router models and four models of laminate trimmers which are specially

Fig. 6-16. 1¼ hp portable "trade" router.

designed small routers for a single purpose. The seven routers vary from ⅞ to 2 hp.

The Stationary Floor Type Router

This machine is sometimes called a router-shaper in that the shaping bits remain in one location and the workpiece moves against the revolving bit or cutter. The essential difference between a shaper and a router-shaper is that the shaping motor is below the table on a shaper and above the table on a router-shaper.

The floor type router-shaper is provided with an adjustable fence of two parts. One part is adjustable toward and away from the cutter while the other fence part is stationary.

The Panel Router

The "Her-Saf" panel router manufactured by *Safranek Enterprises* (158) is made in two sizes: 50″ total vertical capacity and 62″ total vertical capacity. It adapts to Black and Decker. Rockwell,

Fig. 6-17. Routermate Deluxe portable router in use.

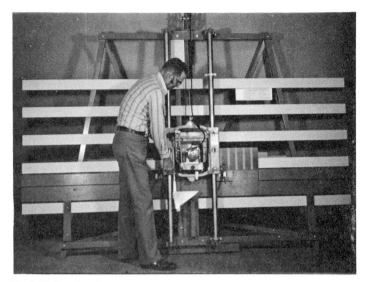

Fig. 6-18. Panel router.

Stanley and air powered units. It routs both vertically and horizontally, in wood, laminated plastic, particle board, etc. Varying material thicknesses are adjusted for with carriage depth control eccentric (Fig. 6-18).

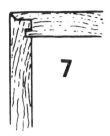

7

Chiseling, Carving, Sculpturing, Scraping and Miscellaneous Tools

Each of the chisel blades listed here is used in conjunction with a specialized task. The thickness of the blade is dependent upon the chore it is required to perform.

CHISEL BLADES

The firmer chisel is any chisel that has a straight cutting edge and the cutting edge face is perfectly flat.

The Gouge. The *gouge* is any chisel with a rounded or U-shaped cross section. Hand gouges are inside and outside ground and are straight across the cutting edge. Lathe turning gouges are outside ground only, and the cutting edge is rounded.

Bevel Edge Chisels. The *bevel edge chisel* blade is easier to use because of the visibility it provides. It is also lighter in weight. Most firmer chisels have beveled edges.

Straight Edge Chisels. *Straight edge chisels* (as opposed to bevel edge chisels) are used where great strength is needed.

CHISEL HANDLES

Chisel handles must stand as much abuse as the chisel blade. The craftsman should take care when selecting a handle to make sure it will stand up to the job at hand.

Tang Handle. Chisels with *tang* handles have a long, sharply pointed projection that fits into a handle with a metal ferrule. Mallets should never be used with tang-handled chisels or gouges.

Socket Handle. The *socket* handle chisel will stand considerable abuse and is quite often used with mallets (wood, rawhide, plastic, rubber, etc.).

Pocket Handle. *Pocket* handle chisels are built for extremely hard usage. They are ideal for school shops. The blade and shank are forged in one piece extending through the handle to a steel cap on the non-cutting end (Fig. 7-1).

SHAPES OF CHISELS AND GOUGES

The three large categories of chisel shapes are *straight, spoon* and *long bend*. Lathe turning chisels have not been included as they are covered in Chapter 5. Carving tools are covered later on in this chapter (Figs. 7-2 and 7-3).

USING CHISELS AND GOUGES

Cutting with chisels and gouges requires a very sharp edge. Sharpening is done in the same fashion as sharpening a plane iron (grind, whet and hone). The stock being chiseled must be securely held in a vise, with clamps, or against a bench hook. The chisel is held in the right hand and the left hand is used to guide and keep the chisel under control. The most common operations are cutting dadoes, tenons and cross-laps.

Remove most of the wood with a socket-firmer chisel and mallet with the bevel side down. This can be done quite rapidly. Stop before you get to within 1/16″ to ⅛″ to the layout line.

Lay aside the socket chisel and use a sharp, tang-handled paring chisel. Paring action requires the handle to be moved back and forth. Pare always toward the center first from one side or edge and then from the other. The bevel side should be up for this step in the operation. Continue paring until the line indicating the depth has been reached. So far, all the work has been across the work and horizontal.

Pare from above (vertical) and across end grain. The bevel of the chisel should be facing away from the edge being pared. Start back from the line at least 1/16″ and do not attempt to remove too much material at a time. Rock the chisel handle back and forth from side to side and keep the chisel blade firmly under control with the thumb and index finger of the left hand. Always strive for a shearing cut.

Keep in mind that all of the chiseling work on dadoes, tenons, cross-laps and the like can be eliminated with a circular saw and a dado head.

The inside ground, straight edge gouge is used when cutting the edge of a curved line from above. The outside ground, straight

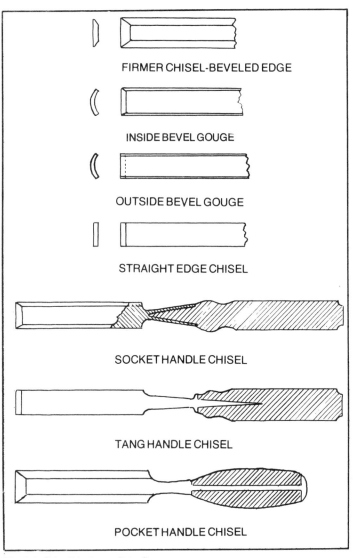

Fig. 7-1. Chisel blades and handles.

edge gouge is used more frequently and is used for carving flutes and in cutting out recesses in trays. Use a mallet and socket-handle gouge for roughing out. Only thing shavings with a paring gouge should be taken as the layout line is approached.

Carving tools are used in about the same way as other chiseling tools. There will be more about carving tools later.

CARVING TOOLS AND THEIR USE

A considerable amount of information found in this section comes from the Fine Tool Shop (68). The range and variety of carving tool sizes and patterns available to the beginning carver are hard to imagine. There are thousands of combinations of size and shape. However, the master wood carver gets along with 100 or less. Of the 100, only about one-third will be used almost

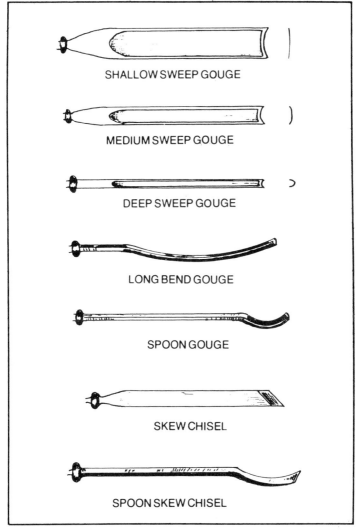

SHALLOW SWEEP GOUGE

MEDIUM SWEEP GOUGE

DEEP SWEEP GOUGE

LONG BEND GOUGE

SPOON GOUGE

SKEW CHISEL

SPOON SKEW CHISEL

Fig. 7-2. Gouge and skew chisel shapes.

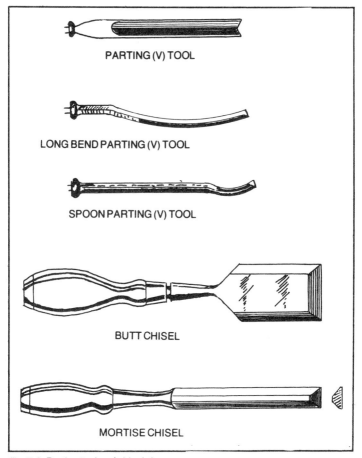

PARTING (V) TOOL

LONG BEND PARTING (V) TOOL

SPOON PARTING (V) TOOL

BUTT CHISEL

MORTISE CHISEL

Fig. 7-3. Parting tool and chisel shapes.

continually. There is no clear-cut distinction between carving tools and chisels and gouges used for other purposes.

Carving tools can be classified in three categories: *length shape* (longitudinal shape)—straight, *curved* and *bent*; *cross section*—curved (gouge), flat (chisel) and "V" shaped (parting); and *size*, the width across the tool, generally in millimeters. Other variations are spade, long spade and shouldered or not shouldered.

Chisels. *Chisels*, beveled on both sides, are either *skew* or *square*. The first grinding will be with rounded heels. This allows the user to perform a back-and-forth rocking motion. Chisels are used for setting in, reaching acute corners and cleaning up recessed backgrounds.

Gouges. *Gouges* are the mainstay of the wood carver. The straight gouge is used for general carving. The size of the sweep (sweep will be discussed further on) will depend on the amount of work expected of the tool. The #8 or #9 sweep is about a 30 mm size and is used to start cleaning out a large area. A smaller sweep is used to clear out the hollows left by the larger gouge.

Parting Tools. *Parting tools*, sometimes called "V" tools, so named because of their shape, are used primarily for cutting grooves, cleaning up inside corners, outlining and lettering.

Veiners Or Veining Tools. *Veining tools* are "U" shaped gouges used for lettering, fluting and similar operations.

Bent Gouges. *Bent gouges* are of two types: *front bent* and *back bent*. The back bent gouge is seldom used, and then only in a restricted area when top clearance is needed. The front bent gouge is used for cutting hollows in rounded shapes and for removing large amounts of wood when carving bowl-shaped objects.

Spoon Gouges. The *spoon gouges* will perform in situations that other gouges will not handle. Their specially designed blades allow them to work in areas that other gouges cannot enter.

Fishtail Gouges. *Fishtail gouges*, which are sometimes called spade gouges, are used primarily for finishing touches without injuring other adjacent edges.

General Sharpening Instructions

Carving tools are sharpened on both sides of the cutting edge. Carving gouges that are used the most have the primary bevel on the outside. A secondary bevel is ground on the inside. The secondary bevel helps to lift the gouge when it is cutting with the hollow side facing down. Otherwise, there would be a tendency for the gouge to be hindered by the wood. The inside bevel also widens the clearance of the tool so that it can make a deep cut more easily.

Sizes and Shapes

The sizes of carving chisels and gouges are identified by the width of the blade in millimeters. Most carving tools range between 6 mm (approximately ¼″) to 25 mm (about 1″); however, Frank Mittermeir (75) lists in his catalog a special large size, Swiss style, fishtail gouge that is 80 mm (about 3¼″ wide).

Shapes of carving tools are identified by numbers, which indicate the *cross section* of the tool and the *length shape*. Chisels with a straight cutting edge are numbered 1, 2, 21, 22 and 23. Numbers 1 and 2 are straight in length shape (longitudinally) while number 21 is a front bent, edge at right angles to the shank, and numbers 22 and 23 identify front bent, left and right hand skew chisels.

Gouges, including fluter and veiner gouges, are classified in nine different cross section numbers for the straight, curved and front bent length shapes, and six different cross section numbers for the back bent length shape.

Straight gouges are numbered from 3 to 11, curved gouges from 12 to 20, front bent gouges from 24 to 32, and back bent gouges from 33 to 38. The gouge numbers are sometimes called "sweep" numbers in that they indicate the amount of curvature of the blade. Numbers 3, 12, 24 and 33 indicate a nearly straight cutting edge with a very large radius. All gouges of a certain number have the same degree of curvature in relation to their width. For example, a number 9 gouge is a half round, semi-circular curve, whatever its width may be. Viewed in another way, all gouges that have the same length shape (straight, curved, front bent and back bent), and have the same cross section, have the same number. Regardless of its width, a number 9 tool is a straight gouge with a half circle cross section. The number 18 is a curved gouge with a half circle cross section and a number 30 is a front bent gouge with a half circle cross section.

Parting "V" tool numbers are numbered 39, 41 and 45 in straight tools; 40, 42 and 46 in curved tools; and 43 and 44 in front bent (Fig. 7-4).

Bottoming Chisels

These chisels are used by gunsmiths for inletting and fitting of side plates on quality guns. Usually available in three shapes, they enable the gunsmith to do the difficult backgrounding on contours of high relief carvings, intaglio carving and recessing for inlays.

Chip Carving Tools

Five classifications of tools are used in chip carving: *chip carving knives, veiners, skew chisels, straight spade tools* and *parting "V" tools.*

Many chip carvers use only knives. More advanced chip carvers use a skew chisel "setting in" tool and a veiner, while others use in addition the "V" tools and/or gouges.

Chip carving often entails the removing of triangular shaped pieces of wood. By working in stages, almost any depth can be attained. The first cut is made down through the central portion of the triangle. Then small chips are removed by holding the knife at 45° and cutting from both sides of the center line.

Chip carving is an excellent method for the beginning carver to learn as he begins to get the feel of the tool. He can observe the wood while it is being carved.

Gravers for Wood Blocks

Gravers for wood engraving are slightly arced for smoother engraving. They also have less tendency for cutting too deeply. The average set has six tools: a knife, a bevel #3, two roughs, #3 and #10, and two flats, #2 and #10.

Stipling Tools

There are many designs of *stipling tools* which are used for embossing the background of carved designs. Stipling is not a carving process and requires little, if any, skill. It is used to enhance the overall effect of the carving. The tool is simply placed at right angles to the work and tapped with a mallet or hammer.

Block Cutting Tools

These tools are used for cutting designs in linoleum. The carved linoleum is often mounted to a wooden block which brings the combined pieces to type height so that they can be used in the printing press.

A typical set consists of a ⅜" straight chisel, a 5/16" bent chisel, a ¼" skew chisel, a 5/16" straight shallow gouge, a ⅛" straight bent gouge and a ⅛" bent deep gouge.

Beginner's Palm Gouges

Woodworkers Supply (211) lists five European palm gouges. These beginner designed tools have handles that give maximum

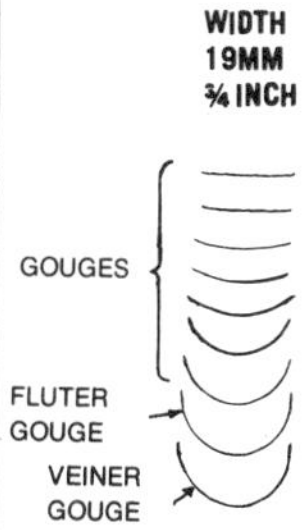

	WIDTH 19MM ¾ INCH	STRAIGHT	CURVED	FRONT BENT	BACK BENT
		#3	#12	#24	#33
		#4	#13	#25	#34
		#5	#14	#26	#35
GOUGES		#6	#15	#27	#36
		#7	#16	#28	#37
		#8	#17	#29	#38
		#9	#18	#30	
FLUTER GOUGE		#10	#19	#31	
VEINER GOUGE		#11		#32	

Fig. 7-4. Gouge numbers.

control of tool and work. The set consists of a 12 mm straight chisel, an 8 mm skew, a 10 mm gouge, an 8 mm bent gouge and a 6 mm "V" parting tool.

Handle Shapes

The most common shapes of chisel and gouges are: *round, octagon, cabinetmaker* and *graver*. The cabinetmaker handles are leather capped with a steel band and varies in length from 4½" to 6". The graver handles are short and stubby varying in length from 1½" to 1¾".

Handle Woods and Sizes

Many different kinds of woods are used for chisels and gouges, but the most popular are beech, boxwood, rosewood, ash, oak and hornbeam.

Sizes of handles are not only identified by the length, but by the size of the ferrule, which varies in diameter from ⅜" to ⅝".

Chisel handle lengths are generally between 4" and 5" long. Longer handles are clumsy to use and shorter handles are difficult to control.

Chisel Identification

Many wood carvers use the handle to quickly identify the chisel being used. Three methods are used for identification:

—Different kinds of wood in the handle,

—Handles of the same kind of wood, but stained in a different color.

—Turning a different number of combination of rings on the handle.

Mallets

Mallets used for wood carving differ from other mallets in that they are shaped like a potato masher. These mallet are always in a position to be used when picked up.

The most common woods used for mallets are *beech* and *lignum vitae*, but other woods such as apple, plum and elm are sometimes used. Lignum vitae mallets should be kept in a plastic bag with a few drops of water added to prevent splitting of this tropical wood. Lignum vitae mallets are available in different weights from 16 ounces to 33 ounces.

The handle of a mallet should extend clear through the head and a little beyond. A wedge should enter the end at 90° to the grain of the head. The wedge is not cut off, but is driven further into the handle as the wood dries, thus tightening up the handle.

Carver's Screw

The *carver's screw* is a device which securely holds the piece being worked on without the use of additional clamps. Square holes in the handle fit a square drive head on the screw so that the handle does double duty as a wrench for starting the tapered pilot screw into the workpiece.

SHARPENING OF GOUGES AND CHISELS

The sharpening of gouges and chisels takes place in three steps: *grinding, whetting* and *honing*.

Grinding

Grinding takes place only when the cutting edge is excessively dulled or nicked; otherwise, only whetting and/or honing will be necessary. Many wood carvers prefer the old-fashioned grindstone, used with water, to the motorized grinder. They hold the opinion that too much metal is removed and the tool edge is apt to burn and lose its temper if ground with a motorized grinder. There is a small, 10″ diameter wet, sandstone grinder that is motorized, but professional carvers are not too impressed with it. The grindstone turns *away* from the tool being sharpened while the motorized grinding wheel turns toward the tool.

If the chisel is excessively dull or nicked, the edge should be held against the wheel to straighten up the edge. Of course, this will dull the tool further, but a true edge will be established to work from.

When grinding straight tools, hold the bevel side down against the grinding wheel, and place the index finger on the underside of it to slide against the rest on the grinder. Naturally, if the grinder is equipped with a tool holder, the "freehand" method is not appropriate.

Take a few passes across the edge of the grinding wheel to see if the correct angle has been established. If not, slide the index finger, up or down, until the right angle is found. During the grinding process, check often for squareness and overheating. If the iron starts turning dark in color, dunk it in water.

When grinding is complete, a wire edge will turn up on the side opposite the bevel. The wire edge will be removed in subsequent whetting.

Grinding or abrasive wheels are usually made of aluminum oxide and are available in fine, medium and coarse. The fine grit wheel is generally best for carving tools. The wheels range in diameter from 4″ to 14″, and in thickness from ½″ to 2″.

Whetting

The whetting of carving tools differs from that for carpenters' and cabinetmakers' tools. The cutting edge of tools, other than carvers' tools, is an extension of the face of the tool; however, the cutting edge of carving tools is toward the middle of the cutting edge.

There is a definite reason for this apparently paradoxical method. The carving chips from a carver's chisel are broken up and are much shorter than they would be from other chisels. This helps to prevent splitting and it is easier to cut across the grain of wood. Furthermore, when the chisel is whetted on the side opposite the bevel (the ground side), more clearance is provided and the chisel has greater leverage.

The *bench stone* is an all-purpose stone. It quite often has a fine grit on one face and a coarse grit on the other. A typical bench stone would measure 8″ x 2″ x 1″ thick.

Gouge stones are used for whetting the inside or outside curves on gouges. The taper in these stones takes care of a wide range of curvatures. Stones are about 6″ long and taper from 2″ wide at one end to ½″ wide at the other. They have both concave and convex surfaces. They are generally available in silicon carbide and aluminum oxide (India).

Slip stones are of different sizes and shapes. They are used to whet the cutting edges on small gouges, parting "V" tools and other edge tools. Sizes vary, but a typical slipstone is 4½″ long and 1¾″ wide. The thickness varies from one edge to the other. The thickest part is in the ¼″ to ½″ range, and the thinnest part is the ⅛″ to 1/16″ range.

The major purpose of whetting stones is to remove the ragged edge (sometimes called wire edge or feather edge) left after the grinding process. On some cutting tools the wire edge is left on. The butcher leaves the wire edge on because it cuts meat better, but a wire edge on carving tools is detrimental to their performance.

"Sharpness" of edge is not necessarily synonymous with "finest" of edge. A long, sharp bevel can be ground on chisel, but it will not be a fine point. It will dull easily and the edge is apt to break under pressure.

The two general classifications of stones are: *synthetic man-made* stones and *natural stones*. Synthetic, man-made stones are made of aluminum oxide, which is also called India stone or aloxite, and of silicon carbide, a dark-grey or black stone, often carrying the name of Carborundum.

The natural stones come from a small area in Arkansas and carry the state's name. The soft white Arkansas stone is relatively inexpensive when compared with the *black hard* Arkansas stone, but more expensive than man-made stones.

Honing

The difference between "honing" and "whetting" is somewhat controversial, but I accept the notion that honing is done only with a *leather strop* or a *buffing wheel*.

The leather strop produces a fine, sharp edge. Strops can be used with or without a specially prepared paste. The combination of a buffing wheel and buffing compound is, by far, the fastest of the honing methods. For the ultimate edge, use the compounds (fine abrasives mixed with wax) in the following order: *grey compound, tripoli compound* and *jeweler's rouge*.

DUPLI-CARVER

The "Dupli-Carver" is available from Laskowski Enterprises (111). The three stages of carving with the Dupli-Carver are: getting ready to carve, carving with the ¼″ bit and finishing the carving.

Getting Ready To Carve. First, a plaster model of the piece to be carved is attached to the turntable on the right side of the Dupli-Carver. The carving block is then attached to the turntable on the left.

Carving With The ¼″ Bit. The plaster model is traced with a ½″ stylus following each contour. A ¼″ bit is placed in the motor router (note stylus/bit size differences) to carve the same contours, but the bit will "under carve" during this step to prevent any chipping that might cut too deeply when the finishing detail is carved. The size difference between bit and stylus causes the "under carving" to leave you excess wood for the next step. As the turntable with the plaster model is rotated, the block of wood rotates to the same degree, permitting all three dimensions of the plaster model to be traced by the stylus and duplicated.

Finishing The Carving. After roughing with the ¼" bit, a 1/32" bit is used to add detail (this time with a stylus of the same size and shape as the bit). Again, the stylus is used to trace the fine detail present in the plaster mold, which is automatically duplicated by the router. The result is a faithful copy in the wood selected (Figs. 7-5 through 7-8).

KURT DUPLICATING WOOD CARVERS

The Kurt Manufacturing Company (110) manufactures four styles of duplicating wood carvers: "Hobbi-Carver," "Kurt Star" carver, Kurt "North Star" carver and Kurt "Master" carver.

The "Hobbi-Carver" operates on a unique, two-level work area with a tracing stylus on the lower level and a cutting router on the top level. The three-dimensional object to be duplicated is placed on the lower level and is traced by the stylus. Corresponding cutting movements are performed by the router cutter on a wood work blank on the top level, thus insuring exact duplication of the work pattern (Fig. 7-9).

The "Kurt Star" carver handles full round 360° carvings up to 10" in diameter by 24" long and flat backed carvings 10" wide by 24" long by 5" thick. The two-spindle machine makes two copies of a pattern per load.

A very outstanding feature of the "Kurt Star" is that the spindles and stylus can be lifted forwards and backwards while running or they may be locked in tilted positions. This feature enables the carver to trace and carve details that cannot be readily traced in the conventional carving machines—such as undercuts. The tilting motor bar is a high quality, accurately machined aluminum casting which holds the two motors and the stylus in precisely built-in locations relative to each other. Work stations are easily added to the "Kurt Star" (Fig. 7-10).

The Kurt "North Star" carver can make up to eight duplicate carvings at one time. It will handle 360° as well as flat work. It has a capability of 72" length and up to 20" in diameter.

The operator simply fastens the pattern to be duplicated into the machine's tracing station. Wood work blanks are fastened in the carving stations, cutters are installed in the carving spindle chucks and a matching stylus is installed in the stylus holder. The operator then traces over the pattern detail with the stylus. Corresponding cutting operations are simultaneously and automatically performed

Fig. 7-5. Sculpturing with Dupli-Carver.

on the work blanks by the rotating cutters. Full 360° rotation of the pattern and blanks is easily accomplished through use of the center turning crank (Fig. 7-11).

The Kurt "Master" carver is designed especially for the mass production of carvings by the industrial user and furniture maker. The smallest "Master" carver is a four spindle machine and the

Fig. 7-6. Stages of sculpturing with Dupli-Carver.

241

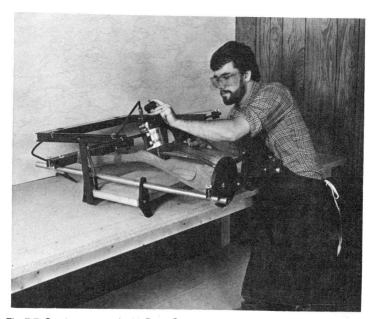

Fig. 7-7. Carving gun stock with Dupli-Carver.

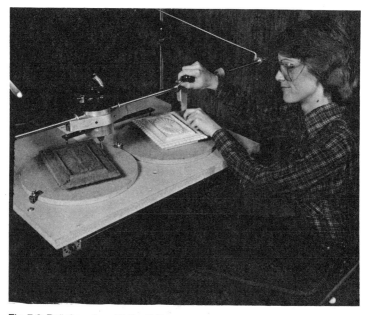

Fig. 7-8. Relief carving with Dupli-Carver.

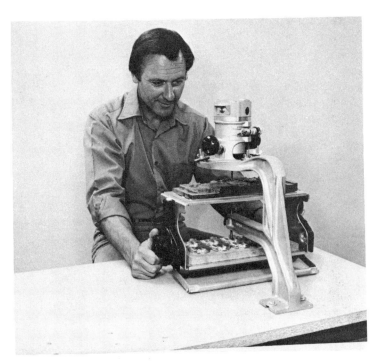

Fig. 7-9. Flat-Work "Hobbi-Carver."

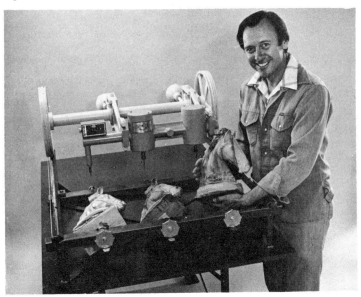

Fig. 7-10. "Kurt Star" carver.

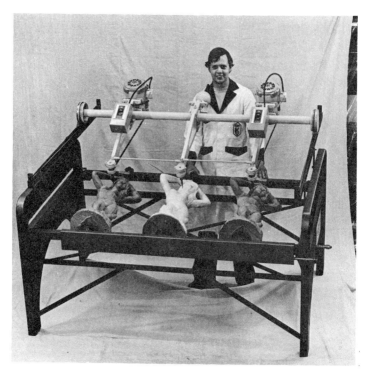

Fig. 7-11. Kurt "Northstar" carver.

largest is a 40 spindle machine. In between are 8, 12, 24, 30, 32 and 36 spindle machines (Fig. 7-12).

HAND CARVED WOOD SCULPTURES FROM BRAZIL

All Brazilians seem to have an innate ability to carve, even with very primitive tools. Figure 7-13 shows a few Brazilian hand carved pieces. From left to right are the following:

■ A *figa*, which is a good-luck charm similar to a rabbit's foot. Brazilians believe that if luck runs out for the owner, a red ribbon tied around the wrist will bring good luck back.

■ A Guarani Indian of southern Brazil. Considered to be much more civilized than their Amazon cousins.

■ A native Bahian (of the state of Bahia) noted for their tall and regal bearing. Very adept at carrying things on their heads.

■ A "caboclo," a backland farmer of mixed blood (Indian, Portuguese and Negro).

■ A smaller "caboclo."

244

WOOD SCULPTURING TOOLS AND THEIR USE

The two general categories of *adzes* are: the *single cutterhead* and the *double cutterhead*. Some double cutterheads are gouges but, more often, one head is a gouge and the other a flat cutter. On some the head is radiused from the eye to each edge to allow the carver to get the maximum bite into the wood. Some adze handles are curved for the same reason.

Sculptor's Adze

Some edges are at right angles and others are parallel to the handle. The cutting edges may be at right angles to each other on the same tool.

The sweep of gouge edge adzes varies from #3 to #8, and the weight ranges from about 10 ounces to four pounds. The cutting edges measure from 1⅛" to 3" in width.

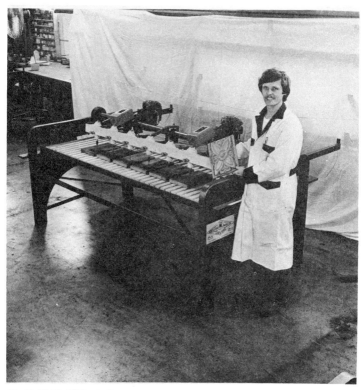

Fig. 7-12. Kurt "Master" carver.

Fig. 7-13. Hand carved sculptures from Brazil.

Some adzes are available in Sheffield and German steel. Adzes are used primarily to remove waste wood rapidly from the carving block.

Power Adze

Sculpture Associates (161) supplies a power driven adze called the *Super Hog-power adze*. It has a 5½″ diameter convex head with three adjustable blades. It is used to remove large chunks of wood rapidly with a minimum of effort, and works well even on end grain. It can be attached to most disc grinders and works at speeds from 2,500 to 8,000 rpm.

Pneumatic Hammer

The *pneumatic hammer* can be used with either wood or stone. This air-driven tool has only one moving part—the piston. The proper chisel or gouge is fitted into the tool, and air pressure forces the piston to strike the shank of the chisel or gouge, causing the cutting tool to penetrate the material being carved. Upon impact the air pressure is diverted, the piston moves back to its original position and the process is repeated. The shuttling of the piston takes place rapidly and automatically. This tool is supplied by Sculpture Associates (161).

Electromagnetic Sculpture Hammer

Sculpture House (162) has for sale a *Pow-R-Tron electromagnetic sculpture hammer* that is designed especially for carved sculpture applications.

The complete kit contains cable, safety goggles, one stone chisel, one metal chisel and one wood chisel. The Pow-R-Tron operates on 115 volts, 60 cycles of electricity.

European Gouges

The *European fish tail gouge*, furnished by Woodworker's Supply (211), has long been a favorite tool used in wood sculpture. It is used primarily for relief carving and background work.

Woodworker's Supply also handles the European *bent gouge*. It is used to remove large amounts of wood in forming concave surfaces. Made of the finest German steel, it is available in three sweeps (#3, #5 and #8) and in widths from 6 mm to 25 mm. All European bent gouges have a heavy, long, octagonal hardwood handle.

Marple's Wood Sculpture Tools

There are five tools to a set with an overall length of 10″. Handles are of a tough, resistant plastic. The set is comprised of: one quick fantail, 1″ gouge; one medium straight ⅝″ gouge; one slow straight ⅜″ gouge; one bent ⅝″ gouge and one ⅝″ skew chisel. All of Marple's tools are made of Sheffield steel. The supplier is Constantine (41).

Marple's Sculpture Gouges

Marple's sculpture gouges are available in two styles: out-cannelled (bevel on the outside of the curve) and in-cannelled (bevel on the inside bevel of the curve). These out-cannelled tools are used for deep cutting rough-in tools and the in-cannelled tools are used for vertical paring of curves and controlled finished cuts.

Both styles are available in six sizes: ¼″, ⅜″, ½″, ⅝″, ¾″ and 1″. These tools are available through Woodworker's Supply (211).

Sorby's Heavy Duty Sculptor's Gouges

Sorby's heavy duty sculptor's gouges are also available in in-cannelled and out-cannelled styles. The handles are durable beechwood and the blades are top-quality Sheffield steel. Sizes are ¼″, ½″, ⅝″, ¾″, 1″ and 1¼″. The supplier is Woodworker's Supply (211).

Sculptor's DeLuxe Carving Set

This very complete carving set contains 19 *KING BRAND* steel tools and a total of 26 items. These custom made steel tools and supplemental items are listed here: 1" fishtail chisel, 1" shallow long bent, ⅝" skew, ¼" chisel, 1" medium gouge, 1½" chisel, ⅝" medium gouge, ⅜" shallow gouge, ½" medium short bent, ¼" deep gouge, ¾" fishtail, 1" deep gouge, ⅝" deep gouge, ⅜" shallow short bent, 3/16" parting tool, ½" parting tool, wood carver's coarse rasp, three wood carving knives, two sharpening stones, one bottle rustproof oil, one can sharpening oil, one carver's adze, one mallet, wood carving book and sandpaper. This carving set, as well as many other carving tools, is available through Sculpture House (162).

Wood Sculpture Set

Greenless (91) has a five-piece set that includes the shapes and sizes most in demand by sculptors. With generous-sized handles of extra tough high impact polycarbonated plastic and "Greenlee Sheffield, England" etched on the blades, these tools are as beautiful as they are practical. The Greenlee five-piece set (other sets are available) has the following chisels and gouges: 1" "quick" fantail gouge, ⅜" "slow" straight gouge, ⅝" medium straight gouge, ⅝" bent gouge and ⅝" skew chisel.

The Fine Tool Shop (68) has a five-piece set with the same sizes and shapes as the Greenlee set.

Swiss Sculptor's Set

This six-tool package by Woodcraft Supply Corp. (204) will take the hard use necessary for roughing out a block and hold the razor edge vital to a clean, crisp surface straight from the tool. The set includes: 1-30 mm chisel, 1-30 mm skew chisel, 1-30 mm #5 sweep gouge, 1-30 mm #7 sweep bent gouge, 1-35 mm #9 sweep gouge, 1-20 mm #12 "V" parting tool, 1-30 ounce, 3½" head lignum vitae mallet and 1-six chisel and gouge carrying roll.

Flexible Shaft System

The secret of this very unique system is that *rotary motion* from a flexible shaft attached to a motor is converted to *reciprocating* action. This unusual piece of equipment by the Fine Tool Shop (68), in addition to a 60" flexible shaft and hand piece, has a ½" chisel blade, a 5/16" gouge blade, a ⅝" gouge blade, a ⅜" bent gouge blade and a ⅜" "V" parting tool.

SCRAPING TOOLS AND THEIR USE

Scrapers are used after a surface has been planed. They help smooth the wood and ready it for sanding. Scrapers are tools of necessity for the craftsman who works with hardwood.

Hand Scraper. The *hand scraper* is a thin, rectangular piece of flexible steel, varying in size from 2½″ by 5″ to 3″ by 6″. The Swedish cabinet scraper (2½″ x 5⅞″) is considered the best of the lot.

Handle Scraper. The *handle scraper* is a highly advertised commercial product that is held in rather low esteem by cabinet-makers. When in use it has two hooked cutting edges that can be reversed to form two more cutting edges. Blades are usually 2½″ wide. It is rather difficult to keep sharpened, although it is probably the most widely used of all scrapers by woodworkers other than cabinetmakers. These scrapers, sometimes called shave hooks, are fitted with handles that will scrape flat, convex, and concave surfaces and corners where other scrapers will not reach.

Cabinet Scraper. The *cabinet scraper* looks like an enlarged spokeshave. The blade is from 2½″ to 2¾″ wide. It is the finest scraper to use on flat surfaces. Due to its solid frame, handles and an established angle, more pressure can be exerted on the blade, thus providing faster cutting. It is a good investment for the home craftsman.

Scraping Plane. The scraping tool is especially suited for smoothing large areas of solid wood or veneer. This place eliminates burned fingers, as well as the chance of digging in on soft grain. It uses a 2¾″ blade, and the blade can be adjusted for different angles.

Hoe Type Scraper. This scraper has a long handle like the handles on lathe chisels. It has a swivel type head and the blade can be adjusted to different angles. The blade sticks out in front so it can be used in corners that other scrapers cannot reach.

Swanneck Scraper. The *swanneck scraper* has many curves of different radii similar to a French curve used in mechanical drafting. It can be used to scrape moldings or such concave surfaces as the bottom of a bowl or tray.

Sharpening a Hand Scraper

Draw file the edge with a flat mill file at 90° to the two surfaces of the scraper. A machinist vise is used to hold the blade, and the file is used in a horizontal position. Remove the file marks by stroking the edges on a stone.

Burnish the edges with a *burnisher*. Start the burnisher in a horizontal position and on each stroke raise the handle slightly. Continue burnishing until an angle of 80° to 85° is reached.

Turn the scraper around in the vise and use the burnisher for the other edge in the same way. The scraping hook produced by the burnisher may be re-established a number of times before the scraper will need refiling.

Sharpening Cabinet Scrapers

Remove the old burr on the flat side of the scraper with the file. Little pressure should be used.

Straighten the edge of the blade if it needs it. File the beveled edge with a flat mill file at an angle of 30° to 40°. File only on the forward stroke and do not drag the file backward over the edge. Continue filing until a burr (wire edge) has been formed on the flat side of the scraper opposite the beveled edge.

Remove the scraper from the vise and hone that beveled edge on a fine oilstone. Turn the scraper over and hone the flat side of the scraper.

Place the scraper back in the vise and start burnishing at about the same angle that was filed on the bevel side. At each stroke across the edge, raise the handle a few degrees until the burnisher is in a horizontal position at right angles to the two faces of the scraper. This process should leave a hook or scraping burr on the scraper.

Using the Hand Scraper

Both hands are used with the hand scraper. It can be either pushed or pulled. The hand scraper is not designed for heavy scraping. If the scraper produces fine sawdust instead of fine, thin, silky shavings, the scraper is dull or it has not been properly sharpened. Several burnishings may be done before it is necessary to file and hone the edges again.

Using Other Scrapers

Cabinet scrapers and scraper planes are generally pushed. The handle scrapers and hoe type scrapers are usually pulled. The swanneck scraper can be either pushed or pulled. If the blade is held at a slight angle, askew to the direction of the cross-grained woods, it will cut better and will hold its edge longer.

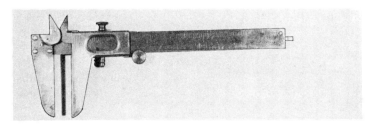

Fig. 7-14. Vernier calipers.

Scrapers are used on cross-grain hardwood or other uniquely grained woods (knotty wood, burl wood, birds-eye maple, and wavy or curly grained woods) and all types of veneer.

The home craftsman who works with hardwoods can hardly do without a scraper. Some woods are impossible to plane smooth.

MISCELLANEOUS WOODWORKING TOOLS

The *profile contour transfer* reproduces contours of irregular shaped objects and eliminates the guesswork by simply pressing one edge against the part to be matched. The 185 spring steel tracer pins automatically match the shape. It is ideal for checking multiple small turnings and a real time saver. Brookstone (32).

Spring-Loaded Center Punch. The spring-loaded center punch makes uniform impressions automatically. There is no need to use a hammer with this center punch. Simply place the point in the desired position and press the handle down. A self-contained hammer mechanism automatically strikes and releases. There is an adjustment screw for light to heavy impressions. Brookstone (32).

Pantograph. The *pantograph* resizes drawings, plans and pictures. This tool reduces or enlarges from one-tenth to 10 times the original size. Brookstone (32).

Honer Guide. This tool makes it simple to sharpen plane irons and chisels. Constant correct angles and square edges are consistently honed. Brookstone (32).

Stanely Combination Layout Tool. This tool is a level, a try square, a miter square, a protractor, a depth gauge, a beam compass, a screw gauge and a scribe. U. S. General Supply (187).

Trammel Head. This device is used for laying out distances between two points or for scribing arcs and circles that are beyond the capacity of a divider. Woodcraft Supply (204).

Rifflers. Rifflers are file-like tools used by wood sculptors, wood carvers and miniaturists. There are many shapes available but the most commonly used are round, flat, square, triangular and half-round. Woodcraft Supply (204).

Baby Sander. This power sander only weighs 4 pounds and takes a 1⅛″ x 21″ sanding belt. The Fine Tool Shop (68).

Vernier. The *vernier calipers* measure in 1/1000″ and 1/10 mm and have a depth gauge that can be read directly on the vernier. Woodworker's Supply (211). The vernier calipers in Fig. 7-14 measure only to 1/128″.

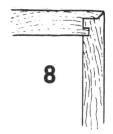

8

Abrasives and Their Use

There are two large categories of coated abrasives: *natural* and *manufactured*. First, let's examine natural abrasives.

NATURAL ABRASIVES

Flint abrasive papers are creamy in color and are of poor quality and durability. Coated abrasives are often incorrectly called sandpaper. Flint is a mined product with the chemical name of silicon dioxide. Flint abrasive paper, the oldest of the so-called "sandpapers," is seldom used because of the development of much higher quality abrasive papers. It is still used occasionally to remove old finishing materials where the clogging of the grit would ruin the more expensive papers.

Garnet, a red mineral found in nature, is probably the best all-round abrasive for the woodworker. Garnet in certain sizes and quality is considered a semi-precious stone and is used in jewelry. Garnet paper is used extensively in the furniture industry because of its lasting qualities and low cost when compared with other similar papers.

Emery, a natural abrasive, is a grey or black mineral. Although extremely hard, its edges are easily dulled. It is used primarily to polish or remove metal. It is often used with some kind of lubricant. It is more often found in the cloth form than in the paper form. Emery cloth is seldom, if ever, used on wood. The home craftsman might well have some on hand to polish up metal tools.

MANUFACTURED ABRASIVES

Aluminum oxide, a tan to brown color, is made in an electric furnace at high temperature. The main ingredient is *bauxite* (a claylike mineral consisting of hydrated aluminum oxide or aluminum ore). Other ingredients such as salt (a flux to bind materials together), sawdust (to burn off the wate materials), sand, coke, iron fillings and *titania* (a deoxidizer) are used, in whole or in part, to impart certain characteristics to the abrasive.

Although aluminum oxide is much harder than garnet, it does not mean that it is better than garnet as a woodworking tool, particularly on the softer woods. Garnet not only is less apt to burn the wood, but in general it is more economical.

Silicon carbide is the hardest of the abrasives. Dark green to black in color, it has grains that are extremely sharp and triangular in shape. Silicon carbide abrasives are seldom used in the coarser grits, but are used extensively in the finer grades for rubbing finishes such as lacquers and varnishes. They are commonly identified as wet-o-dry abrasive papers.

ABRASIVE BACKINGS

Here are some types of paper backing:

■ "A" weight (40 pound paper) is used principally for finishing.

■ "C" weight (70 pound paper) is used when strength and some pliability is required.

■ "D" weight (100 pound paper) is used for medium and coarse grit numbers.

■ "E" weight (130 pound paper) is used for rolls, belts and very coarse grit numbers of sheet abrasive paper.

The following is a list of kinds of cloth backing:

■ "X" grade is used for all ordinary machine sanding operations.

■ "J" grade, a lighter weight and more flexible cloth, is used where flexibility is more important than work value or volume. It is used extensively with the stroke belt sander for sanding contoured moldings.

GRIT SIZE NUMBERS

The grit size numbers in the new system indicate the number of holes per square inch of screen used to sort the grains of abrasive into individual sizes. In the new system the larger the number, the finer the sandpaper. In the old system, the grain size became smaller as the number of 0s increased. See Table 8-1.

HARDNESS AND TOUGHNESS OF ABRASIVES

Lyle Laske, with some assistance from 3M Company and Norton Company, prepared an interesting and enlightening article entitled "Some Abrasive Facts" for the March/April 1980 issue of *Fine Woodworking*. The second paragraph of the article is quoted here.

"Abrasive hardness is routinely measured on two scales. The Mohs scale runs from 1 (talc) to 10 (diamond). Ratings are determined by abrading a soft mineral with a harder one; they do not indicate equal or proportional differences. The Knoop scale, which goes from 1 to 8500 determined with a pressure indenter, more accurately measures the proportional hardness of minerals. Toughness, which differs from hardness, is determined by a ball-mill test: rotating a given grit in a steel drum with steel balls for a standard period of time and noting how much of the grit survives at the original size."

Table 8-2 is the result of information supplied by Laske in the article.

ABRASIVE PAPER AND CLOTH

Garnet cabinet paper comes in standard sheets 9″ x 11″. The 100, 120, and 150 grits are sold in packages of 100; all other grits are sold in packages of 50. See Table 8-3.

Table 8-1. Grit Size Classification.

Type	Old System	New System
Very Coarse	2	36
	1 1/2	40
	1	50
Coarse	1/2	60
	0	80
	2/0	100
	3/0	120
	4/0	150
Fine	5/0	180
	6/0	220
	7/0	240
	8/0	280
Very Fine	9/0	320
	10/0	400
		500
		600

Table 8-2. Information on Hardness and Toughness of Abrasives.

Toughness (Percentages)	Moh's Hardness Scale	Knoop's Hardness Scale
	Diamond 10	8500
55%	Silicon Carbide 9.6	2480
75%	Aluminum Oxide 9.4	2050
80%	Emery 8.5 to 9.0	1750
60%	Garnet 7.5 to 8.5	1360
20%	Flint 6.8 to 7.0	820

Garnet Finishing Paper. Standard sheets 9″ x 11″. Grit numbers 100, 120, 150, 180, 220, 240 and 280 sold only in packages of 100.

Aluminum Oxide Open Coat Paper. Standard sheets 9″ x 11″. Grit numbers 36, 40, 50, 60 and 80 sold in lots of 50. Grit numbers 100, 120, 150 and 220 sold in lots of 100.

Flint Paper (Common Sandpaper For Hand Sanding Only). Standard sheets 9″ x 11″. See Table 8-4.

Silicon Carbide Waterproof Finishing Paper (For Rubbing Lacquer, Varnish, Enamel And Other Finishes). Standard sheet 9″ x 11″. Can be used either wet or dry. Grit numbers are 60, 80, 100, 120, 150, 180, 220, 240, 280, 320, 360, 400, 500 and 600.

Aluminum Oxide Open Coat Oscillating Sander Sheets. Size 3⅔″ x 9″, available in grit numbers 50, 60, 80, 100, 120 and 140. Size 3′ x 8″, available only in 40, 60 and 80 grit numbers.

Aluminum Oxide Belts. Sizes vary in a wide range from 2″ x 21″ to 6″ x 60″. Belts are available in grit sizes 36, 40, 50, 60, 80, 100 and 120.

Table 8-3. Garnet cabinet Paper Grit Size Numbers.

Old Number	New Number
2	36
1 1/2	40
1	50
1/2	60
0	80
2/0	100
3/0	120
4/0	150

Aluminum Oxide Rolls. Aluminum oxide rolls are 50 yards long and available with paper or cloth backing. Widths are 4″ and 6″. Grit sizes are the same as for the aluminum oxide belts.

Abrasive Sleeves. Abrasive sleeves vary in diameter from ½″ to 3″ and in length from 1″ to 9″. Belts are made of both paper and cloth and are available in garnet and aluminum oxide. Grit sizes are 40, 50, 60 and 80.

Aluminum Oxide, Pressure-Sensitive Adhesive Discs. These open coat discs prevent loading and insure long life. May be purchased in 5″ and 6″ diameters. Grit sizes are: 80, 100, 120, 150, 180, 220, 240, 280 and 320, all with "A" backing.

ABRASIVE ADHESIVES

Two methods are used to adhere grains of adhesives to the backing: *electrostatic electricity* and *gravity*. The backing is first coated with *resin* glue or *animal hide* glue. In the electrostatic process the electrical field causes the sharp ends of the abrasive grains to face outward.

Many times a second coat of resin or glue is applied after the abrasive and the first coat have dried. Animal hide glue as an adhesive has serious drawbacks. It is a hydroscopic material and during humid weather tends to pick up enough moisture to soften the bond, with poorer sanding quality the result. Naturally, animal glue bonds cannot be used for operations requiring water as a lubricant in sanding.

FACTORS AFFECTING THE QUALITY OF A SANDED WOOD SURFACE

In accepted sanding techniques, a satisfactory surface is one obtained by the removal of all visible blemishes, including machine marks, clamp marks, dents, fuzziness, surface spots and scratches. This is usually accomplished by the use of a sequence of successively finer grits, each one in turn reducing the magnitude of the scratches produced by the preceding grit. The quality of the sanded surface is often predetermined by the quality of the

Table 8-4. Grit Information for Flint Paper.

Grit	Sold In Packages of
Extra Coarse	50
Coarse	50
Medium	100
Fine	100
Extra Fine	100

subsequent finish application or the selling price of the finish product. In all cases, whatever clear finish is applied to a sanded surface does not serve to mask defective sanding. Rather, the finish will tend to increase the apparent magnitude of the defect.

The quality of a sanded surface is either directly or indirectly affected by several factors, which can conveniently be divided into two groups: those determined by the *abrasives* and their application and those pertaining to the *wood* itself. Among the most important of the first group are: abrasive mineral, backing for abrasive, bonding used, type of coating, size of abrasive particles, pressures used in sanding, type and condition of sanding machine and speed of abrasive.

The second group contains such factors as: the moisture content of the wood, the species being sanded, the alignment of the wood elements with respect to the surface being sanded, the direction of travel of the abrasive with respect to the alignment of the wood elements, and the type and arrangement of the wood elements. The factors in group two are of prime importance because they are not as easily controlled as those in group one.

The cutting action of an abrasive particle is somewhat different from the cutting action of normal wood machining tools. Actually, wood particles are removed by a pushing action. The grit particles no doubt press downward proportionately as much as they push sideways to remove stock. Downward pressure tends to push down or crush the walls of the wood cells, particularly where the cell is cut at an angle, and the result is a thin or feather edge. The action is decidedly different from cutting with a sharp knife. Considerable surface heat is generated at the time of abrasive contact of the grit with the wood. This heat, in conjunction with abrasive action, no doubt deforms the cell walls and "sets" them in a down position. Subsequently, moisture or certain solvents used in stands will tend to swell the deformed cells and restore them to their original shape. This creates raised grain, either before staining (by exposure to humid atmosphere) or by action of the stain solvent. If the stain does not raise the grain, these crushed cells will tend to inhibit the proper penetration of the filler, with resultant trapping of air and solvent in the pores. This will lead to pinholing of the finish coat in later finish applications.

If the wood fibers or cells were stiffened by artificial means before sanding, they will break off more cleanly, thus minimizing the tendency toward raised grain. This is accomplished in industry by "sizing" the wood prior to final polishing. The "sizing" used may be shellac, dextrin, or more usually a thin solution of animal hide glue. Sizing may be done following drum sanding or between first and second belt sanding operations. Sizes are applied by various means: spraying, sponging, brushing, roller coating and dipping being the most common. This method adds somewhat to the final cost of the product, but that fact is normally offset by proportionate increase in quality of finish appearance and slightly easier sanding in the "white". See Chapter 10 for additional information on "sizing" and subsequent finishing operations.

USING ABRASIVES

Sandpaper is generally available to the home craftsman in sheets 9" x 11". The sheet should be torn (over the edge of an old saw blade or over the corner of the table of a circular saw) into four equal parts.

Sanding a Flat Surface

A sandpaper block of appropriate size can be made of scrap wood. It should be 1½" to 1¾" thick and the working face should be covered with a cushiony material such as felt, rubber, foam rubber or leather. Some commercial blocks are made entirely of rubber. An old blackboard eraser makes a fair sanding block, although a little too soft. Fold and crease the sandpaper where the corners of the working face of block are located. Some pieces of wood of the appropriate size may be secured in a vise or anchored to a flat surface with clamps.

Grip the sandpaper and the block with the thumb on the left side and the little finger on the right. The remaining fingers apply pressure to the top of the block.

Very small pieces are sanded by rubbing the pieces over a full sheet of sandpaper laid on a flat surface, or held against the belt of an upside-down portable belt sander (Fig. 8-1).

Sand the entire surface with the same number of strokes and pressure, unless it is necessary to remove a particular blemish. Remove the sanding dust from time to time during sanding in order to inspect the surface. *Never* sand across the grain.

Start with coarse sandpaper and end with fine sandpaper. As a general rule, never skip more than three grit sizes in moving from coarse to fine sandpaper. Do not sand too close to the edge of the stock or the edge may be rolled. At least one half of the sandpaper block should be over the face of stock at all times. *Never* sand surfaces that are to be glued.

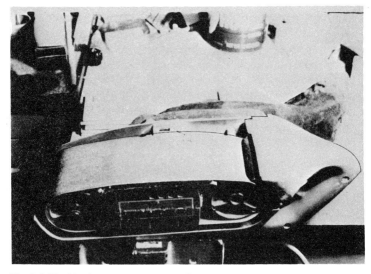

Fig. 8-1. Upside-down portable belt sander.

Sanding An Edge

Sanding an edge, particularly if it is a narrow one, is not an easy operation. After placing stock in a vise, with the edge to be sanded in the up position, take the sanding block in both hands. Let at least one finger of each hand slide along the two surfaces at right angles to the edge being sanded. The fingers act as guides to keep the sanding block square with the sides.

Sanding Convex Surfaces

The sandpaper and the fingers are all that are needed when sanding small convex surfaces found on moldings or molded edges. Large convex edges and surfaces are sanded in the same manner as flat edges and surfaces.

When sanding thin (⅜″ or less) edges on convex surfaces, fold the sandpaper and bend it over the two ends of the thumbs as they are placed together. Hold the sandpaper with the thumbs and index fingers. Sand the convex edge with the major pressure on the center of the edge being sanded. The outside edges will take care of themselves.

Sanding Concave Surfaces or Edges

Place the sandpaper over a cylindrical object. A piece of dowel works fine for smaller curves. The diameter of the cylinder must be somewhat smaller than the diameter of the concave surface or edge.

POWER SANDERS AND THEIR USE

The *portable belt sander* is a valuable tool for the home shop worker. Most portable belt sanders are equipped with their own dust collectors. Belts are usually 21″ or 24″ long and 3″ wide; however, belts are available in 2″ to 4″ widths.

Portable Belt Sanders

Usually a spring-tensioned lever allows belts to be changed easily. Each belt has a mark indicating the direction of the rotation, and this instruction should be followed. After changing a belt, it must be centered while running. All portable belt sanders are equipped with a centering device. The belt should never be allowed to rub against the metal parts of the sander. It will rapidly cut into the metal parts—usually of aluminum—and the belt will be harmed. Here are a few suggestions and precautions.

■ Keep the electric cord away from the sander.
■ Hold the sander firmly with both hands.
■ Be sure the belt is revolving in the right direction.
■ Keep the sander moving, particularly if the belt is a coarse grit; otherwise, a depression will be formed in the wood.
■ Allow the heel of the sander to touch the wood first.
■ Move the sander in a straight line.
■ Empty the dust bag from time to time
■ Never pick up the sander by the electrical cord.

According to Rick Silverman of East Calais, Vermont, and reported in the January/February issue of *Fine Woodworking* , 3M resin-bond closed-coat belts are the best. Although the initial cost is greater, in the long run they are less expensive because of their longer life.

A portable belt sander with a low center of gravity is always superior to centers that are higher. It is much more stable and will prevent rocking and gouging. The controls for changing belts and center tracking are up in front for easy accessibility. This 3″ x 24″ sander runs at 1200 surface feet per minute. This ¾ hp machine has a dust collector bag that is easily removed, emptied and replaced (Figs. 8-2 and 8-3).

Portable Finishing Sanders

Finishing sanders are used for two purposes: for final sanding of wood before finish is applied, and for sanding of finishing coats

Fig. 8-2. 3″ x 24″ dust collecting, low center of gravity, portable belt sander.

such as lacquer, varnish and enamels. Only fine grit sandpaper is used on portable finishing sanders.

There are two types of portable finishing sanders: the *oscillating* or straight-line sanders and the *orbital* type. The oscillating sander moves back and forth in the same manner as hand sanding, while the orbital sander revolves in a ⅛″, 3/16″ or ¼″ diameter circular motion.

There is considerable controversy concerning the two types of sanders. Proponents of the orbital type contend that this type works faster and better, and that the fault appears when too coarse a sandpaper is used.

Advocates of the oscillating type claim that this type sands work as it should be sanded—with the grain. I am inclined to support the oscillating type because industry seldom, if ever, uses the orbital type. The woodworking and furniture industries use air powered straight-line action sanders which are light in weight and do not overheat as electrical sanders. Many of these air powered sanders have two pads which oscillate in opposite directions.

The Black and Decker dual action all-purpose finishing sander is unique in that it is both an orbital and oscillating sander. This ⅓ hp tool has a built-in fan and a dust collector. It uses half of a standard sheet of abrasive (Fig. 8-4).

Disc Sanders

A *disc sander* consists of a revolving wheel to which a disc of sandpaper is mounted, and both are powered by a motor. Most disc sanders have an adjustable table that tilts at different angles in reference to the wheel. The table often has a slot into which a miter gauge may be placed.

Some abrasive discs have pressure-sensitive adhesive backs for easy application. Other discs are applied with a disc cement. The cement remains tacky so that discs can be replaced several times with one application of cement.

Edward A. Lenz of Saratoga Springs, NY states that old fashioned water glass is a good sandpaper disc adhesive. He got the tip from an old cabinetmaker and reported his findings in the Nov./Dec. 1979 issue of *Fine Woodworking*.

The primary function of the disc sander is to sand the edges and ends of stock. The operator should avoid having the work touched by the back half of the disc because this can lead to troubles. The work should be constantly moved to prevent burns and the wearing out of the sandpaper disc in one place. Special jigs and patterns may be devised for sanding multiple parts (Fig. 8-5).

There are portable disc sanders, but their use for woodworking is very limited. There are many disc sander attachments that

Fig. 8-3. Portable belt sander in action.

Fig. 8-4. 1/3 hp dual action finishing sander.

may be purchased or made to be used in conjunction with other woodworking power tools such as lathes, circular saws, drill presses, etc.

Combination Disc and Belt Sanders

Rockwell International (155) manufactures a 6″ belt and 12″ disc combination sander with an optional dust collector attachment. It has two tilting tables with a miter gauge slot and is powered by a 1½ hp motor.

American Machine and Tool (5) manufactures an inexpensive combination disc and belt sander. This versatile tool can be adjusted to be a horizontal or vertical belt sander. Relatively accurate sanding work can be done with the disc sander attachment along with the miter gauge available with it.

The outboard end of the drive shaft with the disc sander removed is adaptable to grinding, wire brushing, drum sanding and other odd and less common requirements. This cast iron and cast aluminum power tool uses 6″ diameter sanding discs and 4″ x 36″ sanding belts. This machine is only partially assembled when delivered (Fig. 8-6).

Powermatic Houdaille (147) builds two models of the combination disc and belt sander—Model 30 and Model 30-A. Model

264

30-A has a built-in dust collector which is optional equipment on Model 30.

Both models are of rugged cast iron construction which virtually eliminates vibration of all contour, angle and flat sanding jobs. Both models have optional miter attachments for straight and angle sanding. The end guard swings away to permit convenient

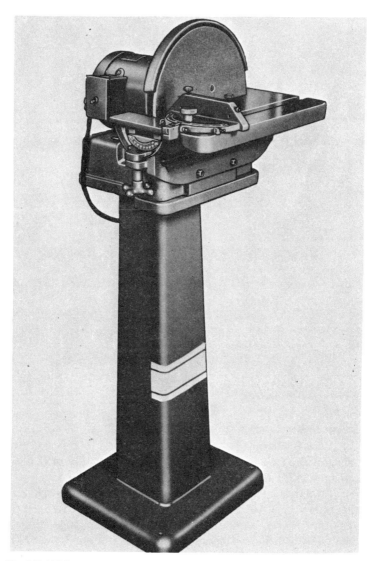

Fig. 8-5. 12″ disc sander, Model 35.

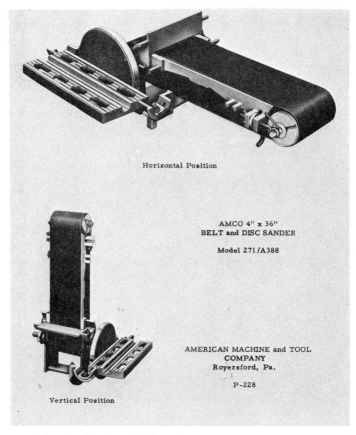

Horizontal Position

AMCO 4" x 36"
BELT and DISC SANDER

Model 271/A388

AMERICAN MACHINE and TOOL
COMPANY
Royersford, Pa.

P-228

Vertical Position

Fig. 8-6. Combination disc and belt sander.

contour sanding. There are removable tilting tables (15° up, 45° down) that can be used with either the disc or belt sander (Figs. 8-7 and 8-8).

Stationary Belt Sanders

Rockwell International (155) manufactures a 6" stationary belt sander with a table fitted with a miter gauge groove. The table tilts 20° up and 45° down. One model is fitted with a dust collector.

Powermatic Houdaille (147) makes a 6" stationary belt sander that operates in four positions from horizontal to vertical. The ample titling table is slotted for an accurate miter gauge attachment. The table tilts and locks at any angle from 0° to 45° out or 15° in. All moving parts are well guarded except the actual working surface (Fig. 8-9).

Combination Disc and Belt Sander/Grinder

Foley's 311 combination disc and belt sander/grinder is a woodworking and metalworking tool. In addition to sanding wood, it is used to sharpen scissors, knives, axes, saw blades, garden tools, lawn mower blades, chisels—most anything. The disc is 8" in diameter and the sanding belt is 1" x 42" (Fig. 8-10).

Belt Sander/Grinder

The Belsaw (21) belt sander/grinder is similar to the Foley combination disc and belt sander/grinder, but it does not have the disc sander. Although designed for tool sharpening, it can be used effectively for sanding wood (Fig. 8-11).

Sanding Wheels

There are two large categories of *sanding wheels*: the *loose-flap* wheels and the *brush* type wheel. The loose-flap wheels consist of narrow strips of abrasive (aluminum oxide or garnet) closely clustered together.

Fig. 8-7. Combination disc and belt sander, Model 30.

Fig. 8-8. Combination belt and disc sander, Model 30-A, with dust collector.

The brush type wheel has a number of inserts around the perimeter of a wheel into which brushes are located to back up the abrasive strips. The brush type wheel is generally considered to be the better wheel.

The Sand-O-Flex wheels supplied by Merit Abrasive Products (123) are one of the most popular and widely used brush type wheels. The center of the Sand-O-Flex is filled with a large roll of adhesive strips, which give many hours of sanding. Simply turning the index knob feeds out new abrasive strips as needed. As the abrasive wears, the ends are cut off. The abrasive strips extend out beyond the brush backup.

There are two sizes of Sand-O-Flex wheels. The 6″ diameter wheel has eight brushes and uses 1″ wide abrasive strips. The 4½″ diameter wheel has six brushes and ¾″ wide abrasive strips.

The firm, cushioning brush bristles force the abrasive strips into, around and over corners, hollow and fluted surfaces and small openings.

Replacement abrasive refills are available in slashed or plain types. The ⅛″ slashed type is for moldings, flutes and irregular shapes while the plain type is for flat or mildly contoured surfaces.

Grits are extra coarse, coarse, medium and fine. All refills are made of aluminum oxide cloth.

Fig. 8-9. Stationary 6″ belt sander, Model 33.

Fig. 8-10. Combination disc and sander/grinder, Model 311.

Drum Sanders

Drum sanders are of two types: *pneumatic* and *solid*. Pneumatic drum sanders, which are filled with compressed air, are the most widely used. The soft, cushiony surfaces allow them to conform to curved and irregular surfaces. The drums are inflated after the abrasive sleeves are fitted to the drums. The air pressure in the drums can vary from high to low depending on the use to which the drum is put.

Conover (40) builds a ½ hp drum sander which is easily mounted on a bench. Both drums are 9½″ long. The smaller is for 3″ diameter abrasives and the larger takes 4½″ sleeves. This

Fig. 8-11. Belt sander/grinder.

Fig. 8-12. ½ hp air wheel (inflated drum) sander.

rugged machine sands both concave and convex shapes with equal ease (Fig. 8-12).

Sand-Rite Mfg. Co. (159) manufactures an all-purpose, double-end pneumatic drum sander. The Sand-Rite sanders are unlimited in their use in the woodworking field. Inflation is regulated through an air valve mounted on the end of the drum and can be fully controlled to provide the right contour to fit the part being sanded. The pneumatic tube is protected by a canvas jacket over which the abrasive sleeve is mounted.

Pneumatic drums are available in 2″, 3″, 4″, 6″ and 8″ diameters and 7″ or 9″ widths. Abrasives sleeves for the Sand-Rite come in grits from 60 to 150 in resin-bond garnet cloth. The Sand-Rite can also be used with brush-back sanding wheels and abrasive discs (Fig. 8-13).

Singley Specialty Co. (166) makes a non-pneumatic, sleeve-less drum sander which eliminates expensive abrasive sleeves by utilizing standard 9″ x 11″ abrasive sheets. The sandpaper is cut to size. The sizes of cylinders are 1″ diameter by 3″ long, 2″ diameter and 3″ long, 2½″ diameter by 3″ long, and 3″ diameter by 3″ long. Paper is cut so that the ends are inserted into a slot in the cylinder and locked in place by an oval aluminum tube, which presses

272

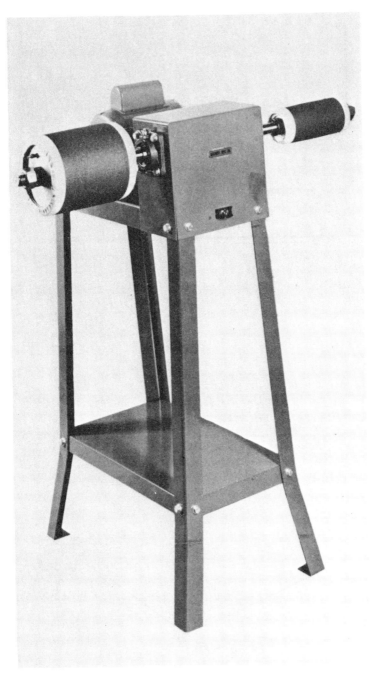

Fig. 8-13. Double-end drum sander.

Fig. 8-14. Adjusting leaves on profile sanding block.

against the ends of the paper in a slot the length of the cylinder. These cylinders may be used in a drill press, lathe, ¼″ electric drill or on the end of a small motor.

Bob Pavey, of Western Springs, Illinois, gives instructions on how to make your own pneumatic drum sander in the March/April 1980 issue of *Fine Woodworking*. In the same issue Harland Smith of Waterloo, Iowa, explains how to make your own lathe sanding drum.

Spindle Sanders

The *spindle sander* operates in a vertical position through a hole in a table. Its unique oscillating-rotating action works well on inside and outside contours. Spindles range in diameter from ¼″ to 3″ and up to 9″ above the table. The large table can be tilted in both directions.

Hand Stroke Belt Sanders

The *hand stroke belt sanders* consist of two wide pulleys, separated some distance apart, over which a wide abrasive belt travels. The height of the table is adjustable. Cross bars on the table prevent the work from slipping when pressure is applied to the belt. Many times adjustable profile sanding blocks are used with the hand stroke belt sander to sand contoured moldings (Figs. 8-14 and 8-15).

McCall House (117) furnishes kits and plans for making your own hand stroke sander. The kit includes a 6″ x 190″ sandbelt, rubber-covered pulley, arbor, graphite-covered sanding block, bolts, T-nuts, cranks, ball-bearing guides for the table to roll in and out, and a fully assembled head including tension, tracking, ball bearings, shaft and rubber covered pulley.

Fig. 8-15. Profile sanding block used with belt sander.

Fig. 8-16 Belt sander for round stock.

M. G. ReKoff, Jr., provides full instructions and drawings for building your own hand stroke belt sander that will accommodate a 30″ by 70″ workpiece without repositioning in *Fine Woodworking Techniques*.

Belt Sander for Round Stock

This unique, specialized sander is used primarily by woodworking industries. See Fig. 8-16.

Thickness Sander

T. R. Warbey describes how he made a low-cost thickness planer that handles stock down to 0.040″. Plywood discs are glued together and mounted on a steel shaft. For complete details, see the March/April 1980 issue of *Fine Woodworking*.

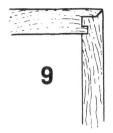

9

Construction and Assembly

This chapter concerns those items that lead up to the preparation for finishing and the finishing process. Included will be basic construction, including joints and carcass construction; adhesives and gluing; clamping and holding devices; and repairing defects and preparing for finish.

Many of the above processes have been covered to some extent in previous chapters. These items will be expanded and further clarified. Very little duplication will take place.

JOINTS

In Chapter 3 a number of joints and cuts were covered. These will not be repeated except to expand on previous information or special treatment of these joints. These joints and cuts are miter joints, rabbet joints, gain and blind dado, tenons (with reversed dado head), the difference between the dado and the groove, and the cutting of a Queen Anne leg.

In Chapter 4 drilling, boring, mortising, tenoning and routing tools and their uses, the blind mortise and tenon, the through mortise and tenon, the haunched mortise and tenon, and how to lay out tenons were covered in considerable detail.

Butt Joint. The *butt joint* is one of the easiest joints to make since butting one member against another and fastening with glue, nails, brads, screws or other fasteners is all that is necessary. However, the butt joint is the weakest joint and should be avoided if strength is a factor. Butt joints must be square and straight. See Fig. 9-1.

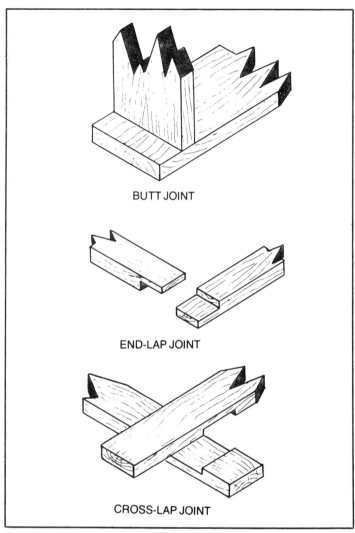

Fig. 9-1. Butt, end-lap and cross-lap joints.

End-Lap Joint. An *end-lap joint* is used on corners where a joint stronger than a butt joint is needed. There are, however, many joints that are much stronger and should always be considered when making a corner joint. See Fig. 9-1.

Cross-Lap Joint. This joint is used a great deal in furniture making and is stronger than either the butt joint or end-lap joint. The *cross-lap joint* is used in joining the faces of two members. See Fig. 9-1.

Edge-Lap Joint. An *edge-lap joint* is similar to the cross-lap joint except the edges are joined together rather than the faces. It is a strong joint and needs only glue and clamping for assembly. See Fig. 9-2.

Middle-Lap Joint. This joint is used when the end of one member is fitted into the middle of another member. See Fig. 9-2.

Half-Lap Joint. The *half-lap joint* is often used when it is necessary to make a long piece from two shorter ones. It should be noted in the construction of the lap joints that half of the thickness

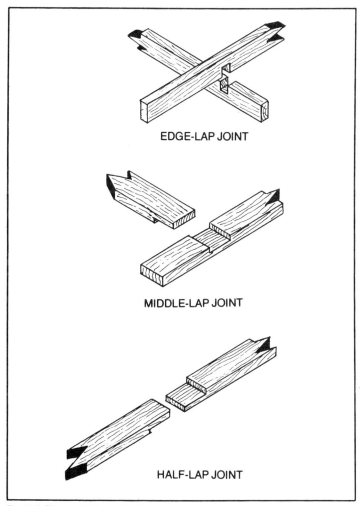

EDGE-LAP JOINT

MIDDLE-LAP JOINT

HALF-LAP JOINT

Fig. 9-2. Edge, middle and half-lap joints.

of the stock is cut away in both members. As a result, the final joint is only as thick as one of the members. See Fig. 9-2.

Mitered Joints. Mitered joints can be divided into two categories: *frame* miters and *corner* miters. Frame miters are right angle miters with each component cut at a 45° angle. The major objective of mitering members is to *cover end grain*.

The frame miter—as the name suggests—is used for making picture frames or other display frames. It is also used in applying moldings to furniture and other woodworking projects. Carpenters often use the frame miter joint in applying trim around windows and doors.

Butt Miter Joint. The *butt miter joint* is the weakest of the frame miters. By using proper metal fasteners and a good glue, it can be converted into a fairly substantial joint. See Fig. 9-3.

Spline Miter Joint. This joint is a strong, sturdy joint that will take a lot of abuse. The combined depth of the two spline slots should be slightly greater than the width of the spline. The grain of the wood should be *across the width* of the spline, not longitudinally. Sometimes thin plywood or other materials are used for splines, which eliminates the problem of grain directions. See Fig. 9-3.

Dowel Miter. A good frame miter joint, but it is often difficult to get the members and dowels to line up correctly without the use of jigs or special devices. See Fig. 9-3.

End-Lap Miter. The *end-lap miter joint* is seldom used for frame construction. It is time-consuming to make and some end grain is left exposed. See Fig. 9-3.

Feather Miter. The *feather miter joint* is almost as strong as the spline miter. The grain of the "feather" should be parallel to the 45° cut. See Fig. 9-3. Corner miters are used in cabinets, boxes and chests. Again, the joint is designed to cover up end grain.

Block Miter. The *block miter joint* is the simplest of all corner miters to make, and it can be a strong joint if properly made. Hot animal glue is applied to two sides of the block and rubbed into place. No nails, brads or screws should be used to hold "rubbed glue" joints. See Fig. 9-4.

Spline Miter. A *spline miter joint* is probably the most popular and most used of the corner miter joints. Careful and precise machine setup is a must in order that all members line up correctly. Again, the spline should be cross grain and the width should be slightly less than the combined depth of the two slots. See Fig. 9-4.

Lock Miter. The *lock miter joint* is a little complicated to make, but it does have the distinct advantage of only requiring clamping in one direction. See Fig. 9-4.

Shaped Lock Miter. The *shaped lock miter* is a double-tongue, symmetrical joint made with a special designed cutter to be used with the shaper or router. Only one cutter is required. One member is run through the shaper in a horizontal position while the other member is held in a vertical position. This joint also has the advantage of only requiring clamping in one direction. See Fig. 9-4.

CONSTRUCTING THE CARCASS

The construction of the carcass (frame) of a piece of furniture is the most exacting, and many times the most frustrating of all the

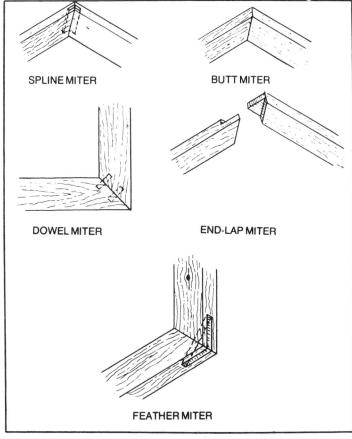

SPLINE MITER

BUTT MITER

DOWEL MITER

END-LAP MITER

FEATHER MITER

Fig. 9-3. Frame miters (spline, butt, dowel, end-lap and feather miters).

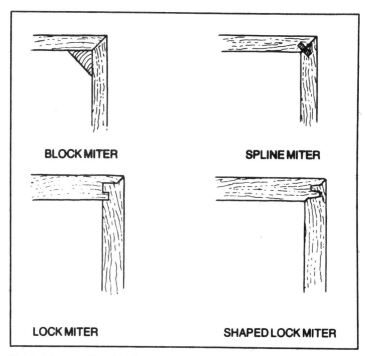

Fig. 9-4. Corner miters (block, spline, lock and shaped miters).

operations, or rather the combinations of many operations imaginable.

The cabinetmaker or craftsman must put into play all the information and skills he has acquired previously with the exception of finishing. One of the most perplexing problems of the wood craftsman is the proper selection of joints to use. The amateur will naturally select the simplest, which may not be necessarily the best, while the experienced and meticulous craftsman may lean the other way and use a complicated joint when it is not necessary.

A typical example of carcass construction would be the making of a chest of drawers. The chest contains a wide variety of joints as well as other aspects of carcass construction. Another very important factor is the proper selection of woods for the different components.

To illustrate all the operations and components of the construction of a carcass, let us use the example of a Chippendale, three-drawer chest made of solid wood, except for drawer bottoms. All operations and components will be in italics. No overall dimensions will be given.

The *top* of the chest is *glued up* and *clamped*. After the glue is dry, the top is *cut* to dimension. The front and two ends are *molded* with a shaper or router. Next the two sides are *glued up, clamped,* and allowed to dry and *cut* to dimensions.

The four *bottom* (base) *rails* are *cut* to size and the ends *mitered* at 45°. Any of the corner miter joints shown in Fig. 9-4 may be used. Before assembling, *make patterns* for the curved portions, *mark patterns* on wood, and cut the *curves* with a band saw or some other curve cutting saw. *Glue, assemble* and *clamp* the bottom rails from front to back and end to end.

The *front* and *back bearer rails* and *runners* (12 pieces) are cut and *assembled* (Fig. 9-5). The *bearer rails* and *runners* form an open shelf on which the *drawers* slide. Very wide drawers often require a center drawer guide. Bearer rails and runners rest on thin strips of wood glued to the inside of the cabinet, or are inserted into dadoes cut into the sides.

Before assembling, gluing and clamping the sides and attaching to the base, shallow rabbets are cut into the sides and the top to accommodate a *dust cover*. The dust cover is often made of *thin plywood, masonite* or *hardboard*.

After the carcass has been glued, assembled, clamped and allowed to dry, the *three drawer fronts* are cut to size. The best joint to fasten the front to the drawer sides is the half-blind dovetail. See Fig. 9-6.

The *drawer sides* are cut to size. The dovetails are cut on the front and one end of a drawer side at the same time, either by hand or with a router and template. *Dadoes* are cut in the ends of the

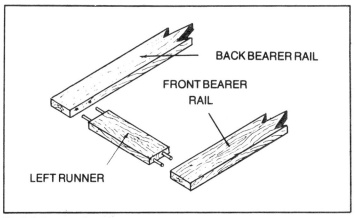

BACK BEARER RAIL

FRONT BEARER RAIL

LEFT RUNNER

Fig. 9-5. Bearer rails and runners.

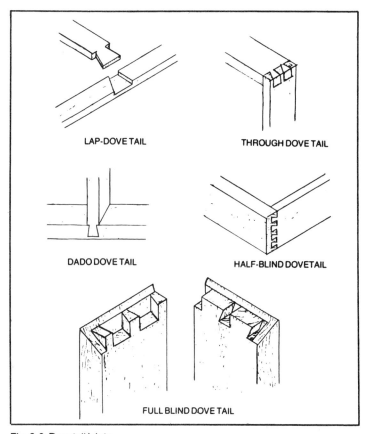

Fig. 9-6. Dovetail joints.

drawer sides, opposite the dovetail ends, to receive the *drawer backs*. Cut *grooves* in the bottom edge of all fronts, sides and backs to receive the *drawer bottoms*.

Test all drawer parts before *gluing* and *clamping* the three drawers. When glue is dry, *fit* the drawers to the carcass. If the drawer binds, proper adjustments must be made.

Attach the necessary *drawer pulls*. After the chest is *finished* with the necessary coats of finishing materials, rub paraffin on drawer runners, drawer guides and the lower part of drawer sides. *Each drawer should move into place with the pressure of one finger on either end of the front of the drawer.*

GLUES AND GLUING

The terms *glues* and *adhesives* are often used interchangeably, but the term adhesive is an "umbrella" name that covers any substance, chemical or in some cases a device that joins together two substances by surface means.

Most adhesives fall into four categories according to the material or function that increases its sticking power.

- ■ Water or liquid solvents (e.g. animal glue).
- ■ Pressure sensitive (e.g. masking tape, Velcro, etc.).
- ■ Hot melts (e.g. bread wrapper).
- ■ Chemically cured (e.g. epoxy).

With the exception of pressure sensitive adhesives, adhesives must set in order to hold. Hot melts are generally called thermoplastics. Application of heat causes the materials to be plastic and the cooling process causes setting.

Natural Glues and Adhesives

There are two large categories of wood glues or adhesives: *natural* and *synthetics*. The synthetic glues have almost completely replaced the natural glues. The following information covers natural glues.

Animal Glue. *Animal glue* is a gelatin-like substance made from hides, hooves, horns and other portions of large domestic animals (cattle, horses, sheep, etc.). Cattle hides makes the highest quality glue. The glue is prepared in a double boiler or an electric pot. The glue is available in *flake* or *ground* form and it must be soaked from eight to 10 hours in cold water before heating. Animal glue works best when it is steaming hot and applied to wood that has been preheated. Clamps must be applied immediately. There is also a liquid, prepared hide glue.

Casein Glue. *Casein* is a water-resistant glue that is made from the protein (curd) of milk. The powdered substance is mixed with water and works best if stirred with an electric mixer. It dries rather slowly and is apt to stain some species of wood.

Fish Glue. *Fish glue* is made of fish scraps and kept in a liquid state by adding an acid. Most liquid glues that come in a tube are of this type. It is a rather low quality glue.

Starch Glue. *Starch glue* is made of cassava starch. It is not used to any great extent by the wood craftsman.

Soybean Glue. *Soybean glue* is similar to casein glue and is used for gluing veneers.

Synthetic Glues and Adhesives

Contact cement is a neoprene-base adhesive that remains elastic after it cures. It is applied to both members (substrates) and allowed to dry before pressure is applied. Great care must be exercised in gluing parts together as there is an immediate, strong bond upon contact which allows no room for error. It is used primarily with plastic laminates (e.g. Formica, Micarta, etc.). Contact cement is water resistant.

Polyvinyl Acetate (PVA). This synthetic resin glue is white in color, (e.g. Elmer's) is ready to use and is very strong. A thermoplastic, it is used extensively in furniture assembly and for general woodworking. It sets quite rapidly at room temperatures; therefore, clamping must take place soon after the glue is applied. Although joints made with PVA are very strong, heat and moisture will adversely affect the bond. Because of its thermoplastic nature, it has a tendency to "cold creep."

Aliphatic Resin Glues. *Aliphatic resin glue* is also polyvinyl acetate based glue, but yellow in color. These glues are of vegetable origin and are highly water resistant as well as heat resistant. They are used extensively for furniture assembly.

Urea Resin Glues. *Urea glue* is made of synthetic urea crystals and formaldehyde. Originally urea glues were made of horse urine which was dehydrated into crystal form. It usually comes in powered form and is used a great deal in the manufacture of plywood. Urea can be made into glue by adding water and a catalyst.

Phenolic Resin Glue. *Phenolic resin glue* is used to glue layers of exterior plywood. It is waterproof and thus is used in boat hull construction. It is marketed in three forms: paper film, dry powder and in a water or alcohol solution. A hot press is used to cure it as the curing temperature is around 300°. The glue line is a dark-reddish color.

Resorcinol Resin Glue. This glue is a reddish liquid which requires a formaldehyde powdered or liquid hardener. It is very strong and resists heat and moisture. It works well for exterior uses.

Epoxy Resin Glues. *Epoxy glue* is probably the strongest of any of the adhesives and will bond together almost all materials including metals. It does not require very high pressure to bond and is very stable with moisture. The resin and the catalyst come in separate, equal size tubes, making them convenient for the home craftsman to use. Equal parts of resin and catalyst must be mixed thoroughly before using. Some epoxies set up in as little as five minutes. Epoxy glues cure at room temperature.

Polyester Resin Glue. *Polyester resin* is similar to epoxy, but not quite as strong, and requires a catalyst. It is used with fiber glass.

Melamine Resin Glue. *Melamine resin* is transparent, is stable to moisture, and is used to impregnate and bond layers of plastic laminates, especially the cover sheet.

Thermoplastic Hot Melt Glue. This glue comes in stick form and is melted in an electric gun for quick application. Clamping pressure must be applied at once because it sets rapidly as it cools. Assembly time can be extended if the parts to be glued are preheated.

Acrylic Glue. This glue is not readily available because its life in the container is fairly short, but it is about the only glue that is successful in gluing end grain to end grain.

Things That Adversely Affect Glue Joints

■ Green wood does not glue well.

■ End grain glues poorly. See the acrylic glue section.

■ Some glues stain some woods.

■ Oily and greasy woods such as teak and rosewood are hard to glue.

■ Glue does not adhere well to burned or glazed wood surfaces due to dull machine knives.

■ Wood that is contaminated with dust, dirt, oil or grease prevents good adhesion.

■ Glue that is spread unevenly will not form a good joint.

■ Wood that has stood too long after machining is apt to be difficult to glue effectively.

■ Glues that have remained too long in the container do not provide optimum adhesion.

■ Glues that are left open in a metal container will lose their strength.

■ If there is not enough clamping pressure, the glue joint will not be at its strongest.

In general, a good glue joint is stronger than the wood that surrounds it, in spite of the glue that might be used.

CLAMPS

The "Jorgensen" hand clamps are among the most versatile clamps in the cabinet shop, and they haven't changed much in the last two centuries. The non-marring jaws are of hard maple and the steel screws have handles of reinforced hardwood. The swivel nuts in the jaws are the one innovation our ancestors didn't have, and they add significantly to versatility. The jaws may be set parallel or, if required, askew. Thus, you can distribute pressure narrowly or widely, and you can clamp angled workpieces. See Table 9-1 and Fig. 9-7.

Klemmsia Cam Clamp

The cam action of these beechwood clamps exerts a surprising amount of pressure—enough for most cabinetmaking needs. Nevertheless, they are gentle enough for veneer and for musical instrument repair and construction. Easy to use, the moveable jaw slides along a steel bar to a loose fit on the workpiece and a flick of the cam lever provides the clamping pressure. The wooden jaws are faced with cork pressure pads. Open sizes range from 7⅞" to 23⅝". See Fair Price Tool Co. (67).

Bar Clamps

There are many sizes and types of bar clamps. A few of them are described here.

Double-Bar Clamps. *Double-bar clamps* are desirable for either very thin stock or extra thick stock. They straddle and pull evenly on both sides of the work, and tend to keep thin stock from buckling. They eliminate the tendency of single bars to bend back under heavy pressure. The fixtures shown in Fig. 9-8 are mounted on a pair of ½" black iron pipes to make a double bar clamp of any desired length.

Single Bar Clamps. The *single bar clamp* shown in Fig. 9-8 is a light-service design clamp, which can be made any length with ½" black iron pipe. The *multiple disc clutch* in the foot grips the pipe automatically at any point, holds it securely and releases it easily by means of extended clutches.

The *Style 40 high speed steel bar clamp* is made of spring steel and has a multiple disc clutch that grips automatically at any point (Fig. 9-9).

Wood bar clamp fixtures are available for attaching to 2 x 4s (1⅝" x 3⅝") for making your own wooden bar clamps. Adjustable Clamp Co. (2) also supplies fixtures for attaching to 1¼" x 2½" cross section wooden bars (Fig. 9-10).

Style 45 "Jorgensen" steel bar clamps have a sliding head and fixed foot with 5" reach from the edge of the bar to the center of the screw. Instant adjustment and secure hold are due to the multiple

Jaw Sizes	Open Sizes
4″	2″
5″	2½″
6″	3″
8″	4½″
10″	6″
12″	8½″
14″	10″
16″	12″

Table 9-1. "Jorgensen" Hand Clamps Information.

disc clutch. The bars are made of spring steel and maximum opening in inches of the different length clamps are 6″, 8″, 12″, 18″, 24″, 30″, and 36″.

The *Style 37, light pattern, "Jorgensen" sliding head, multiple-disc clutch, round handle* is a very lightweight, inexpensive, instant-acting bar clamp that is ideal for woodworkers, patternmakers and home craftsmen where moderate pressure is adequate to do the job. Maximum open capacity sizes are 6″, 12″, 18″, 24″, 30″, and 36″.

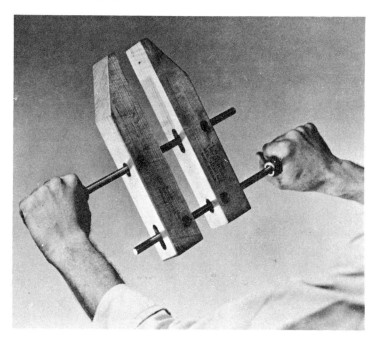

Fig. 9-7. "Jorgensen" hard maple, steel spindle handscrew.

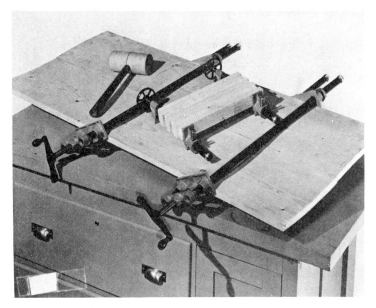

Fig. 9-8. "Pony" multiple-disc clutch, single bar clamps with optional handle and "Pony" multiple-disc clutch, double bar clamps.

The *Style 41, "Jorgensen", miltiple-disc clutch, wing handle bar clamp* is for light service and quick operation. It is a fixed head type with the center of screw 2″ from the edge of the bar. Maximum open capacity sizes range from 6″ to 30″ (Fig. 9-11).

The *Wetzler construction bar clamps* are designed for the heaviest type of work. Castings are made of extra heavy high quality malleable iron. Handles are fixed, two-prong wing type, or upon request they can be screw modified to accept a ¾″ socket wrench. They are available in size openings from 8″ to 60″ (Fig. 9-12).

Miscellaneous Clamps

The lightweight, deep throat clamp gets plenty of use in the average shop. Options in handles are the sliding pin type or the smooth hardwood handle (Fig. 9-13).

The *Wetzler clampettes* have a 2½″ jaw depth and are ideal for applications where light pressure is required. Three sizes open to 5″, 8″, and 12″ (Fig. 9-14).

The Wetzler, *Style No. 4 quick action* clamps have a jaw depth of 4″. Styles No. 5 and No. 7 have jaw depths of 5″ and 7″ respectively. Handles are available in both the wood handle and

Fig. 9-9. Style 40, high speed, "Jorgensen" multiple-disc clutch bar clamps.

wing nut. Cross clamps which are easily attached to these clamps are available for side gluing operations. Sizes of styles 4, 5, and 7 range from 8″ to 60″ openings (Fig. 9-15).

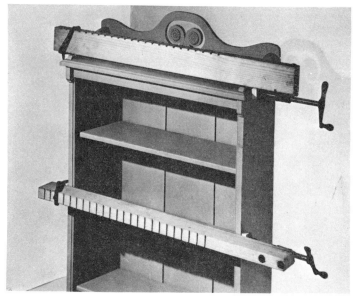

Fig. 9-10. Wood bar clamps.

Fig. 9-11. Style 41, "Jorgensen" stationary head, multiple-disc clutch, wing handle bar clamp.

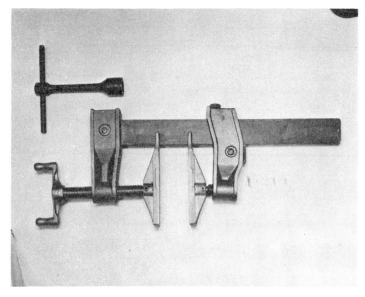

Fig. 9-12. Construction bar clamp.

292

Universal clamps are used for miter and corner work. Two pressure clamps hold pieces to be joined. Freely movable swivel tips adjust easily to curved or beveled edges. The horizontal screw pulls the joints together for a side adjustment of 5″. This can be done with one hand while the other hand is free gluing (Fig. 9-16).

Press screws are used for making your own veneer press frames, case clamps, panel clamps or special jigs for gluing. A removable swivel permits easy installation for any job-design changeovers. A threaded nut drives into a 1″ round hole and may be

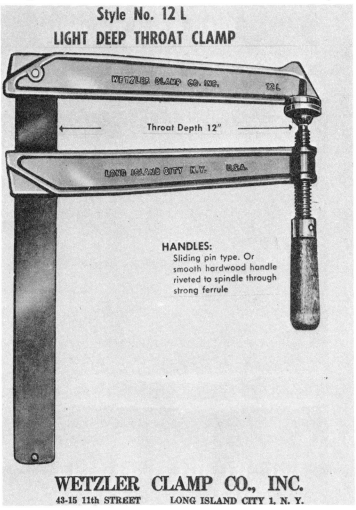

Fig. 9-13. Light, deep throat, quick action clamp.

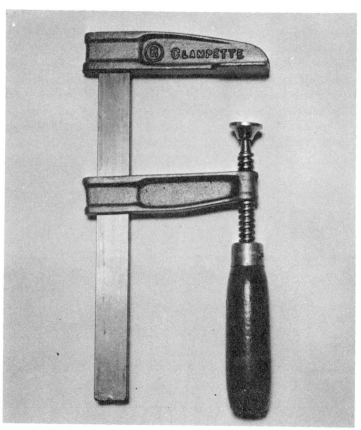

Fig. 9-14. Quick action clampette.

further secured with screws. They are available in 9″, 12″ and 18″ long screws (Fig. 9-17).

Veneer-press frames are also available completely assembled and made of structural steel instead of wood. There are two sizes of frames available. The two spindle type—shown in Fig. 9-18—has an inside width of 18″. The four spindle type has an inside width of 36″. Both have a capacity height of 6½″ (Fig. 9-18).

Band clamps solve the special problems of clamping large irregular or round shapes such as furniture frames, aircraft or boat assemblies, tanks or columns. The band encircles the work and is pulled tight from either end through the screw-head. Self-locking cams hold the band securely without slippage while final screw pressure is applied. Slight pressure on the cam extensions releases the band instantly. They are available in lengths from 10′

to 30' in 5' intervals (Fig. 9-19). The *Wetzler band clamp* has the same specifications as the "Jorgensen" (Fig. 9-20).

Hold-down clamps simplify the holding of any object to a bench top or a machine. The clamp shown in Fig. 9-21 has an opening capacity of 4¼".

Spring clamps are designed for quick clamping. They are ideal for flat surfaces where relatively light pressure is required and fast application and removal are essential. Sizes range from 1" opening to 4" opening in 1" intervals. Plastic tips are available to prevent marring (Fig. 9-22).

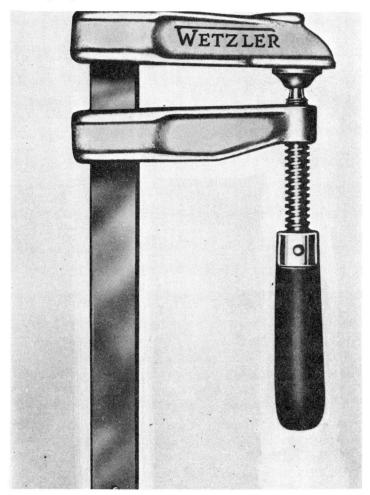

Fig. 9-15. Style 4, quick action clamp.

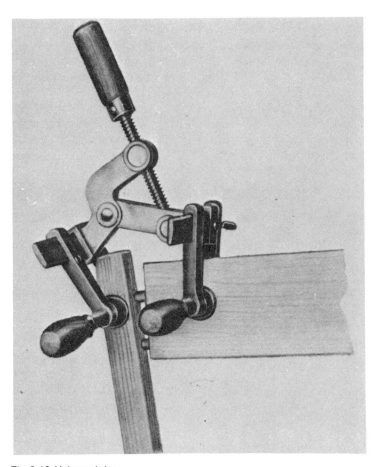

Fig. 9-16. Universal clamp.

HOLDING DEVICES

Holding devices are of many sizes, shapes and design, but all of them make the job of the woodworker much easier. Two such devices and their modifications are described here.

Her-Saf Air-Vac-Clamp

There are two models of the *Air-Vac-Clamp*: the AV1 and AV2-S. The AV1 has a fixed holding plate and stand, while the AV2-S has a holding plate which revolves freely or locks in any of eight different positions. The AV2-S is shown in Fig. 9-23. Either clamp is ideal for holding materials for sanding, trimming, gluing, shaping, assembly, etc.

296

Fig. 9-17. "Jorgensen" press screws used in a veneer press frame.

The Air-Vac-Clamp will hold both porous and non-porous materials, such as hardboard, masonite, flakeboard, plywood and plastic. It has no moving parts and is maintenance free, with a self-contained unit that is controlled by a foot valve (Fig. 9-23).

Fig. 9-18. Veneer press frame.

Fig. 9-19. "Jorgensen" band clamp.

Black and Decker Workmate

The *Black and Decker Workmate* is a combination of work-bench vise and sawhorse (Fig. 9-24). The *Workmate portable work center* and *vise-clampdown 35" Model* has vice jaws that function in horizontal, vertical and 45° positions. The 35" vise jaws open to 19¼" wide. Individually adjustable handles permit wedge shapes to be held in vise jaws. This work center folds for carrying and storage and wheels permit rolling on a smooth surface (Fig. 9-25).

BENDING SOLID STOCK

Historically, the bending of solid wood was accomplished by steaming or immersion in boiling water. Cutting curved parts from solid wood on a band saw, or other curve-cutting tool, leaves much to be desired. Some part of the curve is bound to be cross grain and therefore has little structural strength.

Fig. 9-20. Band clamp.

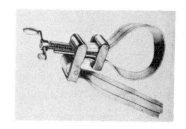

Fig. 9-21. "Jorgensen" hold-down clamps.

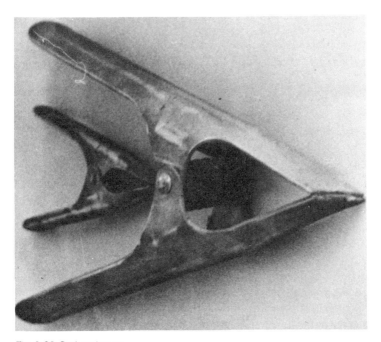

Fig. 9-22. Spring clamps.

Fig. 9-23. Her-Saf Air-Vac-Clamp.

There are two methods for bending solid wood: *steaming* and *soaking*. If one is fortunate to have a steam-heat building, steam can be piped to a metal enclosure in which the pieces to be bent have been placed. However, for most home craftsmen they will have to resort to the soaking method. A large milk can, a metal drum, a large diameter metal pipe with one end closed, or any enclosure that will stand high temperatures can be used. The enclosure must be set at an angle with the closed end somewhat lower than the open end. The enclosure is partially filled with water and heat is applied at the lower end. As soon as the water comes to a boil, the pieces to be bent may be inserted into the tank. Some kind of a cover is placed over the open end to partially contain the steam. The cover should not be a tight fit. The amount of time that it takes to soften (plasticize) the wood depends on the species and the cross section of the stock.

The bending stock should be free of cross grain, twisted grain and knots. Bending stock that has a moisture content (MC) between 12.9 to 20% requires steaming or soaking. Although green wood can be bent to produce most curved members, difficulties are introduced in drying and fixing the bent piece and reducing the moisture content to a level suited for the end use. The sharper the bend in the stock, the higher must be the moisture content.

When the wood has softened to the required degree, it is removed from the boiler and placed in a jig which is generally of two parts conforming to the desired shape. The two parts are gradually forced toward each other. First, a tension strap of metal (stainless steel is preferred) must be placed over the convex side of the stock and end pressure is applied. The tension strap is necessary because when wood is bent along its length, it is stretched in tension along the convex side of the bend and compressed along the concave side. In bending, therefore, the wood must be compressed lengthwise while restraining it from stretching along the convex

Fig. 9-24. Workmate portable work center.

Fig. 9-25. Workmate portable work center and vise-clampdown, 35″ Model.

side. Bent members must be held in place until the stock is thoroughly cooled and dried. When the bent member has dried to a moisture content consistent with its use, it is removed from the jig and it will hold its curved shape.

In general, hardwoods possess better bending quality than softwoods. The species of wood commonly used to produce solid bent members are white oak, red oak, elm, hickory, ash, beech, birch, maple, walnut, sweetgum and mahogany.

Thick members can be bent rather easily by making saw kerfs on the concave side. The sharper the bend, the closer the saw kerfs should be together. It should be kept in mind that the piece is weakened considerably by this method, so that the piece should be reinforced by other structural members. Sometimes veneer strips are glued to the concave side to add strength.

LAMINATED WOOD

With the advent of the newer synthetic resin glues, the practice of bending solid wood began to take a back seat. The

302

essential difference between *laminated* wood and *plywood* is that all layers of laminated wood run in the same direction, while layers in plywood run at right angles to each other. Laminated wood is usually curved. Laminated wood is used for furniture parts, fishing net frames, tennis rackets, sporting goods, etc.

Veneers or resawed lumber are the materials most often used by the home craftsman to form laminated parts. The sharper the curve, the thinner the stock. On the other hand, it is a waste of time and energy to cut a number of thin layers when the curved part has a large radius. If members are a little too thick for bending, they may be soaked in hot water.

Gluing of Laminates

Polyvinyl acetate (PVA), a white synthetic resin glue or urea-formaldehyde glue, is a good glue for laminating purposes. Casein glue may also be used if the stain of the glue is not objectionable.

The glue is applied rather quickly with a brush or roller and stacked. The outside layers should be defect-free. The form or jig should be protected with a plastic sheet, wax paper or some other protective coating to prevent getting glue on the form or jig.

Staggered Joints

Any length member may be made by staggering joints. Each layer must overlap the joint below it. No joints should be directly over another. The ends of each layer should be squared and fit closely to the end of the adjacent piece.

Clamping Devices

A veneer press is an excellent device for laminating curved stock. The male-female forms are placed in the press, with the laminated stock in between each part of the form. Gradual pressure can be exerted with the veneer press clamp. The wood forms must be properly protected with shellac, lacquer or varnish.

Curing Time In The Form

The laminate should be allowed to stay in the form or jig long enough for the glue to thoroughly dry and cure. Generally this will require an overnight waiting period, but if there is any doubt, leave the laminates in a longer period. By increasing the temperature of the jig or form, the curing time will be greatly decreased.

After the laminates have been removed from the clamping devices, they should be set aside for at least a week. The moisture in the glue will have raised to the moisture content and will take time for the laminate to stabilize.

Cutting, Shaping and Finishing

After the laminate has stabilized, it can be cut or shaped. Woodworking hand and machine tools may be used; however, if there is a considerable amount of cutting or shaping, the cutting blades should be carbide-tipped because of the abrasive action of the glue.

Finishing is accomplished by using the same methods and materials used on other wood products.

MOLDED PLYWOOD

Molded plywood is simply placing regular plywood in molds and creating pressure to form the curves. Molded plywood with compound curves often found in contemporary chairs can be formed in industry with large pneumatic or hydraulic presses. Single curved members may be formed in the home workshop by using wooden jigs or forms in conjunction with the proper clamping devices.

STACKING

Stacking is an unusual method of lamination. Stacking is done with two basic materials: *solid wood* and *plywood*.

Solid wood in thick sections are stacked and glued in brick-like fashion to form a block large enough for carving and sculpturing. Many of these large forms are left hollow in the center to cut down on weight and material.

John Kelsey reports on stacking as a technique of building up wood forms for carving in *Fine Woodworking Techniques* . He states, "Since the last century, carousel horses have been carved from laminated blocks of wood." In the same book Ellen Swartz describes how beautiful contemporary furniture can be made with stacked plywood.

REPAIRING DEFECTS AND PREPARING FOR FINISH

Holes that are fairly round and deep may be repaired by whittling a tapered peg of the same kind of wood as the project being repaired. Glue is placed on the end of the peg and it is then driven into the wood, leaving the top end intact until the glue is dry. The top end is then cut off at the surface with a sharp chisel. If the hole is large, the grain in the peg must run in the same direction as the wood in the project.

One of the best, and least expensive, of hole fillers is made of fine, powdery sandings from the same kind of wood, mixed with glue. Sawdust should not be used as it is too coarse.

Plastic wood comes in different colors and may be used to fill holes. As it has a tendency to shrink, it should be piled up above the surface of the wood. When it is dry, it may be sanded flush with the surface. Plastic wood is also made of fine sandings, but the sandings are mixed with lacquer rather than glue. If plastic wood starts to dry up in the can, simply add a little lacquer thinner.

Stick shellac and stick lacquer are also used to repair holes, but they are more apt to be used after the project is partially or completely finished. They are available in many wood colors and shades. Stick shellac and lacquer are "burned" into the wood by using an electric burning-in knife or a knife heated over an alcohol lamp. Expert furniture finishing specialists prefer the alcohol lamp.

Holes in veneer are repaired by punching out a section of the veneer with special veneer punches. These punches are irregular in shape and vary in four sizes from 32mm to 60mm. They are made of high quality hardened steel and cut through veneer with ease. A metal striker on the handle permits hitting with a mallet. All that is necessary for veneer repair is to punch out the defect with the punch and replace it with a punch-out from the same species of veneer, making sure that the grain runs in the same direction.

There are many other pastes, compounds and putties that may be used to fill holes. Each has its own characteristics and the craftsman should be selective.

Repairing Dents

Dents are a result of the crushing of fibers. If the fibers are restored to their original position, the dent will disappear. Repairing small dents requires only a sharp needle and some hot water. Dip the needle in the water and prick, very lightly, the surface of the dent. The hot water will cause the fibers to swell and expand. After the repair spot is completely dry, the surface may be sanded and the dent will have disappeared.

Repairing large dents requires the point of an electric iron or a soldering iron and a dampened cloth. The dampened cloth is placed over the dent and the hot iron is applied to the cloth directly over the dent. Only the deepest dents will resist this treatment.

Final Sanding

Generally all hardware is fitted to the project of this stage and then removed for the final sanding and finishing operations. Final sanding should be done by hand and 150-4/0 to 240-7/0 sandpaper, usually garnet, is used. As always, sanding must be done in the direction of the grain. After sanding, all sanding dust must be removed with a vacuum cleaner or brush. A tack rag (a cheesecloth piece saturated with thin varnish) is applied to the whole project to pick up all small particles of dust.

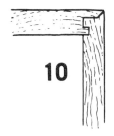

10

Finishing Materials and Their Use

The home craftsman may not have a separate finishing room, but every attempt should be made to have finishing materials well organized and in a safe place. Storage should be provided for volatile materials. (See the introduction at the front part of the book concerning the color coding of safety containers and other information concerning the storage of finishing materials.)

REPRESENTATIVE FINISHING MATERIALS

Here is a list of finishing materials organized alphabetically.

Benzine. Used with oil stains.

Brushes. The craftsman will need a variety of brushes. Glue brushes are round and are fitted with a wire bridle. When the bristles wear down, the bridle is removed and you have a new glue brush. A graining brush from ox hair, a fitch or nylon brush for varnish, a stiff brush for filler, and a number of inexpensive brushes for shellac will be needed. Brushes are also made of horse hair, Chinese hog bristles and cactus fibers.

Colors. They are ground in oil and are used with fillers, stains, enamel, paints and other finishing materials to alter the colors or to make colored finishes from scratch.

Whites are formed by using flake white, white lead or zinc. *Blacks* are made of lamp black and drop black. *Browns* are made with raw and burnt umber, raw and burnt sienna and Vandyke brown. *Greens* are made of chrome. *Blues* are mixed from cobalt blue, Prussian blue and ultramarine. *Reds* are formed from vermilion, Venetian red, rose lake, red lake and Indian red. Colors in oil are generally sold in tubes.

Denatured Alcohol. Used with shellac and spirit stains.

Japan Drier. May be used to hasten the drying of varnish and other oil base materials.

Lacquer Thinner. Is used as a thinner for lacquer and lacquer sealer.

Linseed Oil. Comes in two varieties. Raw linseed oil is used with exterior paints. Boiled linseed oil is used with interior oil-base finishes.

Masking Tape. Used for masking parts between sections having different finishes and for covering parts that are to be glued.

Naptha. Is the best thinner to use with filler.

Pumice Stone. Is used for rubbing down transparent finishes (shellac, varnish, lacquer and polyurethane). It comes in these grades: F coarse, FF medium, FFF fine and FFFF extra fine. Pumice stone and water cut down the finish faster, but the finish is not as smooth as when pumice stone is used with oil. *Rottenstone* and oil will produce an extra high gloss surface, even smoother than FFFF pumice stone.

Rubbing Compounds. Are often used with lacquer and lacquer-based finishes for producing a smooth, glossy surface. Felt pads are used with rubbing materials and compounds.

Rubbing Oil. A light oil, usually of a paraffin base, especially designed for the purpose. Besides being used with pumice stone and rottenstone, it is also used with fine grit, wet-o-dry sandpaper for rubbing finish coats.

Safety Cans. Are used for storing small amounts of volatile liquids. The cap is spring-loaded which automatically closes when the can is not in use.

Tack Rag. Is a chemically treated rag to remove the finest dust particles before varnishing or lacquering. A homemade tack rag may be made with a piece of cheesecloth to which turpentine and a few drops of varnish are added.

Tung Oil. At one time known as China wood oil, it is one of the hardest quickest drying, and most resistant to impurities of any oil. Tung oil or tung oil base transparent finishes are deep penetrating rubbed-in finish materials and are used on gunstocks, bar tops and other members of furniture that take a lot of abuse.

Turpentine. Is used as a thinner mainly for oil stain, wood filler, varnish, enamel and paint. *Mineral spirits* are often used as a substitute for turpentine. Turpentine is also used as a medicine.

Waste Cans. Are essential in any shop using dangerous inflammable materials such as oily waste rags, paper, etc. These cans are often mounted on casters and the cover opens with a foot lever.

Water. Is used with water stain and glue size.

Waxes. Either colored or clear can be used as a final finish over varnish or lacquer. Colored waxes are used to add another dimension (depth) to the finish. Colored waxes must be compatible with the colors underneath (stain, filler, glazes, etc.). Carnauba wax is considered the best base for waxes.

White Vinegar. Is mixed with hot water, one to one, for removing wood bleach.

APPLYING QUALITY FINISH TO OPEN GRAIN WOODS

Open grain woods such as oak, walnut and mahogany require special treatment in the finishing process. The eleven steps illustrated in Figs. 10-1 through 10-3 emphasize the fact that the quality finishing of wood is a rather complex operation. But the beauty and depth of the finish is well worth the effort. These steps are essentially the same as used by manufacturers of fine furniture. The home craftsman should note that the apparent depth of finish is due to the very small amounts of color added to transparent finishes.

Step 1 in Fig. 10-1 depicts one enlarged pore of open grain wood. The finishing process generally starts after the wood is sanded with 2/0-100 sandpaper. Raw lumber direct from the mill or lumber company will require that a coarser paper be used before the 2/0 paper. Unfinished furniture is usually sanded with 3/0 sandpaper. Of course, the sanding should be done with the grain only.

The application of glue size (step 2 in Fig. 10-1) takes place after all planer marks, chip marks, clamp marks and other blemishes have been removed. It is permissible to leave shallow dents or depressions as the glue size will raise the surface. Ten to 13 parts of hot water are added to one part of animal glue— LePage's or Franklin's liquid glue will do. The water should be as hot as the hands will tolerate. The penetration of glue size into wood is probably greater than any other finish process due to the fact that it is hot.

A natural or synthetic sponge is ideal for the application of glue size. On large, flat surfaces, sponging should be done both with and across the grain. This is particularly important if water stain is used, as it will raise the grain of the wood not covered by the glue size. The sponge should carry enough glue size so that the

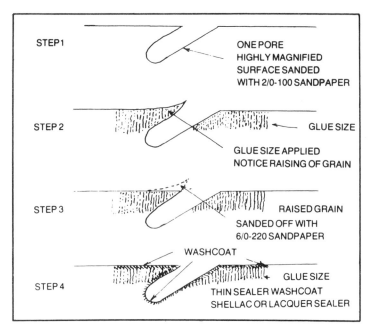

STEP 1 — ONE PORE
HIGHLY MAGNIFIED
SURFACE SANDED
WITH 2/0-100 SANDPAPER

STEP 2 — GLUE SIZE
GLUE SIZE APPLIED
NOTICE RAISING OF GRAIN

STEP 3 — RAISED GRAIN
SANDED OFF WITH
6/0-220 SANDPAPER

STEP 4 — WASHCOAT
GLUE SIZE
THIN SEALER WASHCOAT
SHELLAC OR LACQUER SEALER

Fig. 10-1. Open grain wood finishing, steps 1-4.

wood is thoroughly moistened, but no puddles should be left standing on the wood. If it appears that the wood is too wet, wring out the sponge and go over the area.

The glue size causes the fibers of the wood to turn upward. Water alone will cause the same effect. The advantage of glue size is that after 24 hours of drying, the fiber is in a fixed position. Subsequent sanding (step 3, Fig. 10-1) eliminates the raised fibers. If water alone is used, the flexible, hair-like fibers simply lay down when the sandpaper passes over them and spring right back up again after the sandpaper passes over. Use 6/0-220 sandpaper for sanding.

During step 4 (Fig. 10-1), a thin sealer washcoat of thin shellac or lacquer sealer is applied. The spraying method works the best. At least twice as much thinner (alcohol for shellac, lacquer thinner for lacquer sealer) should be mixed with the finish material.

The purpose of the washcoat is twofold. First, it provides a base for the stain; otherwise the stain will sink in more rapidly in some places than others, causing a blotchy appearance. Second, it provides a casing or pocket for the filler, which prevents the oil in the filler from soaking into the wood too rapidly. This causes the filler to shrink away from the sides of the pore, which results in many problems in subsequent finishing operations.

Stain, along with filler and glaze, adds the most color to wood products. Stains used in furniture manufacturing are usually applied with a spray gun. See step 5 in Fig. 10-2.

On most traditional or period furniture, the filler is colored darker than the stain. Filler should be thinned with naptha, mineral spirits or turpentine to about the consistency of coffee cream. Use a brush or air hose (low pressure) to get rid of all dust particles before filling. Brush the filler into the pores with the grain of the wood with a stiff brush. Work the filler thoroughly into the pores. When the filler starts to appear dull in appearance (about five minutes), rub the surface in all directions with the lower part of the palm of the hand. This further packs the filler into pores. Use old rags or burlap to follow up the hand process. Rub back and forth

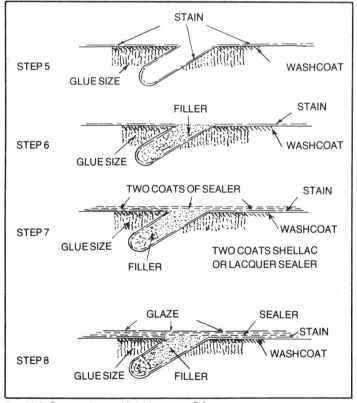

Fig. 10-2. Open grain wood finishing, steps 5-8.

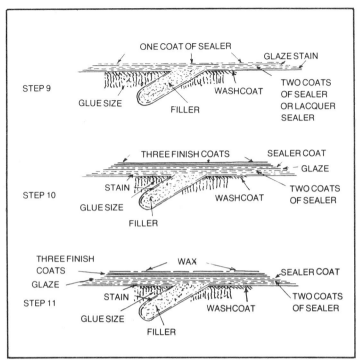

Fig. 10-3. Open grain wood finishing, steps 9-11.

across the grain to eliminate the possibility of removing the filler from the pores. Follow the rags with a clean cloth to remove the remaining filler and oil. With a rag over a sharpened stick, remove excess filler from carvings, moldings or other recesses. Allow the filler to dry over night. See step 6 in Fig. 10-2.

Two thin coats of lacquer sealer or shellac (step 7 in Fig. 10-2) are applied over the filler. Lacquer sealer is best applied with a spray gun. Sand lightly with 8/0-280 or 9/0-320 abrasive paper. Use very fine (0000) steel wool on carvings and turnings. Shellac will have to be sanded a little more than lacquer sealer. Two coats of lacquer sealer actually merge into one coat; white shellac stays as two separate coats. Sand only enough to remove embedded dust particles and any runs or streaks in the finish. Add a very small amount of color, compatible with the entire finishing schedule, to these coats of sealer to add depth to the finish. The tint is barely visible but the overall effect is one of depth.

Glaze on traditional furniture does more to enhance the finish than any other process. See step 8 in Fig. 10-2.

312

Apply one coat of shellac or lacquer sealer. This coat must be applied with a spray gun or aerosol spray can. Add a trace of color if a spray gun is used. The glaze will smear if the shellac or lacquer sealer is brushed on. When the coat is dry, sand with 9/0-320 sandpaper abrasive or rub with fine steel wool. Be careful not to sand through the sealer into the glaze. See step 9, Fig. 10-3.

Varnish, polyurethane or lacquer coats are applied next as in step 10 of Fig. 10-3. *Never* apply lacquer over varnish. Varnish coats are thicker than lacquer coats, but lacquer coats are harder and require less time for drying. Furniture manufacturers sometimes heat the lacquer so that it can be applied in heavier coats. Lacquer requires little sanding as all coats merge into one. Do not add any color to the last coat. If a flat or dull finish is desired, do not apply the flat varnish or lacquer until the last coat, as it does not have the body of gloss varnish or lacquer.

A straight-line sander used with Wet-o-Dry paper and a liquid works best to obtain a perfectly flat surface. Mineral spirits or water can be used as the liquid.

If a high gloss is desired, use rottenstone and oil or a rubbing compound. If a flat finish is wanted, use coarse pumice stone and water or steel wool.

Waxing, step 11 in Fig. 10-3, is the final step, although waxing is frequently omitted on flat finishes. Waxes with a high percentage of paraffin should be avoided. In a completely coordinated and matched system, the colors should be consistent and compatible in all coats. This also holds true for wax. Some of the waxes used in the furniture industry look a little like shoe polish. Buff the wax until a smooth and even polish is attained.

STAINS AND STAINING

Originally all stains were of natural origin. The American Indian used berries, roots, bark, flowers and moss to make stains after they were mashed and soaked to provide a variety of colors. Blood of animals was used to decorate items of wearing apparel. In addition, Indians used colored earth, burnt bones and fungus to create colorful war paint and to decorate ceremonial attire.

The majority of the primitive stains had many shortcomings, among these being lack of brilliance, tendency to fade badly, non-uniform color and short life in general. Present day stains solve all of these problems.

Stains are used for a number of different reasons, a few of which are listed here:

■ To imitate the colors of other woods.

■ To put in grain and figure in otherwise plain wood.

■ To enhance the color contrast of natural figure in wood and to enhance the grain pattern.

■ To even up the overall color when several woods are used in one construction. Bleaching does the same thing, only it lightens the wood.

■ To give a weathered appearance or used look (antique finishes and weathered ash).

There are many woods (ebony, cherry, rosewood, red cedar, purplehart, etc.) that do not necessarily need staining. In general, all woods can have their color enhanced and beauty increased by staining to some degree. Some woods require only the color given in the filling operation, while others require a combination of colors to achieve the ultimate in beauty for the wood used.

Water Stains

Most *water stains* are derivatives of coal tar. Water stains are the lowest in cost of all stains, primarily because of the solvent used. In powder form, either as base colors (red, yellow, blue, etc.) or in standard colors of mahogany, maple, walnut, etc., they cost as much as any other powdered stain.

There are many advantages to using water stain: brilliance and clarity, permanence (very little fading in sunlight or through age), low cost because of the inexpensive solvent, ease of application and non-bleeding under normal finish coats.

There are, however, several disadvantages associated with their use. Raised grain after staining is always a problem, more so on certain woods than on others. This can be minimized by the use of a glue size just before the final sanding before staining.

Care must be taken in applying glue size and water stain over veneers that may be bonded with a non-moisture resistant glue. All moisture added in the staining operation must be removed by air-drying for at least 24 hours.

Preparation of water stain is important. Usual concentrations run from 1 to 4 ounces per gallon of water depending on the desired color. The powder is added to water at or near the boiling point (200 to 212° F). The *exact* amount of powder and the *exact* temperature must be recorded so that succeeding mixes will be alike; otherwise, the color will not be consistent. After the stain is mixed for eight to 10 minutes, it is allowed to cool to room temperature before using. If the stain is not allowed to cool, the color will be too dark.

Oil Stains

Oil stains are perhaps the most widely used of all stains by the home craftsman, probably because of their availability. Oil stains are solutions of coal tar dyes in solvents such as xylol, toluol or benzol, to which may be added such similar compounds as mineral spirits, turpentine or naptha. They can be applied to dip, spray, rags or brush.

Colors for oil stains are relatively brilliant, but only moderately permanent. Fading of colors has always been their drawback. The stains are relatively inexpensive, do not raise the grain of the wood, and have little effect on glue lines of veneered stock.

After application of oil stain, at least eight hours should be allowed for dry time. "Bleeding," muddiness and slow drying will occur if the oil stain is not allowed to dry thoroughly, particularly if a varnish is applied. A sealer coat of one pound cut shellac applied before the varnish will help to alleviate this condition.

Spirit Stains

The solvent in *spirit stains* is alcohol. Spirit stains are seldom used for the base staining of wood, but are used after one or more coats of finish have been applied.

Examples of their special uses include the following:

—For touch-up or "rub-throughs" in the dried coatings.

—Distressing by the use of concentrated dark color on the edge of a crimped can edge, clinker or brush flick method.

—Padding into or between topcoats to accentuate natural coloring.

—Tinting shellac coatings or hole fillers.

—"Frenching-in" colors after finish repairs are made by "burning-in" stick shellac or lacquer.

N.G.R. (Non-Grain Raising) Stains

N.G.R. stains are merely selected water stained powders dissolved in solvents other than water. The solvents selected do not swell wood fibers and therefore raised grain after staining is not a serious problem. By the use of these solutions, glue sizing before staining and washcoating after staining can be eliminated; however, if filler is to be used, a washcoat should be applied to prevent the smearing of the filler over the stained surface.

The advantages of N.G.R. stains are they do not "bleed," they dry in one hour, they are permanent and brilliant, and they do not raise the grain. The disadvantages of N.G.R. stains are a spray gun must be used for application, high costs (when compared with water stain), and they are seldom found on the retail market. See Gaston Wood Finishes (78).

Pigmented Wiping Stains

These stains are used quite widely in the home workshop. A pigmented stain is, in essence, a thin varnish to which have been added ingredients to provide color on the surface to which it is applied.

To use these materials, simply brush them over a surface to be stained. Allow the major portion of the volatiles to "flash off" and then wipe the stain with a dry cloth. Drying time before wiping may vary with different products, ranging from two minutes up to 20 minutes. Allowing the stain to dry too long will create a "tacky" condition on the surface and make uniform coloration and wiping difficult. Allowing too short a time between application and wiping will result in removal of too much pigment, and only light coloration will be had. Rubbing with too much pressure or too little pressure will also vary results. Pigmented wiping stains are primarily used on woods which ordinarily do not require a filler.

SEALERS

After the wood has been stained or (bleached), washcoated and then filled, it is ready for the application of the sealing coats. In most cases where a filler has been used, this is followed by a lacquer type of sealer; however, in some cases, shellac is selected for this purpose.

There are three types of shellac in common use. *Orange* shellac produces a cloudy, colored solution. *White* shellac is the bleached variety. *Dewaxed* shellac produces a clear, pale solution and is used where the highest type of paleness and clarity is necessary in order to enhance the final appearance.

The orange shellac is used whenever the existence of a slight discoloration in the sealer coat can be overlooked, while the white shellac should not be applied in stronger concentration than a two pound cut (the regular four pound cut thinned with an equal amount of alcohol). Heavy coats of shellac are not recommended since they lead to a premature checking and peeling of the lacquer topcoats.

316

Four-Pound Cuts

The most popular marketed types of shellac solutions are known as the *four-pound cuts,* and these contain four pounds of dry shellac dispersed in each gallon of alcohol. When used as a sealer, this solution is reduced with an equal volume of denatured alcohol, producing the equivalent of a two pound cut. This sealer can be successfully brushed, but it is best applied by spraying. After allowing a drying period which varies between one and four hours, the film can be sanded with No. 5/0 or 6/0 sandpaper.

Shellac Mixing Lacquer

In order to improve drying time, flow and the toughness of shellac, a *nitrocellulose* mixing lacquer is blended with it. It is mixed by combining two parts of shellac with one part of lacquer and then adding two parts of alcohol. The nitrocellulose mixing lacquer is specially formulated so as to be able to receive high amounts of alcohol without any resulting incompatibility. This type of blended sealer possesses the advantages of shellac combined with those of cellulose lacquer, and has greater adhesive qualities toward the lacquer topcoats than pure shellac alone.

Varnish Sealers

Varnish type *sealers* cannot be employed under lacquers, since they are attacked by the lacquer solvents; however, they are very satisfactory when used under vanishes of both the oleo-resinous and the synthetic types. The solid content of these varnish sealers vary from about 30 to 35% when thinned ready for spraying. Quick-evaporating hydrocarbon types of thinners are used for the reducing purposes. They dry satisfactorily for sanding overnight, or they can be forced dried in one to two hours at 150°F. They contain enough lubricating agents in their formulation to enable them to be dry sanded smooth. They are economical to use and give excellent toughness and adhesion with the varnish type topcoats.

Lacquer Compositions

The most commonly used types of sealers encountered in the furniture industry are the *lacquer compositions,* and these are generally applied with the spray gun at about 40 to 50 pounds pressure. In some cases dipping is found to be more convenient. The material is usually marketed in the correct consistency for immediate use, but may require reducing with solvents of the lacquer type. The use of an incorrect thinner may affect the drying, flowing and leveling qualities. It is best that lacquer sealer, lacquer and lacquer thinner be purchased from the same manufacturer or supplier and carry the same trade name.

Sealer Drying Time

The air drying time of sealers varies from 30 minutes to two hours. When a conveyor system of operations is used, it is recommended that the sealer be force dried for 10 to 20 minutes at 110 to 120°F. This will remove most of the solvents and permit easier sanding. In some conveyor systems the installation is arranged so that after the sealer has been sprayed on there is a period of 30 minutes before it reaches the sanding area. In these cases, force drying is unnecessary.

FILLERS

The primary purpose of wood fillers is to produce a level surface of the same porosity as the non-porous parts of the wood. A secondary purpose of fillers is the addition of *color* to the wood.

The composition of a typical filler, such as would be purchased at a local paint store, is as follows: a thin varnish composed of linseed oil, resins and driers (to promote hardening). A filler also includes pigments:

—*Silex* (ground quartz). This is the major portion of the filler: grey in color, non-shrinking and very hard.

—Earth colors (siennas, ochres, umbers, etc.) Added to create permanent color in the pores, they are held on the surface of the silex by their varnish coating.

—Soluble colors. These are generally oil stains (aniline dyes) soluble in linseed oil and may be present or absent, dependent on the degree of surface coloring desired.

Thinner or Reducer

The most acceptable *reducer* for fillers is V.M. and P. naphtha *(Varnish Makers and Pointers* naphtha). The reducer is that portion of the filler which is added to produce fluidity, allowing the filler to flow into the porous structure of the wood. It evaporates, usually in about 15 minutes, leaving a crumbly, spongy coating of the filler ingredient on the surface of the wood. White gasoline may be used, but with care. Inflammability of white gas requires more precautions in regard to fires. Normally it evaporates faster than V.M. and P. naphtha and requires faster wiping time.

318

On hot, dry days, the filler may "dry and wipe" at a rapid rate. If large areas are to be filled, it may be deemed necessary to slow down the drying rate of the filler somewhat by the addition of a slower drying solvent, namely mineral spirits. Small amounts, about 10% of the total, are sufficient.

There is a tendency on the part of some finishes to add kerosene to the mixture. It is advisable to avoid the use of *kerosene* in any finishing operation.

Fillers are supplied to the public, usually in several standard colors, mainly "natural," "mahogany," "walnut" and "white." "Natural' filler is a grey-white colored filler and is the mainstay of the home craftsman. It may be tinted to the color desired with colors ground in oil. Colors in oil (boiled linseed oil) are available at any paint store. A small tube of each of the primary colors and earth colors is normally all that is necessary to produce the filler shade desired. Where a large group of items are to be finished, it is always well to attempt to purchase a standard color of filler, since duplication is easier at a later date.

Filler Application

Fillers are normally reduced with V.M. and P. naphtha, at the rate of 8 pounds per gallon of solvent for spraying, and 10 to 12 pounds per gallon for brushing. If no scales are available, mix to the consistency of heavy cream. Brushing, although slower, is less apt to miss spots and will push the filler into the pores more efficiently. Fillers should be stirred well before and during use, since rapid separation of the ingredients is possible.

Woods like maple, birch, beech, basswood, gum, pines, etc., require no filling. Woods with large open pores like oak, chestnut, ash and elm may require a double filling operation. The second filling may be done, preferably, after the first is hardened or immediately after wiping the initial coat. Mahogany, walnut and similar woods can usually be filled flush in one operation.

Applying Filler

Spray or brush the filler over an area that can be wiped in a few minutes. Do not coat extremely large areas at one time; the filler may become too stiff to wipe and will pull out of the pores leaving unsightly cavities.

Allow the filler to "flash off" (solvent elimination) until a finger, pressed on the surface and drawn across it, will indicate a crumbly, non-greasy condition. This will normally be a period of 10 to 20 minutes. Wipe, with moderate pressure, across the grain of the wood, pushing downward to pack the filler into the pores. Use clean burlap, jute tow, cotton rags, waste or similar materials.

Wipe lightly with the grain to eliminate any cross grain streaks of filler. Extreme care at this point is essential to a beautiful finish.

Allow the filler to dry for a minimum of four hours, preferably eight hours, in a warm, ventilated area. It is then ready for sealing and top coating. Filler should not be sanded.

LACQUER

Lacquer comes close to being the best clear topcoat furniture finish. Most lacquers have a nitrocellulose base made from cotton. Other ingredients are added to lacquer to give it more body and elasticity.

Lacquer is quick-drying, moisture resistant and exceptionally hard. Lacquer is also available in colors.

Clear lacquer, as a topcoat, has been used in furniture manufacturing for many years. The big drawback for the home craftsman is the fact that lacquer is hard to apply with a brush. Spray equipment is needed to apply lacquer to large pieces, and the cost of exhaust fans and a spray booth is not cheap. Of course, portable spray equipment may be used outdoors if the weather permits.

Lacquer in an aerosol spray can is one of the most convenient ways of finishing small and medium-sized projects. It goes on professionally smooth and dries rapidly.

Lacquer, as a clear topcoat, comes in gloss, semi, and dull or flat. Flat lacquer is used only as a last coat. Earlier coats are gloss lacquer. Gloss builds up faster than flat lacquer.

Lacquer thinner is used to thin lacquer. Only use lacquer thinner manufactured by the company that makes the lacquer. Sanding between coats is held to a minimum because all lacquer coats and sealer merge into one.

Lacquer should never be applied over varnish or other oil base finishes. All distressing and glazing should be completed before topcoats are applied.

Gloss Lacquers. Regular, heavy body, heavy body alcohol proof, all purpose, acid and heat proof table top lacquer, gloss 21% (solid content), gloss 27%, water white gloss and gloss brushing lacquer.

Semi-Gloss Lacquers. Semi gloss 21%, semi gloss 27% and water white semi gloss.

Flat Lacquers. Regular, heavy body, all purpose, flat brushing lacquer, flat 21%, flat 27% and water white flat.

Lacquer Tinting Colors. Red, green, yellow, blue, black, orange and brown.

Lacquer Shading Stains. Walnut, mahogany and maple.

Colored Spraying Lacquer. Available in most standard colors.

Good Qualities of Lacquer

- Good durability.
- Fast drying.
- Fairly easy to repair damage to the surface.
- Easy to sand, rub, wax and polish.
- The coat is clear and not too "bulky."
- Does not get sticky in extreme humidity or high temperatures.

Poor Qualities of Lacquer

- Very difficult to brush.
- High moisture may cause lacquer to separate from wood.
- Some of the more current synthetic finishes are tougher.
- Not resistant to lacquer base materials such as nail polish remover.

Heated Lacquer

Industrial woodworking finishers have used heated lacquer for many years. The result is that it is possible to lay on a heavy coat in only one application. Home craftsmen who use this method should place an open container of lacquer in hot water and keep it away from open flames as lacquer is highly inflammable.

VARNISH

Varnish of some kind has been used for centuries as a finishing material and, until the advent of lacquer and other synthetic finishes, was the universal topcoat for furniture finishing. The scientific term for these natural finishes was *oleoresinous,* which means a combination of oil (linseed oil, China tung oil, etc.) and resins (fossil gums). The addition of China tung oil to the early varnish gave it greater durability and water resistance qualities.

Synthetic resins in a number of varieties are now used and are far superior to the natural fossil gums resins in speed of drying and in toughness and durability. The most important of these resins is the phenolformaldehyde (Bakelite) synthetics. Bakelite, named after its inventor, L. H. Baekeland, is widely used as an electrical insulator.

Alkyd Varnish

This synthetic varnish is a fast-drying topcoat composed of linseed oil, soybean oil, glycerine and *phthalic acid anhydride.* It is used a great deal in the manufacture of enamels.

Polyurethane Varnish

Polyurethane has a life span greater than varnish or lacquer. It will not chip or peel and is resistant to water stains, alcohol, detergents and food. It can be used for both interior and exterior finish. In addition to brushing polyurethane, it is available in aerosol spray cans.

United Gilsonite Laboratories (185) manufactures five polyurethane finishes under the trade name ZAR: gloss ZAR, a high gloss durable finish; satin ZAR, a finish with a soft luster; antique ZAR, a flat, durable finish for interior use; imperial ZAR, a high gloss exterior finish; and quick drying ZAR, a fast drying gloss finish.

Deft (53) has a gloss and satin polyurethane for brushing or in an aerosol spray can. The Deft spray can is unique in that the spray valve can be rotated 90° to provide both a vertical and horizontal fan spray.

Acrylic Clear Topcoat

Deft (53) also provides a crystal clear, non-yellowing, tough and durable acrylic coating designed to protect and seal interior wood under the name of "Wood Armor." It is resistant to oils, greases, food and water. It is not available in aerosol spray cans. Brushes can be cleaned with soap and water.

Epoxy Resin Topcoat

This is an excellent finish when extra toughness and durability are required. The finish comes in two containers and must be mixed in equal parts shortly before applying (the same as epoxy glue). The directions on the cans should be carefully followed.

Polyester Resin Topcoat

This finish provides a thick layer of finish material. The polyester resin is mixed with a catalyst under carefully controlled conditions and for that reason it is seldom used except in industrial woodworking.

PENETRATING FINISHES

Penetrating finishes are ideal for the home craftsman. He does not have to worry about special finishing facilities and they eliminate dust problems. Brushes and spray equipment are not needed which gets rid of another problem. Many of these wipe-on and penetrating finishes are synthetic chemical ingredients, which not only penetrate the surface but actually combine chemically with the wood. They do not react chemically but combine to form a substance with a different molecular weight which is known as *polymerization.*

Watco Danish oil—Watco-Dennis Corp. (192)—is a popular penetrating polymerizing oil finish particularly adapted to contemporary and Scandinavian furniture. It *primes, hardens, seals finishes* and *protects* in one simple application. It completely and deeply penetrates with its five-in-one action, then changes from a liquid into a permanent solid *inside* the wood, not on it.

Watco Danish oil is available in natural and medium, dark and black walnut colors. It is designed for new wood, but may be used on old wood if the finish is completely removed. It works best on hardwoods (walnut, teak, rosewood, maple, cherry and birch), but can be used on softwoods (knotty pine, cedar, redwood, etc.).

Watco Danish oil finish will not gum out in warm temperatures, and it cannot chip, peel or wear away. Because of its sealing action, it lessens warping, swelling, splintering and checking. Watco-Dennis also manufactures many other wood, tile, marble and *terrazzo* finishing materials.

Sealacell—General Finishes (82) provides a 1-2-3 process of penetrating wood finishes. The preparation of the wood is important, because finishing accents imperfections as well as the beauty of the wood. Raw wood should be sanded with 4/0-180 garnet paper followed by 8/0-280 paper.

Sealacell #1

As the first coat on all woods, it should be applied very liberally with a cloth. If staining is desired, *Seal-A-Stain* may be used in place of *Sealacell #1.* Allow to dry about 12 hours and then buff lightly with 000 steel wool, with the grain, to remove any roughness. Wipe with a clean dry cloth.

Varnowax #2

Varnowax is applied sparingly over the Sealacell #1 and rubbed in circular motion with a small pad of cloth, using only enough material to lightly cover surface. Wipe off the excess finish with the grain of the wood. Allow 12 hours to dry, then buff lightly with 000 steel wool, with the grain, to remove any roughness. Wipe with a dry, clean cloth.

Royal Finish #3

Apply *Royal Finish* #3 over Varnowax #2 in the same manner as Varnowax #2. Allow Royal Finish #3 to dry at least 12 hours, then buff lightly with 000 steel wool, with the grain, to remove any roughness. To increase the depth and luster, additional coats of Royal Finish #3 may be applied, allowing 12 hours drying time between coats and buffing lightly between coats with 000 steel wool.

John Harra Wood and Supply Co. (106) markets a DPS (Deep Penetrating Sealer) that penetrates deeply, seals, stabilizes and applies easily. It retards the movement of moisture from inside and outside by lining the cellular wall and sealing those cells via a chemical (polymerization) process. Polymerization is complete in 72 hours, resulting in a dry, clear, non-toxic, waterproof, long-lasting finish. DPS penetrates ¼″ deep on end grain, and up to ⅛″ deep on surface grain.

DPS can be applied by rag, brush, spray or by dipping. It enhances the wood's natural color and can be mixed with any oil based stain. Varnish, shellac, lacquer, enamels or polyurethane may be applied over DPS.

Applying Penofin Oil—Sealer and Finish

Sand the wood, using 180 grit or finer sandpaper for final cut, and then wipe clean. Apply *Penofin oil*, completely soaking all surfaces. Continue to add Penofin oil to dry areas as they appear for a period of 30 minutes. Reapply Penofin oil to all surfaces, allowing an additional 15 minutes for penetration.

Wipe off any excess oil remaining on suface with a soft dry cloth. Oiled surfaces should be wiped dry within 45 minutes of initial application to avoid surface buildup and tackiness, these conditions may be removed by rubbing affected area with fine steel wool lubricated with fresh Penofin oil. Wipe dry immediately.

When the surface feels dry, additional coats of Penofin oil may be applied to enhance the finish. Wipe dry as before. Allow finished wood to dry at least 12 hours before putting into use.

Burns, mars and scratches may be removed by light sanding with fine sandpaper or steel wool and local application of Penofin oil. Wood may be reoiled as needed after removal of any wax or polish.

Penofin oil may be applied with fine steel wool, brush, spray, cloth or by dipping. Penofin oil should not be thinned.

Minwax

Minwax (Minwax Co., Clinton, NJ 07014) is a penetrating sealer and wax, often combined with a stain, that is applied only to surfaces completely free of other finishes. This penetrating material should be used only on raw wood or over itself. No primer or sealer should be used. Two coats are recommended.

The contents should be mixed thoroughly and the first coat is applied with a brush or cloth. It is allowed to penetrate five to 15 minutes, removing excess with a clean cloth.

After 12 hours, a second coat can be applied in the same manner. Twenty-four hours after the second coat is applied, a paste finishing wax can be applied and polished.

If a harder finish is desired, Minwax's antique oil finish or polyurethane may be used instead of paste wax. Minwax is available in mahogany, walnut, maple, oak and pine colors.

SPRAYING EQUIPMENT AND ITS USE

The home craftsman will need the following minimum pieces of equipment for spraying a finish: a spray gun, a compressor, hose, a fireproof booth, an exhaust fan that will meet code specifications and a turntable.

Types of Spray Guns

Spray guns are either *siphon* or *pressure* feed. A siphon feed gun has a vent hole in the cover of the spray gun cup. Pressure feed guns have a portion of the air side tracked to the *closed* container so that the liquid is forced upward to the gun.

Spray guns are also identified as *bleeder* or *non-bleeder*. The bleeder gun has air passing through at all times which prevents excessive pressure from exploding the safety valve.

The non-bleeder gun allows air to enter gun only when the trigger is pulled, in which case the compressor must be controlled.

Spray nozzles are of two types: the external mix and the internal mix. If the gun is a siphon feed gun, it will have an external mix nozzle, if pressure feed, it will be internal mix.

The siphon feed gun is probably the best for the furniture maker, as it handles lacquers and other lightweight finishing materials with ease. It is adaptable to quick and numerous color and material changes. If heavy materials such as house paint, wall paints, or heavy enamels are the finishing materials, the pressure feed gun is by far the best.

Siphon Feed System. Especially useful when many color changes are involved. The best system for the home craftsman. Air pressure is regulated at the oil and water extractor. The amount of fluid is controlled by a screw on the gun.

Pressure Feed Cup System. Air pressure is controlled at the extractor and fluid pressure is controlled by a cup regulator.

Pressure Feed Tank System (Single Regulator). Designed for medium production. Air pressure is controlled at the extractor, and the pressure of the fluid at a tank regulator.

Pressure Feed Tank System (Double Regulator). Designed for portable spraying, the air and fluid pressures are regulated by two different air regulators on the tank.

Pressure Feed Circulating System. This system is designed for heavy, continuous, production spraying. Air pressure is regulated at the extractor and fluid pressure by the fluid regulator.

Compressor Maintenance

The *air filter* should be washed in a solvent when it becomes contaminated, and the compressor should be housed in a clean place.

The motor should not be switched on if there is pressure in the hose. This extra load may be too much for it to handle.

Ordinary extension cords should not be used. Extension cords 25' and under should be #16 wire. Extension cords of 50' should be #14 wire. If these specifications are not followed, there is apt to be a decided drop in the voltage.

SPRAYING FAULTS

Sags and runs suggest improper spraying technique. Amateurs should experiment on a test panel before starting work on a project.

Streaks are usually the result of poor overlapping of spraying strokes. *Fogging* or *misting* is generally the result of using cheap or incompatible thinner, or holding the gun too far away from the work. *Orange* peel is usually caused by not applying a full, wet coat of finish.

A *rough* or *sandy finish* is usually the result of overspraying. The overspray collects on a newly sprayed surface. Overspray should be directed away from freshly surfaced areas.

APPLYING LACQUER-BASED FINISHES

Although a spray gun may be used to apply enamels, paints, varnish, shellac and other non-lacquer-based finishes, it is almost a necessity for applying lacquers. The spray gun also applies finishes faster, with a smooth and even finish, particularly on carvings, moldings and hard to reach areas. Here is the procedure for applying lacquer-based finishes.

Pour sufficient material into the siphon spray gun cup to cover the project. Add up to 50% lacquer thinner and stir vigorously. If any lumps or foreign particles appear, the lacquer should be strained. A nylon stocking works well.

Attach the cup to the spray gun, and switch on the compressor. A constant pressure should be maintained while the gun is being used. The pressure will depend on the consistency of the material.

Apply the material with the trigger of the gun held back in a slow, steady motion similar to brush strokes. Spray the entire length of the surface and release the trigger just before reaching the end of the stroke. This will keep the material from piling up at the end of the stroke and will save the lacquer.

Keep the gun nozzle at a uniform distance from the work. The worker's body should sway with the gun rather than remain in a fixed position (Fig. 10-4).

Start with the lower parts of the project first and work upward. Leave the top until last.

Remove the cup from the gun after each coat. Insert the siphon pipe of the gun in lacquer thinner. Pull back the trigger forcing thinner through the gun and cleaning it.

If a considerable amount of lacquer is applied, it is best to disassemble the gun and clean it thoroughly. Take a toothbrush and clean inside of the cup lid. Wipe off the needle. Insert a sharpened match stick through the fluid tip. Push a broom straw through the horn holes. *Never use a wire for cleaning.*

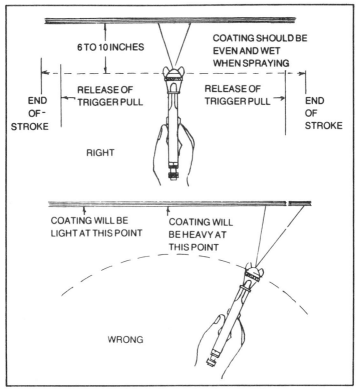

Fig. 10-4. Right and wrong spraying strokes.

Lubricate the fluid needle packing, the air valve packing and the trigger bearing screw. Allow one-and-one-half to two hours for each coat to dry. Generally three or four coats are sufficient (Figs. 10-5 through 10-11).

REFINISHING MATERIALS AND THEIR USE

Refinishing involves many different systems and techniques: from the simple process of sanding the finish lightly with fine sandpaper, followed by washing with warm soda water and finally rubbing with fine steel wool, to the more drastic measure of applying a paint and varnish remover, which removes all finishes down to the bare wood.

For varnished or lacquered finishes that are old and checkered, crazed or "alligatored," an *amalgamator* is used to "melt" the old topcoat and renew it to its original condition. The amalgamator is applied to the surface with a full brush. Sometimes another coat or two of the original finish is applied after the amalgamator is thoroughly dry and sanded lightly with fine sandpaper. Some amalgamators may be applied with a spray gun.

The older paint and varnish removers contained denatured alcohol, benzol and paraffin, but many of the newer removers contain no wax and are noninflammable. Remover should be used on only a small area at a time. After setting for two or three minutes, the finish can be peeled off in large chunks with a wide putty knife. Steel wool should be used for cleaning up carbings, moldings and turnings. A second coat of remover should be applied if the first coat does not do the trick. After the major portion of old finish has been removed, the entire project should be washed with

Fig. 10-5. Binks Model 15 touch-up spray gun in action.

Fig. 10-6. Binks No. 98-320 industrial spraying outfit with pressure tank.

white gasoline or benzine. Allow the surface to dry about five hours and sand lightly with fine sandpaper. Refinish the same as for new wood (stain, seal, fill, apply topcoats, etc.). *Apply paint and varnish remover, benzine, gasoline and other highly inflammable liquids outdoors or in a well-ventilated area.*

REFINISHING KITS

Brodhead-Garrett (30) has two refinishing kits: one for the amateur and one for the master refinisher. The major items in the master kit are gelled stain, gloss finish, sealer, rubbing oil, filler, lemon oil finish, solvent, Danish oil, rubbing pad, cleaning cups, dry stain, stir sticks, pick stick, brushes, disposable gloves, steel wool, cheesecloth, garnet and Wet-O-Dry sandpaper, steel wool wax, tack rag, rottenstone and pumice stone.

Formby's (73) *master refinishing kit* contains one gallon of furniture refinisher, 8 ounces of tung oil varnish, steel wool, 8 ounces of lemon oil, furniture treatment, one pan and one heavy-duty plastic drop cloth.

Amity (8) markets an *Amity 1-2-3 tung oil* refinishing kit which was developed as a clean and safe way to seal wood and produce finished wood products with that "hand rubbed" satin luster.

This system combines all the advantages of the traditional penetrating tung oil finish, with a new breakthrough—a quick drying agent that allows the home refinisher the finest wood finish in a fraction of the time and effort required in years past. Amity also manufactures and sells many other finishing materials and accessories.

Gillespie (86) provides a refinishing kit somewhat similar to Formby's. It contains one quart of refinisher, 8 ounces of lemon oil treatment, 8 ounces of furniture cleaner, 8 ounces of tung oil, steel

Fig. 10-7. Binks No. 98-1081 industrial standard spray outfit.

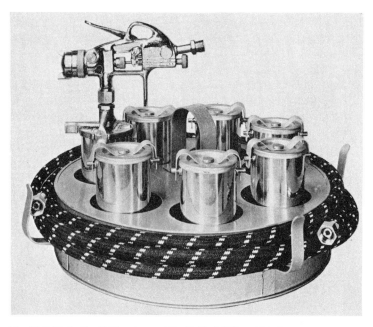

Fig. 10-8. Binks No. 6-4 touch-up outfit with Model 15 spray gun.

wool, refinishing pan, filigree brush, gloves, plastic floor cover and instruction booklet.

FRENCH POLISHING

French polishing is essentially the applying of extremely thin coats of shellac. Due to the large number of coats needed and the amount of hard work involved, its practice is generally confined to small projects or patching defects in a previous finish.

The main tool for applying French polish is a cone-shaped pad. A linen handkerchief or other lint-free material, about 6″ square, is the outside cover. Most any material may be used for the filler, but many finishers consider wool to be the best. The filler material is placed in the center of the lint-free outside covering.

The conical pad is soaked with one pound cut shellac by alternately squeezing and unleasing until the rubbing pad is uniformly moist, but in no case should the shellac be dripping. A few drops of linseed oil, machine oil or other rubbing oil is placed on the conical pad. Once rubbing is started, it must be continued until the shellac is used up, at which time the pad is removed while still in motion. More shellac and oil is added to the pad and the

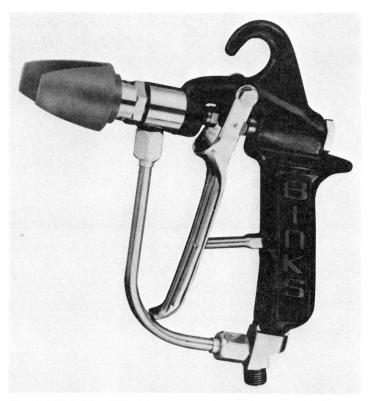

Fig. 10-9. Binks Model 700 airless spray gun to use with Model 98-990 Super BEE outfit.

Fig. 10-10. Binks Model 98-356 touch-up outfit for small or limited spraying jobs.

Fig. 10-11. Binks electric airless Model 98-990.

circular motion starts before the surface is touched. Rubbing is continued until the whole project is covered.

Permit the project to dry overnight. French polish should be continued each day until a substantial finish is built up. After the final application of French polish and drying time, the residual oil left on the finish is removed with a clean cloth and alcohol.

PATCHING DEFECTS BY BURNING IN

"Burning in" is the process of filling defects by filling the area with stick shellac or stick lacquer. "Burn ins" can be made at any time during the finishing process, but are more apt to be made after the final finish has been applied.

There are many different kinds of "burning in" knives. The one preferred by the professional is a heavy, production knife that holds the heat (Fig. 10-2).

Burn-in patching knives should be heated in pairs (one heating while the other one is in use). Some patchers prefer the alcohol lamp for heating while others prefer an electric knife heater that will hold two knives. Some knife heaters are provided with a pilot light.

A small amount of stick shellac or stick lacquer is picked up on the tip of the burning-in knife. The knife is then rolled over and a small amount of stick shellac or stick lacquer will be dropped into place with the backstroke (step 1, Fig. 10-12).

While the burning-in material is still in a liquid, pull the material into the defect with the return stroke. *Keep the knife in motion at all times* (step 2, Fig. 10-12). Continue the stroke to wipe

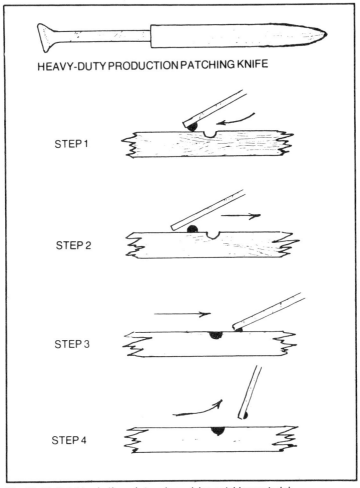

Fig. 10-12. Patching knife and steps in applying patching material.

the excess into a very thin film with the knife held at a low angle (step 3, Fig. 10-12).

Move the knife to a more vertical position and lift from the surface. The excess material will stick to the knife (step 4, Fig. 10-12).

The spot is then sanded with 320-9/0 sandpaper, rubbed with 0000 steel wool, and rubbed with pumice stone and water. If a high gloss is desired, rub with rottenstone and oil.

SUPPLIERS/MANUFACTURERS

Here are suppliers/manufacturers of finishing materials: Amity (8), Deft (53), Flecto (69), Formby's (73), Gaston (78), General Finishes (82), Gillespie (86), John Harra (106), K. P. Distributors (109), Penofin (141), PPG Industries (148), Star Chemical (173), United Gilsonite Laboratories (185) and Watco-Dennis Corp. (192). See the Appendix.

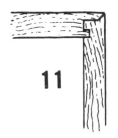

11

Miniature
Woodworking
Tools and Their Use

One of the most popular power tools in the miniature making field is the *Dremel Moto-Shop* (57). This 15″ jigsaw has a disc sander attached to it which increases its capability. In addition, a flexible shaft and accessories are available at extra cost. Drilling, routing, deburring, grinding, sharpening and carving are operations possible with this extra attachment.

DREMEL MOTO-SHOP

This multi-purpose saw will cut stock up to 1¾″ thick softwood and ½″ thick hardwood. The table raises and lowers to utilize the full length of the blade, and it also tilts to 45° on both sides of the perpendicular. The saw will cut to the center of a 30″ circle.

When cutting thick wood, the blade guard may have to be removed. It should be replaced when cutting thinner stock.

Jigsaw blades for the Dremel Moto-Shop have a pin in each end, and the distance from pin center to pin center is 2¾″. Blades are available in three grades: fine, medium and coarse. The coarse blade is wider and has 16 teeth to the inch. It should be used for straight cuts and curves with larger radii. An assortment of blades should be kept on hand at all times. Although they seldom break, they become dull and should be changed when any indication of this nature is noticed. It is false economy and a waste of time and effort to work with a dull blade when the cost factor is so low.

The Dremel jigsaw is a happy and practical compromise between the tiny vibrating jigsaw and the large, heavy, industrial type jigsaw with separate motor and belt driven. The extra expense and lack of portability in the larger saw is a definite drawback. At the other end of the scale, the vibrating type jigsaws are far from satisfactory. The blades cut very unevenly and slowly.

The serious miniature craftsman will find the Dremel Moto-Shop a good investment and it will pay for itself in short order. This high priority multi-purpose tool is not only enjoyable to use, but it takes most of the drudgery out of curve cutting (Fig. 11-1).

CUTTING INTERIOR CURVES WITH THE JIGSAW

Bore or drill one or more holes, large enough for the blade to be pushed through, in the center portion to be sawed out (waste stock). Keep the holes as far as possible from the scribed lines.

Remove the blade from the jigsaw. Place the hole just drilled over the throat of the jigsaw between the upper (spring loaded) chuck and the lower chuck. Insert the blade through the hole in the work, *teeth pointed down*, and place the ends of the blade in the two chucks.

Start sawing. The saw should angle gradually toward the line to be sawed.

If it is necessary to saw sharp corners, it is best to cut clear to the corner. Then back off and cut a well-rounded corner into the part at right angles to the corner cut. Run the saw to the nearest hole (if more than one) and cut the corner from the opposite direction.

SAWING SMALL OBJECTS ON THE JIGSAW

Draw an outline of the piece on self-adhesive paper with a sharp pencil. It is much easier to follow a line more accurately if fine lines are on paper than to follow lines on wood.

Place the drawing on the stock to be cut out with the adhesive side next to the stock. Rubber cement may be used with the pattern outlined on plain paper.

Adhere the pattern, with double-face adhesive paper or rubber cement, and the stock to a much larger piece of scrap wood about ¼″ thick. A circular piece between 3″ and 4″ in diameter is ideal because the craftsman has complete control of the work. The larger protective and control piece will prevent splintering out on the underside of the work.

DREMEL MOTO-LATHE

This light weight, inexpensive, precision mini-lathe made by Dremel (57) is just what hobbyists and miniaturists ordered. There are other small lathes, primarily designed for metal cutting, but the prices are almost prohibitive.

This lathe turns at 3450 rpm and will handle turnings up to 6″ in length and 1½″ diameter. It will also handle faceplate work.

It is an ideal tool for turning dollhouse newel posts, spindles for stair railings, "widow's walk" and turned dollhouse furniture parts. After using this tool for a number of houses, I could find only two minor faults which are greatly outweighed by its many excellent features. The constant speed motor runs a mite too fast for 1½″ diameter stock, and a trifle too slow for stock under ¼″ in diameter. Also, the handles on the four lathe turning tools (60° blade chisel, 30° blade chisel, round chisel and parting chisel) were too short. This situation can be remedied by turning a longer handle or by adding extensions to the original handles.

A small disc sander can be made to use with the lathe by turning a small disc attached to a faceplate. The disc sander is used primarily for sanding edges, not for sanding flat surfaces. Only the half of the disc that rotates *downward* is used. The piece should be kept in motion continuously and lightly against the disc so that the workpiece is not burned and the sandpaper on the disc is not clogged up with sandings or with gum from the workpiece.

When using small disc sanders, the circular sandpaper piece should be attached to the disc with rubber cement so that worn sandpaper can be replaced with new sandpaper without too much difficulty.

Fig. 11-1. Dremel Moto-Shop.

A cylindrical sander may be constructed to use with the *Dremel Moto-Lathe* by turning a cylinder between centers and covering it with sandpaper (Fig. 11-2).

DREMEL MOTO-TOOL

Although the major component of the *Dremel Moto-Tool* (57) is a small, portable electric drill, with all the accessories it becomes a versatile, multi-purpose tool. The variable speed rotary tool has a range of 5000 to 25,000 rpm.

The most economical way to purchase this tool is in the kit form. Although the kit does not include all the accessories available, it does contain 34 of the most used, including abrasive wheels and stones, mandrels, sanding discs and bands, collets, brushes and many others. The kit comes in an attractive plastic case.

As a drill, the Moto-Tool becomes much more flexible when used with the light weight drill press stand. The motor is easily attached to the Dremel drill press with two knurled knobs (Fig. 11-3).

The drill press differs from the conventional drill press table in that the work is lifted against the bit with a table lifting mechanism. Conventional drills move the drill bit downward into the workpiece. The table lifting mechanism is controlled (raised or lowered) by a knob on the right, lower part of the drill press.

On the left, lower part of the drill press is a similar knob which locks the table in position when performing operations other than drilling. There is a table stop in the center, lower part of the drill press which prevents the workpiece from ascending too far. In the table itself are four slots that can be used to fasten guides or hold-down clamps. Three-eighths inch carriage bolts of the proper length are used. Wing nuts are threaded on the top end of bolts. There is a height adjustment for the motor, which moves up and down on the column.

Sanding, routing, grooving, sawing, grinding and other operations may be done on the Dremel Moto-Tool drill press besides drilling.

Another useful addition is the router attachment. It is particularly useful in routing edges and cutting letters in wood or plastic signs. There are six router bits available. A six router bit kit contains three straight cutter bits (1/8", 3/16" and 1/4" in diameter), one convex bit, one veining bit and one "V" groove bit.

The universal stand attachment (another accessory) holds the motor at any angle leaving both hands free to hold the work. When

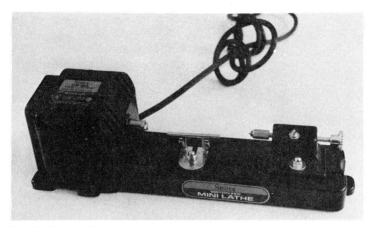

Fig. 11-2. Dremel Moto-Lathe.

used with cutting burrs and other cutters, the Moto-Tool becomes a miniature spindle carver similar to spindle carvers used in the furniture industry.

A few of the many accessories available for the Dremel Moto-Tool are as follows: routers, engraving cutters, high speed steel cutters, silicon grinding points, mounted wheel point set, steel saws, carbide cutters, mandrels, bristle brushes, drum

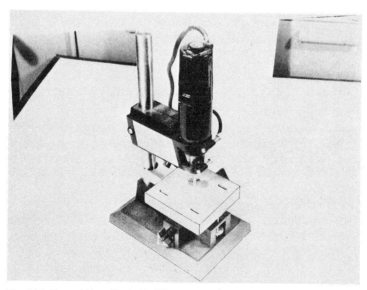

Fig. 11-3. Dremel Moto-Tool with drill press stand.

sanders, sander bands, cutoff wheels, sanding discs, polishing wheels, chuck collets, cloth wheels and steel brushes.

The Dremel Moto-Tool is used by many career specialists. The gunsmith, the model maker, patternmaker, engraver, sculptor, jeweler and dental technician are professionals that use or could use this tool to advantage.

Dovetailer

Percy and Marcy Fisher of "Scale of Twelve," 31203 Huntley Square East Birmingham, Michigan, 48009, market a dovetail jig that works like a charm with the Moto-Tool. The front and side of a drawer can be dovetailed at the same time. The fishers also supply the special dovetail bits (Fig. 11-4).

Dialing The Correct Speed With The Dremel Moto-Tool

Speeds can be dialed from 5000 to 25,000 rpm. The speed selected varies according to the material being worked on. As a general rule, soft and delicate pieces require slower speeds. If possible, try out the speed on waste or scrap stock. The perfect speed will be in a range of a few hundred rpms. Only by experimenting will the craftsman arrive at the perfect speed. When the correct speed is ascertained, the miniaturist should make a written note of the material and the correct speed.

Hard materials such as metal, glass and some of the harder woods require faster speeds. Very fast speeds are required for routing, rabbeting, grooving, dadoing and some shaping operations. Safety instructions come with the kit and should be carefully observed.

Dental Drill

The *dental drill* has certain advantages over other drills. There is a wider selection of burrs and cutters, and the small, pencil-like drill is less cumbersome. It can be used for long periods of time without undue strain on fingers, hand, wrist and forearm. It is, by far, the best tool for executing small, delicate carvings (Fig. 11-5).

HAND TOOLS

Although vises and holding devices are not true tools, they are essential to quality craftsmanship.

Rapid Positioning Vise

If the miniature furniture maker must settle for one vise, the *rapid positioning vise* is probably the best selection. The vise jaw

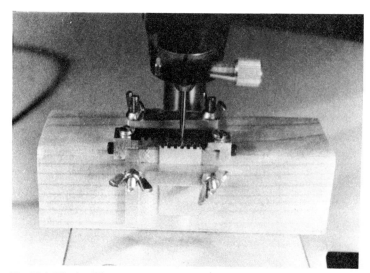

Fig. 11-4. "Scale of Twelve" dovetailer and Dremel Moto-Tool.

widths are 2″ and 2¼″. There are three selections of the "ball-and-socket" rapid positioning bases: 2½″, 3⅝″ and 4½″ diameter.

There are also "third hand" clamps available which may attach to the rapid positioning bases. These handy accessories hold the workpiece securely and the miniaturist is free to work with both hands. "Third hands" speed up the work and protect the piece from

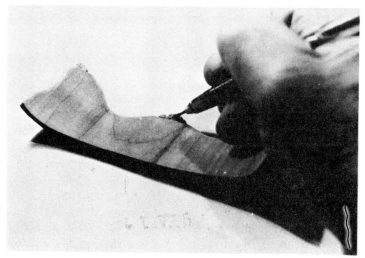

Fig. 11-5. Carving back of Victorian sofa with a dental drill.

damage. *X-acto* makes an X-acto *X-tra Hands* device fitted with alligator clips and a heavy base to prevent tipping. It can be held in a vise or clamped to a bench top.

Pana-Vise

The *Pana-Vise*, manufactured by Colbert Die Cast Co., South Gate, California, is similar to the rapid positioning vise. It swivels 360°, tilts 90° and locks tight in any position. It is available with either nylon or steel jaws. This vise makes impossible jobs possible and possible jobs easy. This vise is widely used by model makers, instrument workers, jewelers and pattern makers.

The jaw width is 2½″ and the jaw maximum opening is 2¼″. The "ball-and-socket" base comes in the bolt-down type and the vacuum base type. The vacuum base type can only be attached to a smooth, flat, hard surface. It is attached by simply turning a lever (Fig. 11-6).

Small Clamps

The *X-acto "C" clamps* are especially designed and engineered for the miniaturist. The thin, flat frame allows the clamp to get into tight places and corners. The screwdriver slot in the handle permits greater pressure than could be applied by using the forefinger and thumb (Fig. 11-7).

Hammers

There are numerous hammers that may be used in miniature furniture construction. About the only requirement is that they be small. Hammers weighing over one-half pound (8 ounces) are apt to be too heavy and cumbersome.

The upholsterer's hammer, the sheet metal riveting hammer and the X-acto mini-hammer all work well with mini-furniture construction.

Most small hammers are fitted with handles that are too long for the user. To overcome this deficiency, cut off ½″ of the handle at a time until it feels right (proper balance) for the user (Fig. 11-8).

Razor Saws

X-acto manufactures a number of fine tooth saw blades ranging in width from ¾″ to 1¼″ and with teeth numbering up to 70 teeth per inch. An angled shank on the blade fits into a collet on a plastic handle. It is similar to the dovetail saw used in conventional full-size furniture making.

344

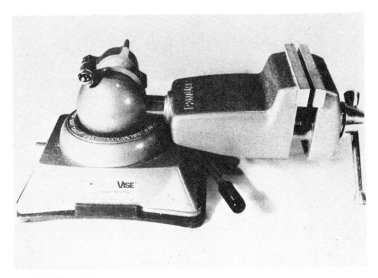

Fig. 11-6. Pana-Vise, vacuum base.

Starting cuts with these saws are best made *toward the user on the backward stroke.* Small strips, moldings and dowels are held in a miter box for sawing to length with the razor saw. The long pieces should be held against the side of the miter box *next to the user.*

Fig. 11-7. X-acto "C" clamps.

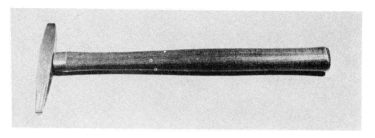

Fig. 11-8. Upholsterer's hammer.

SUMMARY

In this short chapter only the major tools for the miniaturist are listed and described. There are many more tools and accessories that are needed to become a serious miniaturist. The dedicated, would-be dollhouse furniture maker should read two of my other books, *How To Build Your Own Fine Doll Houses & Furnishings* (TAB Book No. 1102) and *Building Antique Doll House Furniture From Scratch* (TAB book No. 1240)

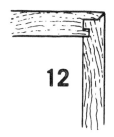

12

Mass Production and Industrial Woodworking

The problems and methods of mass production of furniture and other industrial woodworking items are quite different from those encountered by home craftsmen, industrial arts students or even by small custom woodworking shops. There are five essential differences between these woodworking activities.

■ The mass producing woodworking factories, as a general rule, use larger, heavier and more specialized equipment.

■ With the exception of cabinet makers and other highly skilled craftsmen, the workers in these industries are skilled in working on only one small segment or operation involved in the making of a larger unit (e.g. a piece of furniture). The home craftsman is involved in all the operations and parts in constructing his project.

■ Another factor is the greater ability of the larger establishments to control all aspects of the manufacturing processes. Some furniture factories have their own wood lots and sawmills, and control the whole production process even to the making of their own trim hardware. Some even have their own trucks for delivering the final product.

■ Greater accuracy must be maintained to provide for the interchangeability of parts.

■ Another characteristic of a large woodworking industry is that of developing a product that is easy to produce, but still meets the criteria of acceptable appearance and structural strength.

Not all woodworking industries are alike in size, scope and kinds of machinery used. Manufacturers of sporting goods equipment, architectural components, millwork, store fixtures and musical instruments are quite different from the furniture industry described in this chapter. However, there are certainly elements of similarity among all woodworking establishments. By changing the sequence of departments through which the products move, or by adding or eliminating a department or two, it is possible to establish an organizational structure for almost any woodworking industry.

The organizational structure covered in this chapter does not represent any particular industry but is a hypothetical composite of many woodworking industries. In all probability some companies include departments not included in Table 12-1.

SAWMILL

Some manufacturers own and operate their own sawmills and, in addition, may own their own wood lots. In some cases, mobile sawmills are used so they may be moved to new locations when the lumber is depleted in one area. It is a big advantage to have the sawmill within a transportable distance from the manufacturer.

YARD DEPARTMENT

The *lumber yard* foreman is responsible for proper storage of rough lumber as it comes from the sawmill. This green lumber is sorted, graded and stacked for air drying. The lumber is stacked so that air can circulate freely around each piece. Each layer of lumber is separated by narrow boards called *stickers*. The lumber is allowed to air dry from a few weeks to a number of months depending on the thickness and species of the lumber.

KILN DEPARTMENT

The *dry kiln department* supervisor or foreman must work very closely with the yard supervisor. Generally, he is notified in advance when certain amounts and species of lumber are to be moved from the yard to the dry kiln. In some cases the green lumber may be moved directly into the kiln as it comes from the sawmill.

PLANNING AND OFFICE DEPARTMENT

The function of *planning* is to design, select and engineer the product. The function of *office services* is to attend to fiscal business, sales, payroll, etc.

The *designer* is the key to the conception of what the product might look like. Appearance is a large factor is salability. There are two types of designers: the super designer whose creative imagination designs a product quite different than any product conceived before, and the run-of-the-mill designer who relies on feedback from consumers, colleagues, cabinetmakers, interior decorators, furniture salesmen, other designers, administrative personnel and others. Each type of designer has his place in the scheme of furniture design. The larger furniture manufacturers often have their own full-time furniture designers, but more often the designer is a free lance operator who may design for a number of companies.

When the manufacturer makes a decision to manufacture a certain product to fulfill a need based on evaluation, in-plant discussion, and market research, the designer takes over. The first step is to make a number of preliminary freehand sketches—often in color. He then shows these sketches to the administration, the sales force, furniture purchasers, engineers and others before making his final sketch based on the feedback he has received. The designer spends much more time and energy on the final sketch than on the preliminary sketches.

After the final sketch has been approved by the administration and all others directly concerned, the designer and/or his assis-

Table 12-1. Anatomy of a Furniture Factory.

```
1. The Saw Mill
2. The Yard Department
3. The Kiln Department
4. The Planning and Office Department
        a. Design
        b. Product Selection
        c. Engineering
        d. Business
        e. Sales
        f. Finance
5. The Cutting and Rough Milling Department
6. The Veneer Department
7. Machine Department
8. Carving Department
9. Machine Sanding Department
10. Cabinet Department
11. Finishing Department
12. Upholstery Department
13. Trim Department
14. Inspection Department
15. Storage, Packaging, Shipping and Receiving Department
```

tants make a detailed full-size drawing. This drawing does not include the engineering aspects or the production problem. It includes only those characteristics which are concerned with the terminal visual impression and function of the object. The detailed full-size drawing must be complete as far as proportion and scale is concerned. In other words, all projections, curved parts, turned members, molding contours, grain direction, upholstered areas, hardware trim, etc., must be accurately portrayed.

This full-size drawing is turned over to the planning or engineering section. This section is the bridge between the designing section and many production departments of the industry.

The engineering section develops drawings of individual parts and sets forth the specifications and other instructions necessary for a smooth flow of parts through the factory. It also compiles material bills and develops working instructions and follow-up documents that follow each batch of furniture components through the shop.

The engineering section's next responsibility is to construct samples of the newly-designed piece of furniture. These samples in essence are "pilot run" models. These samples are put on exhibition. Furniture retail store purchasers visit these exhibitions and make the necessary purchases. These exhibitions are held at only certain times during a year.

Traveling furniture salesmen, representing a manufacturer, sell from artists' drawings or photographs the remainder of the time. At one time, in the latter part of the 19th century and the early part of the 20th century, traveling furniture salesmen carried miniature replicas of the actual pieces with them on their journeys. See pages 307-310 in my book entitled *How To Build Your Own Fine Doll Houses & Furnishings* (TAB book No. 1102).

During and after the samples are made, the engineering section is constantly checking the specifications and drawings, comparing them with the samples. All of the documentation (route sheets, part drawings, etc.) must be absolutely accurate before a production run can be made in the factory. Once this documentation is completed, it is not necessary to repeat the process for subsequent production runs, except for small changes that occur because someone has discovered a small error or has developed a better way to produce a component.

350

Material Bill

Material bills or parts lists are generally of two types: lumber bills and purchased items (hardware, fasteners, drawer guides, etc.). Regarding the lumber parts, an engineer, or one of his assistants, looks over the detail drawing very closely to ascertain the exact dimensions of the lumber components necessary to make one piece of furniture.

Each bill of material for lumber, in addition to a description of the part, has a part number or some code identification, finished sizes (length, width and thickness), number of board feet, species of wood, remarks or special instructions and the number of pieces required for each unit. A bill of material for veneers includes the number of plies. The rough dimensions are added to the lumber bill, or the machine department is allowed to use its own discretion as to the amount to be added to the finished dimensions so that the parts will "clean-up" in the machine operations.

All the bills of material are derived from the designer's detailed drawing and are used for the construction of the pilot run (samples) and for production runs after all the "bugs" have been eliminated.

Samples are made for exhibition purposes. In addition to the exhibition pieces, it is common practice to make a few extras for reference purposes in the engineering section or elsewhere.

The sample models are not made by the production departments, but are made in a sample making room. The equipment is quite comparable to tools found in a sophisticated home woodworking shop or custom furniture shop. A great deal of hand work is done on samples.

Samples are used to sell furniture, to observe the piece in three dimensions so that corrections might be made, and to work out the "bugs" of fitting, machining, joining and problems of assembly before actual production runs are started.

Drawings and dimensions must be much more precise for production runs than for making samples. All hand work must be eliminated or held to an absolute minimum. Hand work is expensive and adds a great deal to the cost of manufacturing and eventually to the cost that the customer must pay. No matter how accurate a drawing might be, it is difficult to transfer dimensions and shapes to the wood. Other methods were devised: the *rod* and the *master drawing*.

The Rod

The *rod* was for many years considered Grand Rapids' "secret weapon" for outproducing its competitors in the manufacture of quality furniture. Other methods have nearly superseded this tool, but it is still used by some furniture and fixture industries.

The rod is a long, thin board of solid or plywood stock. The outline of the parts are very accurately drawn in with a sharp knife point. These knife lines are then inscribed with black ink or with a sharp pencil. The rod is finally protected with a coat of clear lacquer or white shellac.

The toy table discussed and depicted in Chapter 1 is again used to illustrate visually what is discussed (refer back to Chapter 1). The orthographic working drawing shows a separate top, front and end (Fig. 12-1).

The rod has some similarities to the orthographic working drawing although the nomenclature of views is quite different. For example, the top portion of the rod directly below the small perspective, which consists of what would be called on the orthographic drawing the top and front view, is called the *plan view* on the rod. The center drawing on the rod is called a *side view* while on the orthographic it would be known as the end view. The bottom drawing on the rod is really a side view tipped up on edge (Fig. 12-2).

It should be noted that there are no dimensions written in on the rod. Whenever a part is needed, the length, width, thickness or height is extended to the working edge (left edge) of the rod, and the machine is set to cut the distance between these extensions. Many times the rod is laid directly on the machine. For example, a saw would be set so that one extension would coincide with the other extension and the saw fence with the other. After a trial piece is cut, it is placed on the rod in order to check its size.

The biggest problem in using a rod—which takes many hours to construct—is that a number of woodworking machine operators may want to use the rod at the same time. The only solution is to construct a number of rods, which is rather costly, or make a number of small rods, each designed for one part only.

In spite of the drawbacks of using a rod, it serves, and is still serving, a useful purpose. Before the use of rods, each machine operator set up his own machine by using his own measuring device (scale, rule, tape, etc.). Many of these measuring devices, particularly the wooden folding rule, could not be counted on for accuracy. In addition, it was easy for the operator to translate, for example, 35¾" on a drawing to 35⅜" on the machine, thus perhaps ruining many pieces of stock before it was discovered.

Master Drawing

The master full-size drawing is a vast improvement over the rod. The drawing is made on glass fiber cloth which is dimensionally stable and is not affected by environmental conditions (heat, cold, moisture, dryness, etc.)

Only the most significant dimensions are listed on the master drawing, that is, the dimension of major parts which affect all the other parts. The master drawing retains all of the factors (appearance, scale, proportion, and fine points of decoration and carving) set forth by the designer. In addition, it has sufficient and accurate information necessary for making quality furniture in any quantity.

Separate drawings are made from the master drawing for each and every part, and these drawings are duplicated in any number necessary. These part drawings accompanied by a *processing tag* follow the parts as they are being cut and shaped from the first cut until the part is assembled into the completed whole. The processing tag has about the same information as would be found on one line of a bill of material, along with a list of operations necessary to complete the piece. In some cases, the jig, fixture, template or rods are listed and the kind of machine is indicated.

Fig. 12-1. Toy table.

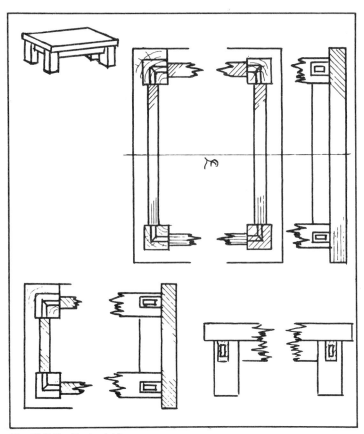

Fig. 12-2. Rod for toy table.

Jigs, Fixtures, Templates and Patterns

Jigs, fixtures, templates and patterns have a great deal in common. They speed up the operation and they maintain consistency in size and shape.

Jigs are often portable holding devices that assist in securing the piece while operations are being performed. Often clamping jigs are used to hold parts under pressure while glue is setting.

A *fixture* is usually a special device permanently attached to a machine and it performs a special function. Templates and patterns are essentially the same thing, although a template is often considered temporary in nature while a pattern is considered a permanent tool.

If all parts of a piece of furniture had rectangular shapes and straight lines, there would be little need for patterns and templates. However, many pieces of furniture have irregular shapes and curved lines which make patterns imperative.

The band saw pattern is the least complicated of patterns. The sawyer lays the pattern on the wood to be cut and marks around it. Patterns and templates are often made of solid wood or plywood. Where close accuracy is required, a parts pattern is made photographically by projecting the image from the glass fiber master drawing onto aluminum or some other metal and shaping the metal carefully to the size and the shape of the image. This provides a permanent and long-lasting pattern unaffected by dimensional changes.

Almost all work done on the shaper and router requires jigs or patterns. Whenever the complete edge of a piece is shaped, it is placed on a pattern or jig and the pattern is forced against the collar of the shaper.

The router pattern has the shape of the completed part on the under part of the pattern. This shape rides against a pin on the table which is directly below the router bit.

Office Section

The office section is responsible for many things. One of the more important functions is the *control of production*.

The administrative personnel notify the production staff (general manager, plant superintendent, the departmental foreman, etc.) as to the number and design of specific pieces to be run by means of an *industry production run*. A definite starting date is established and a completion time is set forth, and on the basis of this, schedule promises can be made to the customers (furniture buyers) as to when delivery can be made.

A production progress board is used to ascertain daily if production quotas are being made. The information is derived from numerous individual employee time cards, work records, job tickets, etc.

Considerable preliminary work must be accomplished before the *industrial production* is sent to the production staff. An inventory must be made of lumber and veneer supplies to determine if enough stock is available to finish the order. A certain percentage must also be allowed for waste. The purchasing agent must start ordering the purchased parts necessary.

The office section performs many other functions (sales, fiscal affairs, payroll, cost estimates, accounting, etc.), but this book is concerned primarily with tools, techniques, tips, and methods and materials relating to the production of woodworking projects.

CUTTING AND ROUGH MILLING DEPARTMENT

The yard department supervisor and kiln department supervisor must work in cooperation with the cutting department foreman or supervisor to make sure there is enough lumber to start, maintain and complete the order. It is not necessary to have the total amount needed on the starting day, but a steady and sufficient supply of material must be assured.

The *cutting and rough milling department* is where actual production begins. The kiln-dried lumber is cut to rough dimensions. All defects (knots, sap wood, blemishes, cracks, splits, etc.) are cut out. Wide boards that may be warped are cut into narrow boards which are glued together and then surfaced to final thickness. Glued-up stock is much more stable and is less apt to warp than solid stock. In addition, widths that would not be available in solid stock can be built up of narrow pieces glued together. Rough stock is always longer and wider than finished stock sizes with the exception of finished narrow stock, such as posts, which are machined to the final width and thickness; however, the length still remains "in the rough."

When the lumber parts leave the cutting room, the color of the wood should be consistent. The parts should be straight and square with no warp or twist. All glued-up joints must be snug. No checks, blemishes or cracks should be evident, and no machine defects should be visible. There should also be at least one working face, or working edge, that can be relied upon as absolutely true.

Band Saw

The resawing operation is done on a large band saw. When thin lumber is needed, it may be possible to get two or three thin pieces out of a thicker piece by splitting the larger piece. Boards are fed into the band saw on edge between large fences or rollers—some of which are power fed—into the band saw.

Yates-American (214) manufactures a large vertical, 60" diameter, band resaw machine with a 5 hp motor that has variable feed drive and controls which offer variable feed rates up to 225' per minute.

Precision Concepts Corp. (150) manufactures a band resaw feed unit which converts standard 30" and larger saws to resaw units. It has a 10 step feed from a low speed of 6' per minute to 90' per minute. It has a roller fence and rubber roll feed unit. Serrated metal rollers are available as optional equipment (Fig. 12-3).

Oliver Machinery Co. (135) makes a 36" bandsaw which is easily converted to a band resaw with the Precision Concepts feed unit or some similar device. This machine is powered by a 5 hp or 7½ hp motor. The band saw is equipped with brakes and has a 36″ x 36″ table 40″ from the floor. The column height may be increased on one model 13″ to give 36″ under the guide (Fig. 12-4).

Cutoff Saw

The first in-line production operation in the cutting and rough milling department is done on the cutoff saw. Lumber is fed to the cutoff saw operator by a slide or conveyor. The cutoff man looks at both sides of the lumber to see if there are defects to be cut out. Only one specie of lumber and only one thickness are cut at a time.

Ekstrom, Carlson and Co. (62) manufactures an automatic, straight line, cutoff saw. The shortest stroke is 6″ and the longest 23″. The forward thrust of the head and ram is cushioned by the air in the cylinder as well as by compression springs. The backward thrust is cushioned by rotary shock absorbers and by two special rubber pumpers mounted on the motor housing. The air operated head and ram, activated by a foot pedal, require 30 pounds per square inch.

An 18″ saw blade will cut through a piece of stock 5″ thick and 18½″ wide. The saw is generally used with infeed and outfeed tables to the right and left of the saw (Fig. 12-5).

Fig. 12-3. Band resaw feed unit to fit band saws 30″ and larger.

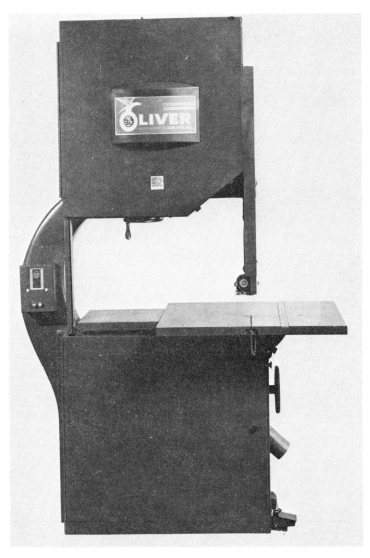

Fig. 12-4. 36" band saw #2416.

C.O. Porter Machinery Co. (42) produces a hydraulically controlled cutoff saw for the woodworking industry. It has variable cutting speeds up to a maximum of 120' per minute. It will cut material up to 6" thick. The machine can be set for feed speeds from 0-120' per minute with constant full speed carriage return. The motor is 7½ hp, 3450 rpm totally enclosed and is fan cooled. The maximum length of stroke on the standard model is 20", but optional models provide for 30″ and 36″ maximum strokes. The standard model calls for an 18″ saw blade and the optional models use a 20″ blade (Fig. 12-6).

Fig. 12-5. Automatic, straight-line, cutoff saw.

Fig. 12-6. Hydraulically controlled cutoff saw.

Goodspeed Machine (89) manufactures a double or triple trim cutoff saw that is hopper fed. This one-man operated machine has an automatic conveyor type hopper which feeds stock to carrier wheels for cutting. This cutoff saw is designed to rapidly trim squares and doweled stock to length before turning or other production operations. It is powered by a 7½ hp motor and takes 14″ carbide saws (Fig. 12-7).

Oliver Machinery Co. (135) makes a hydraulically operated "straitline" cutoff saw which saws up to 20″ in diameter and will cut stock up to 6″ thick. The maximum stroke length is 20″, which can be repeated at the rate of 23 strokes per minute. The saw cycle is actuated by touching the large palm button and can be stopped at any point in the forward stroke by again touching the palm button. The saw is powered by a 7½ hp motor. The hydraulic pump motor is one hp and delivers 150 pounds pressure with 8 gallon tank capacity (Fig. 12-8).

No. 1 Ripsaw

The No. 1 ripsaw in the production line in the rough mill is usually a chain-fed ripsaw. Some chain fed ripsaws have the saw above the stock while others have the saw underneath. All have a large, flat, smoothly polished table, with a short fence or guide that steers the lumber into the chain. The chain operates on both sides of the saw and the saw must be parallel to the chain. There are rolls which exert pressure against the stock to hold it against the chains.

The rip sawyer's first priority is to cut wide boards into narrow ones to eliminate warpage, twist, high spots, etc. A wide board ripped into narrow ones will go through the surface without the removal of an excess amount of wood. The rip sawyer's second priority is to help (along with the cutoff man) eliminate defects in the lumber.

Yates-American (214) manufactures a multiple undercut ripsaw. This versatile machine is designed to do a number of ripping operations exceedingly well. It can be used as a straight-line single as well as a multiple ripsaw. The feed drive motor is 5 hp with a 60

Fig. 12-7. Double or triple trim cutoff saw.

Fig. 12-8. Hydraulic "Straitline" cutoff saw #94.

hp motor driving the saws. Feeds are from 75 to 300′ per minute. The table is 56″ long by 4″ wide.

Precision Concepts Corp. (150) produces a straight line ripsaw with three sets of anti-kickback fingers, an adjustable fence with a scale in both inches and millimeters, and variable feed speeds up to 100′ per minute (Fig. 12-9).

Ekstrom, Carlson and Co. (62) makes two models of undercutting, straight line, chain feed, glue joint ripsaws. The short arm model has a capacity of 25¾″ from the blade to the arm, while the wide arm model has a capacity of 48¼″ for the distance from the blade to the arm. The wide arm model will easily handle a 4′ x 8′ plywood panel. Both models handle an 18″ blade and are powered by motors up to 30 hp.

Both saws are undercutting as a result of tests conducted by the Forest Products Laboratory at Madison, Wisconsin. The lab recommends that the saw blade protrude about ½″ through the stock for best results. This is only possible with an undercutting saw. With the undercutting saw with its downward cutting blade and its safer clockwise rotation, the teeth tend to hold the ripped-off stock down against the chain (Figs. 12-10 and 12-11).

Planer

After the stock is ripped into narrow pieces, it must be surfaced to a uniform thickness. Sometimes a small planer is used to get a working face, and a much larger, heavier planer is used to cut the stock to thickness. Some industries use double surfacers which surface both faces at once. They have cutting heads both below and above the stock. Others use the "Straitoplane" which is jointer and planer combined into one. With this machine it is

362

possible to surface a twisted, cupped and warped piece of lumber into a perfectly straight, flat and smooth piece of stock with just one pass through the machine. The secret is the use of cams instead of rollers. They do not flatten the stock as rollers do. The board passes over a cutter head which acts as a jointer. The equivalent of a single surfacer is a part of the outboard table. This cutterhead surfaces the upper surface.

The Oliver Machinery Co. (135) "Straitoplane" is offered in sizes of 18″, 24″ and 36″. Boards as short as 18″ and as thick as 12″ may be machined at speeds up to 120′ per minute. Maximum widths of boards or of glued up panels is 36″ with 42″, 52″, 64″ and 76″ widths available on special order. Motors up to 100 hp can be used for the top cutters and up to 75 hp can be used for the bottom cutters.

A full 72″ allows most glued-up panels to clear the lower head before being engaged by the upper head. This contributes vastly to the smoothness, straightness and flatness of the finish. This allows

Fig. 12-9. Straight line ripsaw.

Fig. 12-10. Short arm, straight line, chain feed, glue joint ripsaw.

the "Straitoplane" to be used as a finishing planer for glued panels and wide boards, as well as in its long-accustomed role as a rough mill plane (Fig. 12-12).

Yates-American Machine Co. (214) manufactures a double surfacer for prefinishing stock in furniture factories, lumber mills, hardwood flooring plants, and sash and door plants. Separate motors mounted on sturdy brackets, are coupled to each cutterhead. There are four motors on this machine. A 2 hp motor raises and lowers the bed a distance of 14". A 10 hp motor drives the feed mechanism from 60 to 160' per minute. The top cutterhead is powered by a 25 hp motor and the lower cutterhead is powered by 15 hp motors.

Oliver Machinery Co. (135) makes two single surfacers. One has a capacity (24" single surfacer) of 24" x 8" and is powered by two motors: 7½ hp for the cutter head and 1½ hp for the feed.

The cylindrical cutterhead is unique in that it has inserted tooth carbide cutters; 84 four-sided bits are inserted in the cutterhead body. It reduces the noise level from that of the straight knife head and provides a considerably longer time between grinds.

The other Oliver planer is a screw bed single surfacer with a 30" x 8" capacity, with a 20 hp cutterhead motor, a 2 hp feed motor and a one-third hp table hoist motor. The feed speeds are 20 to 60' per minute.

Other Ripsaws and the Hand Jointer

Many woodworkers feel that a good glue joint must be produced with a jointer. Others contend that the straight line, chain feed ripsaw will make an acceptable glue joint.

364

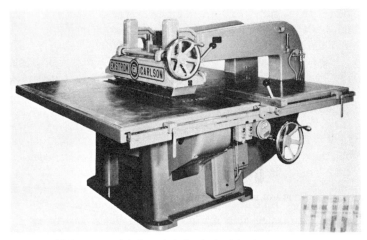

Fig. 12-11. Wide arm, straight line, chain feed, glue joint ripsaw.

To be on the safe side, many woodworking industries use a power feed glue-jointer. Many plants run all of their ripped stock through the glue-jointer regardless of whether the parts are to be glued or not, because of the smoother edges on the stock. The power-feed glue jointer has an endless feed chain in the center. The rollers which put pressure on the stock are on the sides. The parts

Fig. 12-12. Straitoplane #2170.

move past a cutterhead which joints one edge. The part moves down one side, is flipped over and moves back on the other side to joint the second edge.

Recall that the No. 1 ripsaw was a chain feed saw and was in the "mainstream" of production or "on line." The terminal or last ripsaws are not "on line" but are adjunct machines to assist the "mainstream" operations. It is the responsibility of these rip sawyers to search and eliminate defects that were not caught on the first "go-a-round." Their first priority is conservation of material and the elimination of waste. Again, the lumber is matched up for color and grain. The stock is placed on carts ready to be glued together.

The old reliable *hand jointer* will be found in many departments (the rough mill, machine room, cabinet department and others). As such, it is not in the mainstream of production but is used as an auxiliary piece of equipment. This versatile machine can be used any place when it is necessary to remove a small amount of wood from the face or edge of a part.

In spite of its flexibility, this is a dangerous machine to use. The operator should be thoroughly instructed and trained in the use of this machine. The guard should never be removed except for maintenance (Fig. 12-13).

Cutting Room Gluing

Proper gluing depends on many factors. Pressure must be applied equally and forcefully at all points. Clamps must be close together. Pressure should not be released until the glue is firmly set. Heating hastens the drying time of animal and synthetic resin glues. The boards must be perfectly flat in the clamps and must be square and straight, and the glue must be spread evenly in sufficient quantity.

Glue Application to Small Parts

Black Brothers (25) makes a small stock gluer that will glue flat stock up to 8″ wide and will edge glue up to the same dimension. The adjustable scraper blade and grooved coating roll combine for controlled adhesive thickness. Standard models are available with resilient coating roll or metal coating roll. Standard models are equipped with a stainless steel reservoir and scraper blade, permitting use of polyvinyl adhesives without the discoloring of adhesives and subsequent discoloring of stock edges. One model is a thermostatically controlled heating element which provides adjustable temperatures up to 415° for application of hot melt adhesives. The 4″ diameter by 8″ long metal roller is activated by a gear head motor with thermal overload protection (Fig. 12-14).

High Frequency Edge Gluers

The stock is glued and is moved by conveyor to the high frequency gluer where the stock is clamped. The glued up piece is then subjected to high frequency electricity which sets the glue almost instantly. The glue is specially prepared with metallic powder which allows the electricity to set the glue.

Revolving Clamp Carrier

The *revolving clamp carrier* is probably the most widely used device for gluing up stock, and it has been so for many years.

The plain revolving machine is the clamp carrier in its simplest and also original form. Such machines have been found to be increasingly useful not only in smaller shops or departments, but also in larger establishments where the work requires only a short time under pressure, or where the assembly time is relatively long. Black Bros. (25) carriers are made in eight, 12 or 14 sections, and all in widths from 6′ 6″ to 22′ 6″.

When more than 14 sections are needed, the extended chain clamp carrier is the best solution. A 60° extended chain clamp carrier has 30 sections 7′ 6″ wide (10 sections are without clamps). There are 102 style D 2½″ deep by 32″ clamps on 17 sections, six clamps on each section. There are 18 style D, 4″ deep by 32″ clamps on three sections.

Fig. 12-13. Hand planer and jointer #166.

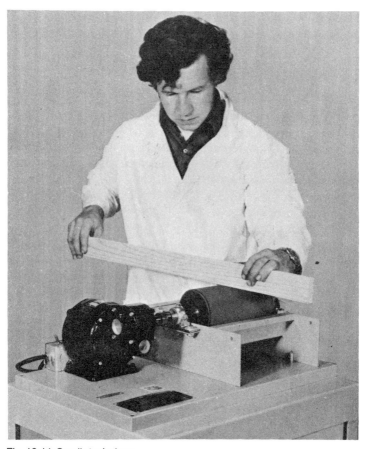

Fig. 12-14. Small stock gluer.

This carrier has two pneumatic hold-downs. Each hold-down has a 2½″ diameter, 4″ stroke air cylinder and is equipped with a pivoting shoe to hold panels flat while clamps are being tightened. It is also equipped with a pneumatic clamp tightener which is an air operated impact wrench suspended from a heavy duty balancer to offset the weight of the wrench for easier handling.

Final Planer (Surfacer) and Molder

The final planing operation is a crucial one. It is the last and most precise process in the cutting room (rough mill department). The final planer plays a dual role. It surfaces the stock to its ultimate and accurate thickness. The stock must be flat, perfectly smooth and of uniform thickness in all points of the stock.

All the other "in line" production department personnel must rely on the accuracy of this one operation. All the subsequent added parts must fit together—not too loose, not too tight—but just right.

The operator of the final planer must be well trained with excellent judgment. For example, if you watch him for a few seconds you will notice that he does not run the stock through the center of the surfacer, but pushes one piece through the left side, the next through the center, and then through the right side. You will also notice that he is apt to run the stock through at a slight angle. The purpose of this technique is to wear the planer knives down at the same rate across the entire length.

The planer operator will not run stock through the planer until he knows that the glue is perfectly and completely dry. Whenever stock is glued up, there is a slight swelling at the joints due to the moisture content. If the glued stock is left a sufficient length of time, the moisture will escape and the swelling subsides. If the stock is planned too soon, the joints will shrink after planning causing sunken joints, which are clearly visible after the stock is sanded and finished.

The molder is generally known by production line workers as the "sticker." In essence, the molder is a double head planer with two side cutter heads.

The molder has the capacity of squaring up four sides of the stock in one pass. It may also cut a contoured shaped on one or more sides in the same process.

As in all other machine operations, there must be one good side or face to work from known as the "working face." The first cutterhead that the work passes is generally the top cutterhead, so the working face is started with the face down.

The entire length of the stock must run through the sticker. If the shape is discontinued at any point along the stock, the shape must be made by some machine other than a molder.

The molder is not designed to shape wide stock; however, some will handle stock up to 1' wide or wider, but these machines are exceptional.

Most stickers are fed by hand, but some machines are hopper fed. The machine extracts one piece from the hopper and feeds it through the machine.

Yates-American (214) manufactures a number of molders which are called "planer-matchers." The A-63 model has a feed capacity up to 1200' per minute. This huge, 16' machine will handle stock 8" thick by 24" wide.

369

The top cutterhead is powered by two 75 hp motors, one on each end of the cutterhead. The bottom cutterhead is activated by one 75 hp motor, the right side cutterhead by a 30 hp motor, and the left side cutterhead by a 50 hp motor.

VENEER DEPARTMENT

The *veneering department* varies in size from one furniture factory to another. Some factories "farm out" their veneered panels while others purchase their plywood from commercial houses. Other closely allied processes such as laminating and bending often are functions of the veneer department.

Lumber core stock for plywood is often glued up and sized in the cutting room. Face veneer and back veneer are glued to the core stock after crossband veneer covers the core stock. The grain of the face veneer and back veneer and the core stock run in the same direction while the crossband veneer is at right angles to the face veneer, back veneer and core stock.

At one time veneered furniture was considered inferior to solid furniture. With the advent of highly developed glue and gluing technology and the need for the conservation of our precious hardwoods, this attitude is pretty well dissipated.

Whenever the edges of plywood panels are to be molded or shaped, a piece of the same kind of wood as the face veneer is glued to the edge. If the edges are flat, strips of face veneer are often glued over the edges to cover the laminations.

Furniture factories usually buy their veneer in flitches (adjacent sheets are adjacent to each other in the log) which have been dried, but sometimes these sheets of veneer must be redried to reach the required moisture content. The veneers are dried by passing the sheets through veneer drying ovens.

Veneers are cut to size on cutters after being jointed on a veneer jointer. The veneer jointer differs from the conventional jointer in that the cutterheads are in a vertical position. A number of layers of veneer are held in a horizontal clamp, which advances past the cutterheads by a motor activated feeding system.

Matched veneer sheets are run through the splicer which applies tape to the joint, or the glued edges are cured with heated strips above and below the glue line. Crossbands, face veneer and back veneers are run through a glue spreader before lamination takes place.

Figure 12-15 shows the infeed operator feeding core stock through a 74″ glue spreader so it receives a controlled thickness of adhesive on *both* sides. The outfeed operator (on the right) is assembling the panel "sandwich" (back sheet, core stock and face sheet) prior to stacking in a cold platen, air operated press. This machine will apply controlled thickness films of almost any liquid adhesive such as urea resin, casein, melamine and polyvinyl as well as specialized adhesives including hot melt, epoxy and contact cement.

One or both sides of almost any flat substrate can be coated including wood, metal, gypsum board, plywood, plastic, cork, hardboard, glass, rubber, particle board, fabric, foil card stock, honeycomb, veneer and vinyl. Substrate may be panels, sheets, webs, dimensional lumber, etc.

The cold platen, air operated press is necessary to supply sufficient pressure to the panels which have been passed through the glue spreader. Black Bros. (25) manufactures such a press that requires only 50 pounds per square inch air pressure. These presses may be end loaded for same size loads and side loaded for different size loads (Fig. 12-16).

Vinyl Laminating Systems and Equipment

Black Bros. (25) provides individual machines or complete systems for laminating rigid or plasticized vinyl to panels of any practical size (particle board, hardboard, etc.) at speeds from 25 to 125′ per minute using epoxy, water base, solvent base and other adhesives.

Black Bros. systems include all support equipment (ovens, conveyors, material handling equipment), plus engineering instal-

Fig. 12-15. Model 22-D glue spreader.

Fig. 12-16. Air operated, platen laminating press.

lation drawings and wire and piping schematics. A schematic of the complete vinyl laminating system is shown in Fig. 12-17.

The *rotary press laminator* is the last machine in the system. The rolls of the rotary press are of many materials and designs. Neoprene is an excellent general purpose roll covering and can be supplied in many hardnesses. Roll coverings are available for heated roll applications where the press is supplied with external infrared roll heaters. Steel rolls are available which can accommodate internal heating or cooling. Rolls can be ordered ground smooth, chrome plated or with Teflon-covered surfaces. Figure 12-18 shows a 62″, pneumatic operated rotary press with an 8¾″ diameter roll.

The *panel cleaner* is the first machine in the vinyl laminating system. The scissors lift, mounted in a pit, automatically adjusts to correct feed height. The panel cleaner cleans both sides of a 5′ wide

372

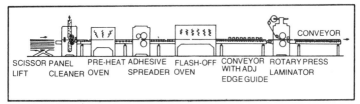

Fig. 12-17. Schematic of vinyl laminating system.

particle board. The "in-line" laminating system turns out vinyl laminated panels at speeds of 60' per minute. The glue spreader, flash-off oven and pneumatic operated rotary press are "down stream."

Panel cleaners remove chips, dust, particles, etc., from both surfaces of flat stock prior to subsequent laminating operation. This greatly reduces the number of laminated panel rejects due to transfer of particles through to the surface of their facing vinyl sheets. In prefinishing operations particles can become trapped on a painted surface (Fig. 12-19).

Shown in Fig. 12-20 is a basic vinyl to hardboard laminating system incorporating panel cleaner, adhesive spreader, control panel for machine speed synchronization and pneumatic rotary press arranged to handle 68″ wide printed vinyl in continuous web form.

Reverse Roll Filling Machines

The *reverse roll fillers* have no connection with the vinyl laminating systems. A wide variety of filling materials are

Fig. 12-18. Rotary press.

Fig. 12-19. Top and bottom panel cleaner.

precisely metered from a crotch-type reservoir by the doctor roll (A) to applicator roll (B), then transferred to the substrate being finished. The wiping roll (D) rotates in reverse direction, removing excess filler and uniformly leveling the surface. Rolls (C) and (E) support the stock and provide a constant feed speed, while the wiping blade (F) removes and recycles the excess filler. Infeed and outfeed idler rolls (G) support and guide the work. Optionally available are an additional wiping blade (H) used with fast drying fillers, and a first revolution scraper blade (I) used when direct roll coating (Fig. 12-21).

The machine handles all modern filling or coating materials. This includes polyester, fillers, stains, colored or clear sealers, paints, primers, lacquers, varnish, enamels or similar materials with either a solvent or water base. The precise coating-wiper action fills nearly every type of sheet stock such as plywood, hardboard, particle board, certain lumber stock and related substrates (Fig. 12-22).

Bending of Wood

Laminated wood is bent in presses similar to the ones described, only special curved forms are made in which the

374

Fig. 12-20. 68″ continuous film laminating systems.

plywood is bent. Solid wood is bent by first being placed in a steaming oven. It is then bent over curved forms or on a bending machine.

MACHINE DEPARTMENT

The machine department is a quasi-in-line department. Some of the machine operations might be considered "in line" while others are adjunct or auxiliary operations.

Some of the machines are the same or similar to those found in the cutting room. They will probably be smaller in some cases because they might not be used continuously.

There are two major functions of the machine room: to finish the necessary operations to conform to the specifications and design, and to try out the adjacent parts to make sure that the cabinet department does not have to do a lot of expensive hand fitting.

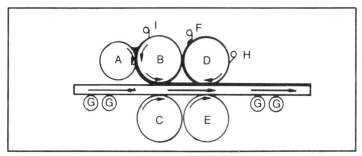

Fig. 12-21. Schematic of reverse roll filling machine.

375

Fig. 12-22. 56" reverse roll filler.

There is one operation that machine department does not do—sanding. Sanding operations are done by the machine sanding department, with hand sanding usually completed in the cabinet department.

The circular saws are of the variety type usually hand operated. Band saws are usually smaller and are never used for resawing. The jointers are of the smaller type and are seldom continuously operated. If it is necessary to do some occasional mass production runs on these hand machines, they are equipped with an automatic feeder.

One such feeder by Forest City Tool Co. (72) has eight rates of speeds, both forward and reverse, from 8½ to 98′ per minute. The automatic feeder may be attached to variety saws, band saws, shapers, sanders, jointers and other machinery.

The unit may be used vertically or horizontally and any angle between. It is powered by a ¾ or one hp motor and is available in either a three or four roller model. The rollers are 4½″ in diameter.

Variety Saw

The Oliver Machinery Co. (135) tilting arbor *variety saw* is a general purpose saw that finds lots of practical uses in the machine room. This two hp machine has a blade that tilts up to 45°. One side of the guard is hinged so that it may be opened to cover the blade when tilted up to 45° (Fig. 12-23).

Double Arbor Bench Saw

The *double arbor bench saw* shown in Fig. 12-24 is also made by Oliver. This type of saw is often called the universal saw. A shaftless motor is built directly on each of the two ball bearing saw arbors in a self-contained compact unit. This saw is designed for shops or departments where both ripping and crosscutting are done on the same machine. Without changing saws, either a ripsaw or a crosscut saw, motor-on-arbor type, may be instantly put in operation by merely turning the handwheel which swings the yoke carrying the two motor driven saw arbors.

One saw arbor carries a 16″ ripsaw, the other a 16″ combination saw. It rips stock 29½″ wide and cuts off stock 36″ wide.

Panel Saw

The Precision Concepts Corp. (150) 14″-16″ sliding table, tilting arbor *panel saw* permits one person to cut panels up to 5′ x

Fig. 12-23. Tilting arbor saw #232.

Fig. 12-24. Double arbor bench saw #260.

10'. The main motor is 9 hp with a ¾ hp scoring unit. The scoring unit minimizes panel chipping. The precision heavy-duty sliding table has a 12' stroke. The saw will handle 14" and 16" blades (Fig. 12-25).

Sawing Center

Powermatic Houdaille (147) manufactures a saw which is similar to the panel saw in that one person can handle full size panels. Large panels, long stock and stack cutting are performed effortlessly with the king size miter gauge which features a quick acting material clamp. A unique spring loaded hold-down prevents panel lift during scoring operations (Fig. 12-26).

Band Saw

The band saw is a necessity in the machine room for cutting external curves. The Oliver Machinery (135) 30" band saw shown in Fig. 12-27 is powered by a 3 hp motor. The saw tension is accurately maintained by an automatic tension control unit. If the tension on the saw blade is too great or too little, the electric control prevents the saw motor from running. If the saw blade

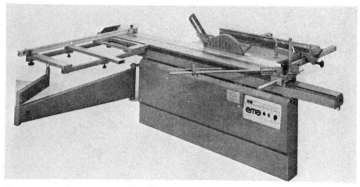

Fig. 12-25. 14″-16″ sliding table, tilting arbor panel saw.

breaks, the tension unit actuates the automatic upper wheel brake and the upper wheel stops immediately. This is a major safety feature as it prevents coiling of the broken blade around the wheel or throwing the broken upper end of the blade against the table.

Heavy-Duty Jigsaw

The heavy-duty, production jigsaw is as different from the small craft jigsaw as a Rolls-Royce is different from a VW. Oliver Machinery makes two types of heavy duty jigsaws. The one has a large curved column arm with a distance of 36½″ between saw and column. It will handle blades from 10″ to 18″ long. The 18″ blade cuts stock up to 10″ thick.

The other model is a ceiling-supported jigsaw which permits unlimited capacity as it does away with the column. The jigsaw is used primarily for internal curved scroll cuts (Fig. 12-28).

Drilling and Boring Machines

The *multiple spindle boring machine* is specifically designed for the woodworking industry to set up in minimum time and

Fig. 12-26. Sawing center, Model 74.

Fig. 12-27. 30" band saw #217.

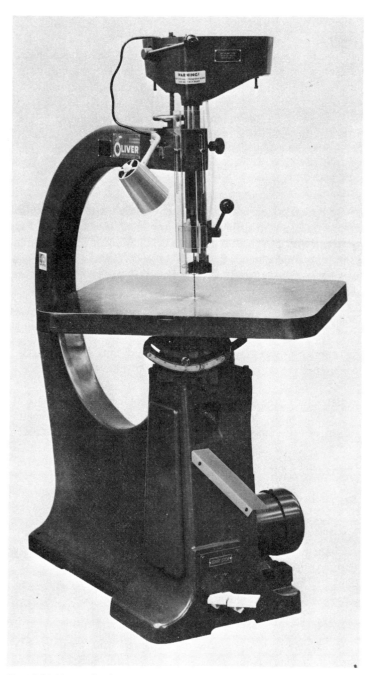

Fig. 12-28. Heavy-duty jigsaw #273.

quickly bore any combination of holes in rectangular workpieces. The machine has an air operated table lift controlled by a foot valve and a rail on which can be placed one to eight spindles. Cluster heads are also available to attach to the spindle. The motor drive on each spindle can be turned on or left to idle independently as needed.

All holes are bored simultaneously. The table is raised and lowered through action of an air cylinder piston. This is actuated through a foot valve. Each spindle is powered by a 1 hp motor. The chucks will handle bits from 1/16″ to ½″ diameter.

Radial Drill

Ekstrom, Carlson manufactures a *radial arm drill*, which comes in handy in drilling to the center of large panels. It is powered with a 1½ hp motor with a spindle speed of from 2500 to 8000 rpm depending on the model ordered. Two of four models may be extended to a 71¼″ radius and can bore holes up to ½″ in diameter (Fig. 12-29).

Hopper Fed, Trim, Chuck and Boring Machine

This machine from Goodspeed Machine Co. (89) is designed for hopper feeding, single or double end trimming, single or double-end chucking, and single, double or triple boring of finished parts such as chair legs. Boring units are quickly and easily adjusted for linear and angular requirements and also for angle of rotation between top and rear units, Hopper loading and automatic return of the completed parts to the front allow the complete operation to be easily handled by a single operator. Production rates using all units average 15 to 20 completed parts per minute (Fig. 12-30).

Deep Hole Drilling Machine

Goodspeed also manufactures a *deep hole drilling machine* which bores smooth and straight holes in end grain lumber up to 3″ in diameter and up to 16″ deep. Holes are drilled with one pass of a carbide tipped non-revolving drill which has an air hole through the center to keep chips clear in the hole during the boring operation. The machine is powered by a 3 hp motor.

Mortisers

There are four categories of mortisers: chain saw mortisers, hollow chisel mortisers, reciprocating bit mortisers and oscillating bit mortisers (Fig. 12-31).

The Oliver Machinery Co. (135) manufactures an industrial type hollow chisel mortiser, powered by a 1 hp motor, which may be tipped 45° degrees to the left or right. The chisel has a maximum vertical travel of 3⅜". The distance from the end of chisel to table is 20" maximum. The mortiser takes chisels up to ½" square.

Shapers

There are many kinds of shapers: single spindle shapers, double spindle shapers, buck shapers, chain and sprocket automatic shapers, circular table automatic shapers and the profile shaper. Oliver Machinery Co. (135) manufactures two heavy, industrial-type single spindle shapers. The smaller #285 model is powered by a 2 hp motor with a 26" x 38" table (Fig. 12-32). The larger #287 model has a 5 hp motor with a 42" square table.

The two spindles of a *double spindle shaper* rotate in opposite directions. As the grain direction changes from shaping with the grain to shaping against the grain, the shaper operator changes the work to the second spindle.

The *buck shaper* is similar to a double-end spindle carver. In fact, it can be used for that purpose to a limited degree. It is quite different from other shapers in that it has horizontal spindles. The buck shaper is used primarily to shape irregular shaped pieces which cannot be clamped or held flat on the regular shaper table.

Fig. 12-29. Radial drill.

Fig. 12-30. Hopper fed, trim, chuck and boring machine.

The sprocket is fitted over the spindle but is driven at a much slower speed than the spindle as it has its own independent source of power. The pattern itself is equipped with a chain which is fastened around the lower edge of the pattern. Mounted in a slide in the table is a pneumatic-operated pressure roller which meshes with the underside of the pattern and presses it against the spindle so that the chain and spocket wheel are always engaged.

A pattern is clamped to the top of a revolving circular table which has slots radiating out from the center. Air clamps hold the stock down on the pattern and are pressed against an overhead cutter while the table is turning. When the completely shaped piece makes its cycle and arrives in front of the operator, the pneumatic clamp holding that piece releases its hold. The operator removes it and inserts a new piece. Many pieces of the same pattern can be cut in one revolution of the table.

Ekstrom, Carlson and Co. (62) makes three sizes of profile shapers which accommodate 44″, 72″ and 96″ lengths: a 15 hp

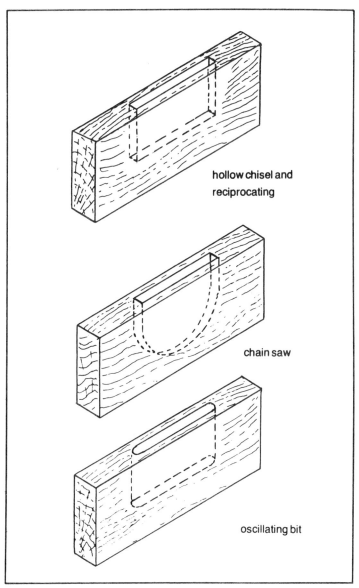

hollow chisel and
reciprocating

chain saw

oscillating bit

Fig. 13-31. Mortise shapes by different mortisers.

Fig. 12-32. Single spindle shaper #285.

motor runs the spindle and a 3 hp motor runs the hydraulic pump on the largest size shaper.

The operation of the profile shaper is similar to that of hand shaping except that both feed and holding power are obtained through hydraulic and pneumatic pressure. On straight line cutting, feed speeds of 15 to 36' per minute are usual when removing ⅛" to ¼" stock, 2" to 3" in height. When shaping profiles of sharp radii, the feed speed must be slowed down to permit the follower guide to remain in contact with the pattern.

Routers

In essence the *router* is a shaper, but the cutting tool is above the table instead of below. This machine is more versatile than a shaper in that it can do internal scroll work as well as outside curve cutting. It can also pinch hit as a carver.

386

The pin router is the one most commonly used by the woodworking industry. Ekstrom, Carlson and Co. (62) has four different models of pin routers, including one model that has a hydraulic, full floating spindle. This standard feature of the 434-H Model provides amazingly accurate routing on serpentine parts and all parts where decorative routing is required. The floating capacity is up to 3½". Three adjustable depth stop positions are provided. The Model 434 comes with either a 5 hp or 7½ hp motor. The table is 24" x 36" and can be raised 10" (Fig. 12-33).

Tenoners

Tenoners are of two types: single-end tenoners and double-end tenoners. The double-end tenoner is actually two machines in one. One machine is in a fixed position like a single-end tenoner.

Fig. 12-33. Pin router with raising and lowering spindle #434.

The other machine may be moved in and out to accommodate different lengths of stock. The stock is moved to the cutoff trim saws and tenon cutterheads by an endless chain.

The double-end tenoner is often called the double-end machine in that it can perform operations other than tenoning. In addition to trim saws and tenon cutterhead, coping heads and dado heads may be added to the machine. Grooves, dadoes, tenons, rabbets, shaped edges, notches, hinge seats and many other shapes can be made on the double-end machine.

Powermatic Houdaille (147) manufactures a single-end tenoner powered by a 2 hp tenon head motor and an optional 1 hp cope motor. Both tenon heads can be instantly adjusted vertically as a unit to cut an identical tenon when changeover to stock of different thickness is made. Both motors have separate controls for individual operation of tenon or cope heads (Fig. 12-34).

Kohler-General (108) manufactures two models of Jenkins double-end tenoners, both of which are in a class by themselves. The Jenkins Model 146 double end machine is fitted with infeed hopper, trim saws, tenon heads, two cam shapers and belt sander. The machine is equipped with dc feed drive to permit gradual automatic adjustment of feed speed while the stock passes through the second cam shaper. It has digital readout on all tooling stations reading to the third decimal.

The Jenkins Model 196 multi-purpose double end machine is a three stand, six station machine with a rugged wide base construction. It is equipped with a 15 hp Trim/Hog motor and belt driven jump scoring saw ahead of the trim saw. Both machines are capable of scoring, trimming, hogging, tenoning, coping, high speed cope and relishing, corner rounding, shaping, notching, boring, routing, belt sanding, wheel sanding, jump dadoing and V-grooving (Fig. 12-35).

The Mereen-Johnson Machine Co. (122) Model 400 is a four station double-end machine with a unit mounted sound enclosure/dust collection system. The adjustable and removable air flow controls doors and single point dust pickup on each enclosure (Fig. 12-36). The Mereen-Johnson Model 600 single station double-end machine has tilting trim motors, interlocking rubber block hold-downs and a handwheel adjusting stock guide.

Lathes

There are a number of lathes used in the woodworking industries. The *pattern and sample lathe* is not a production lathe. It

Fig. 12-34. Single end tenoner, Model 2-A.

often turns patterns used in setting up the automatic or back knife lathe. In some ways it resembles a metal lathe more than a wood turning lathe, in that some lathes are equipped with a power feeding carriage. This lathe is also used for making jig and fixture parts as well as maintenance work.

The Goodspeed Machine Co. (89) hopper fed, hydraulic *back knife lathe* has a turning rate of up to 600 pieces per hour depending on size and shape, with a 10 hp headspindle drive and a 2 hp hydraulic drive. It will turn 1″ to 3″ squares or dowels with lengths

Fig. 12-35. Jenkins (Model 196) multi-purpose double-end machine.

Fig. 12-36. Double-end machine #400.

from 9″ through 30″ long. Spindle speeds vary from 2250 to 4625 rpm (Fig. 12-37).

The Goodspeed *hollow spindle variety lathe* was designed for producing a variety of small diameter wooden parts at high production rates such as golf tees, balls, plugs, beads, etc. It is a combination air and cam operated machine allowing one operator to tend as many as six machines. Dowel stock is hopper fed through a hollow type spindle using a rapid opening and closing collet type chuck for driving the dowel stock for turning. Air dried white birch, maple or birch dowels give excellent results. This machine will turn up to 100 parts per minute.

The *automatic lathe,* sometimes known as the *shaping lathe,* is quite different in design and function from other production lathes. It is widely used in many furniture industries because of its versatility. Other lathes produce only round turnings, but the automatic lathe can shape, too. Both centers of the automatic lathe are powered by a separate motor which turns the centers at the same slow speed.

The arbor, with the cutterheads attached, is powered by a powerful, high speed motor. Each cutterhead is fitted with from two or three up to a half dozen or more knives, which are secured in such a fashion as to produce a shearing cut, thus assuring smooth surfaces that require a minimum of sanding.

A separate knife marking fixture is necessary to mark the knives. The knives are carefully grounded to the marked outlines and precisely balanced before being attached to the arbor.

390

The head and tailstock carriage, with the stock between the two centers, is advanced very slowly toward the high speed cutters while the stock is revolving very slowly. The stock is pushed against the cutterheads by hand lever.

When turnings other than round are desired, special castings (square hexagonal, etc.) of the same shape are attached to the headstock. This special shaped casting rides against a guide on the arbor which moves the carriage forward or away from the cutterhead knives.

CARVING DEPARTMENT

Carving is the process of ornamenting or decorating the surface of wood with tools. In some ways, it approaches the art of the sculptor who works in clay.

In most cases, three types of carving will be taking place in the carving department: Hand carving, multiple-spindle carving and spindle carving. This section will confine its discussion to industrial furniture spindle carving.

There are many tools that shape wood and assist and back up the carving process, although they are not in the category of carving tools. The shaper, router, band saw, jigsaw, and lathe are tools that would be in that back up category.

Hand carving is the most demanding of the carving processes. The craftsman must be highly skilled with many years of appren-

Fig. 12-37. Hopper fed, hydraulic, back knife lathe.

ticeship and experience before he reaches the apex of achievement. In the early part of this century there was a plentiful supply of professional carvers from Europe, particularly in the German, English and Dutch areas, but most of these specialists have either died or retired. There are some training programs—Baker Furniture (17) for example—which are formal apprenticeship programs but, in general, do not meet the demand. As a result, hand carving is, by far, the most expensive of the carving operations.

Although other methods have cut down on the need for hand carvers, there is no way that they can be eliminated from the furniture manufacturing process. Pilot run pieces and samples require a hand carver. There is no way that a machine can do undercutting or execute crisp, sharp carvings. After assembly in the cabinet department, the hand carver is often called upon to eliminate the abruptness of two adjacent shapes or carvings after the piece of furniture is completed. The transition from one part to the other must be subtle and unnoticeable.

The spindle carver duplicates many cuts made by the hand carver but at a much higher speed. The spindle carver presses the radial, multiple-bladed cutting tools against the work. Because of the high speed generated by the spindle carver, the work is done very quickly. The spindle carver must be a careful and safe worker. The speeding blade cuts fingers much easier than it cuts wood.

The *spindle sander* is very much like the spindle carver, but the spindle sander turns considerably slower—roughly at about half the speed. The spindle is powered by a belted motor drive.

The spindle is threaded for a sanding extension point which is screwed onto the spindle. To this sanding extension point may be attached felt sanding wheels or rubber sanding rolls. The spindle sander performs its function in two fashions: sanding, using shaped felt wheels which are covered with slotted discs of sandcloth; and sanding using rubber rolls, over which are slid sandpaper tubes. Small, straight or curved shapings are many times sanded with the spindle sander. This is the only way that stopped (does not extend to the edge of a piece) shapes, flutes, beads and covings can be sanded except by the hand sanding method. This is accomplished by using the felt wheel/slotted sandcloth discs combination.

The felt wheel is molded to fit the shaped part. It is then placed between washers on the tip of the sander. The wheel is covered by the slitted sandcloth disc which is lapped over the edge of the felt wheel.

The felt used for the wheels is purchased by the yard and is 2″ thick. There are four consistencies: soft, medium hard, hard and rock hard. Wheels vary in thickness from ¼″ to 1½″. After the felt is split to the correct thickness, the circular wheels are cut on a band saw or jigsaw. A hole is then bored for the spindle. The shape is formed by holding a piece of rough abrasive paper against the wheel while it is revolving in the spindle sander.

The sandpaper tubes that are used over the rubber rolls are made of paper purchased in the desired width—usually 8″ or 10″—which is the length of the tube. Each operator makes up his own supply of tubes by rolling strips of sandpaper onto wooden rollers of the correct diameter. The sandpaper is secured at the ends with veneer tape.

To attach the sandpaper tube to the spindle sander, the nut which holds the rubber roll to the sander point is loosened. The tube is then slid over the rubber roll and the nut is tightened with a socket wrench, which expands the rubber roll against the wall of the tube, thus holding it securely in place.

MACHINE SANDING DEPARTMENT

Sanding takes place in several factory departments, but the *machine sanding department* carries the majority of the load. Sanding done in this department cuts down on the sanding done in other departments, which is most often hand sanding—the most expensive kind.

The main objective of sanding is to get the stock ready for the finishing department. All scratches, dents, blemishes and marks must be removed before finishes are applied. After stock has been machined and before it is sent to the cabinet department for assembly, it must be sanded. Band sawn edges that are to be shaped are sanded before the pieces go to the shaper to remove all irregularities, because the shaper reproduces these irregularities. In other cases, subassemblies that are put together in the cabinet department are sent back to the sanding department for further sanding.

The sanding of the dovetail corners on drawers to remove the glue is done on a belt sander in the cabinet department—not in the machine department. Drawers are just too cumbersome to be moved back and forth.

Considerable sanding is done in the finishing department, which will be discussed in connection with that department.

Sanding before the finishing operation is often referred to as "sanding in the white."

A lot of experience is needed to be a good sander. A keen sense of touch must be developed. There are several factors that must be considered: speed of the machine, which in most cases cannot be changed; and the amount of pressure and the length of time that pressure is applied. Greater pressure can be applied to hardwoods than to softwoods. Softwoods are more apt to "load up" or gum the sandpaper. If the speed can be changed to a lower rate, this defect can be lessened or eliminated. This slowing of speed will also help eliminate burning of stock. Drum sanders, automatic finishing sanders, belt sanders and other machines are used.

CABINET DEPARTMENT

The *cabinet department* is the place where all the component parts come together to be assembled into a completed whole. It is also the place where final touchup is made in preparation for the finish coats. This work is done by highly skilled cabinetmakers who are also necessary for the precise fitting of parts together. Their main job in case-good manufacture is the careful fitting of drawers to the carcass, and the finish sanding (sometimes called polishing) after the glue size has been applied and dried. Drawers should move smoothly into the carcass by applying one-finger pressure to either extreme end of the drawer.

There are many types of clamping devices used in the cabinet department, many of which are power operated. These devices are used to hold parts together while the glue has a chance to set (Fig. 12-38).

A *glue gun* is sometimes used in gluing up furniture parts. A hose is fastened to the gun through which ready-mixed glue is forced. The gun not only opens and closes the flow, but it can control the rate of flow through the gun.

There are many types of stapling and nailing devices used in industry. One large automatic nailing piece of equipment drives screw-like nails formed from rolls of wire at up to nearly 200 nails per minute. The head of the nail is countersunk so other operations may be performed on the assembly or subassembly. A foot pedal triggers the nailing. Portable staplers and nails are also used in the cabinet room.

Other portable power tools such as hand sanders, portable electric or air-driven drills, and powered screwdrivers are only a few that find their way to the cabinet room.

FINISHING DEPARTMENT

The operations associated with this department have been covered in Chapter 10. Any further discussion would be repetitious and superfluous.

UPHOLSTERY DEPARTMENT

Frames for upholstered furniture are finished before entering the *upholstery department;* however, upholstered furniture with wood exposed parts often has to have the finished wood touched up after the upholstery is completed. The upholstery department of a large furniture factory is not essentially different from a small custom shop—the difference is only in scale and the use of power assisted machinery.

High speed power sewing machines are used with many attachments for piping and *ruching (plaited* or frilled edges) and for closing cushion openings. Electric shears and electric cutting machines are widely used to cut many layers of upholstery material at a time.

Cushion making machines are used to form interior spring cushions. Nailing and stapling machines, both portable and stationary, are widely used. Some of these are air-powered.

There are a multitude of hand tools used: upholsterer's hammer, heavy shears, web stretchers, ripping chisel, needles, regulators and work trestles. Materials used are upholstery materials, webbing, spring canvas, stuffings, tacks, wadding, gimp, twine, round head nails, foam, springs and many others.

TRIM DEPARTMENT

Furniture hardware (drawer pulls, handles, hinges, etc.) is applied in the *trim department.* The trimmer must be very careful and meticulous to avoid any mars or scratches on the newly finished furniture and hardware. Sometimes his job requires

Fig. 12-38. Manually operated, two-way frame clamp.

Fig. 12-39. Warehouse at Brodhead-Garrett Manufacturing Complex, Malta, Ohio.

applying the final coat of wax or polish. Pure lemon oil is often used for this purpose.

INSPECTION DEPARTMENT

This department is often a subsidiary part of another department (trim department or packaging and shipping department). The inspector should have a free hand in judging the quality of workmanship and not be unduly influenced by the heads of other departments. He is often responsible for seeing to it that furniture is properly moved to the packaging and shipping department.

STORAGE, PACKAGING, SHIPPING AND RECEIVING DEPARTMENT

Perhaps the major responsibility of the supervisor or foreman of this department is to check carefully with the production manager or the general manager as to whether the furniture coming through should be immediately packaged and shipped to meet delivery dates which have been promised, or should the furniture be packaged and stored to meet some future delivery date (Fig. 12-39).

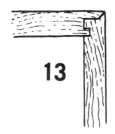

13

Projects, Kits, Plans and Patterns

This chapter is devoted to the making of projects from *scratch*, from *kits*, and from commercial *plans* and *patterns*.

The core or major project is the classical and traditional *wig stand planter*. Originally the wig stand was topped by a large egg-shaped ball over which our ancestors placed their wigs for combing, powdering and storing. Someone conceived the idea of converting this early American piece into a planter and as such it remains a jewel in the Colonial inspired home. It will be found in almost any style home except the ultra-contemporary. This exceptionally well-designed piece of the middle 1700s, Williamsburg area was cherished by southern Colonial gentry.

I selected this piece of furniture because with a minimum of precious wood (walnut or mahogany) the craftsman can build a valuable heirloom that will last indefinitely. Another reason for the selection is the large number of operations represented (straight sawing, curved sawing, spindle turning, faceplate turning, dovetailing, laminating, etc.).

Many craftsmen complain that not enough details and information are included in project procedure. I have tried to correct this problem and have included many small but relevant details. Perhaps I have gone overboard in this respect, but this was a risk that had to be taken.

WIG STAND PLANTER

The wig stand planter may be built of any of the more common cabinet woods (mahogany, walnut or cherry); however mahogany is considered the best choice (Fig. 13-1). The wig stand planter shown in Fig. 13-2 is made of mahogany. See Fig. 13-3 and Table 13-1.

Laminated Ring

Cut a backing piece of 13/16″ white pine, or some similar material, at least 11⅝″ in diameter (Fig. 13-4). Draw two circles with a compass, one 11⅝″ in diameter and one 8½″ in diameter, on the backing piece using the same center mark.

Glue a piece of heavy paper on each side of the center, but do not cover the center mark. The 120° overlay segments will be glued to the ring, which has been glued to the backing piece. After the ring is turned on the lathe, the ring is pried loose from the backing piece. Half of the paper will adhere to the backing piece and half will adhere to the ring. The paper on the ring will be sanded off.

Drill a 1/32″ hole through the backing piece at the center. This hole will assist in lining up the faceplate later.

Glue up one layer of laminated sections at a time. There are four layers (16 laminated sections) in all. Be sure there are enough clamps available before gluing is started. Attach faceplate to the backing piece and laminated rings with flat head screws.

File a registration mark on the faceplate and mark another registration mark on the backing piece with a pencil or ball-point pen. This precautionary measure assures that the faceplate and workpiece will be properly aligned if it is necessary to detach the faceplate. See Fig. 13-5 showing the two registration marks. The lighter wood is the backing piece and the laminated ring is the dark wood at the bottom of the photo.

Make a pattern of the cross section of the ring on heavy paper to check the turning of the ring. See the lower drawing on Fig. 13-4.

Place the faceplate and workpiece on the outboard end of the lathe. If the lathe will swing a 12″ diameter on the inboard side, it may be used. It is easier to turn faceplate work on the outboard end of the lathe.

Set the speed of the lathe at its lowest rate of rotation. Turn the ring. Be sure that the lathe tools are sharp. Shape the profile slowly, making shallow cuts. Check with the pattern frequently.

Sand the laminated ring while it is rotating. Use successive grades of sandpaper. For best results, fold the sandpaper.

Remove the fing from the paper and backing piece with a sharp chisel. Work slowly and carefully around the perimeter of the ring. Sand off the paper that adhered to the ring (Fig. 13-6).

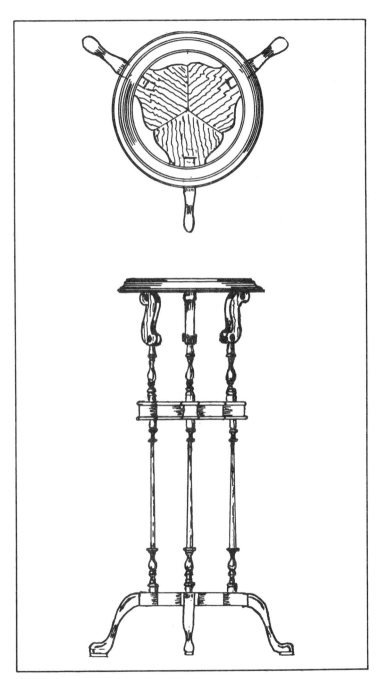

Fig. 13-1. Wig stand planter diagram.

Fig. 13-2. Wig stand planter with plants and accessories.

"S" Scroll Ring Support

Make a pattern for the "S" scroll from heavy paper. The laminated ring sits on top of the three "S" scroll ring supports (Fig. 13-7).

Fig. 13-3. Wig stand planter.

Table 13-1. Materials List for the Wig Stand Planter (Rough Dimensions Only).

No. of Pcs.	Description	Size	Material
16	Laminated Ring	1/4" x 3 1/2" x 8 1/2"	Walnut or Mahogany
3	"S" Scroll Ring Support	7/8" x 2 1/2" x 5 1/8"	Walnut or Mahogany
3	Short Turning for Ring Support	1 1/4" x 1 1/4" x 5 1/2"	Walnut or Mahogany
1	Top Shelf	1 3/8" x 8" x 9 1/2"	Walnut or Mahogany
6	120° Overlays	3/16" x 4 1/2" x 6"	Walnut or Mahogany
3	Long Turnings	1 1/8" x 1 1/8" x 15"	Walnut or Mahogany
1	Bottom Shelf	1 5/8" x 8" 9 1/2"	Walnut or Mahogany
3	Legs	1 1/8" x 3" x 9 1/2"	Walnut or Mahogany
12	Rosettes	3/16" x 3/4" x 3/4"	Walnut or Mahogany

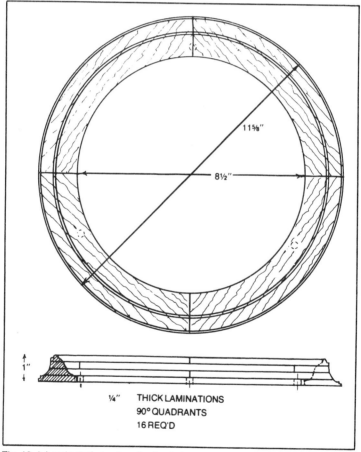

11 5/8"

8 1/2"

1"

¼" THICK LAMINATIONS
90° QUADRANTS
16 REQ'D

Fig. 13-4. Laminated ring for wig stand planter.

402

Transfer the outline of the pattern to self-adhesive paper. Apply self-adhesive patterns to stock (Fig. 13-8).

Saw out "S" scrolls with a band saw. In order to cut the short radius curves at the two ends, it is necessary to make a series of saw kerfs to the edge of the curves unless a very narrow band saw blade is used (Fig. 13-9).

Sand the "S" scroll with successive grades of sandpaper. Bore the hole for ¼" dowel at the top of the scroll and a ⅜" hole at the bottom of the scroll (Fig. 13-7).

Short Turning For Ring Support

Cut the stock for the ring support turnings (Table 13-1). Mark diagonals across the ends of the cut stock with a centering jig or with a scale (Fig. 13-10). The centering jig can be used on both round and square stock.

Saw a saw kerf about ⅛" deep on one end of the stock using the pencil marks that were inscribed (discussed in the previous paragraph) as a guide. Drill a 1/16" diameter hole where the two kerfs intersect to accommodate the center of the spur drive center. If the hole is not drilled, the spur center is apt to split the wood when the spur center is driven into the saw kerfs.

Drill a small hole (about 1/32" in diameter) where the two pencil lines intersect on the other end of the stock. This hole is to accommodate the tailstock center (Fig. 13-11).

Fig. 13-5. Registration marks.

Fig. 13-6. Turning laminated ring on outboard end of Myford lathe.

Remove the spur drive center and tailstock centers from the lathe and drive them into the stock held in a vise until the centers are firmly seated. Use a mallet for driving in the centers. Never use a hammer. The stock should never be driven into the center while the center is in the lathe because it might do damage to the lathe bearings. Insert the centers and stock into the lathe and with a gouge turn the stock until it is round (Fig. 13-12).

Make a template of thin wood to indicate the major incisions and critical diameters. A "V" cut should be made at the edge of the template at every marked point to allow a sharp-pointed pencil to slide into the rotating stock without wandering. *Never use a scale or rule against rotating stock.* Mark the incisions and diameters on rotating stock (Fig. 13-13).

Select the lathe tools for making the incisions. The parting tool is the one most generally used.

Set calipers to the correct dimensions. The caliper adjusting nut should be held away from the operator and between the middle finger and the finger adjacent to the little finger. This prevents the

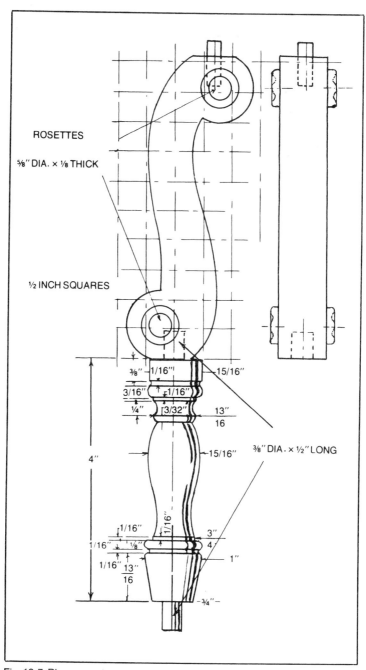

ROSETTES

⅝″ DIA. × ⅛ THICK

½ INCH SQUARES

⅜″
1/16″'
15/16″
3/16″
1/16″
¼″
3/32″
13″
16

15/16″

⅜″ DIA. × ½″ LONG

4″

1/16″
1/16″
1/16″
⅛″
1/16″
13″
16

1/16″

3″
4
1″

¾″

Fig. 13-7. Ring support.

405

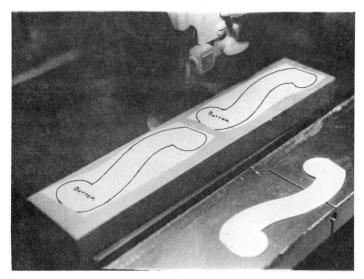

Fig. 13-8. Self-adhesive patterns attached to stock.

nut from vibrating and losing the correct setting. The handle of the lathe tool should be held along the forearm of the left arm (for right-handed people).

After each cut with the lathe tool, check the diameter with calipers. Continue using the lathe tool and calipers alternatively until the calipers barely slip over the turning. Never use calipers on stock that is not perfectly round. It could lead to a serious injury.

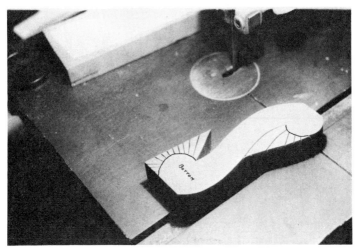

Fig. 13-9. Saw kerfs to assist cutting short radii curves.

406

Fig. 13-10. Centering jig.

Make all the necessary incision cuts. Finish turning the piece with appropriate lathe tools. Sand rotating stock with successive grades of folded sandpaper (Fig. 13-14).

Fig. 13-11. Spur drive and tail stock centers.

Fig. 13-12. Turning to the round.

Top Shelf

Study Fig. 13-15. Note carefully how the grain runs in the six 120° overlays (three on top and three on the bottom). The top and bottom shelves are essentially the same as far as the outside contour is concerned.

Make the pattern of the shelf on heavy paper. Lay the pattern on 1⅛″ thick stock and mark the contour. Saw the curves with a band saw. Sand the curves with an upside-down belt sander held in a vise (Fig. 13-16).

Make six 120° overlay segments. Be sure the angles are exactly 120°.

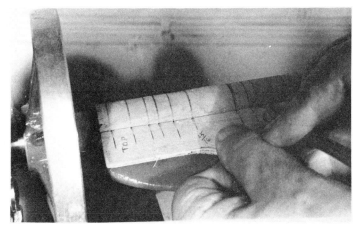

Fig. 13-13. Marking incisions on short turning.

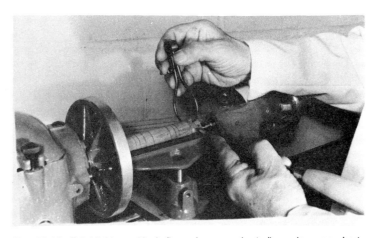

Fig. 13-14. Establishing critical dimensions on short dimensions on short turning.

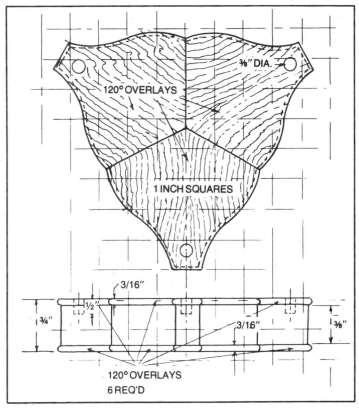

Fig. 13-15. Top shelf of wig stand planter.

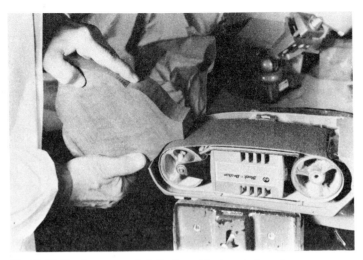
Fig. 13-16. Sanding curves of shelf with upside-down belt sander.

Tape three overlay segments for the top as shown in Fig. 13-17. Tape the other three overlay segments for the bottom overlay.

Make the pattern of overlay segments about 3/16″ larger all the way around than the 1 3/8″ thick base shelf pattern. Trace the pattern on the overlay segments and cut the outline on the band saw. Roll all the edge with rasp, file and different grades of sandpaper.

Glue the overlay segments to the base shelf with white glue. Be sure there are enough clamps available to do the job. Place wooden pads under each clamp's jaws. Glue bottom segments in the same fashion.

Sand the top and bottom by hand, orbital or finishing sander. A portable belt sander is hard to control on a piece this small (Fig. 13-18).

Long Turning

Make a template for long turning. See Fig. 13-19 and the bottom of Fig. 13-20. Cut stock to rough size, 1⅛″ x 1⅛″ x 15″. Mark diagonals on ends and saw recess for spurs on the drive center.

Place stock in the lathe and turn on the motor. Mark the incision points with a template while the lathe is running, after the stock has been turned to the round. Establish critical dimensions with calipers as shown in Fig. 13-14.

Fig. 13-17. Taping overlay segments.

Finish turning the piece with appropriate lathe tools. Sand the rotating stock with successive grades of folded sandpaper.

Bottom Shelf

Cut stock for the bottom shelf. Mark with the same pattern as used to mark the top shelf. Cut contour with a band saw. Sand edges as described in Fig. 13-16. See Fig. 13-21.

Lay out dovetail mortises for legs on the underside of the bottom shelf. The dovetail is ⅝" long, ¾" across the wider part and ½" across the narrow part.

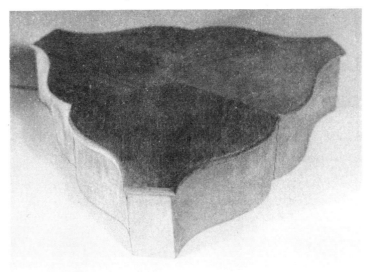

Fig. 13-18. Top shelf with top overlay segments in place.

411

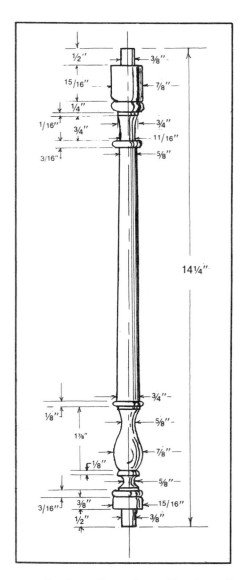

1/2″

15/16″

1/4″

1/16″   3/4″

3/16″

3/8″

7/8″

3/4″

11/16″

5/8″

14 1/4″

Fig. 13-19. Long turning
for wig stand planter.

3/4″

1/8″

1 7/8″

1/8″

3/16″   3/8″

1/2″

5/8″

7/8″

5/8″

15/16″

3/8″

Cut dovetail mortises with a dovetail saw. Leave a little stock to be removed when the legs are fitted (Fig. 13-22).

Fasten the side with the dovetail mortises to the faceplate. Be sure that it is properly centered. Turn the recessed portion to the dimensions indicated in Fig. 13-21. Sand the recessed portion on the lathe while the piece is turning. Then sand the two flat faces by hand after removing the piece from the lathe.

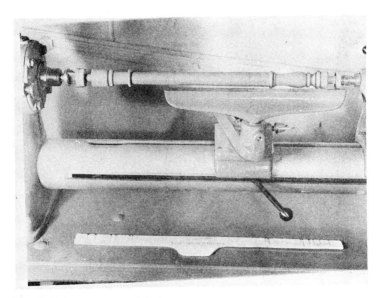

Fig. 13-20. Long turning in Myford lathe.

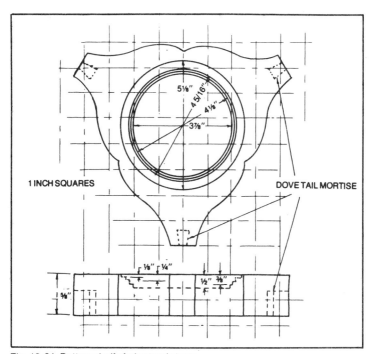

Fig. 13-21. Bottom shelf of wig stand planter.

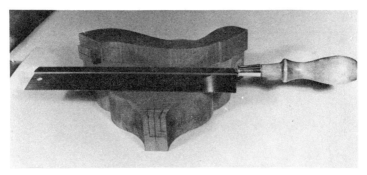

Fig. 13-22. Layout for dovetail mortise, leg and dovetail saw.

Legs

Make the pattern for the leg as shown in Fig. 13-23. Trace the pattern on 1⅛″ thick stock. Cut out rough blanks for legs on the band saw (Fig. 13-24).

Cut the dovetail tenons with the dovetail saw (Fig. 13-25). Shape the legs to conform to the dimensions shown in Fig. 13-26

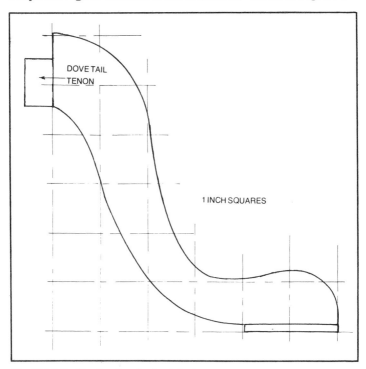

DOVE TAIL
TENON

1 INCH SQUARES

Fig. 13-23. Profile of leg for wig stand planter.

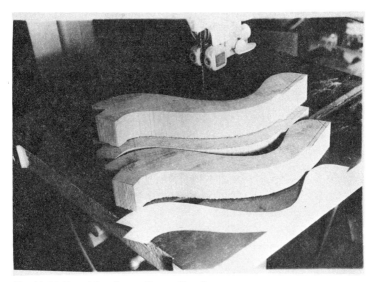

Fig. 13-24. Rough band sawed legs with pattern.

with spokeshave, Surform, rasps and sandpaper. A drum sander or the end of an upside-down portable belt sander can be used to advantage here.

Fit the leg dovetail tenons into the dovetail mortises in the bottom shelf. Glue the legs to the bottom shelf (Fig. 13-27).

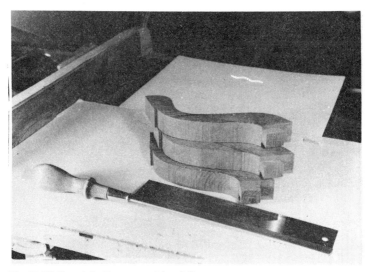

Fig. 13-25. Dovetailed tenons and dovetail saw.

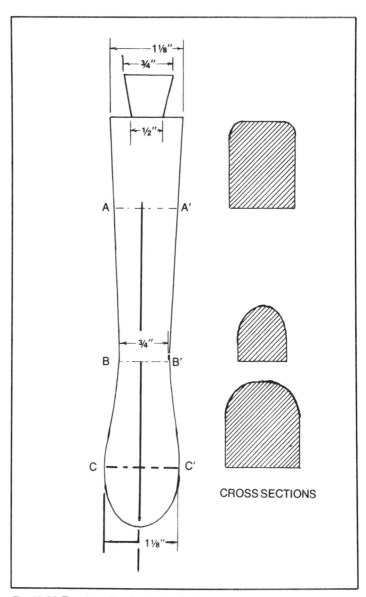

CROSS SECTIONS

Fig. 13-26. Top view of leg for wig stand planter.

Rosettes

Cut enough 3/16" thick stock for 12 rosettes. Draw 12 circles ¾" in diameter on the stock. Cut the circles with a jigsaw or coping saw.

416

Cut a circle of ½″ stock on the band saw or jigsaw at least 2″ in diameter and mount to faceplate. The lathe used to turn the rosettes in this case was a Dremel Mini-Lathe.

True up the wood faceplate and inscribe a ⅝″ diameter circle on the wood faceplate while it is turning in the lathe. Drive three small brads into the faceplate inside the inscribed circle. Cut off the heads of the brads, leaving about 1/16″ of the brad protruding. File the brads to a sharp point (Fig. 13-28).

Drive the rosette stock on to the pins with a wood mallet and turn the rosette to conform to dimensions in Fig. 13-7. Glue the 12 rosettes to the "S" scroll supports as shown in Fig. 13-7. See Fig. 13-29.

Assembly

Bore ¼″ diameter holes in tops of "S" scrolls ½″ deep. Cut ½″ diameter dowels to fit in "S" scrolls.

Drive dowels into the holes after glue has been applied. One-quarter inch of dowel should protrude from the top of scroll. Bore ⅜″ holes ½″ deep in the bottom of the "S" scrolls to receive the dowel turned ends of the short turnings. Bore three holes ¼″ in diameter and ¼″ deep in the laminated ring as shown in Fig. 13-4.

Glue the short turnings to the "S" scrolls. Glue the short turning/"S" scroll subassembly into the laminated ring. The top of the "S" scroll should point away from the center. See Figs. 13-1 and 13-3.

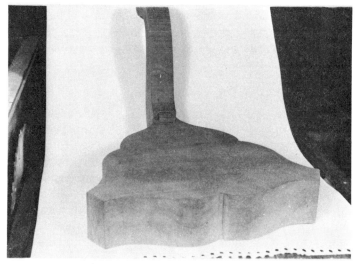

Fig. 13-27. Leg dovetail tenon being fitted to shelf dovetail mortise.

Fig. 13-28. Pins in wood faceplate to hold rosette stock.

Before the glue has had a chance to harden, set the subassembly on top of the top shelf. It might be necessary to force the short turning/"S" scroll assembly into position before the glue is set. When it is properly positioned over the three "horns" of the shelf, draw circles around the turned ends of the short turnings. Mark the centers with an awl and bore ⅜″ diameter holes ½″ deep in the top of the top shelf. Bore the three ⅜″ diameter holes ½″ deep on the underside of the top shelf and on top of the bottom shelf.

Test assemble the entire wig stand. Dissassemble, glue, reassemble and clamp.

Finish

After glue has set overnight, sand the project with 4/0-150 sandpaper. Make a glue size of hot water mixed with LePage's or Franklin liquid animal glue, about 13 parts of hot water to one part of glue. Apply to the entire project with a natural or synthetic sponge. Apply only enough size to moisten the wood—no puddles. This step is particularly important if water stain is to be applied. After eight to 10 hours, sand the project with 6/0-220 sandpaper.

Apply a sealer washcoat of thin shellac or lacquer sealer. At least twice as much thinner should be mixed with the finish material. This washcoat prevents the stain from sinking in more rapidly in some places than others, and provides a casing around the filler which prevents the oil from the filler from sinking into the wood too rapidly.

Apply stain. If the project is made of walnut and contains no sapwood, it might be advisable not to stain.

Apply filler. For walnut and mahogany, the filler should be darker than the stained wood. When the filler starts to dull, rub it in with the lower part of the palm of your hand. Use rags or burlap to follow, rubbing across grain. Remove the filler from incisions and corners with a rag over a sharpened stick.

Apply two thin coats of lacquer sealer or shellac. When dry, sand lightly with 8/0-280 or 9/0-320 abrasive paper. Use #0000 steel wool on turnings.

Apply glaze if so desired. It does a lot to enhance the finish.

Apply one coat of shellac or lacquer sealer or spray *Deft* over the glaze coat. This coat must be applied with a spray gun or aerosol can; otherwise the glaze will smear.

Apply three coats of lacquer or varnish (natural or synthetic resin). If a flat or dull finish is desired, do not apply the flat varnish or lacquer until the last coat, as it does not have the body of the gloss finishes.

Apply wax if a gloss finish is desired. Avoid waxes with a paraffin base. Buff the wax until an even polish is attained.

If you cannot find a basin or bowl to fit the laminated ring, one can be spun from sheet brass or copper. I spun one from brass (Fig. 13-30). A wooden form the shape of the inside of the bowl is turned

Fig. 13-29. Turned rosette on Dremel Mini-Lathe.

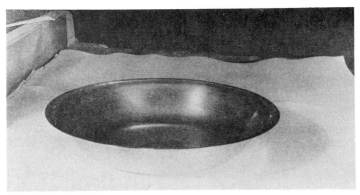

Fig. 13-30. Spun brass bowl to fit laminated ring.

on the lathe faceplate. Special tools and a revolving tailstock are required. See your local library for books on metal spinning. Do not spin the bowl on your wood turning lathe unless you know that the headstock bearings will handle the extra strain.

OPTIONAL DESIGNS TO FIT THE ENVIRONMENT

Many craftsmen often see pieces of furniture and accessories in stores and home other than their own that appeal to their aesthetic taste. They discard the idea immediately as a possibility for reproduction for use in their own home because the piece will not fit into the surroundings. The craftsman feels, and rightly so in most cases, that the piece will clash with the general decor and style of the home. The enterprising designer-craftsman will take the idea and turn it into an object of beauty that *will* fit into the environment.

The main objective of an accessory is to fill some need. As a prelude to the projects that follow, it is assumed that a need existed for a place to store incoming and outgoing letters. a place to store such small items as stamps, rubber bands, paper clips, etc., or a place for a plant.

There are two letter racks or letter rack planters that will be ideal in the Early American or Colonial home. The other two letter wall racks are designed strictly for the contemporary home, one in the African motif and the other in the Egyptian motif.

EARLY AMERICAN PINE LETTER RACK AND STAMP DRAWER

The user of this project may elect to use the drawer as a planter. See Fig. 13-31 and Table 13-2.

Make patterns for the back and sides on heavy paper. If folded paper is used, only half of the pattern needs to be drawn. Cut the folded paper. When unfolded, a complete pattern is evolved. This procedure applies only to the back.

Cut stock for back, sides, top, bottom and shelves. Lay patterns on back and sides and trace around patterns. No patterns are needed for top and bottom shelves or for drawer parts.

Cut out the back and sides with a band saw, jigsaw, saber saw or coping saw. Sand and roll the exposed edges. Drill a small hole for hanging near the top of the back.

Cut stock for the letter holder. Lay out letter slots and cut on the band saw. Round the front with plane and sandpaper. Shape the top and bottom *finials* with a band saw, round wood rasp and sandpaper. Cut 5/16″ dadoes, 1/8″ deep, in the sides to receive the top and bottom drawer shelves.

Attach letter holder to the back with small flat head screws and glue. Glue the top and bottom drawer shelves into dadoes in the sides. Attach this assembly to the back with small brads and

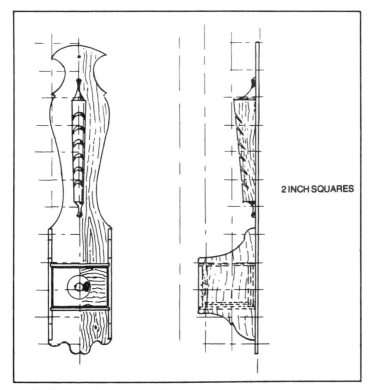

2 INCH SQUARES

Fig. 13-31. Early American pine letter rack with stamp drawer.

No. of Pcs.	Description	Size	Material
1	Back	5/16" x 4 1/2" x 23"	White Pine
1	Letter Holder	1 1/8" x 1 1/8" x 10 1/2"	White Pine
2	Sides	5/16" x 4 1/4" x 8 1/2"	White Pine
2	Top and Bottom Shelves for Drawers	5/16" x 4 1/4" x 4 1/4"	White Pine
1	Drawer Front	1/2" x 3" x 4"	White Pine
2	Drawer Sides	1/4" x 3 1/4" x 3 3/4"	Birch or Fir Plywood
1	Drawer Bottom	1/4" x 4 1/8" x 3 3/4"	Birth or Fir Plywood
1	Drawer Back	1/4" x 3" x 4"	Birch or Fir Plywood

glue. Be sure that the top and bottom drawer shelves are at right angles to the sides.

Cut drawer front to size. Make a special, knob turning chisel from an old file (Fig. 13-32). See pages 108 to 115 in my book *66 Weekend Wood Furniture Projects* (TAB book No. 974).

Fasten drawer front stock to the lathe faceplate. Mark a 2" diameter circle for recess and a ¾" diameter circle for the top of the knob while the lathe is turning.

Insert the special chisel into the space between the two scribed circles. Move the chisel back and forth until the scribed circles are reached. Sand the recess with folded sandpaper, first with 1-50 grit followed by 3/0-120 grit.

Remove the drawer front from the faceplate. Cut ¼" wide, ¼" deep rabbets on the two ends of the drawer front to receive the drawer sides, and cut a ¼" wide, ¼" deep groove ⅛" from the bottom to receive the drawer bottom. Cut ¼" wide by ⅛" deep dadoes on the ends of the drawer sides ¼" from the ends.

Assemble and glue up the drawer. Fit the drawer between the top and bottom drawer shelves. See the next project, the Early American pine letter rack planter, for instructions regarding distressing and finishing. See Figs. 13-33 and 13-34.

EARLY AMERICAN PINE LETTER RACK PLANTER

See Table 13-3. Make patterns for the back and planter front. Cut stock for the back, planter front, planter ends and planter bottom.

Lay patterns on back and planter front and trace around patterns. No patterns are needed for the planter ends and bottom.

Cut out the back and planter front with a band saw, jigsaw, saber saw or coping saw. Sand and roll the edges of the back down

Fig. 13-32. Special chisel and turned recessed knob.

to where the back is attached to the planter. Sand and roll the top edge of the planter front.

Cut stock for the letter holder. Lay out letter slots and cut on the band saw. Taper the sides with a plane and round the front with

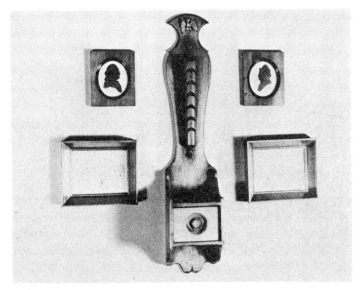

Fig. 13-33. Early American pine letter rack with stamp drawer.

423

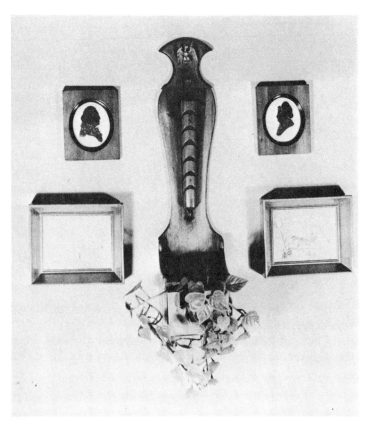

Fig. 13-34. Early American pine letter rack with stamp drawer converted to planter.

the plane and sandpaper. Shape the top and bottom finials with the band saw, round wood rasp and sandpaper.

Cut ¼″ dadoes ¼″ from the bottom of the planter ends to receive the planter bottom. The dadoes should be ⅛″ deep. Drill ⅛″ hole near the top for hanging.

Attach the letter holder to the back with small screws and glue. Attach the planter ends to the planter front with small brads and glue.

Slide the planter bottom into the dadoes. Attach the planter assembly to the back with small brads and glue.

Distressing may be done at this stage if desired. Worm holes may be simulated with an ice pick or awl. Bruises, nicks and dents can be made by lashing with a piece of chain or by pressing the surface with a furnace clinker.

Apply a very thin coat of walnut stain. The stain should discolor the wood only slightly. Allow stain to dry.

Spray on one coat of lacquer sealer or "Deft" from a spray can. Sand with 4/0-150 sandpaper after the sealer is dry. Apply a second coat of sealer. Sand again with the same grit sandpaper after the sealer is dry.

Apply a glaze made of burnt umber (color ground in oil) mixed with turpentine or mineral spirits. It should be about the consistency of coffee cream. Apply glaze to the project with a rather stiff brush. Immediately wipe off the glaze with a soft cloth. Do not apply much pressure when wiping off the glaze. If a darker effect is desired, leave the glaze on longer before wiping. Do not attempt to remove the glaze from corners or recesses.

Blending is the most important step in glazing and the most difficult. Using a soft brush (badger or fitch), blend the heavy accumulation of glaze away from the corners and recesses. The shading should be gradual from dark to light. There should be no pronounced demarcation between the two. It would be wise to practice on scrap stock beforehand.

Apply one spray coat of lacquer sealer or "Deft." Allow to dry for at least three hours. Sand with 6/0-220 sandpaper and rub with #0000 steel wool. Apply at least three coats of spray lacquer. Allow at least four hours between coats and overnight on the last coat. Sand each coat with 9/0-320 sandpaper and rub with #0000 steel wool. Apply two coats of paste wax and buff (Fig. 13-35).

To make an optional design of the Early American pine letter rack planter, follow the same procedure as for the Early American pine letter rack planter. See Figs. 13-36 and 13-37.

AFRICAN MOTIF LETTER RACK

This letter rack should be made of walnut or some other dark hardwood. Maple or birch may be substituted but should be stained a very dark brown or black. See Table 13-4.

Table 13-3. Materials List for Fig. 13-34 (Rough Dimensions Only).

No. of Pcs.	Description	Size	Material
1	Back	¼″ x 5¾″ x 16¾″	White Pine
1	Letter Holder	1⅛″ x 1½″ x 10″	White Pine
1	Planter Front	¼″ x 2⅝″ x 5¾″	White Pine
2	Planter Ends	¼″ x 2½″ x 3″	White Pine
1	Planter Bottom	¼″ x 2½″ x 4¼″	Masonite

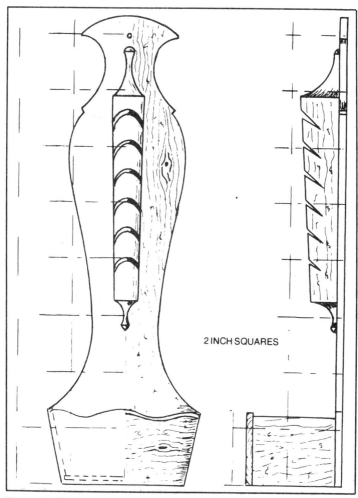

Fig. 13-35. Early American pine letter rack planter.

Cut rough stock for the letter holder. Shape contour with the band saw.

Finish shaping with spokeshave, Surform, rasps and sandpaper. A drum sander can be used to advantage. Cut in the letter holding incisions with a backsaw or dovetail saw.

Glue up a blank (1⅞″ x 12″ x 12″) for the turned container. Only a portion has to be of walnut. The rest can be any hardwood.

Cut the blank to a 12″ diameter circle on the band saw. Mount the blank on the lathe faceplate and turn to dimensions as indicated in Fig. 13-38. Sand the turning while it is rotating.

After the turning is completed, cut off the container slab on the band saw after it has been removed from the faceplate. Turn the bowl upside-down on the band saw table to make the cut.

Cut a "V"-shaped cut in the container to receive the lower portion of the letter holder with the band saw. The container should be fitted to the letter holder with chisels, a small rasp and sandpaper.

Bore holes for ¼″ brass hinge pins in the container. Glue the container to the letter holder.

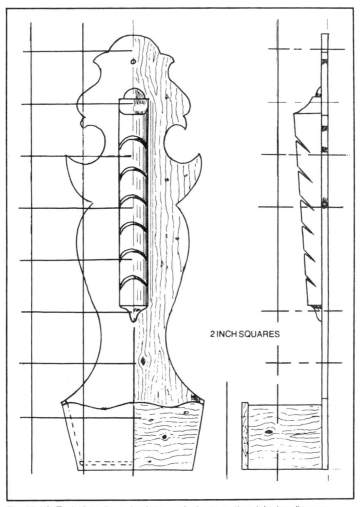

2 INCH SQUARES

Fig. 13-36. Early American pine letter rack planter optional design diagram.

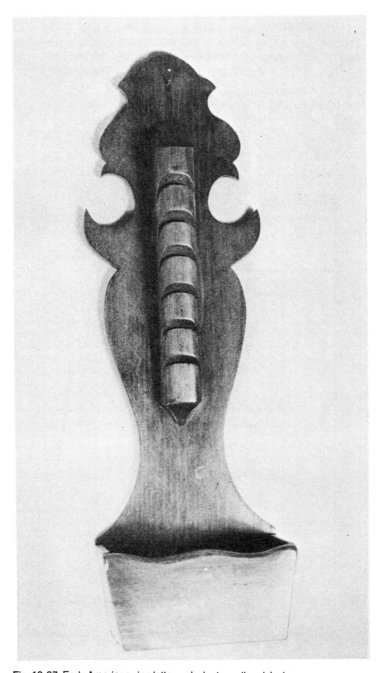

Fig. 13-37. Early American pine letter rack planter optional design.

428

Cut ¼″ stock for the container covers. Make a pattern for the container covers. Be sure that the pattern fits around the lower part of the letter holder. Trace around the pattern on the ¼″ stock and cut container covers on a jigsaw or bandsaw.

Bore holes for the ¼″ brass hinge pins. Cut two brass rods about ⅜″ long. Glue the rods into the container covers with epoxy glue.

Chisel out the finger nail depressions with a small gouge. Cut thin veneer or thin plywood for the back and fit into place.

Sand the entire project with 6/0-220 sandpaper. Finish with a penetrating oil finish. Apply a number of coats. A few penetrating oil finish suppliers are listed here: Watco Danish oil finish (192), Penofin oil finish (141), Sealacell (82) and DPS (Deep Penetration Sealer) (106).

EGYPTIAN MOTIF LETTER RACK

See Table 13-5. Saw the letter holder to rough dimensions. Saw the two slanting faces on the circular saw while the stock is still rectangular in cross section. Saw the incisions to hold the letters on the band saw.

Make the pattern for the contoured shape. Trace the pattern on stock. Cut the contour on the band saw.

Finish shaping with plane, Surform, rasp and sandpaper. Sand the letter incisions with a piece of sandpaper over a thin piece of wood.

Cut the drawer support to rough rectangular shape. Smooth the underside. Make two drawer guides and glue to the underside.

Cut the drawer front to rough rectangular shape. Cut out the finger depression.

Cut the two ⅛″ deep dadoes across each end to receive the tenons on the end. Cut the two ends to rough rectangular shape. Cut the dadoes to receive the back, and cut a rabbet to form the tenons to fit into the front.

Table 13-4. Materials List for the African Motif Letter Rack (Rough Dimensions Only).

No. of Pcs.	Description	Size	Material
1	Letter Holder	1½″ x 1¾″ x 19″	Walnut
1	Turned Container	1⅞″ x 12″ x 12″	Walnut
2	Container Covers	¼″ x 2½″ x 4¼″	Walnut
1	Back		Thin Veneer or Plywood, Any Species

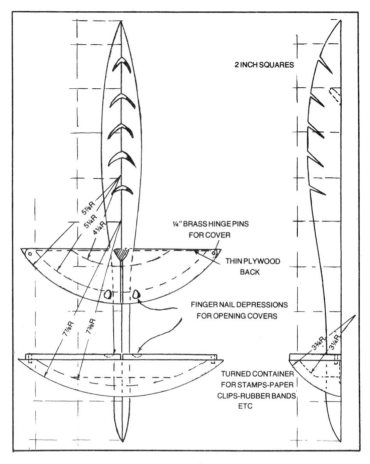

Fig. 13-38. Contemporary letter wall rack, African motif.

Cut the back to fit into the dadoes in the end. Cut the bottom to rough rectangular shape. Cut the drawer guides and glue to the ends. Make sure that they mesh with the drawer guides on the drawer support.

Assemble and glue the drawer front, drawer ends, bottom and back together. After the glue is dry, slide the drawer onto the guides on the drawer support. Make sure that all rectangular parts line up.

Clamp the drawer support to the drawer, being careful not to exert enough pressure to break the drawer guides. Remove the waste and contour the shape with a drum sander or with Surform, rasps and different grades of sandpaper.

430

Remove the drawer from the drawer support. Bore a hole for a flat head screw in the center of the back of the drawer support.

Contour the lower end of the letter holder so that it fits the drawer support. Drive in a screw to hold the drawer support to the letter holder after glue has been applied to the joint. Reinsert the drawer and sand the entire project with different grades of sandpaper, ending up with 4/0-150 abrasive paper.

Stain the project with NGR (non-grain raising) red mahogany. Fill the project with a very dark red filler. Apply four coats of spray "Deft." Rub lightly between coats with #0000 steel wool. Wax and polish (Fig. 13-39).

FURNITURE KITS

Cohasset Colonial kits by Haggerty are faithful reproductions of traditional museum pieces (Metropolitan Museum, Museum of Fine Arts, Boston; Old Sturbridge Village, Sturbridge; Fruitland Museum, Harvard, etc.). The furniture comes as a complete kit. All parts are accurately handcrafted and sanded, ready to assemble. Glue, screws, hardware, sandpaper, stain and instructions are included.

Cohasset Colonial kits include chairs, clocks, chests, desks, hutch cabinets, four poster beds, mirrors, shelves, stools and wall racks. Woods used are clear, *select rock maple* and *Easter white pine*. Cohasset also markets metal accessories and curtain fabrics.

Rollingswood Furniture Kits (156)

Rollingswood offers a wide range of classical, traditional reproductions in *Honduras mahogany,* Pennsylvania *cherry* and *American black walnut.*

Rollingswood feels that the "kit" is misleading, if not totally improper. A Rollingswood kit is truly a fine piece of furniture

Table 13-5. Materials List for the Egyptian Motif Letter Rack (Rough Dimensions Only).

No. of Pcs.	Description	Size	Material
1	Letter Holder	1″ x 2 1/2″ x 14″	Mahogany
1	Drawer Support	5/8″ x 2 1/2″ x 8 3/8″	Mahogany
1	Drawer Front	3/4″ x 1 1/4″ x 8 3/8″	Mahogany
2	Drawer Ends	3/8″ x 1 1/4″ x 1 7/8″	Mahogany
4	Drawer Guides	Make to Fit From	Mahogany
1	Drawer Bottom	1/2″ x 2 1/2″ x 8 3/8″	Mahogany
1	Drawer Back	3/16″ x 7/8″ x 8 3/8″	Mahogany

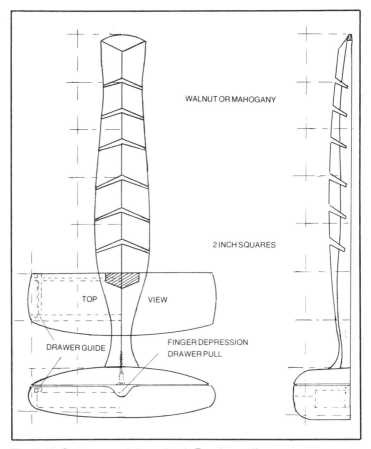

Fig. 13-39. Contemporary letter wall rack, Egyptian motif.

offered unassembled and unfinished. Rollingswood also offers furniture completely assembled and finished.

The projects include candlesticks, chests-of-drawers, high-boys, dressing benches, fern stands, spoon racks and a large variety of tables. Excellent hand carving is executed on pieces that call for this embellishment.

Construction often calls for dovetailing and mortise and tenon joints. Solid brass pulls and escutcheons are used on drawer fronts.

Bartley Furniture Kits from the Bartley Collection, Ltd. (19)

These 18th century antique furniture reproduction kits are available in cherry and Honduras mahogany. The Reproduction Committee of the Henry Ford Museum and Greenfield Village has selected The Bartley Collection, Ltd., as the exclusive manufacturer of a number of exceptionally fine pieces from the magnificent Henry Ford Museum furniture collection.

Bartley pieces are available either unassembled and ready-to-finish or assembled and hand-finished. Projects include benches, candlestands, chairs, cupboards, block front chests, butler trays, lowboys, English muffin stands and a large variety of tables. Brass hardware is hand cast, precisely copied from the original.

FURNITURE PLANS AND PATTERNS

Colonial Workshop offers 200 shop tested plans individually on heavy paper. They are fully detailed in clear, easy-to-follow scale drawings, with many "exploded" diagrams.

Projects include chests, letter racks, footstools, dry sinks, tables, magazine racks, desks, gun cabinets and gun racks, spice cabinets, shelves, workbenches, outdoor projects, bookcases, Shaker furniture, trophy cases and tool cabinets. Colonial also supplies a wide range of jigsaw patterns.

Craftplans (44)

Craftplans offers easy-to-follow plans and full-size furniture designs. Full-size furniture plans include beds, buffets, chairs and rockers, magazine racks, settees, tables and tea carts. A complete list of materials, including hardware, is on each plan. In addition, an "exploded" perspective sketch shows at a glance how all parts are assembled.

Plans for smaller projects and accessories include shadow boxes, toys, doll furniture, duck decoys, lawn novelties, flower boxes, lathe projects, spinning wheels, looms, clocks, birdhouses and feeders, jigsaw patterns and lawn novelties.

Delcraft, Inc. (50)

Delcraft offers 237 full-size blueprint plans making decorative accents, dining room, bedroom and family room furniture in Early American, Spanish and Modern American designs. Recommended woods are pine, maple and oak.

The Designery (55)

The *Designery* specializes in furnishing well-designed contemporary furniture plans. The 240 furniture plans include a wide variety of beds, benches, bookshelves, cabinets, chairs, chests of drawers, desks, ottomans, screens, shelves, sofas, stereo cabinets and stools. The furniture pieces are designed by Doug Lambrecht and Jerry Mandell, who are well known and highly acclaimed for their work in the field of furniture design. Examples of their designs are found in studios, offices and private collections from coast to coast in over 30 states.

Furniture Designs (77)

Furniture Designs supplies 277 full-size furniture plans. Patterns can be traced on to the wood directly from the plans. A complete list of materials, including hardware, is on each plan, saving time in gathering the necessary parts. Exploded views show how projects are assembled.

Furniture plans include bars, beds, benches, bookcases, chairs and rockers, chests of drawers, *chifforobes*, commodes, cradles, credenzas, cribs, cupboards, desks, dressers, dry sinks, gun cabinets, hall trees, hostess carts, hutches, love seats, magazine stands, mirrors, night stands, settees, settles, shelves, sofas, spinning wheels, stools, tables, and tea carts.

Other suppliers of kits and plans are *Aerogon Industries, Inc.* (3), which furnishes bedroom kits; *Mart Wood Products* (118), which markets full-size plans for children's furniture; *Mastercraft* (119), which sells gift and novelty patterns; and Mayco Sales (121), which offers 700 furniture, toy and novelty plans.

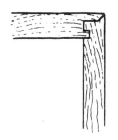

Appendix:
Suppliers/Manufacturers

(1)**A Cut Above**
P. O. Box 139
Greensburg, OH 44232

Veneer supplies

(2)**Adjustable Clamp Co.**
431 N. Ashland Ave.
Chicago, IL 60622

*Many varieties
of clamps and
manufacturers of
"Pony" Kerf
Keeper and
"Jorgensen" and
"Pony" trademarks*

(3)**Aerogen Industries, Inc.**
6309 Westline Drive
Houston, TX 77036

*Bedroom furniture
kits*

(4)**A.L.I. (Automatic Lubrication Inc.)**
2735 Tanager Drive
Willmington, DE 19808

*Hegner Heavy-
Duty, German made
jigsaw*

(5)**American Machine and Tool Co.**
4th and Spring St.
Royersford, PA 19468

*Power Woodworking
tools*

(6)**American Woodcrafters**
Box 919
Piqua, OH 45356

*Veneers, hard-
woods, carving
and turning
blocks, hand and
power tools,
hardware, mar-
quetry supplies,
finishing materi-
als, etc*

(7)**American Wood Working Co.**
Montello, WI 53949

*Domestic hard-
woods and manu-
facturer of
wood parts*

(8)**Amity**
Box 2204
Madison, WI 53707

*Professional
wood finishes*

(9)**Armor Products**
P. O. Box 290
Deer Park, NY 11729

*Hardware plans
for furniture,
clocks and wooden
toys, clock
movements and
dials*

(10)**Anson Industries**
414 W. Cypress St.
Glendale, CA 91204

Inca tools

(11)**Arco Products Corp.**
110 W. Sheffield Ave.
Englewood, NJ 07631

*Screw drills,
dowel centers,
dial-a-dado
washers*

(12)**Arizona Industrial Tools**
5002 S. 40th St.
Phoenix, AZ 85040

*Drill press and
bench grinders*

(13)**Artistry In Veneers**
633 Montauk Ave.
Brooklyn, NY 11208

*Veneers, inlays
and tools, furni-
ture designs and
finishing
materials*

436

(14)**Astro Wood Planer Co. Inc.**
58 Jerome Ave.
Bristol, CT 06010

Astro 10%"
thickness planer

(15)**Atlas Press Co.**
2019 N. Pitcher
Kalamazoo, MI 49007

Power and hand
tools

(16)**Austin Hardwoods, Inc.**
2125 Goodrich
Austin, TX 78704

Domestic and
imported lumber

(17)**Baker Furniture**
24th S. and Columbia
Holland, MI 49423

Quality
furniture

(18)**Barap Specialties**
835 Bellows
Frankfort, MI 49635

Hard to find
supplies

(19)**Bartley Collection, Ltd.**
747 Oakwood Ave.
Lake Forest, IL 60045

Ready-to-assemble
and finish 18th
century furniture

(20)**Beauty-Wood Industries**
339 Lakeshore Rd. E.
Mississauga, ON
  Canada

Hardwoods and
softwoods

(21)**Belsaw Power Tools Co.,**
9079 Field Bldg.
Kansas City, MO 64111

Three-in-one pow-
er tool, saw
mills, belt
grinder, sharp-
ening tools and
devices

(22)**Bingaman Plans**
P. O. Box 74
Langhorne, PA 19047

Gothic, Early
American and
Colonial Wood-
working plans

(23)**Binks Mfg. Co.**
9201 W. Belmont Ave.
Franklin Park, IL 60131

*Spray guns and
related equipment*

(24)**Bimex, Inc.**
487 Armour Circle, N.E.
Atlanta, GA 30324

*Heavy-duty quick-
action clamps,
power routers,
carbide bits, and
many other tools,
machine knives
and power tools*

(25)**Black Bros.**
501 9th Ave.
Mendota, IL 61342

*Flat stock lami-
nating and pre-
finishing equip-
ment for the
Furniture and
Allied Woodwork-
ing Industries*

(26)**Black and Decker**
Black and Decker (U.S.) Inc.
701 East Joppa Rd.
Towson, MD 21204

*Tools and
holding devices*

(27)**The Board Store**
Box 205
Bangor, WI 54164

*Kiln-dried
hardwoods*

(28)**Bob Morgan Wood**
1123 Bardstown RD.
Louisville, KY 40204

Iron-on veneers

(29)**The Brink and Cotton Mfg. Co.**
77 Poland St.
Bridgeport, CT 06605

Clamps and vises

(30)**Brodhead-Garrett**
4560 East 71st. St.
Cleveland, OH 44105

Suppliers of woodworking tools, supplies and lumber to educational institutions

(31)**Brookside Veneers, Ltd.**
107 Trumbull St.
Bldg. R-8
Elizabeth, NJ 07206

Exotic hardwood veneers and carving blocks

(32)**Brookstone Co.**
Vose Farm Rd.
Peterborough, NH 03458

Hard-to-find tools

(33)**Bryden Inc.**
2407 Ardn Dr.
Champaign, IL 61820

Parts to make your own router-shaper table

(34)**Carter Products Co.**
23 Ottawa Ave., N.W.
Grand Rapids, MI 49503

Band saw accessories and guide-line lights

(35)**Chem-Tech**
4669 Lander Road
Chagrin Falls, OH 44022

Wood binding epoxy adhesives

(36)**Chester B. Stem, Inc.**
2708 Grant Line Road
New Albany, IN 47150

Foreign and domestic hardwood lumber and veneer

(37)**Classic Grain Hardwood Co.**
902 E. Hughes Access Rd.
Tucson, AZ 85706

Hardwoods, wholesale only

439

(38)Cohasset Colonials By Hagerty
337 Ship St.
Cohasset, MA 02025

Early American furniture kits

(39)Colonial Workshop
P. O. Box 41032
Sacramento, CA 95841

200 woodworking plans

(40)Conover Woodcraft Specialties, Inc.
18124 Madison Rd.
Parkman, OH 44080

Wood bits, wood threading box and tap set, and power woodworking tools

(41)Constantine and Son, Inc.
2065 B Eastchester Rd.
Bronx, NY 10461

Veneers, marquetry, inlays, furniture woods, hardware, miniature power tools, finishing and refinishing materials. PEG (polyethylene glycol 1000)

(42)C. O. Porter
522 Plymouth Rd. N.E.
Grand Rapids, MI 49505

Industrial Woodworking machinery

(43) Craftmark Products, Inc.
P. O. Box 6308
Marietta, Ga 30065

Wood and leather branding irons

(44)Craftplans
Rogers, MN 55374

Plans and patterns

(45)Craftsman Wood Service Co.
2727 South Mary St.
Chicago IL 60608

Inlays, veneers, picture framing, tools, hardwood, hardware. Also PEG (polyethylene glycol 1000)

(46)Craft Value Center
P.O. Box 1637
Wayne, NJ 07470

Wood trim and novelties

(47)Craftwoods
(Division of O'Shea Lumber Co.)
York Rd. and Beaver Run Lane
Cockeysville, MD 21303

Foreign hardwoods, domestic hardwoods, veneer and cabinet plywood

(48)The Crand Creek Co.
Box 5553
Madison, WI 53705

Polyethylene Glycol 1000 wood stabilizer and chemical seasoning agent. Retail and in bulk

(49)The Cutting Edge
295 S. Robertson Blvd.
Beverly Hills, CA 90211

Hand and power tools. No mail orders

(50)Dalcraft, Inc.
600 Hogan
P.O. Box 746
Starkville, MS 39759

Full-size furniture plans

(51)D. A. Buckley
R 1, W.
Valley NY 14171

Native american hardwoods

(52)The Decorative Hardware Studio
160 King St.
Chappaqua, NY 10514

Furniture hardware

(53)Deft
17451 Von Karman Ave.
Irvine, CA 92714
    or
411 East Keystone Ave.
Alliance, OH 44601

Finishing materials

(54)**Delmhorst Instrument Co.**   *Wood moisture*
908 Cedar St.   *content dector*
Boonton, NJ 07005

(55)**The Designery**   *Contemporary*
521 W. Kirkwood Ave.   *furniture plans*
Bloomington, IN 47401

(56)**Diamond Maching Technology, Inc.**   *Diamond embedded*
34 Tower St.   *whetstones*
Hudson, MA 01749

(57)**Dremel**   *Small power wood-*
    (Div. of Emerson Electric Co.)   *working tools*
Racine, WI 53406

(58)**D.R.I. Industries, Inc.**   *Tools, nuts,*
6864 Washington Ave., South   *bolts, screws,*
Eden Prairie, MN 55344   *washers, etc*

(59)**Du-Er Tools**   *Power wood-*
5448 Edina Ind. Blvd.   *working tools*
Minneapolis, MN 55435

(60)**Dupli-Carver**   *Duplicating*
4004 West 10th St.   *carving device*
Indianapolis, IN 46222

(61)**Educational Lumber Co. Inc.**   *Appalachian hard-*
21 Meadow Ct.   *woods and veneers*
Asheville, NC 28803

442

(62)Ekstrom, Carlson & Co.
1400 Railroad Ave.
Rockford, IL 61110

Industrial wood-
working machinery

(63)Electrodyne Inc.
2126 Adams St.
Milwaukie, OR 97222

Portable mois-
ture meters

(64)Elu Machine Co.
9040 Dutton Drive
Twinsburg, OH 44087

Combination table
saw and miter saw

(65)Ecmo-Lux Corp.
2050 Fairwood Ave.
Columbus, OH 43107

Universal combi-
nation power
woodworking tools

(66)Eric Riebling Co. Inc.
106 Miller Place
Mt. Vernon, NY 10550

Klemmsia quick-
grip clamp

(67)Fair Price Tool Co.
La Canada, CA 91011

Jorgensen hand
clamps, work-
benches, vises,
chisels, hand
tools, books,
sharpening stones

(68)The Fine Tool Shop
1200 E. Post Rd.
Westport, CT 06880

Cutting and carv-
ing tools, sharp-
ening stones,
hand planes,
handsaws, mea-
suring and layout
tools, power
tools, clamping
tools, drilling
accessories and
books

(69)**Flecto Co. Inc.**
P. O. Box 12955
Oakland, CA 94604

Varathane wood
stain

(70)**Foley Mfg. Co.**
3300 Fifth St. N.E.
Minneapolis, MN 55418

Combination
planer-molder and
sharpening
equipment

(71)**The Foredom Electric Co.**
Bethel, CT 06801

Brett safety
guard for table
saws. Flexible
shaft machines

(72)**Forest City Tool Co.**
(Ex-Cell-O Corp.)
P. O. Box 788
Hickory, NC 28601

Woodworking ma-
chines, saws, cut-
ters, knives and
mill supplies

(73)**Formby's**
P. O. Box 667
Olive Branch, MS 38654

Finishing and
Refinishing
materials

(74)**Fox Super Shop, Inc.**
6701 W. 110 St.
Bloomington, MN 55438

7-in-1 Super Shop
multi-purpose
power tool

(75)**Frank Mittermeir, Inc.**
3577 E. Tremont Ave.
Bronx, NY 10456

Quality imported
hand tools

(76)**Frog Tool. Co. Ltd.**
548 North Wells St.
Chicago, IL 60610

Quality hand
woodworking tools.
including bow
saws, representa-
tive for Myford
wood turning
lathe

(77)**Furniture Designs**
1425 Sherman Ave.
Evanston, IL 60201

*Full-size
furniture plans*

(78)**Garden Way Research**
Charlotte, VT 05445

Workbenches

(79)**Garrett-Wade Co.**
302 Fifth Ave.
New York, NY 10001

*Quality hand
tools, Inca Swiss
planers and saws*

(80)**Gaston Wood Finishes, Inc.**
3630 E. 10th St.
P.O. Box 1246
Bloomington, IN 47402

*Wood finishes
and hardware*

(81)**Gebr. Busch**
P.O. Box 130254
D 5630 Remsheid 1
West Germany

*Wood carving
Tools*

(82)**General Finishes**
Box 14363
Milwaukee, WI 53214

*Sealacell finish-
ing system*

(83)**General Mfg. Co.**
835 Cherrier
Drummondville, PQ, Canada

*Woodworking
tools*

(84)**General Woodcraft**
100 Blinman St.
New London, CT 06320

*Hardwood, plywood
and veneers*

(85)**George Koch Sons, Inc.**
P.O. Box 358
Evansville, IN 47744

*Industrial furni-
ture finishing
conveyors*

(86)**Gillespie**
Box 1879
Memphis, TN 38101

*Old furniture
refinisher*

(87)**Gilliom Mfg. Co.**
St. Charles, MO 63301

*Power tool kits
to build your own
power tools*

(88)**Glenn Wing**
1437 S. Woodward Ave.
Birmingham, MI 48011

*Power tools
(Rockwell, Bosch
and Stanley)*

(89)**Goodspeed Machine Co.**
15 Elm St.
Winchendon, MA 01475

*Industrial wood-
working machinery*

(90)**Granberg Industries, Inc.**
202 South Garrard Blvd.
Richmond, CA 94804

*Chain saw lumber
mill*

(91)**Greenlee Tool Co.**
2136 12th St.
Rockford, IL 61101

*Quality wood-
crafting tools*

(92)**Haddon Tools**
4719 W. Rte. 120, Dept W
McHenry, IL 60050

*Lumber making
chain saw
accessory*

(93)**Handcrafted Tool and Supply**
744 W. Fullerton Pkwy.
Chicago, IL 60614

*Wood carving sets,
maple benches and
Greenlee wood-
crafting tools*

(94)**Henegan's Wood Shed**
7760 Southern Blvd.
West Palm Beach, FL 33471

Lumber

(95)**Holz Machine Co.**
45 Halladay St.
Jersey City, NJ 07304

*Power woodworking
tools*

(96)**Homecraft Veneer**
901 West Way
Latrobe, PA 15650

Veneer

(97)Horton Brasses
P.O. Box 95
Nooks Hill Road
Cromwell, CT 06416

*Cabinet and furni-
ture hardware*

(98)House of Hardwoods
610 Freeman St.
Orange, NJ 07052

*Hardwood, plywood,
veneers, carving
blocks and burls*

(99)I. Miller Enterprises
Box 772
Manchester, MO 63011

*Wood branding
irons*

(100)Independent Nail, Inc.
Bridgewater, MA 02324

*Specially design-
ed nails and nail-
like parts*

(101)Industrial Abrasives Co.
644 North Eighth St.
Reading, PA 19603

*Sanding belts and
sheet abrasives*

(102)Industrial Arts Supply Co.
5724 W. 36th St.
Minneapolis, MN 55416

*PEG (polyethylene
glycol 1000)*

(103)Interstate Hardwood Co. Inc.
850 Flora St.
Elizabeth, NJ 07201

*Hardwood. No mail
orders*

(104)Irwin
Wilmington, OH 45177

Drill bits

(105)John Congdon Cabinetmaker
P.O. Box 493
Moretown, VT 05660

*All wood hand
screw clamps*

(106)**John Harra Wood and Supply Co.**
39 West 19th St.
New York NY 10011

Hardwood, tools, deep penetrating sealer, etc

(107)**Kimball Woodcarver Co.**
2602 Whitaker St.
Savannah, GA 31401

Wood carver, sign machines and templates

(108)**Kohler-General**
100 Clark St.
Sheboygan Falls, WI 53085

Jenkins double end tenoners, industrial woodworking machinery

(109)**K.P. Distributors**
P.O. Box 3211
Fort Pierce, FL 33450

Old world aniline dye stains and other finishing materials

(110) **Kurt Manufacturing Co.**
1720 Marshall St. N.E.
Minneapolis, MN 55413

Woodcarving machines

(111)**Laskowski Enterprises**
(Dupli-Carver)
2346 Fisher Ave.
Indianapolis, IN 46224

Device for duplicating carvings

(112)**Leichtung, Inc.**
701 Beta Drive
Cleveland, OH 44143

Professional (German) woodbits and depth adjusting collars. Workbenches

(113)**Lamont Specialties**
Box 271
Lamont, PA 16851

PEG (polyethylene glycol 1000)

(114)**Lion Miter Trimmer**
R R 2
Windsor, VT 05089

Miter trimmer

(115)**L.L. Enterprises**
P.O. Box 35203
Phoenix, AZ 85069

Plans for outdoor furniture, children's toys, children's play furniture, workbenches, shelves, cabinets and novelties

(116)**Love-Built Toys and Crafts**
2907 Lake Forest Rd.
P.O. Box 5459
101 Tahoe City, CA 95730

Wood toy patterns

(117)**McCall House**
Box 1950
Lenoir, NC 28645

Table stroke sanders

(118)**Martin Wood Products**
224-A North Main
Republic, MO 65738

Full-size plans for children's furniture

(119)**Mastercraft**
P.O. Box 631
Park Ridge, IL 60068

Gift and novelty patterns

(120)**Maurice L. Condon Co. Inc.**
248 Ferris Ave.
White Plains, NY 10603

Domestic and foreign hardwoods and softwoods

(121)**Mayco Sales**
P.O. Box 2931
Mesa, AZ 85204

700 furniture, toys and novelty plans

(122)**Mereen-Johnson Machine Co.**
4401 Lyndale Ave., North
Minneapolis, MN 55412

Industrial woodworking machinery

(123)Merit Abrasive Products, Inc.
201 W. Manville,
Box 5447
Compton, CA 90224

Sand-O-Fox sanders

(124)Michigan Production Grinding Co.
(Div. of Core Industries, Inc.)
P. O. Box 628
1 Core Way Drive
Pioneer, OH 43554

Soss invisible hinges

(125)M. and H. Wood Products, Inc.
Box 310
Claremont, CA 91711

Burl table slabs

(126)Minnesota Woodworkers Supply Co.
21801 Industrial Blvd.
Rogers, MN 55374

Creative and un- usual woodworking supplies

(127)Mobile Mfg. Co.
P. O. Box 258
Troutdale, OR 97060

One-man portable sawmill powered by a VW engine

(128)Moisture Register Co.
1510 W. Chestnut St.
Alhambra, CA 91802

Portable moisture meters

(129)The Newell Workshop
128 Drawer
Hinsdale, IL 60521

Chair caning kits

(130)Nor Cal Walnut Products
1265 Walnut Ave.
Redding, CA 96001

Walnut lathe blocks

(131)**North American Products Corp.**   *Cutting tools*
Suite 226/120
Interstate North Parkway
Atlanta, GA 30339

(132)**Northfield Foundry and Machine Co.**   *Power woodworking*
Northfield, MN 55057   *tools*

(133)**The Nutty Co. Inc.**   *Specialists in*
135 Main St.   *wood screws*
Derby, CT 06418

(134)**Ohio Woodshop Specialties**   *Coated abrasives*
190 Anderson Drive
Jackson, OH 45640

(135)**Oliver Machine Co.**
445 6th St.
Grand Rapids, MI 49504

(136)**Old South Patterns**   *Full-size*
P. O. Box 11143   *working patterns*
Charlotte, NC 28209

(137)**The Olson Saw Co.**   *Precision made*
(Div. of Black-   *saw blades includ-*
 stone Industries,   *ing bow saw blades*
 Inc.)
Bethel, CT 06801

(138)**Otner-Botner**   *Solid brass*
P. O. Box 6023   *(whale) finger*
Providence, RI 02940   *planes*

(139) **The Parks Woodworking Machine Co.** *Thickness planers*
501 Knowlton St. *and other machine*
Cincinnati, OH 45223 *tools*

(140) **Paxton** *Furniture*
Upper Falls, MD 21156 *hardware*

(141) **Penofin Co.** *Penetrating oil*
819 J Street *finishes*
Sacramento, CA 95814

(142) **Period Furniture Hardware Co. Inc.** *Furniture*
123 Charles St. *hardware*
Boston, MA 02114

(143) **Poitras, Danckaert Wood-** *Power woodworking*
working Machine Co. *tools*
891 Howell Mill Road, N.W.
Atlanta, GA 30318

(144) **Polamco** *Power woodworking*
755 Greenleaf Ave. *tools*
Elk Grove Village, IL 60007

(145) **Pootatuck Corp.** *Miter trimmer*
R R 2 Box 18 *and measuring*
Windsor, VT 05089 *attachment for*
picture framing

(146) **Portalign Tool Corp.** *Precision drill*
P.O. Box A-80547 *guides and shaper*
San Diego, CA 52138 *bits*

(147)**Powermatic Division, Houdaille** *Power woodworking*
   Ind. Inc.   *tools*
   Morrison Road, Box 70
   McMinnville, TN 37110

(148)**PPG Industries, Inc.**   *REZ stains*
   Gateway Center
   Pittsburgh, PA 15222

(149)**Prakto, Inc.**   *Tool sharpeners*
   P. O. Box 1023
   Birmingham, MI 48012

(150)**Precision Concepts**   *Power wood-*
   4200 Westgrove, Box 918   *working tools*
   Addison, TX 75001

(151)**The Princeton Co.**   *English handsaw*
   P. O. Box 276-29   *sharpener*
   Princeton, MA 01541

(152)**Rima Mfg. Co.**   *Chisel sharpening*
   P. O. Box 99   *jig*
   Quaker Hill, CT 06375

(153)**Ritter and Son Hardware**   *Old antique*
   Dept. 461   *hinges and*
   Gualada, CA 95445   *latches*

(154)**Robert M. Albrecht**   *PEG (polyethy-*
   8635 Yolanda Ave.   *lene glycol 1000)*
   Northbridge, CA   91324

(155)**Rockwell International**   *Power wood-*
   400 N. Lexington Ave.   *working tools*
   Pittsburgh, PA 15208

(156)**Rollingwood**
Box 404
Grayslake, IL 60030

Classic furniture kit reproductions

(157)**Russ Zimmerman**
RFD 3, Box 57A
Putney, VT 05346

Myford ML8B English wood turning lathe

(158)**Safranek Enterprises**
4005 El Camino Real
Astascadero, CA 93422

Panel router and Air-Vac-Clamp

(159)**Sand-Rite Mfg. Co.**
1611 N. Sheffield Ave.
Chicago, IL 60614

Pneumatic drum sanders and sanding drums

(160)**The Sawmill**
P. O. Box 329
Nazareth, PA 18064

Exotic and precious woods. Wholesale only

(161)**Sculpture Associates, Ltd., Inc.**
114 East 25th St.
New York, NY 10010

German wood carving tools

(162)**Sculpture House, Inc.**
38 East 30th St.
New York, NY 10016

Old world tools

(163)**Sears, Roebuck and Co.**
Dept. 141, 925 S. Homan Ave.
Chicago, IL 60607

Woodworking tools and supplies

(164)**Shop Smith, Inc.**
750 Center Drive
Vandalia, OH 45377

Five major power tools packaged into one

(165) **Silvo Hardware Co.** *Brand name tools*
2205 Richmond St.
Philadelphia, PA 19125

(166) **Singley Specialty Co. Inc.** *Drum sanders*
P. O. Box 771
Henderson, NC 28739

(167) **Sligh Furniture** *Quality furniture*
174 E. 11th St. *manufacturers*
Holland, MI 49423

(168) **Smith's Knife and Stone** *North Arkansas*
262 Central Ave. *stones*
Hot Springs, AR 71901

(169) **Soss Mfg. Co.** *Soss invisible*
Division of Core Industries, Inc. *hinges*
P. O. Box 8200
Detroit, MI 48213

(170) **Sperber Tool Works, Inc.** *Portable chain*
Box 1224 *saw mills*
West Caldwell, NJ 07006

(171) **Spielman's Wood Works** *PEG (polythylene*
188 Gibraltar Rd. *glycol 1000)*
Fish Creek, WI 54212

(172) **Sprunger Corp.** *Power woodworking*
Box 1621 *tools*
Elkhart, IN 46515

(173) **Star Chemical Co. Inc.** *Wood finishing*
4500 W. Cermak Rd. *supplies and*
Chicago, IL 60623 *equipment*

(174)**Sunshine Plans**
P. O. Box 134-B
West Gramby, CT 06090
Furniture patterns and plans

(175)**Swanson Tool Co.**
P. O. Box 434
Oak Lawn, IL 60453
Speed square and saw set

(176)**Tannewitz**
3940 Clay Ave., S. W.
Grand Rapids, MI 49508
Power woodworking tools

(177)**Three Crowns**
3850 Monroe Ave.
Pittsford, NY 14534
Bow saws

(178)**Toolcraft**
700 Plainfield St.
Chicopee, MA 01013
Tools

(179)**Toolmark Co.**
6840 Shingle Creek Pkwy.
Minneapolis, MN 55400
Lathe duplicator attachment

(180)**The Toolroom**
East Oxbow Rd.
Shelburne Falls, MA 01370
Wood bits and depth collars

(181)**The Tool Works**
76 Ninth Ave.
New York, NY 10011
Tools parts and supplies

(182)**Tremont Nail Co.**
P. O. Box 111
Wareham, MA 02571
Authentic antique decorative nails

(183)**Turn-O-Carve Tool Co.**
P. O. Box 8315
Tampa, FL 33674
Lathe-top turning duplicators

(184)**Unicorn Universal Woods, Ltd.**
137 John St.
Toronto, Canada
M5V2E4 363 1162

Foreign and do-mestic hardwoods, softwoods and veneers

(185)**United Gilsonite Laboratories**
Scranton, PA 18501

ZAR woodfinishing products

(186)**Universal Clamp Corp.**
6905 Cedros Ave.
Van Nuys, CA 91405

Home workbench and special clamps

(187)**U.S. General Supply Corp.**
100 General Place
Jericho, NY 11753

Large assortment of tools and hardware

(188)**Valley Products and Design**
Box 396
Milford, PA 18337

Portable electric moisture meters

(189)**Violette Plywood Corp.**
W. Northfield Rd.
Lunenburg, MA 01462

Plywood

(190)**Wadkin Ltd.**
Green Lane Wks.
Leicester, England LE5 4PF

Power wood-working tools

(191)**Warren Tool Co. Inc.**
Rt. 1. Box 12-B
Rhinebeck, NY 12572

High carbon tool steel chisels

(192)**Watco-Dennis Corp.**
Michigan Avenue and 22nd St.
Santa Monica, CA 90404

Danish oil wood finish

(193)**Weird Wood**
Box 190
Chester, VT 05143

*Hardwoods and
softwoods in
boards, slabs
and free form
cut ovals*

(194)**Western Commercial Products**
P. O. Box 1202
Tulare, CA 93274

*"Saw helper"
safety guide*

(195)**Wetzler Clamp Co. Inc.**
43-15 Eleventh St.
Long Island City, NY 11101

*Clamps and clamp-
ing devices*

(196)**Wholesale Tool Co.**
12155 Stevens Drive
Warren, MI 48090

*Taps and dies for
wood. Other tools*

(197)**W.I.G. ("Wood Is Good") Co.**
Box 477
Lakewood, CA 90174

*Wood carving
tools and blocks*

(198)**Wikkmann House**
Box 501
Chatsworth, CA 91311

*Home workbenches
and insertable
attachments and
special clamps*

(199)**Wilkens-Anderson Co.**
4525 West Division St.
Chicago, IL 60651

*PEG (polyethylene
glycol 1000)*

(200)**Willard Brothers Woodcutters**
300 Basin Road
Trenton, NJ 08619

*Wood flitches,
slabs, mantle
clocks, carving
blocks, dimension
and unusual woods*

(201) **Williams and Hussey Machine Co.**
Dept. 5
Milford, NH 03055

*Combination mold-
er, planer and
edger*

(202)**Wisner Tools**
259 Whaley St.
Freeport, NY 11520

*Edge-trimming
block planes and
precision corner
mortise chisels*

(203)**Wood Carvers Supply**
3112 W. 28th St.
Minneapolis, MN 55416

*Wood carving
tools*

(204)**Woodcraft Supply Corp.**
313 Montvale Ave.
Woburn, MA 01888

*Tools, materials
and projects sup-
plies, books and
workbenches*

(205)**Woodline**
1004 Central Ave.
Almeda, CA 94501

*Japanese sharp-
ening and honing
stones*

(206)**Wood Shed**
1807 Elmwood Ave.
Dept. 4
Buffalo, NY 14207

*Veneers and
hardwoods*

(207)**Woodstream Hardwoods**
Box 11471
Knoxville, TN 37919

*Exotic and do-
mestic hardwoods
retail and
wholesale*

(208)**The Woodworker's Store**
21801 Industrial Blvd.
Rogers, MN 55374

*3000 woodworking
items*

(209)**Woodshop Specialties**
Box 1013
East Middlebury, VT 05740

*Stationary wood-
working machines
and related
accessories*

(210)**Wood World**
9006 Waukegan Rd.
Morton Grove, IL 60053

*Foreign and do-
mestic hardwood*

(211)**Woodworker's Supply, Inc.**   *Woodworking*
      P. O. Box 14117   *tools*
      Albuquerque, NM 87112

(212)**Woodworks**   *Hardwoods*
      Box 79238   *and dowels*
      Saginaw, TX 76179

(213)**Woodworker's Tool Works**   *Tools*
      222-224 So. Jefferson St.
      Chicago, IL 60606

(214)**Yates-American Machine Co.**   *Power woodworking*
      Roscoe, IL 61073   *machines and in-*
                               dustrial woodwork-
                               ing machines.
                               Cutterheads
                               and knives

(215)**Black Bros. Co.**   *Clamping, gluing,*
      301 Ninth Ave.   *laminating and*
      Mendota, IL 61342   *flat stock fin-*
                               ishing equipment

(216)**Drexel Heritage Furnishing, Inc.**   *Furniture*
      Drexel, NC 28619   *manufacturers*

(217)**J. M. Lancaster, Inc.**   *Air operated fur-*
      2949 Lee's Chapel Road   *niture clamping*
      Drawer 5280   *equipment*
      Greensboro, NC 27403

Index

461

462

Edited By: Robert E. Ostrander